The Politics of Domestic Authority in Britain since 1800

The Politics of Domestic Authority in Britain since 1800

Edited by

Lucy Delap
Fellow and Director of Studies in History, St Catharine's College, Cambridge

Ben Griffin
Fellow and Director of Studies in History, Girton College, Cambridge, and Lecturer in History, Fitzwilliam College, Cambridge

and

Abigail Wills
Postdoctoral Fellow in History, Brasenose College, Oxford

palgrave
macmillan

First published 2009 by
PALGRAVE MACMILLAN

Palgrave Macmillan in the UK is an imprint of Macmillan Publishers Limited,
registered in England, company number 785998, of Houndmills, Basingstoke,
Hampshire RG21 6XS.

Palgrave Macmillan in the US is a division of St Martin's Press LLC,
175 Fifth Avenue, New York, NY 10010.

Palgrave Macmillan is the global academic imprint of the above companies
and has companies and representatives throughout the world.

Palgrave® and Macmillan® are registered trademarks in the United States,
the United Kingdom, Europe and other countries.

ISBN-13: 978–0–230–57994–1 hardback

This book is printed on paper suitable for recycling and made from fully
managed and sustained forest sources. Logging, pulping and manufacturing
processes are expected to conform to the environmental regulations of the
country of origin.

A catalogue record for this book is available from the British Library.

A catalog record for this book is available from the Library of Congress.

10   9   8   7   6   5   4   3   2   1
18   17   16   15   14   13   12   11   10   09

Printed and bound in Great Britain by
CPI Antony Rowe, Chippenham and Eastbourne

Contents

List of Figures   vii

Notes on Contributors   viii

Introduction: The Politics of Domestic Authority in Britain
 Since 1800   1
Ben Griffin, Lucy Delap and Abigail Wills

Part I Violence and the Law

1 'I am master here': Illegitimacy, Masculinity, and Violence in
   Victorian England   27
   Ginger Frost

2 '...the instrument of an animal function': Marital Rape and
   Sexual Cruelty in the Divorce Court, 1858–1908   43
   Gail Savage

Part II Poverty and the State

3 Irish Orphans and the Politics of Domestic Authority   61
   Anna Clark

4 Fatherhood and Family Shame: Masculinity, Welfare and the
   Workhouse in Late Nineteenth-Century England   84
   Megan Doolittle

Part III Domesticity

5 'Tiresome trips downstairs': Middle-Class Domestic Space and
   Family Relationships in England, 1850–1910   111
   Jane Hamlett

6 Love and Authority in Mid-Twentieth-Century Marriages:
   Sharing and Caring   132
   Simon Szreter and Kate Fisher

7 'A paradise on earth, a foretaste of heaven': English Catholic
   Understandings of Domesticity and Marriage, 1945–1965   155
   Alana Harris

Part IV Domestic Service

 8 Domestic Servants as Poachers of Print: Reading, Authority
    and Resistance in Late Victorian Britain   185
    Margaret Beetham

 9 Authority, Dependence and Power in Accounts of
    Twentieth-Century Domestic Service   204
    Judy Giles

Part V Parenting and Childhood

10 Child Care and Neglect: A Comparative Local Study of Late
    Nineteenth-Century Parental Authority   223
    Siân Pooley

11 Godfathering: The Politics of Victorian Family Relations   243
    Valerie Sanders

12 "Beating Children is Wrong": Domestic Life, Psychological
    Thinking and the Permissive Turn   261
    Deborah Thom

Index   284

List of Figures

5.1 Illustration showing an empty nursery from J. E. Panton
(1884) *Nooks and Corners* (London: Ward and Downey)   116

5.2 The nursery of the home of the Garsten family in London,
Greater Manchester County Record Office, Documentary
Photography Archive, 2357/143   117

5.3 Photograph of 'Museum' at Frondeg, Greater Manchester
County Record Office, Documentary Photography Archive,
1642/30, 1/U12/25   124

5.4 Photograph from Shaw Storey family of Bursledon, family
album, Hampshire Record Office, 58A01/1.   125

7.1 Tim Madden (1965) *How's the Family? Cartoons from the
Catholic Herald* (London: Burns and Oates), n.p. [Reproduced
with permission from Bodleian Library, University of
Oxford]   161

7.2 A Durham miner leading his family in the rosary.
Reproduced from 'Crusader for Prayer', *Picture Post*, 26 July
1952, p. 5 [with permission of Getty Images]   168

7.3 Tim Madden (1965), *How's the Family?* (London: Burns and
Oates), n.p. [Reproduced with permission from Bodleian
Library, University of Oxford]   171

7.4 'St Joseph the Workman', *Catholic Times*, 6 May 1955, p. 9
[Reproduced with permission from Bodleian Library,
University of Oxford]   172

10.1 Extract from a page of advertisements for a range of
children's medicines, published in *The Burnley Gazette and
East Lancashire Advertise*, 26 November 1898. At this date an
average of around five such advertisements was published
each week   231

10.2 Advertisement for 'Scott's Emulsion', published in *The
Burnley Gazette and East Lancashire Advertise*, 24 December
1898. 'Scott's Emulsion' was advertised in most editions of
the Burnley newspaper in the late 1890s and early 1900s,
with different illustrated and emotive stories of the curative
powers of the medicine. It was not promoted to Auckland
parents   232

Notes on Contributors

Margaret Beetham recently retired as Reader in the Department of English at Manchester Metropolitan University. Her publications include *A Magazine of Her Own: Domesticity and Desire in the Women's Magazine* (1996), *Victorian Women's Magazines; An Anthology* (2001) with Kay Boardman, and articles on Victorian recipe book, Lancashire periodicals and issues of popular reading and gender. She is an associate editor of the *Dictionary of Nineteenth Century Journalism* (2008).

Anna Clark is Samuel Russell Chair in the Humanities at the University of Minnesota, and the editor of the *Journal of British Studies* until 2010. She is the author of several books, including *Desire: A History of European Sexuality* (2008), *Scandal: The Sexual Politics of the British Constitution* (2003) and *The Struggle for the Breeches: Gender and the Making of the British Working* Class (University of California Press, 1995) as well as numerous articles.

Lucy Delap is a fellow of St Catharine's College, Cambridge, and a member of the History Faculty, University of Cambridge. Her book *The Feminist Avant-Garde: Transatlantic Encounters of the Early Twentieth Century* (2007) won the 2008 Women's History Network Prize, and explores the intellectual history and cultural politics of feminism set within Anglo-American exchanges of the early twentieth century. She has recently published a collection of primary sources, *Feminism and the Periodical Press, 1900–1918* (2006), co-edited with Maria DiCenzo and Leila Ryan. She is also an associate editor of *History and Policy*, and is currently working on a forthcoming monograph, *Domestic Service in Twentieth Century Britain* (Oxford, 2010).

Megan Doolittle is a senior lecturer in Social Policy at the Open University. Her published work includes 'Fatherhood, Religious Belief and the Protection of Children in Nineteenth-Century English Families' in *Gender and Fatherhood in the Nineteenth Century*, ed. Trev Lynn Broughton and Helen Rogers (2007) and *The Family Story: Blood, Contract and Intimacy in Modern England, 1840–1960*, with Leonore Davidoff, Janet Fink and Katherine Holden (1999). Her research interests lie in the areas of fatherhood and masculinity, contemporary families and their alternatives, domestic space and family life, and the relationships between law, social policy and the family.

Kate Fisher is Senior Lecturer in History at the University of Exeter. Her research focuses on the history of sexuality in the nineteenth and twentieth centuries and she is the author of *Birth Control, Sex and Marriage in Britain, 1918–1960* (2006) and *Private Lives: Love, Sex and Marriage in Britain, 1918–1960* (with Simon Szreter, forthcoming). She is currently collaborating with the Classicist Rebecca Langlands on an interdisciplinary project 'Sexual Knowledge, Sexual History' which explores the uses of ancient cultures within the history of sexuality.

Ginger Frost is Professor of History at Samford University in Birmingham, Alabama. She is the author of *Promises Broken: Courtship, Class and Gender in Victorian England* (1995), and numerous articles, all focusing on family dynamics in crisis periods and the role of the Victorian courts in the family. Her forthcoming works continue this emphasis and include *Living in Sin: Cohabiting as Husband and Wife in Nineteenth-Century England* (2008) and *Victorian Childhoods* (ca. 2009).

Judy Giles is Professor Emeritus at York St John University. She has published extensively on women and domesticity in the first half of the twentieth century and is committed to an interdisciplinary approach to the study of the past. Her major publications are *Women, Identity and Private Life in Britain, 1918–50* (1995) and *The Parlour and the Suburb* (2004).

Ben Griffin is a fellow of Girton College, Cambridge, and Lecturer in History at Girton College and Fitzwilliam College. He is currently working on a book entitled *Feminism, Masculinity and Politics in Victorian Britain*, which reassesses the relationship between Victorian feminism, liberalism and conservatism, and which explores how competing models of masculinity shaped the actions of nineteenth-century politicians. He is also working on a history of child custody law in the nineteenth century. In 2005 his doctoral thesis was awarded Cambridge University's Prince Consort and Thirlwall Prize and the Seeley Historical Medal.

Jane Hamlett is Lecturer in Modern British History at Royal Holloway University of London. She completed her PhD in 2005 and a book based on her doctoral research, *Material Relations: Domestic Interiors and the Family in England 1850–1910* will be published in Autumn 2009. Her research interests lie in the field of nineteenth- and twentieth-century social and cultural history, in particular in the material and visual cultures and in gender, intimacy and the family. She was formerly ESRC Postdoctoral Research Fellow at the University of Manchester and has taught at the Universities of Manchester, Oxford and London.

Alana Harris is the Hardie Postdoctoral Fellow in Modern History at Lincoln College, Oxford. Her recently co-authored and co-edited book *Redefining Christian Britain: Post-1945 Perspectives* (2007) brings together writers from the disciplines of history, sociology and theology to reassess the role of Christianity in twentieth-century Britain. Other journal publications have included an exploration of 1950s religious revivals in Britain and a comparative study of changes in the Anglican and Roman Catholic liturgies from the 1960s. Her current research interests are exploring the methodological and subjective aspects of contemporary 'lived religion', including an inter-religious case study of the faith lives of migrants in East London from the 1960s, and contemporary reasons for and experiences of pilgrimage to Lourdes, Fatima, Glastonbury and Stonehenge.

Siân Pooley is a postgraduate research student in History at St John's College, Cambridge. Her doctoral thesis is on parenthood and child-rearing in England, c. 1860–1910. From October 2009 she will be the Mark Kaplanoff Research Fellow at Pembroke College, Cambridge, where she will begin a new project on intergenerational intimacy in modern Britain. Her wider research interests relate to the history of the family, gender, class, and welfare. She recently published 'Domestic servants and their urban employers: a case study of Lancaster 1880–1914', *Economic History Review* (May 2009).

Valerie Sanders is Professor of English at the University of Hull, specializing in Victorian literature. She has published on Harriet Martineau, anti-feminist women novelists, Victorian women's autobiography, and, most recently, *The Brother-Sister Culture in Nineteenth-Century Literature from Austen to Woolf* (2002). Her book, *The Tragi-Comedy of Victorian Fatherhood* (2009), questions the popular stereotype of the harsh paterfamilias, drawing on the personal responses of father-figures themselves, including Dickens, Darwin and Gladstone.

Gail Savage is a professor of History at St. Mary's College of Maryland. She has published widely on the history of social policy, including *The Social Construction of Expertise: The English Civil Service and Its Influence, 1919–1939* (1996), and she is currently completing a book manuscript on the history of divorce in England entitled 'Breaking up is Hard to Do: Divorce and Divorce Law Reform in England, 1828–1937'.

Simon Szreter is Reader in History and Public Policy, University of Cambridge, Fellow and Director of Studies in History, St John's College Cambridge, and Editor, www.historyandpolicy.org. He has authored and edited books and articles in the fields of modern social and demographic history, the history of demography and the social sciences, and in public health and development. His principal publications have been *Fertility, Class and Gender in Britain 1860–1940* (1996); *Changing Family Size in England and Wales 1891–1911: Place, Class and Demography*, co-authored with E. Garrett, A. Reid and K. Schurer (2001); and *Categories and Contexts. Anthropological* *and Historical Studies in Critical Demography*, co-edited with H. Sholkamy and A. Dharmalingam (2004); and *Health and Wealth. Studies in History and Policy* (2005). He and Kate Fisher are currently completing a book for publication, provisionally titled *Private Lives. Sex, Love and Marriage in England 1918–1963*.

Deborah Thom is a college lecturer at Robinson College, Cambridge. She teaches twentieth-century British and European social and cultural history in the faculties of History, Social and Political Sciences and History and Philosophy of Science at Cambridge. Her first book was *Nice Girls and Rude Girls* about women's work in the First World War published in 1998. She has published on gender and history, war, photography, child psychology and education and is currently writing a book on the history of corporal punishment of children in Britain since 1899.

Abigail Wills is a postdoctoral Career Development Fellow in History at Brasenose College, Oxford. She completed her PhD at Clare College, Cambridge, in 2005. Her publications include 'Delinquency, Masculinity and Citizenship in England, 1950–1970', *Past and Present* 187 (2005); 'Historical Myth-making in Juvenile Justice Policy', *History and Policy* (2007); 'Resistance, Identity and Historical Change in Residential Institutions for Juvenile Delinquents' in H. Johnston (ed.), *Punishment and Control in Historical Perspective* (2008). Her current research project explores the history of childhood nutrition and health visiting between 1930 and 1970, continuing her interest in questions of gender, professional expertise, subjectivity and social policy in twentieth-century Britain.

Introduction: The Politics of Domestic Authority in Britain Since 1800

Ben Griffin, Lucy Delap and Abigail Wills

Beatrice Webb, born in 1858 to a servant-keeping family, recalled her development of consciousness of social station through observing her mother's exercise of domestic authority. Webb wrote, 'As life unfolded I became aware that I belonged to a class of persons who habitually gave orders, but who seldom, if ever, executed the orders of other people. My mother sat in her boudoir and gave orders – orders that brooked neither delay nor evasion.'[1] The power to give voice to one's will and compel obedience over others has long been a central part of personal and social identity, and consequently domestic authority has been a powerful and controversial theme in the political, social and cultural history of the nineteenth and twentieth centuries. Whether deployed by husbands, by public bodies such as Poor Law Guardians, Members of Parliament and judges, by masters and mistresses, by servants or by parents, claims to exercise domestic authority have been of central importance to the history of modern Britain.

As the influential work of Catharine Hall and Leonore Davidoff has shown, domestic authority played a vital role in the formation of social class in the nineteenth century, serving as a means through which social station might be established, enacted and contested.[2] Moreover, domestic authority formed an emotional resource and was implicated in the formation of individual subjectivities, as the work of Carolyn Steedman and Alison Light has shown.[3] It was central to the relatively restricted social positions open to women that they could construct themselves as authorities in the home, though to do so sometimes brought them into conflict with others who also laid claim to such authority. The home has been a key location for struggles around these issues, through negotiation and advice, manipulation and outright physical force, but the power-play of the home was also central to public political discourse, serving both as a metaphor and as a material constraint on who could be associated with political agency.[4] This aspect of domestic authority continued to mark British society and political culture. Writing of interwar Britain, Alison Light has pointed out the paradox that the most personal and intimate spaces should also be capable of being read

1

as the most national and public territories, sites at which gender norms and narratives of class and nation were acted out.[5] The chapters of this book take up the challenge of thinking about domestic authority in all its myriad forms. In the process, they add important insights to our understanding of 'domestic authority', both in terms of how it has played out historically in Britain over the past 200 years and as a theoretical construct.

The first aspect of this involves thinking in new ways about the meanings of familial authority, and in particular how it relates to other defining aspects of domestic relations, such as love, reciprocity, and consanguinity. Szreter and Fisher's chapter on the growth of 'companionate' marriage in mid-twentieth-century Britain suggests ways in which relations of equality and of authority were not mutually exclusive, but rather existed in creative tension. 'Love' was acknowledged to have complex meanings within relationships, and a commitment to mutuality could coexist with a continued gendered division of labour within the family. This suggests that subjective understandings of 'authority' within the family did not necessarily correspond to what one might expect, given the unequal distribution of power or resources.

Margaret Beetham expands on this link between authority and subjectivity in her chapter on reading and domestic service in the Victorian era. Beetham's discussion focuses our attention on the cultural and symbolic dimensions of the 'servant problem'. The management of servants took on a deeper significance than simply the ordering of individual households, illustrated through her account of the profound challenge that the 'reading servant' offered to the social and gendered order. Beetham's findings suggest that the control of the reading matter of domestic servants can be understood as an attempt to minimise opportunities for interiority as a strategy of asserting domestic authority. Reading, as she notes, was 'a place for the production of ... the self', and was thus seen as a threat to the established hierarchies of the household. By reading to the children of the household and helping themselves to their employers' books, servants could disrupt the link between knowledge and power in a similarly threatening way. Domestic authority, then, did not just play out in material culture, but involved a complex interaction between culturally sanctioned hierarchies of power.

Related to this point is the question of how domestic authority extended beyond the family, most particularly in the context of growing state intervention into the family from the mid-nineteenth century onwards. Anna Clark and Megan Doolittle, for example, look at the role of the state as 'substitute parent'. Doolittle makes the point that state recognition of domestic authority was contingent on the financial autonomy of the head of the household. Where this was absent, domestic authority could be practically and symbolically withdrawn: state welfare, as she puts it, was 'formulated as ... a form of substitute fatherhood'. In this argument, the burgeoning welfare state did as much to undermine the working-class family as it did to bolster it, forcing families into defensive positions. Ginger Frost, in her chapter on illegitimacy in Victorian England, makes a similar point about the ambiguity of public definitions of authority, and the difficulties this created for fathers – leading some to extreme violence in defence of their position as heads of family.

Yet at another level, as Siân Pooley notes in her chapter on parental authority in late nineteenth- and early twentieth-century Auckland and Burnley, the nascent welfare state provided an arena within which parental power was actively solicited. She argues that ideas of 'professional parent-hood' developing in the early twentieth century meant that parents were expected to assert their authority vis-à-vis the welfare state. Moreover, as Deborah Thom suggests, the family also continued to be understood as essentially 'private' in significant ways well into the second half of the twentieth century. Her study of corporal punishment in twentieth-century Britain notes that despite a developing consensus against the practice within domestic advice literature, children continued to be punished physically in a majority of homes. Here, relations of authority and autonomy within families functioned as a force for continuity in socio-cultural norms. The idea of parental authority as independent of and ultimately superior to the state had powerful political and public support throughout the period under study.

The origins and meanings of such prevailing cultural models of domestic authority are a further important theme. Alana Harris, in her chapter on Catholic understandings of domesticity in post-war England, looks at the changing intellectual underpinnings of different models of family authority. She argues that the relationship between religious and 'official' understandings of family was far from unproblematic, and shows how Catholic model of family provided a resource for both reinforcing and challenging official norms. Valerie Sanders thinks in similar terms about family rituals, notably baptism, and explores their role in both bolstering and undermining established lines of authority. Christening ceremonies, she argues, were used by male heads of household as an occasion for 'secular networking', undermining the church and women's domestic authority.

Cultural norms could be quite distinct from legal precept when it came to domestic life. Gail Savage makes the point that in the second half of the nineteenth century, the legal authority of a man over his wife was in practice conditional on the extent to which his behaviour was seen as culturally acceptable. Thus while the law did not recognise that a husband could rape his wife, divorce could be granted to wives based on claims of cruelty by 'husbands who attempted to enforce their marital rights violently'. Judges' interpretations of legal doctrine were thus informed by wider cultural norms of appropriate husbandly behaviour. The construction of 'hegemonic' norms of domestic authority was a complex process, in which law, custom and evolving familial practices interacted.

Finally, several chapters call attention to the need to think about space – both within the home and within different localities – in understanding the lived experience of domestic authority. The nineteenth- and twentieth-century 'servant question', for example, made continual reference to the difficulties of managing the circulation of servants, guests and children within domestic space. 'Domestic space' is a construction that, as Davidoff and Hall suggested, and numerous other historians have elaborated, is particularly charged and changeable over the nineteenth and twentieth centuries.[6] Siân Pooley draws attention to the local dimensions of familial relations, noting that 'national' prescriptive models of childrearing were taken up in very different ways in different parts of the country. In Burnley, for example, ideas of 'professional parenting' had purchase as early as the 1860s, whereas in the coal-mining district of Auckland, these had little influence even by 1900. Jane Hamlett explores the spatial dimensions of familial life within the confines of the home, showing how 'parents controlled and constructed their relationship with their children by permitting or restricting their access to adult spaces in the home'. This study of space usefully brings to light 'hidden' or transgressive aspects of the network of family relationships, such as sibling rivalry, the arithmetic of parental attention, and the undermining of parental and class authority by servants. The mobility of different actors within these spaces, and how this shaped their interaction within them, is central to an account of authority and power within the home. As Hamlett's chapter suggests, children proved to be particularly adept at crossing boundaries, while also being prone to attempts to segregate them from other areas of the home, or from associating with servants. The chapter by Judy Giles points to the powers of servants to pervade many or all areas of domestic space, though mistresses often sought to limit their powers of circulation, or to render them invisible through manipulation of names and clothes.

The aim of this collection is thus both to acknowledge the flourishing nature of the study of authority practices and to enable a broad historical review of the household as a site of the 'micropolitics' of the negotiation of authority – the power to speak, to spend, to consume, to name, to command, to trespass and cross boundaries. The concept of domestic authority helps us to reconceive the home as an arena of active negotiation, agency and remembering. It should be seen as a site of flux for some central social identities, rather than a realm of constraint and timeless domestic labour. The contributions also point beyond the boundaries of the home to explore the way in which domestic authority was also being negotiated and contested in wider realms such as the courts, Parliament, the workhouse or the church.

The transformation of domestic authority?

A crucial part of this enterprise is to chart the changing contexts in which contests over domestic authority took place. The meanings of concepts like 'home', 'family', 'public' and 'private' are not historical constants, while both prescriptive ideals and the practice of domestic authority have changed considerably since the late eighteenth century. This second half of this introduction will therefore chart some of the major transformations in the history of domesticity in the early nineteenth century in order to provide both a historical and a historiographical context for the chapters that follow, most of which deal with the period after 1850.

The agenda for historical research on domestic authority was set by Leonore Davidoff and Catherine Hall's pioneering book *Family Fortunes: Men and Women of the English Middle Class, 1780–1850*. Davidoff and Hall argued that the period between 1780 and 1850 saw the formation of a middle class in Britain which distinguished itself from the working class and the aristocracy by its claims to moral and religious authority, much of which derived from the evangelical revival of the late eighteenth century. Because evangelicals saw the world as full of temptation and sin they valued the home as a refuge from the sinfulness of the public sphere and increasingly sought to separate the public sphere of work and politics from the private sphere of the home. This separation of spheres was profoundly gendered: men were seen as better able to cope with the trials of the public sphere, while women were supposed to maintain their purity by remaining in the private sphere, where they could create a domestic environment in which family religion could prosper. By the 1840s they argued, these ideas 'which had originally been particularly linked to Evangelicalism had become the common sense of the English middle class'.[7] Since the publication of *Family Fortunes* all writing about the history of gender politics has taken place in the shadow of the debate about whether or not gender relations can be said to have been characterised by 'separate spheres', and this conceptual framework has informed nearly all studies of domestic authority in the nineteenth and twentieth centuries.[8]

Regrettably, 'separate spheres' has become a straw man, a reductive caricature of an argument that presents an easy target for historiographical potshots.[9] A more constructive approach than attacking this straw man is to develop the agenda for further research set by Davidoff and Hall's book. Their argument about the development of 'separate spheres' referred to a number of distinct developments, each of which had its own chronology: an ideology of domesticity, the practice of a sexual division of labour, changes in patterns of women's work, the association of a conceptual division between public and private with male and female, and the separation of home and work. Some of these areas remain relatively unexplored even 20 years after the publication of *Family Fortunes*, while much confusion has been caused by the conflation of these separate features, as arguments about any one of these developments have been assumed to rebut theories about 'separate spheres' *tout court*.[10] There is a need for more detailed research on each of these areas, but it is possible to venture some suggestions based on the most recent research which support Davidoff and Hall's view that gender relations underwent significant changes in the late eighteenth and early

nineteenth centuries while at the same time qualifying some of its arguments. We will suggest that despite arguments in favour of a 'long eighteenth
century' there are good reasons to treat the period since 1780 separately,
and suggest that the meaning of domesticity and family life underwent
major changes that raised difficult questions about how households should
be ordered.

The recent surge of research on the eighteenth century has had an important effect on our understanding of developments which until recently
nineteenth-century specialists called their own. Amanda Vickery's famous
review article posited two fundamental challenges to Davidoff and Hall's
chronology.[11] First, she argued that the rhetoric of 'separate spheres' was
nothing new. This is incontestable, though it leaves open questions of
whether or not there were changes in how these traditional ideas were
understood, propagated and received – the purchase of separate spheres ideology on particular groups.[12] Second, Vickery pointed out that Davidoff
and Hall's picture of class formation was incompatible with the growing
scepticism about an 'industrial revolution' taking place in the late eighteenth and early nineteenth centuries.[13] Although some have attempted to
rehabilitate the idea of an industrial revolution, the latest research has pow-
erfully reinforced the basic picture that the British economy grew slowly
but steadily in the seventeenth and eighteenth centuries from a relatively
high base, and only entered a 'take-off' phase in the 1820s.[14] The implications of this work promise a profound transformation of our understanding
of the political and social history of Britain, but for our purposes it is sufficient merely to note that arguments about long-term continuities have
prompted Davidoff and Hall to retreat from their earlier claims about class
formation.[15]

And yet despite these arguments in favour of long-term continuities, the
more that we learn about gender in the eighteenth century, the more different it seems from the nineteenth century. The codes of 'politeness' and
'sensibility' that had regulated eighteenth-century masculinity did not survive the political and cultural upheavals of the fin de siècle and by the
middle of the nineteenth century 'refinement' had given way to 'character' as the crucial component of respectable manliness (though the legacy of
'politeness' and 'sensibility' on ideals of femininity perhaps lasted longer).[16]
Philip Carter has noted that one aspect of this transformation was 'a desire
to move...to more exclusive and intimate forms of sociability'; the assem-
bly or public walk now gave way to the home as a site for sociability and
'the dining- and drawing-room became key locations for genteel contact'.[17]
This retreat to the domestic arena was encouraged by the evangelical revival,
which increasingly came to see the public sphere as a source of moral danger.
While it is difficult to support claims that as a result of these developments
women were increasingly confined to the home in practice, it is certainly
true that in the period after 1780 public space was differentiated from the

home with increasing sharpness and this process can be traced through two significant semantic transformations.

The first change concerns that most basic of concepts, 'the family', which underwent a significant change some time after 1800. As Naomi Tadmor has demonstrated, when people in the eighteenth century spoke about 'families' they could have intended to refer to groups of kin, but more often 'what they had in mind was a household unit, which could comprise related and non-related dependants living under the authority of a householder: it might include a spouse, children, other relations, servants, apprentices, boarders, sojourners, or only some of these.'[18] At some point after 1800 this clearly changed as the word became more closely associated with the nuclear family. The second semantic transformation has been suggested by Lawrence Klein, who has argued that 'generally in the eighteenth century, the distinction between the private and the public did not correspond to the distinction between home and not-home.' Consequently, privacy was ascribed to forms of behaviour that we would consider public and time spent at home was not necessarily time spent in private, while the gendering of the various meanings of 'public' that Klein identifies was far more complicated than the existing literature has allowed.[19] That is to say that during the period covered by this book, distinctively modern ideas about a distinction between public and private developed. The years after 1800 saw significant changes in the way that key terms like 'family', 'public' and 'private' were conceptualised, even if the practice of work and family life remained much the same for large parts of the population. This process was fundamentally gendered, as Davidoff and Hall demonstrated: the home was increasingly seen as not only 'private' but also as a 'feminine' space. John Tosh's pioneering work has demonstrated that an essential feature of middle-class masculinities was the need to negotiate this shifting boundary, as men tried to find a domestic role within this feminised sphere alongside their responsibilities as breadwinners in the public sphere.[20]

Further research on the development of the concepts of 'the private' or 'the domestic' is needed, especially for the twentieth century: work that should be mindful of the fact that economic, political and social transformations were all changing the meanings attached to work, civil society and the state, creating multiple and shifting 'publics' against which to define the domestic.[21] The fierce controversies over the state in its relations with the Church throughout the nineteenth century clearly indicate the problems of defining the boundaries of 'the state', civil society and the private individual.[22] This complicates any attempt to claim that women were engaged in more 'public' activities in the nineteenth century than the eighteenth century, because we cannot assume that the meanings of either 'public' or 'private' activities were stable. Rather, the new activities and agencies that developed after 1800 were not self-evidently 'public' or 'private' to contemporaries, and at the heart of nineteenth-century gender politics were battles over the public or private character of, say, the voluntary societies of the 1830s and 1840s, the anti-slavery campaigns, or new agencies of local government like school boards.[23] Was sitting on a school board an extension of women's domestic maternal role or an intrusion into the public sphere? At what point did participation in philanthropic societies become a public role? The creation of 'separate spheres' was not a dramatic change in lifestyles so much as a dynamic and never-completed process of labelling that shaped the terms in which men and women understood their social world. The struggle for domestic authority therefore took place in a domestic sphere whose boundaries were uncertain, changing, and constantly contested, but in a context after the 1770s when it was thought increasingly important to make the attempt to distinguish between 'public' and 'private'.

The case for seeing the 1780s as a point of departure has been made most forcibly by Dror Wahrman, who has argued that in the final two decades of the eighteenth century there was a revolution in the way that people conceived of personal identity. Across a range of discourses he identifies a shift from 'gender play' to 'gender panic': a mentalité 'which allowed eighteenth-century categories of gender to be imagined as occasionally mutable, potentially unfixed, and even as a matter of choice, disappeared with remarkable speed'. As part of this process, 'long-standing forms and practices that had formerly capitalized on (and sometimes wallowed in) the acknowledged limitations of gender boundaries now became socially unacceptable and culturally unintelligible.'[24] The explanation for this sudden change, he suggests, was the American War of Independence, a conflict which contemporaries found difficult to explain in terms of prevalent notions of identity, and consequently an event that prompted an effort to place categories of identity – especially race, class and gender – on more stable foundations. One aspect of this was an effort to reassert clear distinctions between gender roles and root them in essential biological differences between the sexes.[25] The belief that the conflict was an unnatural civil war 'was frequently expressed through images of an unnatural family affair or domestic strife', and the restoration of household harmony through the reassertion of clear gender roles and female submission therefore became a pressing concern.[26] In this respect 'gender panic' forms just one part of that broader movement for the reformation of manners that followed defeat in America – that national effort to set Britain's house in order and re-establish the nation's virtue by enforcing stricter adherence to particular moral codes.[27] The domestic values that were propagated were by no means new – the need for patriarchal authority and female submission – what was new was the urgency with which they were pressed on the attention of the public and the perceived risks of ignoring the increasingly strident warnings. This is reflected in the sheer scale of the production of literature urging the benefits of domesticity between 1780 and 1850.[28]

The evangelical revival lay at the heart of the movement for the reformation of manners and it was evangelicalism that raised the moral stakes so high in the rhetoric of domesticity, driving the relentless urge to categorise activities as either 'public' or 'private' and promoting the idea that women were innately morally purer than men. The evangelical belief that the home should be a refuge from the sinfulness of the public sphere exerted a powerful hold on the nineteenth-century imagination and made nineteenth-century conduct literature qualitatively different from what had gone before.[29] A conduct manual from 1850 was typical in insisting that 'It is home...to which we must retreat from the bustle of life, if we would find enjoyment. It is in the serene employments of that blessed sanctuary, that we must fortify our spirits against temptation, and prepare for a better world on high.'[30] It was at home that a man could find 'the strength by which he is able successfully to combat life's temptations'.[31] In this context it is possible to understand the obsessive concern that nineteenth-century men and women displayed about household discord. Given the centrality of the home to the moral and religious health of the nation, it was obvious that 'few arguments will be needed to enforce the common obligation to guard its sanctity with trembling care, and to watch against everything that threatens its harmony.'[32]

The pressing question was then how to preserve household harmony. The most basic answer was that harmony should be obtained through submission to the will of the male head of the household. Women were allowed to exercise 'influence', but decision-making was to be left to their husbands.[33] The core of nineteenth-century domestic ideology was the internal logic which reconciled male authority with the ideal of marital unity and household harmony by assuming that women would happily surrender their own opinions.[34] Elizabeth Sandford, for instance, wrote in the 1830s that 'Where want of congeniality impairs domestic comfort...it is for woman, not for man, to make the sacrifice'.[35] In response women like Sarah Stickney Ellis tried to manipulate separate spheres ideology to carve out a space for female autonomy in the home. She thought that a husband ought to leave domestic arrangements alone 'simply because the operations necessary to be carried on in that department of his household, are alike foreign to his understanding and his tastes'. 'Thus, unless a husband can feel sufficient confidence in his wife, to allow her to rule with undisputed authority in this little sphere, her case must be a pitiable one indeed.'[36] If women's natural role was the care of others and if women were naturally sources of beneficent moral influence then it became difficult to deny them authority in the home and possibly beyond.[37] This female subversion of separate spheres can be seen at one level as an alternative answer to the problem of maintaining household harmony: establishing a rigid sexual division of labour would minimise conflict between spouses, but it was not a position which challenged male authority head-on.

This is small wonder when we consider the powerful religious ideas legitimating male authority: in a deeply religious age these cannot be under-estimated. Not only did wives normally make a religious vow to obey their husbands as part of the marriage service, but such submission was enjoined by scripture. In the book of Genesis wives were told that 'thy desire shall be to thy husband, and he shall rule over thee', while St. Paul's letter to the Colossians unequivocally instructed, 'Wives, submit to your husbands, as is fitting in the Lord.'[38] It is little surprise that the most radical alternatives to patriarchal marriage were developed by groups far removed from the religious mainstream. Robert Owen's vision of communal childcare and easy divorce was made easier by his militant atheism.[39] Similarly, it is no surprise that the egalitarian vision of marriage that found its fullest expression in John Stuart Mill's essay on *The subjection of women* was developed in the 1830s by the circle of liberal Anglicans and Unitarians who clustered around W. J. Fox's chapel at South Place in London – precisely those groups who felt least bound by literal interpretations of scripture.[40] In this light it seems plausible to suggest that changing attitudes towards domesticity and domes-tic authority followed changing patterns of religious belief, although the lack of research on this is striking, given the importance that the secondary lit-erature attaches to evangelicalism in the creation of domestic ideology. The transition from a primarily religious to a primarily secular understanding of gender roles is arguably one of the most significant changes in modern gen-der history. Even so, we should not get carried away by arguments about secularisation; as Alana Harris's chapter reminds us, religious language con-tinued to inform ideas about domesticity long after the Victorian age. A more nuanced approach is needed that acknowledges variety and change within religious discourse. For instance, the transformation that Boyd Hilton has identified between the evangelical emphasis on the Atonement that dom-inated early nineteenth-century culture and the greater emphasis on the Incarnation that came to dominate after mid-century seems fundamental, not least because it brought in its wake new attitudes to 'manliness'.[41]

If domesticity rested in part on religious foundations then we should expect some differences in domestic ideology and practice between denom-inational groups. Linda Wilson's study of non-conformist women between 1825 and 1875 supports this contention, though further research is required to explore the differences between pre-millenialist and post-millenialist vari-eties of evangelicalism and the range of positions within the Church of England.[42] Wilson has found that women who were Congregationalists (like Sarah Stickney Ellis) or Baptists seem to have internalised the clas-sic Victorian ideal of submissive, religious, domestic womanhood more than Wesleyans or Primitive Methodists.[43] Sandra Stanley Holton's study of Quaker women complements this by drawing attention to the unusual prominence of single women within the strong Quaker commitment to domesticity and family.[44] This raises the question of the purchase of the domestic ideal described above – how many people were affected by 'separate spheres' ideology and the accompanying concerns about domestic authority?

Class has formed the basis of most answers to this problem, with Davidoff and Hall famously arguing that 'separate spheres' was characteristic of the emerging middle class. Subsequent research has shown that domestic ideology, separation of spheres and evangelicalism were by no means restricted to one sociological group, but this does not mean that class is not a useful concept. If we treat class as one category of identity that contemporaries used to interpret the social order rather than as a heuristic retrospective sociological category then class can still be productively brought to bear on the history of domesticity.[45] Historians of the early modern period have suggested that during the eighteenth and nineteenth centuries behaviour that had characterised certain types of masculinity became increasingly associated with emerging class identities. Over time certain models of early modern manhood 'rooted in values ranging across prodigality, excess, bravado, brawn, transience, and collectivism, were positively claimed by, and became increasingly associated (often pejoratively) with the "meaner" sorts of men'. Similarly, 'some of the attributes of patriarchal manhood in terms of orderly, rational self-control ... were realigned with distinctions of social status, and became exclusively associated with the "better" or "middling" sorts'.[46] Domesticity should be seen in this light: as Dror Wahrman has convincingly argued, it was only after the debates on the 1832 Reform Act that the domestic ideal came to be seen as distinctively middle-class, part of the process by which the category of 'middle-class' became firmly entrenched in political discourse.[47] Since the meaning of 'domesticity' was no more fixed than the meaning of 'middle-class' the rhetoric of domesticity interacted in complex ways with fluid categories of social identity, as actors sought to locate themselves and others in schemes of social categorisation and hierarchy. The outcomes of these struggles were not simply political in their own right but also shaped a range of practices. For instance, Anna Clark's work has shown how working-class radicals abandoned older understandings of domesticity and tried to appropriate the evangelical ideal during the Chartist campaigns of the 1830s and 1840s.[48] Similarly, Elizabeth Foyster has shown how in the nineteenth century domestic violence became seen as primarily a working-class phenomenon, while Ben Griffin has argued that these perceptions of the abuse of male authority shaped parliament's reactions to demands for women's rights in the final third of the nineteenth century.[49]

It therefore makes no sense to set up 'separate spheres' as a straw man – a theory whose only utility lies in the insights we can develop by disproving it. The task of historians is to examine how the rhetoric of domesticity operated and was made meaningful in particular contexts, how contemporaries used it to make sense of their experiences, how it shaped the actions of particular individuals or groups, and how it changed over time. What is needed then is a more sophisticated approach to the relationship between social identities, domestic ideology understood as a set of prescriptive norms, and the range of behaviours involved in the practice of everyday life. In this context Simon Szreter's model of changing patterns of fertility provides a helpful way of thinking about patterns of domestic practice. Szreter has argued that 'roles, norms and social identities...are constructed by and embedded in the shared social practices and values of social groups or what might more accurately be termed "communication communities" '.[50] Local neighbourhood or street communities, churches or chapels, schools, workplaces and the national media have all been sites where individuals participate in communication communities and where individuals are socialised into different sets of expectations, norms and values. At its most basic we can see this in the differences between the hard-drinking manual labourers and the self-improving artisans who populate Anna Clark's study of the early nineteenth-century working class: each had distinctive patterns of socialisation which were reflected in different models of masculinity.[51] Seen in this way it is clear that the middle classes participated in national communication communities, through national printed media and particular educational institutions for example, whereas working-class communication communities were predominantly rooted in shared localities, often with their own dialects, and face to face contact.[52] That is to say that the middle classes were exposed to a nationally standardised set of ideas about domestic practices through the vast outpourings of pamphlets and books on household management and marriage, while working-class domesticity was governed by local norms enforced by 'rough music'.[53] The intersection of these two cultures among the lower-middle-classes could produce serious strains as couples struggled to rework middle-class ideals, prompting the kind of ridicule visited upon Mr Pooter by George and Weedon Grossmith in *The Diary of a Nobody*.[54] Szreter has demonstrated that there were substantial variations in the norms and practices associated with fertility between different regional and occupational communities; for instance, between the Potteries, with its widespread domestic industry performed by household units, and mining areas like South Wales, where men earned high wages and there were few employment opportunities for women.[55] There is every reason to suspect that there were also different approaches to the exercise of domestic authority that can only be explored through the kind of regional case studies presented by Siân Pooley and Simon Szreter and Kate Fisher in this volume.

This focus on multiple domestic ideals and practices should not however obscure large-scale trends. The evangelical-influenced model of domestic authority described above *was* culturally dominant among the educated classes in the first half of the nineteenth century but came under increasing pressure in the second half. Growing concerns about negligent and violent husbands, abusive and irresponsible parents, not to mention the dangers of unbridled male sexuality, prompted serious re-evaluation of the limits of male domestic authority.[56] The chapters that follow by Ginger Frost and Gail Savage pay eloquent testimony to this point. In a quieter way men were becoming dissatisfied with the emotional rewards of patriarchy as it had been practised by their fathers in the final decades of the nineteenth century, leading John Tosh to identify a 'flight from domesticity' for middle-class men in his major study of Victorian masculinity.[57] Other men experimented with new forms of emotional and sexual intimacy, leading some historians to propose 'companionate marriage' as a large-scale trend characterising the close of the nineteenth century.

Claims to novelty must be treated with caution. It is troubling that the move towards a more nuclear, socially isolated family and towards 'companionship' between couples in the home has been heralded and yet later 'rediscovered' on numerous occasions. Companionate marriage seems to be such a slippery and capacious concept that it offers little purchase for historians trying to map change over time. Ambitious accounts of courtship and marriage such as that offered by John Gillis have ended up posing continuity between the nineteenth and twentieth centuries, failing to find a shift towards intimacy and understanding between spouses.[58] As suggested above, part of this problem is due to the failure to distinguish between various aspects of the social history of domesticity, which need to be carefully disaggregated, and their relationship to complicated and constantly changing ideologies of marriage and domesticity. The uncertain purchase of 'companionate marriage' points to some serious gaps in the historiography of domestic authority in the twentieth century, which lacks ambitious overarching texts such as *Family Fortunes* or explanatory frameworks such as 'separate spheres'. While there is a wealth of detailed empirical work, there are fewer more general concepts which attempt to capture social change on a broad scale. If our understanding of the development of Victorian domestic ideology is well developed, our understanding of its decline is still remarkably sketchy and the contributions to this book aim to fill some of the gaps.

'Companionate marriage' (or variants of this concept such as Marcus Collins' idea of 'mutualism'[59]) was clearly conceived of in the eighteenth and nineteenth centuries, but it has been seen by many as becoming broadly accepted and practised in the twentieth century. The tone of advice manuals became much more insistently dogmatic concerning the need to establish a marital complementarity that would enable deeper forms of intimacy, including sexual intimacy. In the nineteenth century the authors of advice literature had been predominantly clergymen or women writers like Sarah Ellis, but in the twentieth century new kinds of 'expert' emerged claiming new forms of knowledge and authority to pronounce on marriage: psychologists, sociologists and agony aunts, for example. The pronouncements of such experts need to be carefully located in their social context. It may be that the twentieth century saw the decline of distinctive local patterns of domestic authority such as those described by Siân Pooley, in favour of a nationally more standardised set of norms and practices. Certainly, companionate marriage can be linked to some of the major changes in domestic living arrangements and fertility norms which do seem to make the twentieth century different. As couples began to produce smaller families earlier in their marriages, and as mortality rates fell, there were extended periods when adult companionship became the central mode of marital interaction. Some historians have argued that this created a more demanding emotional profile for marriage, and opened the door to more egalitarian family dynamics.[60] But demographic changes alone cannot account for the complexity of subjectivities and experiences that were encountered and produced through the discourse of companionate marriage. Relations of power, authority and intimacy between couples shifted with the new availability of sexual knowledge in the interwar decades, with women's changed citizen status in 1918 and 1928 and the feminist politicisation of domestic organisation that accompanied it. New patterns of paid employment taken up by women in manufacturing industries and the expanding service sector were also significant in refiguring marriages.[61] And the recent historical attention to masculinity suggests that it was not only women's work, but also the jobs taken up by men in new industries had the power to change profoundly relationships of domestic authority, as Pat Ayer's work on the balance between familial and personal consumption by men in different sectors of employment suggests.[62] Finally, the twentieth-century state came to interact with individuals in the domestic realm through new avenues – health visitors, midwives, teachers, nurses – which again reshaped the idea of authority in the home.[63]

One of the most profound transformations of domestic authority in the twentieth century was the changing institution of domestic service. Service formed a key realm in which middle-class women, and occasionally men, attempted to shape themselves as authorities within the home, and engaged with 'domesticity'. It was also an institution through which working-class women frequently subverted that authority and asserted their own. In the literature on domestic service, a similarly slippery concept to that of companionate marriage has been the idea of a shift from 'status' to 'contract', or from personalised service and its intense authority relations to a more professional or 'modern' relationship in which personal authority was, ideally, left out of play. Like companionate marriage, this 'shift' has been posited as a key symbolic moment, characterising the move to 'modernity', or a shift from 'community' to 'civil society', as a basis for social interaction. The changing legal norms of employment in domestic service, however, tell us little about how such a process of professionalisation might have been achieved.[64] The idea of contract is used by historians to indicate a far deeper change, in realms beyond that of service employment. It has been used, for example, to shed light on the changes in twentieth-century marriage, from a realm of, ideally, material support and companionship, to romantic love, and finally to what Anthony Giddens has termed the 'confluent love' of the late twentieth century 'separating and divorcing society'.[65] But this shift to 'contract' in all its guises is variously located between the late eighteenth and the late twentieth centuries, and cannot easily be tied down to any particular evidential basis. It is clear that there has been a transformation of intimacy and authority within the home during the twentieth century, but that the basis of this is multifaceted and needs to be thoroughly historicised.

Historians of domestic service have tended to see the two World Wars as marking watersheds, in creating conditions allowing for a diminution of deference and personalised authority in the home, and with this, a growing refusal to serve in private residential service.[66] But we should be wary of overstating the nature of the change; there was no 'inevitable' decline of domestic service, understood as linked to the creation of a 'modern' nuclear family that no longer included the wide variety of kin, dependents and workers who had been found in households of earlier centuries. Indeed, households continued to be complex affairs, comprising lodgers, kin and domestic workers in the twentieth century, and domestic authority thus continued to be a contested and locally diverse set of prescriptions and practices. There was, however, a transfer of domestic labour from live-in service to more casual and marginalised domestic help – chars, cleaners and au pairs – that went with the transformation of middle-class feminine identity from 'mistress' to 'housewife'.

With this shift went a change in the symbolic value of the domestic interior and the practices of housekeeping. Becky Conekin has argued that in post-war Britain, the household and its material artefacts became a significant site of 'modernity', through discourses of design, taste and efficiency.[67] The workers who continued to 'help' housewives have tended to be historically invisible, eclipsed by the new importance attributed to the refrigerator or the 'hoover'. There has been little attempt to chart their experiences with the same fascination and attention that has been given to the maids, nannies and cooks that characterised the sector before the First World War. The contribution by Judy Giles to this volume examines such workers alongside more traditional 'servants', and provides a sense of the evolution of the 'servant problem' beyond the Second World War and into the second half of the twentieth century. While service was prominent in the first half of the twentieth century, the sharp fall in households employing servants after the Second World War has led historians to neglect this later period. However, both the persistence of casual cleaners *and* the continuing cultural prominence of servants lead us to look afresh at this later period, and to ask why the idea of domestic service has continued to have such salience and visibility in post-war British society.

Amongst the non-servant keeping classes, varieties of domestic authority were tempered and supported in the nineteenth and early twentieth centuries by the power of neighbours and relatives to enforce and regulate communal norms, and to police any 'irregularities', particularly in poorer communities where housing conditions allowed for more intrusion.[68] The power of wives and mothers within households has been argued by Melanie Tebbutt to have depended on the degree to which they were able to tap into the networks of gossip and 'wary mutuality' that characterised working-class communities.[69] Access to these kinds of resources was strongly determined by ethnicity, gender and class. Neighbourliness was a major source of support to some working-class women, but, Tebbutt argues, was found intrusive by many working-class men, and increasingly, was avoided by families with aspirations for social mobility.[70] The experiences of immigrant families were varied, with neighbourly support being denied within some hostile neighbourhoods, and being a resource developed within immigrant communities themselves, to enable discrimination to be parried.[71] As the twentieth century brought technical and sanitary advances, and changes in the spatial layout and location of working-class housing, the ways in which neighbours and communities might intervene in or influence domestic authority became less marked. The increasing availability of council housing in new estates in the interwar decades, and of mass owner-occupation after the Second World War, created new domestic spaces that allowed for the reframing of social relationships and the undermining of the localised communication communities that had characterised working-class sociability. With the decline of multiple occupancy houses, there was a new isolation from the extended family and community in the domestic realm from the 1930s.

But this story is not one of a simple shift to a more intense and private version of 'domesticity', despite the common assertion of more domestic versions of both masculinity and femininity becoming popular in the interwar years. As Martin Francis has suggested, both men and women felt ambivalent about the idealised versions of domesticity presented to them in the interwar decades, and in revised form in the 1940s and 1950s. Companionate marriage provided no easy blueprint explaining how to construct intimate relationships, as men indulged in homosocial fantasies of 'flight from commitment', and women increasingly experimented with combinations of paid work and motherhood.[72] At the same time as some experienced more freedom to transform their domestic norms, some family forms became pathologised – the working mother in the 1950s, the single mother in the 1980s – and these marginalised households found it periodically hard to assert their authority vis-à-vis the state, kinship networks and communities.[73]

These tensions over authority played out in relation to neighbourhood, space and domesticity were perhaps most pronounced when it came to the exercise of authority between generations. Recent work by Selina Todd has suggested that as younger women became more likely to take paid employment outside of the home in the interwar decades, their wages became a resource in determining their ability to marshal authority within the home.[74] Shifts in the nature of resources used to construct domestic authority from the mid-twentieth century led to strong generational divides, with tensions emerging between the divergent expectations and aspirations of parents and children. Such shifts were particularly marked in the south-east, where suburbanisation and changes in retail were widespread and greater mobility made for a more privatised family life. These changes reproduced similar tensions to those found between husbands and wives as married women had achieved greater economic independence in the course of the nineteenth century.[75]

We can also see a change in the authority exercised by older generations towards younger ones in the twentieth century, as pensions and decreased mortality allowed grandparents to be present and to marshal resources for longer in twentieth-century households. The small pensions available to the elderly poor from 1908 sometimes made them the sole breadwinners in households experiencing unemployment or ill-health, and until other welfare benefits became more widely available, pensions gave older generations new avenues of authority. The new role that grandparents took in caring for their grandchildren as more women worked in the early to mid-twentieth century also created new interdependencies, intimacies and points of conflict in households. These care relationships declined towards the middle to end of the twentieth century, as geographical mobility made grandparents less likely to live near their wider families, and as grandmothers became more likely to be working themselves when their grandchildren arrived.

Despite the appearance of such patterns of generational change and division, the historiography of intergenerational relations in nineteenth- and twentieth-century Britain is still lacking in grand narrative frameworks. Two key transitions have emerged, and are held to have taken place first at the turn of the twentieth century and second in the 1960s. Viviana Zelizer's pioneering work, first published in 1985, established the notion of the new 'sacralisation' of childhood in early twentieth-century America, arguing that as the economic worth of children waned with the decline in child employment, so the emotional worth of the child within the family grew exponentially.[76] And with this shift went an intensification of parental authority over children, as 'care' of children intensified.[77] The second key transformation in parent–child relations is located during the 1960s, with the notion of the 'permissive shift'. The increasing consumer power of children and young people led to the growth of 'youth culture', which – it is assumed – led to the overthrow of traditional relations of authority between parents and their children.

Yet both these shifts need further elaboration. Their precise chronology is hazy. The focus of work on the 1960s in particular has been primarily 'public', with intergenerational relations studied through the lens of national or metropolitan cultural movements such as rock'n'roll and the beat poets, and through the activities of obviously 'rebellious' groups such as students and hippies.[78] This focus has ignored the importance of the domestic setting in coming to an understanding of 'public' generational conflicts. Historians such as Frank Mort and Peter Bailey have begun to explore the private dimensions of what they see as the radical intergenerational shifts of the post-Second World War period, looking in particular at the role of grammar schools in forging new class identities.[79] The contributions of this book highlight the importance of further detailed empirical work on this subject. Deborah Thom, for example, suggests that changing professional discourses on family – which are the focus of most historical research in this field – bear no straightforward relationship to practices within families. This in turn forces a reconsideration of the established chronologies of intergenerational relations in the later half of the twentieth century, and particularly the notion of a 1960s 'revolution' in parent–child authority.

More generally, we have encouraged contributions to this collection which look at some of the neglected actors and relationships of the domestic realm. Leonore Davidoff has suggested that historians should pay more attention to the domestic relationships that depart from the imagined ideal of the 'nuclear' family – the role of lodgers and landladies for example – or to those relationships that have escaped historical attention, such as sibling relationships.[80] Jane Hamlett's discussion of middle-class childhood takes up Davidoff's challenge to think about the relationships between siblings, and in her discussion of godparenting, Valerie Sanders sheds light on a historically neglected identity. It is notable, however, that certain groups still lack a presence in the historiography; most notably, the elderly represent an obvious gap in this collection. There is a pressing need to build on the work of Pat Thane in locating the elderly in the complex and reciprocal realm of the domestic.[81] Attention to issues of domestic authority that arise in households affected by migration would also seem a promising area of further research.[82]

However, while these neglected areas call for further attention, this should not be at the expense of a more holistic account of homes and households. Jane Hamlett points to the limitations of historical investigations which take certain relationships in isolation rather than situating them as part of a 'structural whole' – in other words, to focus on the elderly, parenting or marriage, at the expense of a wider landscape of the multiple relationships which go to make up 'the domestic'. This collection aims to remedy this gap in the literature both by offering accounts inspired by a broadly defined sense of domestic authority and by juxtaposing the chapters collected here so that an account of corporal punishment is set alongside one of godparenting or the 'domestic' authority of school teachers. We hope to create a fruitful space for exploring the inter-relations of these different areas of research, and in doing so to think in broader terms about the historiographical framework we can use to make sense of issues of domestic authority.

Notes

1. B. Webb quoted in K. Muggeridge (1967) *Beatrice Webb: A Life* (London: Secker and Warburg), p. 37.
2. L. Davidoff and C. Hall (1987) *Family Fortunes: Men and Women of the English Middle Class, 1780–1850* (Chicago: University of Chicago Press).
3. C. Steedman (1986) *Landscape for a Good Woman: A Story of Two Lives* (London: Virago); idem (2003) 'Servants and Their Relationship to the Unconscious', *Journal of British Studies* 42, pp. 316–50; A. Light (2007) *Mrs Woolf and the Servants* (London: Penguin).
4. A. Clark (1995) *The Struggle for the Breeches: Gender and the Making of the British Working Class* (Berkeley: University of California Press); H. Rogers (2000) *Women and the People: Authority, Authorship and the Radical Tradition in Nineteenth Century England* (Aldershot: Ashgate). See also A. August (2001) 'A Culture of Consolation? Rethinking Politics in Working-Class London, 1870–1914', *Historical Research* 74, p. 184 for an account of later controversies over domestic authority in London working-class communities.
5. A. Light (1991) *Forever England: Femininity, Literature and Conservatism Between the Wars* (London: Routledge), p. 12.
6. On the 'spatial turn', see F. Mort (1996) *Cultures of Consumption: Masculinities and Social Space in Late Twentieth Century Britain* (London: Routledge); M. Houlbrook (2001) 'Towards a Historical Geography of Sexuality', *Journal of Urban History* 27, p. 44.
7. Davidoff and Hall, *Family Fortunes*, p. 149.
8. A sensible overview of the debate over 'separate spheres' can be found in R. B. Shoemaker (1998) *Gender in English Society, 1650–1850. The Emergence of Separate Spheres?* (London: Longman Press).
9. For an incisive attack on this tendency, see Anna Clark's review of Amanda Vickery's book *The Gentleman's Daughter. Women's Lives in Georgian England* (New Haven: Yale University Press, 1998), www.history.ac.uk/reviews/paper/anna.html.
10. For the most detailed recent study of the separation of home and work, see E. Gordon and G. Nair (2003) *Public Lives. Women, Family and Society in Victorian Britain* (New Haven: Yale University Press), ch. 3, which echoes many of the findings of *Family Fortunes*, pp. 364–9.
11. A. Vickery (1993) 'Golden Age to Separate Spheres? A Review of the Categories and Chronology of English Women's History', *Historical Journal* 36, pp. 383–414.
12. On the difficulty of establishing the purchase of ideas, see P. Mandler (2004) 'The Problem with Cultural History', *Cultural and Social History* 1, pp. 94–117. On the continuities in domestic ideology between the eighteenth and nineteenth centuries, see M. Hunt (1996) *The Middling Sort: Commerce, Gender and the Family in England, 1680–1780* (Berkeley: University of California Press).
13. The classic statement of this position is found in N. F. R. Crafts (1985) *British Economic Growth During the Industrial Revolution* (Oxford: Clarendon Press). The

vast literature is summarised in J. Mokyr (2004) 'Accounting for the Industrial Revolution', in R. Floud and P. Johnson (eds), *The Cambridge Economic History of Modern Britain. Volume 1: Industrialisation, 1700–1860* (Cambridge: Cambridge University Press), pp. 1–27.

14. This is one of the findings of the ESRC research project on *The Changing Occupational Structure of Nineteenth Century Britain*, www-hpss.geog.cam.ac.uk/research/projects/occupations.

15. An indication of how subversive this new story could be for political historians is given by R. Brent (1992) 'New Whigs in Old Bottles', *Parliamentary History* 11, p. 156. Davidoff and Hall retreat from their earlier position about class formation in L. Davidoff and C. Hall (2002) *Family Fortunes: Men and Women of the English Middle Class, 1780–1850*, 2nd edn (London: Routledge), p. xxxi.

16. P. Carter (2001) *Men and the Emergence of Polite Society, Britain 1660–1800* (Harlow: Longman), pp. 213–14; J. Tosh, 'The Old Adam and the New Man: Emerging Themes in the History of English Masculinities, 1750–1850' and 'Gentlemanly Politeness and Manly Simplicity in Victorian England' in J. Tosh (2005) *Manliness and Masculinities in Nineteenth Century Britain: Essays on Gender, Family and Empire* (Harlow: Pearson Longman), pp. 61–82, 83–102.

17. Carter, *Men and the Emergence of Polite Society*, p. 213.

18. N. Tadmor, *Family and Friends in Eighteenth-Century England. Household, Kinship and Patronage* (Cambridge: Cambridge University Press, 2001), p. 272.

19. L. E. Klein (1996) 'Gender and the Public/Private Distinction in the Eighteenth Century: Some Questions about Evidence and Analytic Procedure', *Eighteenth Century Studies* 29, p. 105.

20. J. Tosh (1999) *A Man's Place. Masculinity and the Middle Class Home in Victorian England* (New Haven: Yale University Press).

21. A start has been made by M. McKeon (2005) *The Secret History of Domesticity: Public, Private and the Division of Knowledge* (Baltimore: Johns Hopkins University Press). On the meanings of 'civil society', see J. Harris (2003) 'From Richard Hooker to Harold Laski: Changing Perceptions of Civil Society in British Political Thought, Late Sixteenth to Early Twentieth Centuries', in J. Harris (ed.), *Civil Society in British History: Ideas, Identities, Institutions* (Oxford: Oxford University Press).

22. For an overview, see G. I. T. Machin (1977) *Politics and the Churches in Great Britain 1832–1868* (Oxford: Oxford University Press).

23. C. Midgley (1992) *Women Against Slavery: the British Campaigns, 1780–1870* (London: Routledge), p. 17; P. Hollis (1987) *Ladies Elect: Women in English Local Government, 1865–1914* (Oxford: Clarendon Press); R. J. Morris (1990) 'Clubs, Societies and Associations', in F. M. L. Thompson (ed.), *The Cambridge Social History of Britain, 1750–1950* (Cambridge: Cambridge University Press), Vol. 3, pp. 395–443.

24. D. Wahrman (2004) *The Making of the Modern Self. Identity and Culture in Eighteenth-Century England* (New Haven: Yale University Press), pp. 40–1.

25. Ibid., pp. 246–7.

26. Ibid. p. 242.

27. J. Innes (1990) 'Politics and Morals: The Reformation of Manners Movement in Later Eighteenth-Century England', in E. Hellmuth (ed.), *The Transformation of Political Culture. England and Germany in the Late Eighteenth Century* (Oxford: Oxford University Press), pp. 57–118.

28. Davidoff and Hall, *Family Fortunes*, 2nd edn, pp. xx–xxiii.
29. Shoemaker, *Gender in English Society*, p. 32.
30. G. Sargent (1851) *Domestic Happiness; Home Education; Politeness, and Good Breeding* (London: Groombridge and Sons), p. 12.
31. T. S. Arthur (1850) *Advice to Young Men on their Duties and Conduct in Life* (Boston: Phillips, Sampson), p. 99.
32. Anon. (1870) *Marriage and Home* (London: Morgan and Chase), pp. 24–5.
33. Davidoff and Hall, *Family Fortunes*, pp. 116–17; S. P. Walker (1998) 'How to Secure Your Husband's Esteem. Accounting and Private Patriarchy in the British Middle Class Household During the Nineteenth Century', *Accounting, Organisation and Society* 23, pp. 485–514.
34. See B. Griffin (2003) 'Class, Gender and Liberalism in Parliament, 1868–1882: The Case of the Married Women's Property Acts', *Historical Journal* 46, pp. 62–4 and *Feminism, Masculinity and Politics in Victorian Britain* (forthcoming), ch. 2.
35. E. Sandford (1831) *Woman, in Her Social and Domestic Character* (London: Longman), pp. 2–3.
36. S. Ellis (1843) *Wives of England: Their Relative Duties, Domestic Influence and Social Obligations* (London: Fisher, Son & Co.), p. 121.
37. For examples, see F. K. Prochaska (1980) *Women and Philanthropy in Nineteenth Century England* (Oxford: Clarendon Press); J. Walkowitz (1980) *Prostitution and Victorian Society: Women, Class and the State* (Cambridge: Cambridge University Press); H. Rogers, *Women and the People*.
38. Gen. ii:16; Colossians, iii, 18. For a discussion of how changes in religious culture affected attitudes to domestic authority, see Griffin, *Feminism, Masculinity and Politics*, chs 2 and 4.
39. B. Taylor (1983) *Eve and the New Jerusalem. Socialism and Feminism in the Nineteenth Century* (Cambridge, MA: Harvard University Press).
40. K. Gleadle (1995) *The Early Feminists: Radical Unitarians and the Emergence of the Women's Rights Movement 1831–1851* (Basingstoke: Macmillan); D. Wigmore-Beddoes (1971) *Yesterday's Radicals: A Study of the Affinity between Unitarianism and Broad Church Anglicanism in the 19th Century* (Cambridge: Cambridge University Press); R. Brent (1987) *Liberal Anglican Politics: Whiggery, Religion and Reform 1830–41* (Oxford: Clarendon Press).
41. B. Hilton (1988) *The Age of Atonement: The Influence of Evangelicalism on Social and Economic Thought, 1785–1865* (Oxford: Clarendon Press), esp. p. 333; idem (1989) 'Manliness, Masculinity and the Mid-Victorian Temperament', in L. Goldman (ed.), *The Blind Victorian: Henry Fawcett and British Liberalism* (Cambridge: Cambridge University Press), pp. 60–70.
42. On the importance of differences between pre-millenialist and post-millenialist varieties of evangelicalism, see Hilton, *Age of Atonement*, ch. 1; for suggestive comments on Anglican views towards sex and marriage, see J. Maynard (1993) *Victorian Discourses on Sexuality and Religion* (Cambridge: Cambridge University Press).
43. L. Wilson (2000) *Constrained by Zeal: Female Spirituality among Nonconformists, 1825–75* (Carlisle: Paternoster), pp. 138–40, 223.
44. S. S. Holton (2007) *Quaker Women: Personal Life, Memory and Radicalism in the Lives of Women Friends, 1780–1930* (London: Routledge).
45. For useful comments on how to approach class, see J. Thompson (1996) 'After the Fall: Class and Political Language in Britain, 1780–1900', *Historical Journal* 39, pp. 785–806.

46. A. Shepard (2003) *Meanings of Manhood in Early Modern England* (Oxford: Oxford University Press), p. 252; E. Foyster (2005) *Marital Violence. An English Family History, 1660–1857* (Cambridge: Cambridge University Press), pp. 72–81.

47. D. Wahrman (1993) 'Middle Class Domesticity Goes Public: Gender, Class and Politics from Queen Caroline to Queen Victoria', *Journal of British Studies* 32, pp. 396–432; see also D. Wahrman (1995) *Imagining the Middle Class: The Political Representation of Class in Britain, c. 1780–1840* (Cambridge: Cambridge University Press).

48. A. Clark (1992) 'The Rhetoric of Chartist Domesticity: Gender, Language and Class in the 1830s and 1840s', *Journal of British Studies* 31, pp. 62–88; idem, *The Struggle for the Breeches*.

49. Foyster, *Marital Violence*, pp. 72–81; Griffin, 'Class, Gender and Liberalism'.

50. S. Szreter (1995) *Fertility, Class and Gender in Britain 1860–1940* (Cambridge: Cambridge University Press), p. 546.

51. Clark, *The Struggle for the Breeches*.

52. Szreter, *Fertility, Class and Gender*, pp. 546–53. On dialect communities, see P. Joyce (1991) *Visions of the People: Industrial England and the Question of Class, 1848–1914* (Cambridge: Cambridge University Press).

53. See A. J. Hammerton (1992) *Cruelty and Companionship: Conflict in Nineteenth Century Married Life* (London: Routledge).

54. A. J. Hammerton (1999) 'Pooterism or Partnership? Marriage and Masculine Identity in the Lower Middle Class, 1870–1920', *Journal of British Studies* 38, pp. 291–321.

55. Szreter, *Fertility, Class and Gender*, pp. 488–503.

56. Hammerton, *Cruelty and Companionship*; Griffin, 'Class, Gender and Liberalism'; G. Behlmer (1982) *Child Abuse and Moral Reform in England 1870–1908* (Stanford: Stanford University Press); L. Bland (1987) 'The Married Woman, the "New Woman" and the Feminist: Sexual Politics in the 1890s', in J. Rendall (ed.), *Equal or Different: Women's Politics 1800–1914* (Oxford: Basil Blackwell), pp. 141–64; J. Walkowitz (1992) *City of Dreadful Delight. Narratives of Sexual Danger in Late-Victorian London* (Chicago: University of Chicago Press). The contribution of the women's movement to this process was vital, but still awaits its historian.

57. Tosh, *A Man's Place*, ch. 8. For a helpful critique of this idea, see M. Francis (2002) 'The Domestication of the Male? Recent Research on Nineteenth- and Twentieth-Century British Masculinity', *Historical Journal* 45, p. 643.

58. J. R. Gillis (1985) *For Better, For Worse: British Marriages, 1600 to the Present* (New York: Oxford University Press).

59. M. Collins (2001) *Modern Love: An Intimate History of Men and Women in Twentieth-Century Britain* (London: Atlantic Press).

60. L. Davidoff, M. Doolittle, J. Fink and K. Holden (1999) *The Family Story: Blood, Contract and Intimacy, 1830–1960* (London: Longman), p. 191.

61. For historical treatments of some of these changes, see E. Yeo (ed.) (1998) *Radical Femininity: Women's Self-Representation in the Public Sphere* (Manchester: Manchester University Press); C. Dyhouse (1989) *Feminism and the Family in England, 1880–1939* (Oxford: Blackwell); M. Glucksmann (1990) *Women Assemble: Women Workers and the New Industries in Inter-War Britain* (London: Routledge); K. Fisher (2006) *Birth Control, Sex and Marriage in Britain 1918–1960* (Oxford: Oxford University Press); H. Cook (2004) *The Long Sexual Revolution: English Women, Sex and Contraception, 1800–1975* (Oxford: Oxford University Press).

62. P. Ayers (2004), 'Work, Culture and Gender: The Making of Masculinities in Post-War Liverpool', *Labour History Review* 69: 2, pp. 153–67.
63. See S. Koven and S. Michel (eds) (1993), *Mothers of a New World* (London: Routledge); E. Ross (1993) *Love and Toil: Motherhood in Outcast London, 1870–1918* (Oxford: Oxford University Press); A. Davin (1996) *Growing up Poor: Home, House and Street in London* (London: Rivers Oram Press).
64. See, however, C. Steedman (2007) *Master and Servant: Love and Labour in the English Industrial Age* (Cambridge: Cambridge University Press), for a discussion of how employment law and the establishment of the Poor Law in the late eighteenth and early nineteenth centuries did effect a substantial change in the social relations of domestic service.
65. A. Giddens (1992) *The Transformation of Intimacy: Sexuality, Love and Eroticism in Modern Societies* (Cambridge: Polity Press), p. 61.
66. Teresa McBride, for example, poses the First World War as a dramatic end point of live-in domestic service; Judy Giles and Pamela Horn give more attention to service in the 1930s and 1940s, but posit the Second World War as a sea change. T. McBride (1976) *The Domestic Revolution* (London: Croom Helm); J. Giles (2004) *The Parlour and the Suburb: Domestic Identities, Class, Femininity and Modernity* (Oxford: Berg); P. Horn (2001) *Life Below Stairs in the Twentieth Century* (Stroud: Sutton Publishing).
67. B. Conekin (1999) ' "Here is the Modern World Itself": The Festival of Britain's Representations of the Future', in Becky Conekin, Frank Mort and Chris Waters (eds), *Moments of Modernity: Reconstructing Britain, 1945–1964* (London: Rivers Oram), pp. 228–46.
68. Ross, *Love and Toil*.
69. R. McKibbin (1998) *Classes and Cultures: England 1918–1951* (Oxford: Oxford University Press), ch. 5; M. Tebbutt (1995) *Women's Talk? A Social History of 'Gossip' in Working-Class Neighbourhoods, 1880–1960* (Aldershot: Scolar Press), pp. 118–121.
70. Tebbutt, *Women's Talk*, pp. 141, 183.
71. See, for example, N. Copsey (2002) 'Anti-Semitism and the Jewish Community of Newcastle-upon-Tyne', *Immigrants & Minorities* 21:3, pp. 52–69.
72. M. Francis (2007) 'A Flight from Commitment? Domesticity, Adventure and the Masculine Imaginary in Britain After the Second World War', *Gender and History* 19, pp. 163–85. See also S. Brooke, 'Gender and Working Class Identity in Britain during the 1950s', *Journal of Social History* 34, pp. 773–95.
73. Davidoff *et al.*, *The Family Story*, p. 203.
74. S. Todd (2005) *Young Women, Work and Family in England, 1918–1950* (Oxford: Oxford University Press).
75. M. B. Combs (2006) '*Cui bono*? The 1870 British Married Women's Property Act, Bargaining Power, and the Distribution of Resources within Marriage', *Feminist Economics* 12, pp. 51–83.
76. V. A. Zelizer (1985) *Pricing the Priceless Child: The Changing Social Value of Children* (New York: Princeton University Press).
77. J. Weeks (1989) *Sex, Politics and Society: The Regulation of Sexuality since 1800* (London: Longman).
78. See, for example, A. Marwick (1998) *The Sixties: Cultural Revolution in Britain, France, Italy and the United States, c.1958–1974* (Oxford: Oxford University Press); A. Clayson (1995) *Beat Merchants: The Origins, History, Impact and Rock Legacy of the 1960's British Pop Groups* (London: Blandford); B. Osgerby (1995) 'From the

Roaring Twenties to the Swinging Sixties: Continuity and Change in British Youth Culture, 1929–1959', in B. Brivati and H. Jones (eds), *What Difference Did the War Make?* (Leicester: Leicester University Press).

79. F. Mort (1999) 'Social and Symbolic Fathers and Sons in Postwar Britain', *Journal of British Studies* 38, pp. 353–84; P. Bailey (1999) 'Jazz at the Spirella. Coming of Age in 1950s Coventry', in Conekin *et al.* (eds), *Moments of Modernity: Reconstructing Britain*, pp. 152–70.

80. L. Davidoff (1995) *Worlds Between: Historical Perspectives on Class and Gender* (New York: Routledge), pp. 151–79, 206–26.

81. P. Thane and P. Johnson (1998) *Old Age from Antiquity to Post-Modernity* (London: Routledge); P. Thane (2000) *Old Age in English History: Past Experiences, Present Issues* (Oxford: Oxford University Press).

82. Work on migration has tended to be concentrated in historical sociology; see, for example, L. Ryan (2004) 'Family Matters: (E)migration, Familial Networks and Irish Women in Britain', *The Sociological Review* 52, pp. 351–70; M. Chamberlain (1995) 'Family Narratives and Migration Dynamics: Barbadians to Britain', *Immigrants and Minorities* 14, pp. 153–69.

Part I

Violence and the Law

1

'I am master here': Illegitimacy, Masculinity, and Violence in Victorian England

Ginger Frost

Recent work on fatherhood in the Victorian period has emphasised its centrality to the concept of masculinity. Being a 'good man' meant providing for a family; even more, at least in the respectable classes, a father should help rear his children. Fathers nursed children when they were ill, played with them during holidays, and disciplined them when necessary. Mothers, of course, were central to the home, but fathers remained the ultimate authorities, legally and socially.[1] Naturally, this picture is idealised and was more common in the middle classes than those above or below. In particular, working-class fathers were more problematic, for their ability to provide was always contingent, and their time with their children was limited. In addition, physical chastisement for children was ubiquitous in this class; 'correcting' children was an essential part of working-class men's authority in their households. Men who were breadwinners demanded respect; if they did not get it, they might enforce their wishes with violence, against both women and children.[2]

More specifically, historians have shown that poor men had a vexed relationship with fatherhood and masculinity. For one thing, providing for a family meant multiple things. It was a duty and legal responsibility, but as Julie-Marie Strange has argued, 'the act of providing for one's family could, in itself, be interpreted as an expression of love and affection'. Sometimes, in fact, it was the only outward show of love from a father to his children. Yet poor fathers also had more difficulty in succeeding as providers. Megan Doolittle, in her chapter in this volume, shows that many could not rely solely on that function as the basis for their authority, due to low wages and spells of un- or underemployment. They, then, might have to find other ways to assert control. On the other hand, at the same time, authoritarian fatherhood was under attack from feminist pressure and radical ideas at the end of the century. As a result, some poor men tried to use 'experiments' in parenting to break away from old models of family life. In short, by 1900, the definition of a 'good' father was in transition.[3]

Because of their peculiar circumstances, illegitimate children offer one way to complicate the picture of fathers and masculinity. According to English law, illegitimates were literally parentless at law; they had neither father nor mother. If intestate, they could not inherit from their parents, nor could their parents inherit from them. Even the subsequent marriage of the parents did not erase the illegitimacy, which remained with the child for life. Mothers did have the responsibility to support illegitimate children, since they could be prosecuted for neglect if they failed to do so. Although technically fathers had no responsibility for such children after the New Poor Law of 1834, the bastardy clause was revised as early as 1844 (mothers could sue for support through the petty courts) and more substantially in 1872 (magistrates themselves could demand payment from putative fathers).[4] Thus, by the end of the century, women commonly sued for support from the fathers of their illegitimate children in a process called affiliation. Men found, sometimes to their surprise, that magistrates did expect them to help support children they had fathered, in or out of wedlock. Still, unlike a legal father, the father of an illegitimate child had no custody rights or enforceable authority. This anomalous position pushed some men to violent acts in an effort to assert themselves, both over their 'unlawful' children and the mothers of those children.

In order to examine men's views of fatherhood and illegitimacy, I have assembled 51 cases of violence/neglect of men against their illegitimate children between 1850 and 1905. Of course, this barely scratches the surface of crimes against children; according to Carolyn Conley, though illegitimate children made up only 4–6 per cent of births in the late Victorian period (1867–92), they were victims in over a third of child homicides in England (excluding murders of newborns).[5] Nevertheless, these cases provide important insights into men's domestic authority, masculinity, and violence against children. The bulk of these cases comes from Lancaster, York, and London and are from both the magistrates' and assize levels (34 high court cases, 16 police court, and 1 inquest). The vast majority concerned the working class (43 of 51, or 84.3 per cent), so the chapter will primarily focus on working-class masculinity and fatherhood, but the five lower-middle-class and two middle-class cases do offer intriguing comparisons.[6]

The motives for violence/neglect fell into five broad categories. Out of 51 men, 21 killed because they could not or they did not want to pay affiliation or to support the children in general (41 per cent). Another nine men harmed the children through a combination of neglect and violence (often because of alcohol consumption), but without strong motives for murder (17.6 per cent). Seven of the men killed or assaulted the children because they 'corrected' or 'chastised' them with excessive force, but not with any real desire to kill; they simply overdid their disciplinary role (13.7 per cent). The final two categories were the most interesting. In six cases, the men wanted to cover up the illicit connections; these usually involved adulterous or incestuous relationships with the mothers, and the men wanted to avoid public exposure (11.7 per cent). And in the last eight cases, the fathers punished the mothers through their children; in other words, these were revenge killings (15.6 per cent). These final cases were the most informative about men's views of fatherhood and masculinity.

Because of space restrictions, I will focus on the three groups of cases that reveal the most about masculinity and fatherhood: those who did not want to support the children, those who wanted to avoid public exposure, and those who wanted revenge. The first group of 21 men either could not or would not support these children. Despite the fact that manhood meant providing, many fathers of illegitimate children deeply resented having to pay for their care, and they were sometimes brutal in their attempts to rid themselves of the obligation. James Flint was a painter in Birmingham who had an 11-month-old illegitimate son. James hired Sarah Barnbrook to care for the child for 3 shillings a week. Sarah could not make ends meet on that amount, and so told James she would need 4 shillings. The extra shilling was too much for James, and he offered Sarah a sovereign to 'make away' with the boy, which she indignantly refused. On the night of 20 February 1888, the two met in a pub in Denbigh, and James tried to get Sarah to sign a paper to take the child permanently for 15 shillings. When Sarah refused, James grabbed the baby and hurled him towards the fire. When that failed, he tried to stomp him to death. The pub customers stopped him and then went for the police. Despite his violence, James had done little damage. He was, thus, tried before the magistrates for assault, going to prison for three months.[7] Though he was ineffectual in his attempts, James's reaction showed his resentment of his financial obligations. Pressed by Sarah's request for more money, James struck out at the child whose existence pointed up his inadequacies as a provider.

Not surprisingly, the men in this group also disliked supporting the illegitimate children of other men. Cecil Chapman, who was a magistrate at the Southwark police court in London for 25 years, claimed that every case of deliberate cruelty that came before him 'had to do with a step-child or an illegitimate child', and certainly my sources provide plenty of support for his view.[8] For example, in the 1860s in York, Mary Ann Lee had cohabited with Thomas Stoughton and had three children with him when she ran off with the lodger, a man named Lee. Lee married her, but he did not want to accept her children. His violence and neglect led to the death of her 2-year-old son, Frederick. According to the landlady, Lee complained that the boy 'was not a child, but a rotten corpse like its rotten father, "Black Tom." . . . He said he was not going to keep any of Black Tom's bastards.'[9] Since the boy died of neglect rather than violence, Lee got only three months at hard labour. Nevertheless, Lee's definition of his responsibilities clearly differed from that of his neighbours, who testified against him, and of the court, which convicted him.

The law stated clearly that when a man married a woman with children, he took on responsibility for the entire family. Despite this, many men disputed the strict interpretation of their providing role. Richard Hale, an Oxford puddler, killed Eliza Sillitoe, the illegitimate daughter of his deceased wife. He appeared annoyed that he had to keep the girl after her mother's death, complaining that 'if the child were dead he could leave the country'. He and his new cohabitee, Cecilia Baker, suffocated the girl in 1864. In the 1850s, George Vickers, similarly, abused his step-daughter Harriet Herbert, after he married her mother, Ann. Harriet was illegitimate, and both of her parents begrudged caring for her. By the age of six, Harriet did a great deal of the housework (including cooking), but this did not spare her constant beatings. At the trial for assault, George justified his behaviour by insisting that 'the child was dirty, lazy, [and] inclined to tell lies', but, as in the case of Mary Ann Lee, the neighbours were appalled at the child's treatment and several testified against him and Ann. Unsurprisingly, men were even less enthusiastic about supporting children they suspected were the products of their wives' infidelity. William Young of Dorchester poisoned and then strangled his wife's child in 1887 because he was convinced the boy was the product of his wife's affair.[10]

These cases indicate that the connection between fatherhood, manliness, and providing was contingent on circumstances. Working-class men would not always accept responsibility for illegitimate children or for step-children, however acquired. Since the Victorian law courts also made distinctions, particularly between legitimate and illegitimate children, men may well have felt justified in drawing these lines. After all, a state that called children parentless at law, but then demanded the parents support those same children, contradicted itself. Men did not dispute their roles as providers, but they narrowed the list of dependents for whom they should have responsibility. When their self-definition conflicted with that of the state, or with that of the mothers of the children, men's frustration sometimes boiled over into violence. In other words, these cases show that though providing was one way a father showed love, the converse was also true; lack of providing was a way of disowning unwanted children and rejecting some forms of fatherhood. These cases also complicate the view that the Victorian authorities had few sanctions against men who did not live up to paternal ideals. In fact, the Poor Law authorities, police courts, and assize courts called fathers to account for any dereliction in providing for and protecting dependents.

The second group of cases were those in which men killed because they wanted to hide the results of illicit sexual relations. Though most works on child-killing have emphasised the unmarried mother's fear of having her 'shame' exposed, men too wanted to avoid being associated with illegitimate children, either because they were already married or because they feared for their social positions. As many historians have noted, the courts sympathised with infanticidal women, rarely convicting them of murder, but instead sending them to prison for one or two years for 'concealment of birth'.[11] Men who killed their illegitimate offspring were a minority, and thus have received far less historical attention. My limited sample indicates that such men got far less leniency when they resorted to violence to conceal their shame. Partly, this was because of the Victorian assumption that men were sexual aggressors who 'seduced' women into 'falling'; they, then, had no right to refuse responsibility for any children born of such connections. And men could not plead postpartum nervous instability, nor could they claim to be poverty-stricken as effectively as women could. Already immoral, these men became irredeemable once they added murderous violence to their list of sins. As Roger Chadwick noted, 'in cases of the murder of children by men . . . we see the Victorian law at its most severe and uncompromising', especially when a man killed his own child, 'since the paternal duty to protect his family was a central tenet' of Victorian domesticity.[12]

A good example of this was the case of William Bartlett, the foreman at a quarry in Cornwall. William was 45, married, and the father of several children when he began an affair with a local widow, Elizabeth Wherry. When Elizabeth became pregnant, William arranged for her to have the baby in Newquay. Afterwards, he persuaded Elizabeth to let him get their daughter, Emma, adopted, so the nurse, a Mrs Knight, brought the child to him on 22 June 1882. After Emma passed through a few more hands (apparently to confuse identification), William took her out on a buggy ride from which she never returned. In July, workers found the baby's body in a disused mine shaft near William's office, and some of her things were concealed nearby. The prosecutor in the subsequent trial pointed out that William's motive was not just the maintenance he had to pay, but also 'that the fact of the child's birth might be kept secret from his wife and family'. At the first trial, in Bodmin, the jurors could not agree, but at the second trial in Exeter, the jury convicted him, and William hanged. An editorial in the *Times* expressed the difficulty for fathers in asking for mercy:

> It is usual to recognize, formally or informally, some claim to mercy in the case of a woman who has given birth to an illegitimate child, and who is driven out of her better self by the misery and shame of her position. For Bartlett no such palliation can be alleged. He went to work in the most deliberate way.

The editorial concluded, 'If there is a tendency among libertines to regard infanticide with leniency as the most simple means of screening their immorality, the fate of Bartlett will, perhaps, provide such with a wholesome warning.'[13]

Similarly, John Dilley, a postman and picture-frame maker, was married and had a family when he had an affair with Mary Rainbow, a servant. He had seduced her in 1869, when she was 17, and she gave birth to a son;

that boy lived with Mary's natal family while she continued to work as a servant. For ten years, Mary avoided John, but he at last succeeded in getting her to see him, and she again got pregnant. When she gave birth to a baby girl, she took care of the child for three weeks in lodgings. John came and fetched the two of them on 10 May 1879, and they went to the train station together. At some point on that journey, the baby died, apparently from a skull fracture, though she had also taken a fatal dose of laudanum. At their trial, the jury found both John and Mary guilty of murder, but recommended Mary to mercy, since they believed her to be acting under John's direction. John hanged for the crime, while Mary served seven years. Again, the need for concealment was paramount. John had a position in his village; in addition, his wife might tolerate one illegitimate child, since its birth was well in the past, but a second, more recent one was different. Moreover, the state's treatment of the woman and man differed. Mary served seven years, but John went to the scaffold. John's fear of exposure was reasonable, but Justice Hawkins insisted that there were 'no extenuating circumstances in the case' for him.[14] Indeed, men killing children had much higher rates of conviction and execution than women throughout the Victorian period.[15]

As these previous examples have made clear, such cases depended on the respectability and class of the man involved. The higher the standing, the bigger the fall if an illegitimate child came to light. In consequence, the few lower-middle-class and middle-class men cluster in this type of case. For instance, a Manchester cotton manufacturer, named Ashworth Read, was tried for the murder of his illegitimate son with Elizabeth Remington, his servant, in 1893. According to Elizabeth, Ashworth paid for her confinement and lodgings, but then tried to suffocate the child and hide the body when he visited. He explained to her 'it would disgrace him, and that he would never hold up his head in Burnley' if anyone found out about their relationship.[16] Ashworth feared for his reputation, just as John Dilley and William Bartlett had done, though Ashworth was not, apparently, married. Clearly, men worried about their social standing, too; an illegitimate child with a servant was not the kind of fatherhood that conferred a high standing. Thus, these cases show the ambivalent relationship of men and fatherhood, and, especially, conflicting notions of masculine responsibility between the courts and the men themselves. Some types of fatherhood gave both responsibilities and prestige, but others were shameful and, in some men's opinion, should not require more money out of their pockets.

These tensions came out most clearly in those cases in which the men seemed to revenge themselves on disobedient or 'unfaithful' women by killing their children.[17] In these instances, the men agreed that they had authority over and responsibility for women and illegitimate children, but because of their ambiguous legal standing, they could not enforce their claims. They were not husbands and so could not command obedience from the women, and they had no custody of the children or even visitation rights. Despite these legal disabilities, courts were not sympathetic to the men's frustrations, since judges and magistrates, as well as most juries, assumed the men themselves were responsible for their liminal position in these families. They had, after all, only to marry the mothers of their children to correct the difficulties. If the men chose not to do so, they had only themselves to blame for any problems. Indeed, even in less serious cases, judges were unimpressed with moral laxity; Justice Cave told Sidney Clay, a shopkeeper on trial for solicitation of murder, that he 'should have been disposed to have dealt more leniently with him if he had taken advantage of the opportunity he had had of making an honest woman' of the mother of his son.[18] Thus, punishments for revenge crimes were harsh; of the eight cases in this group, six of the men hanged, one was found insane, and only one was convicted of the lesser offence of manslaughter.[19] Men who wanted to remain free of domestic ties, then, learned that such freedom came at a price. If not married, a man forfeited his authority and control of the family, and any attempts to regain it through violence led to the gallows.

I will centre on four examples which show various facets to this type of violence. The first example is the case of Thomas Day. Thomas was a soldier when he met Caroline Meek, a servant, in November 1877. The two were engaged when Caroline gave birth to their daughter on 18 July 1879, but Thomas did not marry her because, he claimed, he could not support her. He visited her and the child once or twice over the next five years, but his entire contribution to Caroline's income was six stamps at Lily's birth and then 5 shillings later on. In 1882, Caroline gave up on Thomas and married William Woodgate, a railway labourer. Thomas was incensed, considering the marriage a betrayal of him. He wrote her several angry letters, reproaching her faithlessness and insisted that he would have married her eventually. Interestingly, Thomas was especially upset that Caroline had wronged Lily: 'you have wilfully deceived that poor innocent child...You have cut the link between yourself, child, and me without any cause.' In another letter, Thomas demanded a photograph of his daughter, and when Caroline did not reply, he accused her of 'contracting' Lily away from her real father, adding, 'She is my blood and bone...the day will come when I shall see the one that is mine in spite of all'.[20]

In August 1883, Thomas Day arrived in Ipswich to see Lily. He met Caroline Meek in the road, and complained 'that she had robbed the child of its parent'. He asked Lily her name, and when the girl replied 'Lilian Woodgate', he corrected her and said, 'No, your name is Meek.' Caroline arranged for him to see Lily that evening when both she and her husband would be present. When Thomas arrived that night, he was calm at first and took Lily on his knee. He again asked her what her name was, and she said both Lily Meek and Lilian Woodgate, clearly confused. 'Then he asked her, "Who is your father." The child at once pointed to William Woodgate. Prisoner said, "Oh! No; I am your father, he's not." ' When Lily seemed to choke on Thomas's tobacco smoke, he told her she would have to put up with 'a lot', and Caroline immediately said that she would not have to put up with much from her or her husband. This led to an argument, during which Thomas called Caroline 'a deceitful whore'. William then told Thomas he would throw him out if he said any more such things. At that point, Thomas said, 'I have got her and I shall do as I like with her.' Then, as both Woodgates watched in horror, Thomas put one hand on Lily's forehead and drew a knife across her throat with the other. In the melée that followed, the neighbours were able to subdue Thomas, but Lily died of loss of blood on the way to the hospital.

At the trial, Thomas Day insisted in his defence that he had accidentally cut Lily with the knife he had out for cutting his tobacco. He also claimed not to have a motive, since if he wanted revenge, he would have killed one or both of the Woodgates. However, he smoked shag tobacco, which did not need to be cut, and he could just as easily revenge himself on Caroline Meek by killing her daughter, as the Justice Fry pointed out. The jury found him guilty after 15 minutes' deliberation, and he hanged, protesting his innocence and his love for his child to the end. Thomas's distress at having no control over either Caroline or Lily was evident throughout this story. He particularly resented having his child 'stolen' from him by Caroline's marriage to another man, and insisted that Lily know her true legal name was Meek rather than Woodgate and that he was her father. Thomas had made almost no financial provision for Lily and had not married Caroline in five years, yet he still thought Lily 'belonged' to him because she was his 'blood and bone'. When William threatened to throw him out of his house, Thomas retaliated the only way he could – with violence. Rather than see William Woodgate as Lily's father, he killed her. He thus was able to defy William's legal authority, and he also got revenge on Caroline. She had taken his daughter from him, so he took that same daughter from her. But the cost was his daughter's, and his own, life.

The second example was the case of Felix Spicer in Chester in 1890. Felix was a rigger on ships and also a small businessman. He met Mary Ann Palin in 1874 when she was only 16. The two cohabited for 16 years and had 7 children, passing as a married couple. By 1890, Mary ran their refreshment rooms and boarding house; in fact, because Felix was often at sea, he put the businesses in her name in 1889. In Easter 1890, Mary discovered that Felix had told their landlord that they were not actually married, and she threw him out of the house. Felix was then in a difficult position, because all the businesses were in Mary's name. He wrote to her twice, begging her to forgive him: 'do consider my broken heart, and have mercy and pity on me'. Mary, however, replied:

> You must be mad to think I shall ever speak to you again, much less make it up. You told Mr. Wright I was not your wife. You mean, contemptible

scrub, did you think of my tears, when, before Felix was born, I asked you
to marry me out of my shame. You laughed at me, but I have waited and
the day has come

Mary Ann Palin now had the means to maintain her children herself, and
she meant to do so without Felix Spicer.[21]

Felix Spicer now had no businesses and no access to his family, and his
pleas for forgiveness had met with harsh rebuff. Yet, legally, he had no
recourse, precisely because he was not married to the mother of his children.
Further, Mary Ann Palin made him even angrier when she called herself
Mary Spicer in the business, to take advantage of the good will of the name.
If she went by Mary Palin, he later said, he would not have been as angry,
'but as he was founder of the business... she had no right to trade on his
name'. He argued with her about this, insisting to her 'There is no Marry
[*sic*] Spicer', to which she replied 'so much the better for me'. Mary continued to send some money to him, which was also humiliating, since he was
living on her handouts. After several days of tension, Felix began sharpen-
ing a wood frame to make it into a battering ram, muttering, 'They will not
have it all their own way. I am Master here.' That night, he broke into Mary's
house and tried to cut her throat with his clasp knife, but she fought him off
and ran for help. Thwarted yet again, Felix went back into the house and slit
the throats of their two sons, though, curiously, he did not hurt their two
daughters, also sleeping in the house.

Felix Spicer denied killing his sons, and certainly witnesses claimed he
was an affectionate father to all his children, putting them to bed and caring
for them if they cried. Alfred Short, a clerk, even testified, 'He was like a
mother to them.' Yet all the evidences pointed to him battering down the
door with the wood frame and then murdering the two boys as they slept.
As Justice Stephen put it in his summation, 'A point had been made out
of the prisoner's fondness for his children, but a man's desire to play with
engaging children was not the kindness of heart that made a man control
his own passions.'[22] Despite his frantic denials, Felix went to the gallows
in August 1890. One must conclude that he asserted his 'mastery' in the
only way left to him, since he had no legal recourse and had not even been
able to subdue Mary physically. He could not stop her running his business;
he could not get custody of their children; and he could not beat her into
submission. Thus, he took the lives of their two sons, in an effort to remove
his impotence in his domestic affairs.

The third and fourth examples both concern men who reacted violently
to women using the law courts to demand support. Both examples were
of extreme violence, showing the high emotionalism that came when a
man combined anger over providing with that of a love affair gone wrong.
Alfred Waddington was an 18-year-old grinder in Sheffield when he met
Sarah Slater, who worked for an edge-tool manufacturer. The two courted,

and Sarah had their child in 1850. She affiliated the baby girl, Elizabeth, on Alfred a month after the birth, and Alfred contributed 2 shillings a week for its maintenance. Sarah continued to work, and the child lived with its maternal grandmother. Alfred and Sarah remained close for a time, but, according to the prosecutor in the subsequent trial, Sarah 'had refused to marry the prisoner unless he would provide her with a home and be steady'. As a result of her hesitation, Alfred 'laboured under the mistaken impression that she had become some rich man's mistress'. Thus, when Elizabeth was approximately 20 months old, Alfred stopped paying his 2 shillings a week. Sarah almost immediately summoned him to the magistrate's court for failure to maintain.[23]

This action infuriated Alfred Waddington even further. He met Sarah on the street of Sheffield two days after the issue of the summons, 'and swore he would never pay another farthing towards the support of the child'. Sarah ignored him and went about her business. That night she went to a class at the Mechanics Institute, leaving Elizabeth with a friend named Barlow. Knowing Sarah would be busy, Alfred found Barlow when she had taken the baby out for a walk on the street, grabbed the infant, and fled. A few hours passed, and Alfred then showed up at the Mechanics Institute and induced Sarah to come with him by claiming that Elizabeth had broken her neck. Once he had her away from the centre of town, however, he confessed to murdering their child and then tried to cut Sarah's throat. She was able to fend him off until a newspaper boy came to her aid, and Alfred ran away. Later, one of her friends also confronted Alfred, and he attacked her as well. Eventually, he turned himself in, confessing to the murder. When the police found the child's corpse, they tried to lift up the body, and the head rolled down the embankment. Alfred had decapitated the baby with a shoemaker's knife.

Alfred Waddington justified the murder by blaming Sarah Slater. He insisted that she had jilted him to be 'a rich man's whore', and complained, 'I was very much attached to her, and I loved my child. I can't think what could possess me to murder the child. I wish it had been Sarah.' Sarah testified that she had gone to London on a trip with her aunt and uncle, but had not found a rich lover, so Alfred's jealousy was badly misplaced. And, of course, he had attacked three people, injuring two adult women, including a friend who had done nothing to him, and killing his daughter. Indeed, even if the accusations against Sarah had been true, they would still not have justified violence against a helpless baby. Justice Talfourd, in particular, was not impressed with Alfred's self-justification. His summation dismissed the defence's attempts to plead insanity, and he also refuted the idea that strong emotion made the crime manslaughter. He insisted to the jury that passionate jealousy was not enough to lessen the charge: 'there could be no question whatever that the crime of murder was committed'. The jury took an hour, but still found Alfred guilty of the capital charge.

Alfred Waddington was furious with Sarah Slater in part because he believed she had betrayed him yet still insisted that he pay for his child. Alfred apparently believed that he only had to support his offspring if the mother intended to marry him (or at least was not in a relationship with anyone else). Again, his definition of his responsibility differed from both the law's and his former fiancée's. He did not attack Sarah immediately after the affiliation; he accepted responsibility for his daughter for over a year and a half. He stopped paying, though, as soon as he became convinced Sarah was seeing another man – and, even worse, a rich man. Alfred felt humiliated and struck out at Sarah by killing the person she loved the most. He may also have intended to make sure his daughter never had anything to do with Sarah's alleged rich lover; in one confession, he incoherently raged: 'Before I will let it [the baby] be a slave to anybody, I will murder it.' Alfred could not make Sarah marry him, nor could he stop her from demanding support for their child. In his rage, he killed Elizabeth and also attempted to kill Sarah. Tragically, his irrational approach led only to the death of his child and himself.

The fourth revenge murder, that of George Place in 1902, was similar to Alfred Waddington's, in that it involved both a dispute over financial support and also a courtship gone wrong. Apparently, the passage of 50 years had not diminished working-class men's insistence on defining their providing responsibilities more narrowly than their neighbours or the state. George Place was a miner who had courted Eliza Chetwynd since his arrival at Baddesly Ensor in January 1901. He eventually became a lodger in her mother's house, leading to an even closer intimacy. On 14 August 1902, when George was 28 and Eliza 20, Eliza had a baby boy. At this point, things went seriously wrong. Eliza's mother, also called Eliza Chetwynd, insisted that her daughter affiliate the child on George. Thus, on 20 August, P. C. Sloss arrived at the house and issued the summons. George was extremely angry; he threw the order into the fire and said, 'I'll show you who is b—y well Boss now'. Joseph Chetwynd, Eliza's brother, replied, 'You won't be boss here', and George responded, 'I'll show you who's boss'. Early in the morning of 23 August, George got up early, loaded his pistol, and then shot Eliza, her mother, and his child in the head. Afterwards, he went into the kitchen where Joseph was sleeping and handed him the gun. The police eventually apprehended him, and he never denied the crime. Instead, he explained, 'They kept asking me to pay and pay, and I have paid them now.' The police concluded that he wanted to 'get rid of the annoyance that the woman and child were to him'.[24]

George Place's case is a good illustration of the fury men could express when asked to support illegitimate offspring. Though he was a miner, and not of a high social standing, he resented the publicity of the affiliation order and the elder Eliza Chetwynd's insistence that he pay for the expenses of the confinement. Clearly, he had a limited income, so the requests for money were troublesome. In fact, he had earlier asked a friend for a loan of six pounds to help defray the costs. In addition, as a lodger, he did not have standing in the house; Eliza's brother Joseph Chetwynd challenged him on who would be 'boss' there. He did not, apparently, want to marry Eliza, but he could not stop her from demanding that he live up to his paternal responsibilities. Interestingly, even after several decades of women affiliating the fathers of their illegitimate children, some men found the procedure humiliating and infuriating. Unable to stop Eliza legally, George resorted to shooting her, their child, and her meddlesome mother. Since he made basically no defence, the conclusion of his trial was not in doubt. George hanged for the triple murder on 30 December 1902.

What do these examples tell us about masculinity, fatherhood, and illegitimacy in the late Victorian period? First, competing definitions of fatherhood existed within the Victorian state, and these contradictions made for deep frustrations for men. The father of an illegitimate child had no legal standing and no custody rights, but the mother could nevertheless affiliate him and force him to support the child. As he was not a husband, he could not control his lover's actions, nor did he have the legal right to 'correct' her, or, for that matter, the children. Women could refuse to share resources, to live with the men, or to allow access to children, and the state would do nothing. Men who did not marry the mothers of their children, then, lost that inherent domestic authority that fathers and husbands assumed. Men connected their masculinity to providing, controlling women and children, and being masters in their homes. Many of these fathers failed on all the three counts, and their response was to try to regain mastery through violence.

This point goes along with much recent work on men, violence, and masculinity. J. Carter Wood has argued, for example, that working-class men had a different view of violence that tolerated far more domestic violence than the idealised middle-class home allowed. This more 'customary' idea died out very slowly, and poor men were particularly likely to consider violent responses to any 'slights'. Strikingly, the four examples of revenge murders centred either on a public humiliation or on a confrontation with another man, as well as with the mothers of the children. Thomas Day argued with William Woodgate, who threatened to throw him out of the house. Felix Spicer's businesses were under his pseudo-wife's name, placarded across the town. Alfred Waddington had been summoned for a failure to maintain, as well as having his former lover refuse to marry him, because, he thought, she had found a better-off man. And George Place not only had to endure a public summons for bastardy, but argued with Joseph Chetwynd about who was 'boss' in the house. Men who thought their honour was impugned were all the more likely to take drastic steps to regain it.[25]

Second, men themselves remained contradictory about fatherhood. One of the main reasons for violence against illegitimates (and their mothers) was that men objected to paying any support for illegal children, despite the close connection between masculinity and providing. Men defined this requirement narrowly, referring largely to legitimate family and those of their own blood. This was particularly the case when a man had another family to support or limited resources. As Megan Doolittle points out in her chapter in this volume, poor families often shared providing duties and authority in practice, since low wages made complete dependence on one breadwinner impossible. Men's prestige, then, was always fragile. Without enough money to meet his obligations, a man's frustrations might result in violence, since his inability to provide emphasised his failures as a father. This was especially true when the problems became public. Men guarded their reputations and disliked the publicity of affiliation orders, even if they were not married to someone else. Though women's reputations were hurt more from sexual irregularities, men, too, feared a connection to a scandal and the subsequent loss of prestige. Certainly, middle-class men were horrified at their sexual 'falls' becoming public knowledge, but both Alfred Waddington and George Place, a grinder and a miner, also felt belittled by the actions of Sarah Slater and Eliza Chetwynd.

Third, the Victorian courts were far less sympathetic to men who killed illegitimate children than to women who did so. Even when both partners were convicted of murder, the man hanged while the woman was reprieved. A woman could excuse her actions as postpartum 'mania' or fear of her shame becoming known. A man had no such excuses, as William Bartlett discovered. He did not give birth, so could not plead physical problems, and the courts assumed that men were less emotionally fraught in any case. Further, a man should protect his dependents, not attack them. Thus, the courts held men strictly accountable for their actions, and did not regard the fear of exposure and 'ruin' as a mitigating circumstance. With regard to violence, the courts assumed that men could exercise self-control and had little sympathy with men who fathered children they then could not support. If a man did not marry the mother of his child, he had only himself to blame when things went wrong. These findings supplement Martin Wiener's work on the Victorian courts' reaction to working-class male violence against women. There, too, judges demanded self-control and 'respectable' manliness and punished harshly when they did not get it. These cases also somewhat modify arguments that the state rarely exerted itself to punish men who failed to live up to the paternal ideal. Clearly, the courts had strong and consistent views on the duties of fathers to provide and protect children and used the power of the bench to punish those who failed to meet those expectations.[26]

In short, fatherhood provoked complicated and sometimes contradictory responses from men and from the Victorian courts. Men's desire to be independent of all controls conflicted with domestic ties. In addition, men's determination to be 'masters' and to uphold their honour against other men, as well as women, influenced their attitude to fatherhood, particularly of illegitimate children. Many men were unwilling to support other men's children, but they could also rage at 'strangers' raising their children as their own. Further, they did not take well to other men insisting they were not 'boss' of their homes. In asserting their rights to provide and act as fathers only as they wished, they came up against social and legal norms that made such control impossible. The results of these collisions were unfortunate for all concerned, most especially the children, but also for their mothers and for the fathers themselves.

Notes

1. J. Tosh (1999), *A Man's Place: Masculinity and the Middle-Class Home in Victorian England* (New Haven: Yale University Press), pp. 79–101; L. Davidoff and C. Hall (1987), *Family Fortunes: Men and Women of the English Middle Class, 1780–1850* (Chicago: University of Chicago Press), pp. 321–56; A. J. Hammerton (1992), *Cruelty and Companionship: Conflict in Nineteenth-Century Married Life* (London: Routledge), pp. 73–101.
2. J. Gillis (1985), *For Better, For Worse: British Marriage, 1600 to the Present* (Oxford: Oxford University Press), pp. 248–59; A. Clark (1995), *The Struggle for the Breeches: Gender and the Making of the British Working Class* (Berkeley: University of California Press), pp. 63–87; G. Behlmer (1998), *Friends of the Family: The English Home and its Guardians, 1850–1940* (Stanford: Stanford University Press), pp. 181–229; Hammerton, *Cruelty and Companionship*, pp. 34–67; E. Ross (1993), *Love and Toil: Motherhood in Outcast London* (Oxford: Oxford University Press), pp. 84–6; S. D'Cruze (1998), *Crimes of Outrage: Sex, Violence, and the Victorian Working Woman* (Dekalb, Illinois: Northen Illinois University Press), pp. 63–80; S. D'Cruze, (ed.) (2000), *Everyday Violence in Britain, 1850–1950: Gender and Class* (New York: Longman); C. Conley (1991), *The Unwritten Law: Criminal Justice in Kent* (New York: Oxford University Press), pp. 68–135; idem (2007), *Certain Other Countries: Homicide, Gender, and National Identity in Late Nineteenth-Century England, Ireland, Scotland, and Wales* (Columbus: The Ohio State University Press), pp. 124–205; J. C. Wood (2004), *Violence and Crime in Nineteenth-Century England: The Shadow of Our Refinement* (London: Routledge), pp. 61–8.
3. J. Strange (2007), ' "Speechless with Grief": Bereavement and the Working-Class Father, c. 1880–1914', in T. L. Broughton and H. Rogers (eds) *Gender and Fatherhood in the Nineteenth Century* (New York: Palgrave Macmillan), pp. 138–49, quote from p. 147; M. Doolittle (2007), 'Fatherhood, Religious Belief and the Protection of Children in Nineteenth-Century English Families', in Broughton and Rogers (eds) *Gender and Fatherhood*, pp. 31–42, quote from p. 39.
4. U. Henriques (1967), 'Bastardy and the New Poor Law', *Past and Present* 37, 103–29.
5. Conley, *Certain Other Countries*, p. 177. I assembled the cases by looking through three sources and reading both the magistrates' court and assize court cases: the *Lancaster Guardian* at five-year intervals from 1850 to 1900; the *York Gazette* in 1850, 1855, 1865, 1870, 1876, 1882, 1885, 1892, 1895, and 1899; and the months February–March and July–August in the *Times* in 1858, 1868, 1878, 1888, and 1898. I supplemented the list with cases from compilations like Steve Fielding (1994) *The Hangman's Record*, 2 vols (Beckenham, Kent: Chancery House Press). Once I had a list, I read the relevant Home Office, Assize, and Old Bailey Reports at the National Archives in Kew. The numbers of cases per decade are as follows: 7

in the 1850s, 7 in the 1860s, 11 in the 1870s, 13 in the 1880s, 9 in the 1890s, and 4 between 1900 and 1905.

6. One man had no class listing or indication of his standing, so I have left this case out of these calculations.

7. *Birmingham Daily Mail*, 21 February 1888, p. 3; *Times*, 22 February 1888, p. 8. For more examples, see K. Watson (2004), *Poisoned Lives: English Poisoners and Their Victims* (London: Hambledon), pp. 78–83; Conley, *Certain Other Countries*, pp. 177–9.

8. C. Chapman (1925), *The Poor Man's Court of Justice: Twenty-Five Years as a Metropolitan Magistrate* (London: Hodder and Stoughton, Ltd), p. 79; see also Conley, *Unwritten Law*, pp. 106–10.

9. *Yorkshire Gazette*, 28 January 1865, p. 10.

10. National Archives, Kew, Home Office Records, Appeals, HO 45/9375/40246; *Oxford Times*, 10 December 1864, p. 2; *Times*, 25 July 1853, p. 8; Fielding. *The Hangman's Record*, I:159. Richard Hale and William Young hanged for their crimes; George Vickers received a month at hard labour, while Ann got three months.

11. Conley, *Unwritten Law*, pp. 110–12; M. Arnot (2000), 'Understanding Women Committing Newborn Child Murder in Victorian England', in D'Cruze (ed.) *Everyday Violence in Britain*, pp. 55–68; and M. Arnot (2002), 'The Murder of Thomas Sandles: Meanings of a Mid-Nineteenth-Century Infanticide', in M. Jackson (ed.) *Infanticide: Historical Perspectives on Child Murder and Concealment, 1550–2000* (Aldershot, Hants: Ashgate), pp. 149–67; H. Marland (2002), 'Getting Away with Murder? Puerperal Insanity, Infanticide and the Defence Plea', in Jackson (ed.) *Infanticide*, pp. 168–92; and T. Ward (2002), 'Legislating for Human Nature: Legal Responses to Infanticide, 1860–1938', in Jackson (ed.) *Infanticide*, pp. 249–69.

12. R. Chadwick (1992), *Bureaucratic Mercy: The Home Office and the Treatment of Capital Cases in Victorian Britain* (New York: Garland), pp. 310–11; quote from 310.

13. *Times*, 38 October 1882, p. 10; *Exeter and Plymouth Gazette Daily Telegram*, 28 October 1882, p. 3; editorial in *Times*, 28 October 1882, p. 9.

14. National Archives, Old Bailey Sessions Papers, PCOM 1/116; HO 144/40/83853; *Times*, 12 June 1879, p. 14; 9 August 1879, p. 11; 11 August 1879, p. 11. John Dilley's experience was not unique. In my sample, I have nine cases where both the mother and father were charged with murder or manslaughter. In two cases, I do not know the outcome, and in two the couple received the same punishment or were both acquitted. But in the five others, the man received a harsher punishment by far than the woman; in four of these, he hanged while the woman served, at most, seven years or got no punishment at all (in two cases, charges against the mother were dismissed). The opposite was true with neglect/cruelty cases; there women received longer sentences five out of eight times. Sian Pooley's chapter in this collection also comments on the differing treatment of men and women in 'neglect' cases.

15. For instance, Margaret Arnot has discovered that only three women were convicted in Sussex of murdering their children between 1840 and 1880; men who murdered children in this same period had higher rates of both conviction and execution. Arnot, 'Murder of Thomas Sandles'; see also M. Wiener (2004), *Men of Blood: Violence, Manliness, and Criminal Justice in Victorian England* (Cambridge: Cambridge University Press), pp. 123–69; Chadwick, *Bureaucratic Mercy*, pp. 289–315; and Conley, *Certain Other Countries*, p. 179.

16. *Times*, 13 October 1893, p. 4; 21 October 1893, p. 9; 24 November 1893, p. 11. Ashworth Read was acquitted for lack of evidence. See also Conley, *Unwritten Law*, pp. 112–13.
17. For other examples of this type of murder, see Conley, *Unwritten Law*, pp. 108–9.
18. *Times*, 1 March 1884, p. 13. Sidney Clay got six months at hard labour for trying to induce the local doctor to murder Sidney's illegitimate child.
19. That one was James Arnold in 1875. His case was different, since he accidentally killed his infant child while he was attacking the child's mother (she was holding the child when he struck out at her). He got two years at hard labour. PCOM 1/107; *Times*, 10 February 1875, p. 12; 4 March 1875, p. 11.
20. Thomas's story taken from ASSI 36/28, Magistrates Depositions, South-eastern Circuit; *Supplement to the Norwich Chronicle and Norwich Gazette*, 3 November 1883, p. 2; *Times*, 27 October 1883, p. 6.
21. HO 144/235/A51593 (Appeals); *Lancaster Guardian*, 31 May 1890, p. 5; 7 June 1890, p. 3; *Times*, 2 August 1890, p. 10; 23 August 1890, p. 10.
22. HO/144/235/A51593/7, *Cheshire Observer*, 2 August 1890 (excerpt in file).
23. *Times*, 20 August 1852, p. 6; 22 December 1852, p. 7.
24. ASSI 13/32, Magistrates Depositions, Midland Circuit; *Times*, 9 December 1902, p. 7; *Warwick and Warwickshire Advertiser*, 13 December 1902, p. 5.
25. Wood, *Violence and Crime*, pp. 47–69; 107–18; see also A. Davis (1998), 'Youth Gangs, Masculinity and Violence in Late Victorian Manchester and Salford', *Journal of Social History* 32, pp. 353–6, 360–4; and C. Emsley (2005), *Hard Men: The English and Violence Since 1750* (London: Hambledon), pp. 35–6, 59–69.
26. Wiener, *Men of Blood*, 123–239; G. Frost (2008), ' "He Could Not Hold His Passions": Domestic Violence and Cohabitation in England, 1850–1900', *Crime, History & Societies* 12, pp. 25–44. See also Doolittle, 'Fatherhood, Religious Belief, and Protection of Children', p. 31.

2
'...the instrument of an animal function': Marital Rape and Sexual Cruelty in the Divorce Court, 1858–1908[1]

Gail Savage

J. S. Mill, in his foundational essay *The Subjection of Women*, identified the authority of the husband to enforce his sexual demands upon his unwilling wife as central to the inequities and horrors of married life. Mill's was not the only expression of protest about this element of the Victorian marital regime. A marital regime that required a wife to submit to sexual advances repugnant to her generated considerable outrage on the part of feminist leaders such as William Thompson and Elizabeth Cady Stanton. Nineteenth-century fiction also vividly portrayed the horror of wives in sexual thrall to their husbands. Helen's plight in *The Tenant of Wildfell Hall* and Gwendolyn's realization about the nature of the marital bargain that she has struck with Grandcourt in *Daniel Deronda* stand out as especially stark examples. Helen Huntingdon resolutely denied her dissolute husband his marital rights and then fled their home taking their son with her.[2] Gwendolyn Grandcourt, who lacked that kind of courage and resolution, had to endure her husband's demands and restrictions until his accidental death by drowning before her eyes released her. More explicitly, John Galsworthy, in *The Man of Property*, confronted the issue of marital rape when he depicted the human destruction that flowed from Soames' assertion of his marital rights over Irene.[3] Soames, reflecting on his victory the night before, reassures himself:

> The incident was really not of great moment; women made a fuss about it in books; but in the cool judgment of right-thinking men, of men of the world, of such as he recollected often received praise in the Divorce Court, he had but done his best to sustain the sanctity of marriage.[4]

John Galsworthy here depicted Soames as engaged in self-justifying rationalization. But by the early twentieth century the views of many 'right-thinking men' would not have necessarily endorsed his behaviour, and the Divorce Court did not provide a sure refuge for husbands who asserted their sexual rights over their wives without regard to their health, their well-being, or even their consent.

The explicit legal grounds for the sexual privileges attributed to husbands dated back to the seventeenth century when Matthew Hale (1609–1676) enunciated the famous and influential dictum about the impossibility of marital rape – the so-called marital rape exemption. He argued that 'the husband cannot be guilty of rape committed by himself upon his lawful wife, for by their mutual matrimonial consent and contract the wife hath given up herself in this kind unto her husband, which she cannot contract'.[5] This created a long-standing precedent that remained stubbornly intact until the very end of the twentieth century. Carole Pateman's *The Sexual Contract* sets out the intellectual context for this understanding of the marriage relationship.[6] Not until a series of cases challenging the traditional view, followed by legislation in the 1990s, was the rape of a wife by her husband explicitly defined as a criminal act.[7] The scholarly literature on this topic, both by historians and by legal scholars, celebrates these late twentieth-century developments as a long over-due triumph, as indeed it was. But this triumphalism seems to assume that in the years before the enactment of such reforms husbands could behave with impunity in requiring sexual services from their wives.[8]

An exclusive focus on the criminal law overlooks other avenues of resistance to a husband's authority over marital sexuality. In seeking divorces and separations, wives could and did charge their husbands with making illegitimate sexual demands upon their bodies. And Divorce Court judges took those claims seriously. Indeed, in assessing acts of sexuality that might be understood as bodily cruelty, the Divorce Court construed acceptable marital sexual practices very narrowly, and the Divorce Court had the power to restrict a husband's sexual demands by depriving him of his status as husband. Drawing upon a systematic sample of divorce petitions filed with the Divorce Court between 1858 and 1908, this chapter will examine those cases in which sexual cruelty figured as an element of the litigation.[9] Divorce cases that involved charges of excessive and unreasonable sexual demands, sodomy, the imposition of birth control, or the transmission of venereal disease show the Divorce Court placing limits on a husband's authority over marital sexuality at the behest of wives' demands for intercession and protection. An analysis of these cases reveals the influential role of prescriptive notions of sexual normality and restraint in disciplining and limiting a husband's power over his wife's body.

Approximately 30 petitions selected from the sample show Divorce Court judges hearing a variety of cases that raised questions about aspects of a husband's sexual behaviour in the marital bedroom. These cases, most of which were initiated by wives, included divorces, judicial separations, and actions for the restitution for conjugal rights. In many of these, wives claimed that their husbands had forced them to have sex. For instance, Eliza Mackle's 1870 petition for divorce explicitly cited her husband's insistence on his sexual rights as the cruelty that formed the basis for her petition. Eliza, the daughter of a merchant and already a widow at the age of 21, had married James O'Neill Mackle, a merchant and the son of a gentleman, in Liverpool in 1866. As Eliza explained in her petition, only three weeks after giving birth to a child and 'in a state of health which rendered it injurious to her health to resume cohabitation', her husband 'did by force and violence have sexual intercourse with your petitioner and thereby seriously injured your petitioner'. Eliza cited other instances of violence, which ultimately caused a miscarriage, and she also charged her husband with adultery. Inside a year, a lapse of time typical for nineteenth-century divorce litigation, the Divorce Court awarded Eliza her divorce.[10]

If a wife could point to her husband's illegitimate sexual demands as a basis for her claim to a divorce, a wife could also utilize such accusations to resist her husband's assertion of his demands that she remain in the marital home. The Divorce Court enforced the requirement that spouses live together through the legal action of restitution of conjugal rights, notoriously at the centre of the 1891 Jackson case.[11] But 20 years earlier, in 1871, Edward Ferris, a clerk employed by the Great Western Railway Company living on the Harrow Road in Middlesex, presented a petition to the Divorce Court for restitution of conjugal rights, claiming that his wife had refused his conjugal rights. Her reply revealed that she did indeed deny him sexual access, but, she explained, her husband insisted on sleeping with her 'contrary to the advice of the medical men then attending her' and so impaired her health. Martha then filed her own petition for divorce later that same year, claiming that her husband was guilty of cruelty and had also, in 1868, committed adultery with one Sarah Alice Letto 'in a railway carriage on the Great Western Railway between the stations of Leamington and Didcot'. Neither spouse pursued this litigation to a conclusion, so the Divorce Court never came to a decision about this ill-sorted couple.[12] A railway carriage also figured in the 1876 divorce case brought by Mary Oppenheimer against her husband George. This case, heard *in camera* according to the report that appeared in the *Times*, came only two years after the marriage and the couple had no children.[13] Mary's petition claimed that her husband had 'degraded' her by 'enforcing his marital rights at <u>unreasonable</u> and improper times and places'. When asked by the Divorce Court to provide more particular details, Mary explained that her husband wished to have sexual relations in railway carriages. The Divorce Court granted the wished-for divorce.[14]

Since a charge of cruelty necessitated that a wife establish some threat to her physical health, a wife might refuse to have intercourse with a husband suffering from venereal disease. For instance, when Charlotte Holland petitioned for a divorce in 1877, she claimed that her husband tried to force her to have sex even though he suffered from venereal disease. Charlotte, the daughter of a farmer, had married William Holland, who worked as a carpenter, in 1865, and they had four children. William's venereal disease helped to establish his adultery, and his abusive and threatening behaviour, which culminated in his attempts to enforce his marital rights despite the threat to his wife's health, established his cruelty. The Divorce Court readily granted the wife both a divorce and custody of the children. In two additional cases of petitions for judicial separation, wives accused their husbands of insisting upon sexual relations even though the husband suffered from venereal disease.[15] And in 1898, Elizabeth Solder of London successfully won a divorce from her husband, Frank, a shoemaker, after she charged that he made her 'wait and attend to him whereby your Petition contracted gonorrheal opthalima'.[16]

By the end of the nineteenth century, wives began to claim cruelty in the face of husbands who attempted to enforce their marital rights violently or by force. The 1886 divorce petition of Margaret Jackson against her husband, Colonel George Jackson of the Bengal Cavalry, did not elaborate any extenuating circumstances for her refusal to have sex with her husband but simply cited his attempt to have intercourse by force and against her will.[17] Similarly, the unfinished divorce action brought in 1902 by Florence Hackett, the daughter of a storekeeper, against her husband Horace, a commercial traveller, listed his attempt to rape her along with other claims of cruel behaviour.[18]

Sometimes, a wife had to defend herself not just against her husband's unwanted sexual attentions, but also against his pressure to engage in sexual practices with others he wished to introduce into the conjugal bed. Jane Singleton, in her successful 1873 petition for a divorce, claimed that her husband offered the sexual favours of both her and her daughter to another man.[19] Mary Parker, in her 1867 petition for divorce, described how her husband brought a young man and a prostitute to their house, suggesting that he sleep with the prostitute while she slept with the man. She promptly left and then found herself locked out of the house. Mary could make use of that same incident to establish her husband's adultery with the prostitute.[20] In an 1876 case, Julia Morrison defended herself against her husband's petition for restitution of conjugal rights by claiming that his threat to make her drunk and sleep with another man gave her reasonable cause to separate herself from him.[21] Marion Goldhill's 1897 successful petition for a judicial separation cited her husband's insistence that other men sleep in the same room with them.[22] In John Kilby's 1899 divorce case, his wife May defended herself against his charges that she engaged in prostitution by describing an incident in which

the Petitioner requested the Respondent to get into bed with a male person of the name of Speedy while the Petitioner should do the like with a female person of the name of Fraser and that upon the Respondent's refusal so to do the Petitioner got into bed with the said Fraser in the Respondent's presence.[23]

The successful 1901 bid by Edith Laycock to divorce her husband Alfred rested on several claims, including the accusation that the husband had 'compelled your Petitioner by threats to permit a woman named Bevans with whom he has admitted that he committed adultery to sleep in the same bed with your Petitioner'. Alfred also forced his wife to permit a servant girl in her bed.[24] Similarly, the successful 1902 divorce petition of Helena Fletcher against her husband Ernest featured her claim that he 'was in the habit of making love to a married woman named Mrs. Quickie in your Petitioner's presence'.[25]

Other divorce petitions similarly made claims based on a variety of non-normative sexual behaviours. Nudity, for instance, appeared to be one marker of problematic sexual demands. Alice Duncan's 1902 petition for divorce provides a particularly good example of what appears to the modern sensibility to be the extreme narrowness of acceptable conventional marital sexuality during the nineteenth century. Alice accused her husband of numerous cruelties: coming home in a drunken state and infecting her with a venereal disease. She also indignantly recorded her husband's cruelty in 'insisting on several occasions sleeping naked'. Although this probably was not the charge that weighed most heavily with the court, Alice won her divorce.[26] Similarly, Ann Ayres alleged that her husband 'on several occasions came into the room in a state of nudity where your Petitioner and her children were the eldest of whom being a daughter was 14 to 15 years of age'. From her account, the petition outlined the career of a man with a significant drinking problem, but not even establishing his period as an inmate in the Insane Ward of St. Pancras Union Workhouse and the Culney Hatch Lunatic Asylum would gain Ann legal protection from her husband. Ann abandoned her suit after obtaining an order for her husband to pay her alimony of 5 shillings per week.[27] In defending herself against her husband's charges in his 1861 suit for restitution for conjugal rights, Emily Westrup described a situation in which her husband prevented her maid from coming to her assistance by undressing himself 'then and there'.[28] Such behaviour wavered on the line between nudity and indecent exposure and sometimes went over that line. For instance, in 1906, Ethel Annie Goldsmith of Tiverton in Devon, the daughter of a land agent, sued her husband William, a farmer, for a judicial separation, making various claims about his cruel and abusive behaviour, including one incident that occurred during her pregnancy when William 'cruelly shocked and insulted your Petitioner by indecently exposing himself in ... the presence of a female nurse'.[29]

Other sexual practices, often described as unnatural in petitions presented to the Divorce Court, also elicited disapproval. The use of condoms, demands for sex during the wife's menstrual cycle, masturbation, oral sex, bestiality, and sodomy all came within the purview of stern judges. Ethelwyn Leveaux, the wife of a theatrical manager, Montagu Vivian Ellis Leveaux, indignantly claimed to the Divorce Court that her husband had 'against your Petitioner's wish and despite her protests insisted upon having inter-course with her in an unnatural manner and thereby seriously affected her health'. When pressed by the Court to define these unnatural prac-tices more explicitly, Ethelwyn revealed that her husband always insisted upon using a 'french letter' whenever they had intercourse, and (not sur-prisingly perhaps) this couple had no children after four years of marriage. The husband also insisted upon oral sex, thus 'causing her great distress and disgust'. As a consequence of the 'grief and distress' this conduct caused, her health broke down and 'she suffered from intense mental and physical depression'. Such allegations about her physical health were crucial for the success of the petition because she had no other cruelties to offer to com-bine with her husband's adultery in order to qualify for a divorce.[30] Mary Esther Oppenheimer, whose husband, as we have already seen, demanded sex in railway carriages, also alleged that her husband 'compelled her to submit to disgusting and unnatural practices'. Her husband behaved cru-elly towards his wife when 'on divers occasions ... the Respondent, by force placed the Petitioner's head and face close to and touching his private parts and attempted to force and occasionally did force his private parts into her mouth'. The Divorce Court accepted Mary's account of her hus-band's behaviour and her claim that it amounted to cruelty, granting her a divorce.[31]

Wives could also use such allegations to defend themselves against a hus-band's suit for divorce. Husbands had not only to prove their wife's adultery to divorce her, but they also had to be able to show themselves innocent of any marital transgression or any conduct which might have conduced to the adultery. When Daniel Barker, a Norwich boot manufacturer, sued his wife for divorce she admitted her adultery but defended herself on the grounds of her husband's desertion and failure to support her as well as his cruelty, which consisted of demanding his conjugal rights within two weeks of her having given birth and of compelling her 'to submit to the injury to her health to marital intercourse with him, although she was menstruating and wholly unfit for sexual relations'. The Barkers abandoned their litigation so the court did not get a chance to rule on the respec-tive merits of these charges and counter-charges.[32] Emily Hunt, in resisting her husband's 1861 suit for restitution of conjugal rights, claimed that her husband had

> insisted on having conjugal intercourse with the Respondent who was then unwell from the recurrence of a monthly period on which ground the Respondent expressly declined to yield to the wishes of the petitioner

who thereupon became very angry, abused her violently, assaulted her, pushed and pinched her, and finally gave her a blow as a child is smacked for correction.[33]

Marion Tatam's suit against her husband, a civil engineer, alleged that he had 'habitually insisted on subjecting your Petitioner to most offensive and indecent and disgusting treatment...'. This consisted of the abuse, threats, and insults routinely detailed in divorce petitions. The Court asked Marion to be more explicit about her husband's 'indecent and disgusting' treatment of her, and she revealed that her husband had 'attempted and very often succeeded notwithstanding the resistance of the Petitioner in passing his hands under her clothes and inserting his fingers into her private parts'. Not only did her husband's proclivities result in her injury, but he also insisted on fondling his daughters in the same way. Marion won her freedom and alimony of £80 per year.[34]

In 1868, Caroline Eliza Hartry of Southampton petitioned for a separation from her husband Thomas, a dentist, listing several grievances that evidenced cruelty. She described her husband as a 'confirmed drunkard' who refused to wash or change clothes. When she tried to sleep separately, he would break into her room, or, alternatively, he would lock her out of their bedroom. He also committed 'acts of gross indecency', and these included bringing a dog to bed, as well as a brood of chickens.[35] After the court empanelled a special jury to hear the case, Caroline failed to press forward with her case.[36]

The 1900 divorce case of Margaret Dent reveals a husband attempting to use marriage to get around the law on age of consent. Margaret had married William Dent, a merchant's son and a man of independent means, in 1893. Although she was only 14 at the time, Margaret, the daughter of a railway porter, performed in the ballet in London theatres, and she had the permission of her father to marry. Margaret had a child in 1894, and then, in 1897, William persuaded Margaret to allow another young girl, Mabel Quantrell, to join their household. William was subsequently charged and convicted of violating the 1885 Criminal Law Amendment Act for his sexual relationship with Mabel. William, in his defence against the divorce petition, unusually filed by his wife's mother rather than by his wife although Margaret was by that time at least 20 years old, claimed that Margaret had engaged in sexual acts with Mabel, but Margaret denied these charges during the Court hearing. These counter-charges failed to have any effect, and the Court readily granted Margaret a divorce from her husband.[37]

Upon occasion, descriptions of assaults by husbands upon their wives make clear the sexual overtones of this violence. Helen Parr, the daughter of an oil importer, married John Parr, an engineer who was the son of a clergyman, in 1899. In 1904, Helen filed for divorce citing her husband's frequent adultery, threats, and assaults, including one she described in some detail, when her husband 'seized your Petitioner violently by the hairs of her private parts and dragged her round the bedroom causing her much pain'. Nine months after she filed her petition, the Divorce Court had granted the divorce.[38] Similarly, Beatrice Tomlinson, the daughter of the manager of a cutlery works, petitioned for a divorce from her husband, Reginald, the son of a draper who had become a bookkeeper, charging him with multiple adulteries and various threats and violent assaults, including one occasion when her husband 'struck your Petitioner in her private parts with the stock of a gun causing her great agony'. Beatrice's petition, like Helen's, received a favourable hearing from the Divorce Court.[39] Although Emma McLellan did not press her 1872 petition for a judicial separation to a conclusion, she accused her husband of indecent assault in public that caused her 'internal injuries, causing a displacement of her womb'.[40]

In five cases wives alleged that they had been the victim of their husbands' forcible commission of sodomy. In the nineteenth century and earlier the term 'sodomy' often was used very generally, encompassing a variety of non-procreative sexual practices.[41] The incidence and the legal status of homosexual sodomy have recently received scholarly attention.[42] These divorce petitions, however, clearly use the word much more precisely to mean heterosexual anal intercourse. For instance, Emma Blakeley complained in her petition for a judicial separation that her husband, a Yorkshire manufacturer, had treated her 'in a bestial manner'. Pressed by the Court to explain her meaning, she elaborated, 'the Respondent under the cover or pretence of having marital intercourse with the Petitioner violently, cruelly and wilfully abused the Petitioner by thrusting or inserting his person into the anus or fundament of the Petitioner, thereby causing her considerable pain and distress'.[43] In a 1901 petition for divorce, Ethel Bishop claimed that her husband committed sodomy on her.[44] In an 1887 petition for divorce, Mary Ann Beardwell also claimed her husband forcibly committed sodomy on her.[45] In her 1895 petition for a judicial separation, Sophia James employed somewhat ambiguous language in her accusations against her husband that nonetheless strongly suggested sodomy. Sophia described William James as a man of 'violent temper', who, since their marriage in 1887, was 'habitually guilty of outrages abominable and unnatural practices upon and against your petitioner and that he thereby caused your petitioner excruciating pain and agony'.[46] None of these cases actually proceeded to a conclusion. But the 1886 Otway case received a full hearing, and newspaper coverage of the case reveals the attitude of the judge towards such allegations and claims.

The Otway divorce case concerned a couple apparently comfortably fixed in life. The couple had married in 1879 and had four children. Their marriage certificate described Adelaide Otway as the daughter of a gentleman and Harold Otway as a gentleman and the son of a gentleman. The couple lived in the London area. In June 1886 Adelaide sued her husband for divorce, claiming that her husband had repeatedly attempted to commit sodomy on her and in 1886 had forcibly succeeded in doing so. She also claimed that he had made indecent assaults on one of their children. Harold not only denied all these accusations, he filed his own petition for divorce in September 1886, accusing his wife of adultery. She countered by denying the adultery and accusing her husband of conniving at her adultery by his behaviour. As it often did in the case of counter-suits, the Divorce Court consolidated the two cases and heard them over the course of three days of testimony in open court on 30 November, 1 December, and 2 December, 1887.[47] The sensational nature of the accusations attracted extensive newspaper coverage, which reported the judge's lengthy statement about the case.

Justice Sir Charles Butt presided over the trial.[48] The observations he made about the Otways as he delivered judgement expressed his deep moral outrage at the behaviour of both parties, although he reserved his strongest condemnation for Harold. Butt had held the proceedings in open court, despite the nature of the accusations made against Harold, because 'he had a strong objection to allowing parties in cases where their conduct had been particularly flagitious to screen themselves from publicity by the very heinousness of the offences they committed'. Nevertheless, Butt did close the court during the testimony pertaining to the charges of the husband's indecent assault on a child. In his final judgement, Butt concluded that both the Otways had committed adultery. He also found that Adelaide had proved her charges of 'ordinary cruelty' and 'personal violence'. Butt was not so convinced by the charges that Harold had connived at the adultery of his wife or the claims about Harold's 'indecent conduct' towards one of his children. Although Butt did not find the direct evidence for these charges fully compelling, he pointed to two letters entered into evidence by Adelaide that revealed Harold's character as so immoral that he would have been capable of such behaviour. Butt described the tenor of these letters as:

> indescribably filthy and abominable. To say that they showed the writer to be unfit for the society of decent people would be to convey an altogether inadequate notion of their contents. He did not hesitate to say that if the writer were turned into any convict prison in the country with those two letters pinned on his back, the inmates, however degraded they might be, would shrink from him with loathing and with horror.

Butt found himself in something of a quandary, as such proven counter-charges of adultery usually meant that neither petition could succeed, as divorce was reserved to an injured but innocent spouse. He decided to grant Adelaide a judicial separation, although it was unusual to do so for a wife guilty of adultery. In defence of this decision, Butt asked, 'was there not a refinement of cruelty in wounding the feelings of the wife through the children?' He also worried that if he refused Adelaide any relief from her marriage then the cruel behaviour of her husband would continue. In addition, granting a judicial separation gave the court control over the custody of the children, who he thought must be kept out of their father's reach. Butt was not entirely happy with leaving the children with their mother, who had also exhibited a weak moral character, but he expressed the hope that 'respectable relations and connexions' of the couple would step forward to apply for custody, saying that he would 'gladly listen to any application for placing those children in the hands of a trustworthy relative'.[49]

In all five of these cases, wives made their charges about sodomy in explicit detail. Although the James, Beardwell, Blakeley, and Bishop cases ended inconclusively, the richer documentation and decisive conclusion of the Otway case shows the revulsion with which the Divorce Court judges reacted to proven charges of deviant sexual behaviour. Sodomy, of course, could also mean homosexual anal intercourse. In only one case in my sample of petitions presented to the Divorce Court does a wife go so far as even to imply that her husband had a sexual relationship with another man. In her 1890 petition for a judicial separation, Mabel Edith, Countess Russell, complained that her husband, John Francis, Earl Russell (Bertrand Russell's older brother), brought a male friend into the house with whom he spent many hours late at night in his guest's room.[50] Russell successfully defended himself against this charge, but his success in this respect meant that his wife's divorce suit failed, and the irreconcilable couple remained married to one another, a personal disaster for them both.[51]

The threat of venereal disease forms a recurrent thread in these cases.[52] A husband suffering from venereal disease obviously represented a material threat to his wife's health and so formed a recognized basis for her to reject his sexual advances. Indeed, an attempt to raise the issue of marital rape as a criminal matter during the nineteenth century featured a wife who had engaged in sexual intercourse with her husband while ignorant of his diseased state. This case, *R. v. Clarence*, which failed, could be taken to express the legal system's support of the husband's sexual rights.[53] That conclusion, however, neglects the way a husband's venereal disease figured in divorce cases.

Given their legal handicaps, only wives placed in the direst circumstances could divorce their husbands. The transmission of venereal disease to the wife by the husband represented one of those circumstances the Divorce Court might find an acceptable basis for a petition for divorce.[54] English law recognized such an offence as an exception to the usual requirement during the eighteenth century that cruelty be violent.[55] Decisions in *Boardman v. Boardman* (1866) and *Brown v. Brown* (1865) laid down the precedents that guided the Divorce Court during the Victorian period. The judgement in the case of *Boardman v. Boardman* explicitly defined the knowing and reckless communication of disease by the husband to the wife as cruelty, while in the case of *Brown v. Brown* the court established the premise that 'the husband's state of health is to be presumed to be within his own knowledge'.[56] These decisions provided wives with the opportunity to claim the court's protection against this particular variety of marital cruelty.

Throughout the Victorian period, petitions filed before the Divorce Court invariably included some in which one spouse accused the other of bringing venereal disease into the home. Although never very numerous, these cases constituted a distinct and recognizable aspect of the court's business throughout the period and an important tactic employed by wives against their husbands. In the early years of the twentieth century, both the Royal Commission on Divorce and the witnesses before it felt the need to address this particular problem explicitly. After a half century of this litigation, the *Lancet*, prompted by yet another such case in 1907, warned its readers to take great care in the diagnosis of gonorrhoea in a married person. Doctors had to be prepared for the likelihood that legal action might follow and that the attending physician would be called upon to give expert testimony in court.[57] These cases formed an important proportion of the court's business – more than 10 per cent of the sample or about 20 per cent of wives' petitions.[58]

In conclusion, the cases reviewed here complicate our understanding of the cultural standing of the sexual rights of husbands and the legal power of the marital rape exemption. Although the marital rape exemption did indeed hold in criminal law until comparatively recently, that did not necessarily mean that wives had no legal recourse at all against the untrammelled sexuality of their husbands. Of course, such recourse was limited by social norms that generally enjoined the sexual submission of wives to husbands and stigmatized those wives who tried to challenge their husbands or bring their grievances to court in seeking divorces or separations or protection from their husbands. But the judges who served the English Divorce Court upheld a strict morality that did not exempt husbands, and some wives could and did turn to the divorce law to defend themselves against their husbands' illegitimate sexual demands. Furthermore, the social norms employed by Divorce Court judges defined sexuality in such limited terms that almost any sexual behaviour out of the ordinary could feature in a wife's petition. Through the second half of the nineteenth century, the increasing strength of domestic ideology enjoining companionate affection and respect on married couples found expression in judges holding husbands much more strictly accountable for their behaviour towards their wives.[59]

These cases, like those featuring male violence against illegitimate children examined by Ginger Frost, show husbands asserting a physical power that did not recognize any limits. If drawn into divorce litigation by their wives, however, husbands had to face Divorce Court judges, a small and elite group of jurists who had the power and authority to define and enforce limits. Their decisions express a remarkable consensus about restraining the uncontrolled husband. But the Divorce Court bench was very small, limited to two judges at any one time until after the First World War. Such a con-certed consensus would break down when these questions moved to larger groups, such as the men who staffed the magistrates' courts.

The broad social range of litigants suggests that the recourse to physical force by a husband to assert his self-perceived right to gratify his sexual desires was not limited to the working class and the poor. Those groups largely lacked the means to bring their marital grievances to the Divorce Court. The contestation of sexual power often entailed physical violence, even if it did not reach the level of lethality that the judges considering cases of murder and grievous bodily harm committed by husbands against their wives and children had to weigh. These cases also suggest the practice of a broader range of sexual behaviours than that prescribed by Victorian social norms. After all, we would not find a married couple of like mind about enjoying a sexual interlude in a railway car among these couples at odds with one another about what form their sexual life together ought to take.

From the perspective of the twenty-first century, the civil law of divorce, even if it did sometimes free wives from violent and abusive husbands, does not appear to us a sufficiently punitive response to the horror of marital rape. But since the nineteenth century the civil law of divorce has changed in counter-point to the changes in the way the criminal law treats violent abuse in marriage. Today divorce has been reduced to virtually an admin-istrative procedure where the courts mainly concern themselves with the equitable arrangement of matters of property and custody rather than reach-ing a judgement about the behaviours of the spouses. In contrast, during the nineteenth century in England divorce was an adversarial procedure that sought to establish guilt and innocence. And, although the Divorce Court could not order a punishment that included incarceration (except for fail-ure to pay court-ordered alimony), divorce actions extracted a high cost of litigants, particularly the transgressing party. Public humiliation, loss of family life, and the punitive aspect of paying costs and alimony formed the weapons the Divorce Court could deploy in their duty to uphold the sanctity of marriage and to discipline the unruly sexuality of men and husbands.

Notes

1. J. S. Mill (1988) *The Subjection of Women*, ed. Susan Moller Okin (Indianapolis: Hackett Publishing Co.), p. 33.
2. A. Bronte (1985) *The Tenant of Wildfell Hall* (London: Penguin Books), pp. 316, 394–400.
3. J. Galsworthy (1969) *The Man of Property* (New York: Charles Scribner's Sons), pp. 246–95. R. M. Ryan (1995) 'The Sex Right; A Legal History of the Marital Rape Exemption', *Law and Social Inquiry* 20 (4), 941–1001, uses this scene to frame her discussion (pp. 951–2), although her essay primarily focuses on developments in nineteenth- and twentieth-century America.

4. Galsworthy, *The Man of Property*, p. 247.
5. Quoted in G. Geis (1978) 'Lord Hale, Witches and Rape', *British Journal of Law and Society* 5, p. 40. This essay gives an interesting treatment of Hale's ideas about women, connecting his view of women in marriage with his view of witches and witchcraft.
6. C. Pateman (1988) *The Sexual Contract* (Stanford: Stanford University Press).
7. See V. Laird (1992) 'Reflections on *R v. R*', *Modern Law Review* 55, pp. 386–92, for a discussion of decision that overturned the marital rape exemption.
8. M. J. Anderson (1988) 'Lawful Wife, Unlawful Sex – Examining the Effect of the Criminalization of Marital Rape in England and the Republic of Ireland', *Georgia Journal of International and Comparative Law* 18; Jill Elaine Hasday (2000) 'Contest and Consent: A Legal History of Marital Rape', *California Law Review* 88, pp. 1373–505.
9. The following analysis is based upon cases drawn from a sample of all petitions filed before the Divorce Court between 1858 and 1908, inclusive. For the first 20 years of the period, I examined every tenth file; for the remainder of the period I examined every twentieth file. Such a systematic sample approaches a random sample in representativeness.
10. The National Archives [TNA], Public Records Office [PRO], J77/108/1760, *Mackle v. Mackle*, 14 December 1870.
11. On the restitution of conjugal rights in general and the Jackson case in particular, see M. Lyndon Shanley (1989) *Feminism, Marriage, and the Law in Victorian England, 1850–1895* (Princeton: Princeton University Press), pp. 156–88; and M. E. Doggett (1993) *Marriage, Wife-Beating and the Law in Victorian England* (Columbia, SC: University of South Carolina Press), pp. 1–2, 103–5.
12. TNA, PRO J77/111/1868, *Ferris v. Ferris*, 27 February 1877.
13. Judges had the power to exclude the public from the courtroom and hear cases privately when entertaining sensitive testimony or testimony that might violate public sensibilities if reported in detail. This was routinely done in nullity cases, but judges took advantage of this option far less often in divorce cases.
14. TNA, PRO J77/171/4252, *Oppenheimer v. Oppenheimer*, 19 February 1876, emphasis in original.
15. TNA, PRO J77/192/5012, *Holland v. Holland*, 25 May 1877; J77/234/6589, *Andrews v. Andrews*, 20 November 1879; J77/236/6670, *Rymer v. Rymer*, 20 January 1880.
16. TNA, PRO J77/653/9906, *Solder v. Solder*, 1 November 1898.
17. TNA, PRO J77/364/1014, *Jackson v. Jackson*, 9 August 1886.
18. TNA, PRO J77/750/2827, *Hackett v. Hackett*, 9 May 1902.
19. TNA, PRO J77/137/2915, *Singleton v. Singleton* & Queen's Proctor intervening, 1 September 1873.
20. TNA, PRO J77/74/424, *Parker v. Parker*, 27 May 1867.
21. TNA, PRO J77/173/4334, *Morrison, J. M. v. Morrison, A. B. and Morrison, A. B. v. Morrison, J. M.*, 7 April 1876.
22. TNA, PRO J77/627/19139, *Goldhill v. Goldhill*, 26 November 1897.
23. TNA, PRO J77/672/423, *Kilby v. Kilby*, 3 July 1899.
24. TNA, PRO J77/714/1727, *Laycock v. Laycock*, 8 March 1901.
25. TNA, PRO J77/767/3351, *Fletcher v. Fletcher*, 6 November 1902.
26. TNA, PRO J77/764/3267, *Duncan v. Duncan*, 15 October 1902.
27. TNA, PRO J77/184/4722, *Ayres v. Ayres*, 11 December 1876.
28. TNA, PRO J77/24/H108, *Hunt v. Hunt*, 6 April 1861.
29. TNA PRO, J77/893/7083, *Goldsmith v. Goldsmith*, 22 October 1906.

30. TNA, PRO J77/869/6403, *Leveaux v. Leveaux*, 27 January 1906.
31. TNA, PRO J77/171/4252, *Oppenheimer v. Oppenheimer*, 19 February 1876.
32. TNA, PRO J77/902/7395, *Barker v. Barker & Phillips*, 15 February 1907.
33. TNA, PRO J77/24/H108, *Hunt v. Hunt*, 6 April 1861.
34. TNA, PRO J77/294/8707, *Tatem v. Tatam*, 13 March 1883.
35. The file does not give details about why Thomas Hartry brought chickens to bed with him, but a leading case in the late nineteenth century struggled with the question of whether or not poultry counted as animals under the statute governing bestiality. G. Parker (1986) 'Is a Duck an Animal? An Exploration of Bestiality as a Crime', *Criminal Justice History* 7, pp. 95–110.
36. TNA, PRO J77/88/960, *Hartry v. Hartry*, 30 November 1868.
37. TNA, PRO J77/684/804, *Dent v. Dent*, 10 January 1900; *Times*, 30 June 1900, p. 17, col. e.
38. TNA PRO, J77/813/4723, *Parr v. Parr*, 6 April 1904.
39. TNA PRO, J77/878/6667, *Tomlinson v. Tomlinson*, 7 May 1906.
40. TNA PRO, J77/125/2446, *McLellan v. McLellan*, 22 July 1872.
41. See Vern L. Bullough and Martha Voght (1973) 'Homosexuality and Its Confusion with the "Secret Sin" in Pre-Freudian America', *Journal of the History of Medicine* 38, pp. 143–55, for a discussion of this.
42. See H. G. Cocks (2003) *Nameless Offences: Homosexual Desire in the 19th Century* (London: I. B. Tauris).
43. TNA, PRO J77/427/3035, *Blakeley v. Blakeley*, 13 June 1889.
44. TNA, PRO J77/719/1860, *Bishop v. Bishop and Witherst* combined with *Bishop v. Bishop*, 14 May 1901.
45. TNA, PRO J77/3740136, *Beardwell v. Beardwell*, 19 January 1887.
46. TNA, PRO J77/575/7562, *James v. James*, 23 December 1895.
47. TNA, J77/362/0931, *Otway v. Otway* and *Otway v. Otway and Hoffer*, 28 June 1886.
48. Sir Charles Parker Butt (1830–1892) was appointed to the Divorce Court in 1883 and became president of the Court in 1891, shortly before his death in 1892.
49. *Times*, 3 December 1887, p. 5, col. b, c, d. The official files on this case do not record any such intervention.
50. TNA, PRO J77/46/4047, *Russell v. Russell*, 29 November 1890. For a discussion of this case, see A. Sumner Holmes (1999) ' "Don't Frighten the Horses": The Russell Divorce Case', in G. Robb and N. Erber (eds) *Disorder in the Court: Trials and Sexual Conflict at the Turn of the Century* (London: Macmillan), pp. 140–63.
51. For Frank Russell's future career, see G. Savage (1996) ' "... Equality from the masculine point of view...": The Earl Russell and Divorce Law Reform', *Russell* 16, pp. 67–84.
52. Seven of the cases discussed above included allegations about venereal disease: *Singleton* (1873), *Morrison* (1876), *Holland* (1877), *Andrews* (1879), *Rymer* (1880), *Solder* (1898), and *Duncan* (1902).
53. On *R. v. Clarence*, see Shanley, *Feminism, Marriage, and the Law*, pp. 18–5; K. Gleeson (2005) 'Sex, Wives, and Prostitutes: Debating *Clarence*', in J. Rowbotham and K. Stevenson (eds) *Criminal Conversations: Victorian Crimes, Social Panic, and Moral Outrage* (Columbus: Ohio State University Press), pp. 215–31.
54. In addition, cruelty alone could be grounds for a judicial separation, and some wives chose that legal avenue, as Lady Campbell did in her suit against her husband in 1884. G. H. Fleming (1989) *Lady Colin Campbell: Victorian 'Sex Goddess'* (Gloucestershire: Windrush Press).

55. J. M. Biggs (1962) *The Concept of Matrimonial Cruelty* (London: Athlone), pp. 131–4.
56. A. P. Stone (1892) *Digest of Cases, 1860–1890* (London: William Clowes and Sons), Vol. 2, col. 1996.
57. 'The Diagnosis of Gonorrhoea [*sic*]', *Lancet* (23 February 1907), p. 515.
58. For a more comprehensive treatment of the way in which Divorce Court treated venereal disease, see G. Savage (1990) ' "The Wilful Communication of a Loath-some Disease": Venereal Disease and Marital Conflict in Victorian England', *Victorian Studies* 34, pp. 35–54.
59. See A. J. Hammerton (1992) *Cruelty and Companionship: Conflict in Nineteenth-Century Life* (London and New York: Routledge) for a discussion of the significance of these developments with respect to abusive behaviour. See also, R. L. Griswold (1986) 'Sexual Cruelty and the Case for Divorce in Victorian American', *Signs* 11, pp. 529–41.

Part II
Poverty and the State

3
Irish Orphans and the Politics of Domestic Authority

Anna Clark

The plight of poor English orphans is familiar to us from Dickens, with Oliver Twist pitifully bleating, 'Please sir, can I have some more?' But the plight of poor Irish orphans is less well known and even more pitiable. For instance, in the Cork workhouse, 18 per cent of the child inmates, many of whom were orphans, died each year. This was not surprising since they were fed watery, bug-ridden vegetable soup and inedible bread. They were forced to labour for many hours a day, clothed in rags and shod in heavy clogs, and when they were let out to exercise, they had to splash in sewage, which pooled in the courtyards where they were confined. Scrofula afflicted many of them, eating away their skin as it infected their necks with tuberculosis. Ophthalmia almost blinded others.[1] Clearly, Irish workhouse children, especially orphans, had little chance of growing up to be healthy adults.

Orphans are a particularly interesting topic for the consideration of domestic authority, because they were deprived of the seemingly natural authority of their fathers and mothers. So who would have domestic authority over them? In nineteenth-century Ireland, several groups used the figure of the orphan to claim authority over children and families. First, the British government over Ireland, in the form of the Poor Law, asserted legal authority over orphans. Second, the Catholic Church challenged the British state for moral authority by asserting the rights of the family over the state, using orphans as a *cause celebre*. Third, female philanthropists claimed their domestic authority as 'ladies.'

All of these groups are quite interesting because since they were not the parents, they did not have 'natural' authority. The British government in Ireland, of course, was a quasi-colonial power, and as such faced many challenges. The Catholic Church was still building and consolidating its power and did not control education and welfare as it did in twentieth-century Ireland. And women were identified with the domestic world: as ladies, they exerted influence over their localities, and authority over their servants, but women were not associated with public authority. How could they translate this private influence and authority into the public realm?

And then there was the question of how authority should be exercised, and for what purpose. Victorian reformers believed that children must be brought up to become self-governing individuals, who would internalize authority, learn how to behave according to the rules, and above all, become independent. But as we shall see, Victorian reformers debated what was the best setting in which to create such independent individuals: large institutions or the family? In the case of orphans, the question was whether they should be raised in the poor law workhouses or schools, or boarded out within foster families. This debate represented a contest between two philosophies of individualization.

The first stemmed from Bentham's behaviourism, but also boarding schools, the Lancaster method of regimented classes and rote learning, as well as prisons and workhouses. In this method, an orderly building, a rigid schedule, classification of inmates, and a system of rewards and punishments would create individuals who would internalize discipline.[2] In mid-Victorian Britain, however, the Benthamite idea of discipline was challenged on several fronts. As Lauren Goodlad observes, John Stuart Mill was one of those who began to challenge the Benthamite model of discipline to emphasize 'the sense in which the exercise of the will against the force of habit was central to the development of the self.'[3] Other groups, such as the Catholic Church and lady philanthropists, interpreted individualism in their own way to argue that institutions brought up children as if they were machines; the family, they believed, was the only way in which children could develop autonomy and discipline. The boarding out of pauper orphans was a central issue in this debate.

The problem of pauper children relates to the larger question of who qualified to be the liberal individual who must be left alone to pursue his or her autonomous ends. Debates raged over whether the poor man could be considered to be an individual with political rights and/or economic responsibilities. Similarly, would the Irish Catholics ever be able to govern themselves? It is sometimes argued that certain populations, such as colonized people, were subjected to the 'rule of difference,' to be disciplined through classification, categorization, and regulation, but not regarded as liberal individuals. However, early nineteenth-century missionaries believed that Jamaican slaves, if freed, could learn to govern themselves and become liberal individuals, that is, disciplined wage-earners.[4] These arguments revolved around the extent to which citizenship and individuality were attainable only by those who were independent of the state. They were also tied to laissez-faire individualism, the idea that the state ought not interfere in the freedom of the individual – and that to earn this freedom the individual ought not be dependent on the state.

Children, and especially Irish pauper children, raised special questions in this philosophy. In *On Liberty* John Stuart Mill argued that both children and 'backwards' peoples could not exercise autonomy. Significantly, he noted that like children 'barbarians' were in the 'nonage' of the race.[5] While he saw 'barbarians' as needing 'despotic' rule, children needed protection. By the 1840s, even political economists conceded that the state could regulate the working hours of children, since they were not free agents. Women, too, raised similar problems; in the 1840s, they were lumped together with children as needing the protective hand of the state in the workforce.[6] However, in other ways some Victorians saw both women and children as exercising potential autonomy as individuals. Mill did stress that children were future adults who must be prepared for freedom by being trained to exercise their spontaneity and their self-will. The Victorian bourgeois woman, as Nancy Armstrong observes, was the 'very model of the auto-inspecting, self-regulating forms of individuality required by liberal forms of government.'[7] Mill pointed out the contradictions in nineteenth-century domesticity, and argued very forcefully (unlike the dominant trend in Victorian society) that women should have autonomy. Feminists in the classical liberal tradition felt strongly that women must be able to exert self-will, be responsible for their own actions, and exercise authority over appropriate dependents. To the chagrin of many working-women trade unionists, they opposed protective legislation and some even supported the bastardy clauses, which made unmarried mothers totally responsible for their illegitimate offspring. Lady philanthropists insisted that girls could not be reared in large, institutional poor law schools, but must be individualized in a family through being subject to the authority of parent substitutes. Of course, the idea that individuality and self-will must be nurtured was in itself another form of discipline.

Orphans and the Poor Law

The plight of the orphaned or deserted child was a central problem in poor law philosophy. In the eighteenth century, for kind-hearted philanthropists, poor children were pitiful, helpless creatures needed to be rescued; to reformers, they were potential soldiers and labourers who could strengthen the state. They established foundling hospitals to take in these poor children. But institutions were no place for very young children, who died in droves, only surviving if they were 'boarded out,' sent out to nurse with families in the country. Workhouses, too, fostered out children informally to local families.[8]

But for Thomas Malthus, the foundling hospitals and poor laws just encouraged people to have children they could not support, in the knowledge they would be taken care of if anything happened. Malthus believed that the poor laws should be totally abolished. Even orphans should be told there was no place for them at nature's banquet. Abolishing the poor laws was not politically feasible, but England's 1834 New Poor Law was very harsh, forcing parents to go into the workhouse to receive relief for their children. There, they would be deprived of domestic authority, as husbands were separated from wives and parents from children.

Before 1838, Ireland had had no formal provision for the poor at all, and much more extreme population pressure. The adult poor depended on charity and begging; unmarried mothers, shamed by the Church, often abandoned their illegitimate infants. Up to 1 per cent of all Irish infants were deserted after birth.[9] Orphaned and deserted children were the responsibility of local parishes, which sent them to nurses or foundling institutions, with the usual problems of high mortality. When the establishment of the Irish poor law was debated in the 1830s, some commentators wanted no relief for either adult or child paupers. One even declared that foundling hospitals and provisions for deserted children encouraged women to have illegitimate children, and should be abolished, even if this drove women to infanticide.[10] The Irish poor were often described in racial terms, as primitive and undisciplined, like the 'wild Indians.'[11] But others advocated the establishment of a poor law and greater industrial development for Ireland. The first Irish poor law commissioners had suggested that orphans and deserted children be boarded outside of the workhouse (to avoid infant mortality) and then sent to the colonies.[12]

Ultimately, the British government imposed a poor law on Ireland that was much like the English New Poor Law of 1834, only more rigid. The British poor law commissioners denied that the Irish poor had any right to relief, and instructed that able-bodied men were to be denied admission to the workhouse. While the 1838 commissioners did not go so far as to abolish relief for children, they refused to allow boarding out, that is, sending out children to be nursed and fostered in families. They believed it would violate the principle that relief should only be given in the workhouse, and encourage Irish women to bear illegitimate children and desert them, instead of facing the consequences of their own 'immorality.'[13] Poor law officials believed that the workhouse would 'elevate [the Irish pauper] in the scale of human existence, and teach him the self-respect to feel the degradation of his position; and make him forbear to propagate his species like the beasts of the field without any thought of provision for his offspring.'[14]

The poor law in both England and Ireland was based on three principles: less eligibility, economy, and institutional discipline. 'Less eligibility' meant that conditions in the workhouse had to be worse than the conditions of the poorest labourer, so that people would only seek help there if they had no alternative. So harsh conditions were mandated even for abandoned children and orphans; otherwise, parents might abandon their children to the workhouse if their lives would be better there. Poor law ideologues also believed that working-class people should not have children unless they could provide for them after their death. And the principle of less eligibility went along nicely with the drive to cut the burgeoning costs of the poor law in the harsh years of the 1830s and 1840s.

But Edwin Chadwick and others influenced by Bentham also thought that the discipline of the workhouse itself would reform the poor and make them independent. Edwin Chadwick argued that if children were boarded out in poor families, they would be exposed to bad influences, and that a well-run workhouse could redeem children from the 'hereditary taint' of pauperism.[15] The model of domestic authority in the workhouse was that of an institution, a Benthamite, depersonalized model of authority. The authority in the workhouse itself derived as much from the physical structure of the building and the schedules of life as it did from the officials. Children, in particular, would learn structured habits by living their lives according to the workhouse bell. A visitor to a strictly run English workhouse gained an overwhelming sense of the institution's 'Power' over the helpless children, enforced by 'endless rules, endless iron-barred windows and padlocked gates.'[16] But it was hard to run a disciplined, efficient workhouse, when officials constantly wanted to cut costs, and when the principle of less eligibility mandated that workhouse conditions had to be worse than the miserable conditions in which the Irish poor lived.

The problem of cost-cutting was particularly acute in Ireland because of the sectarian divide, encouraged by the British state. English Protestant commissioners tightly regulated the Irish poor law with constant surveillance. Local Protestant elites dominated local boards of guardians, and tried to keep expenditure to a minimum, since most of the poor were Catholic, seen as alien and other. However, some Catholics were also elected as guardians; although they tended to be in a minority, they could draw upon popular support and sometimes challenge the English-dominated state.[17] Workhouses tended to be riven by sectarian conflict, with patronage, contracts and appointments allocated on religious lines. This meant that local officials could often evade discipline for incompetence, abusive violence and corruption if they could exert their sectarian clout; the commissioners would rebuke them in private, but support them in public. Both Catholic and Protestant guardians tended to pinch pennies, reducing the allocation of food and clothing even further than the commissioners mandated.

As a result of this frugality, as well as the inherent problems of institutionalization, children died in droves in Irish workhouses. In 1842, 35.33 per cent of all the children admitted to the North Dublin Union died; few infants survived. Mothers, pauper wet nurses, and children were crammed into a damp, ill-ventilated, low-ceilinged room with almost no light. Mothers had to breast-feed their infants while picking oakum (heavy, tarry ropes), which filled the air with flecks of fibre. Wet nurses and nursing mothers went without food from five in the evening to ten in the morning. Not surprisingly, the surviving children were 'generally pale, with a soft flaccid state of the limbs.' Even the guardians were outraged. But the poor law commissioners sent in their own doctors, who tried to claim (without much credibility) that these living conditions, and this high mortality, were no worse, and indeed somewhat better, than the conditions of the young children of the poor in the Irish slums. The principle of 'less eligibility,' therefore, mandated this squalor and disease.[18]

During the famine, the rigid policy of limiting relief in the workhouse crumbled, as these institutions filled with starving and sick people. But afterwards, the Irish poor law system still gave much less outdoor relief than the English equivalent. Women, the aged and infirm, and especially, famine orphans, inhabited the workhouses. Infant mortality continued to be a terrible problem. As a result, in the 1840s and 1850s some Irish guardians began to petition the poor law commissioners to allow children to be raised outside the workhouses. They looked to Scotland for a precedent. The Scottish poor law minimized the use of the workhouse as too expensive. Instead, it continued the practice of boarding out, because it was much cheaper than keeping children in workhouses or schools. The Scottish advocates of boarding out tended to idealize the rural family, where independent cottagers would welcome children into their homes with rough affection, and train them into habits of labour.[19] However, the Irish commissioners obdurately refused to follow the Scottish example, in part because they were so wedded to the deterrence of the workhouse, perhaps for Malthusian reasons, and perhaps because they rightly feared that children sent out to nurse would die.[20]

In the larger British context, however, officials also feared that contrary to Chadwick's hopes, the workhouse would not reform pauper children, but instead, contaminate them with the company of adult paupers, especially mothers of illegitimate children and other 'profligate' characters; they would become 'a separate caste, in some respect unfitted for mixing hereafter in the world.'[21] So they advocated industrial or district schools instead, which were large institutions in the country for pauper children, separate and distant from the workhouse.[22] Their advocate, James Kay Shuttleworth, had argued that the orphaned or deserted boy educated in the workhouse was 'generally unfitted for earning his livelihood by labour'; having 'acquired no skill ... he would be effeminate' because he lacked a 'frugal and industrious father' to teach him. To substitute for the domestic authority of the father, he wanted a centralized system; pauper children would be taught industry in regimented schools which would be inspected by experts.[23] While the schools would be quite different than the horrors of the Benthamite workhouse, they were based on a similar notion of individuals disciplined by structure and by schedule. Early nineteenth-century education relied on rote learning and the monitorial system which meant that few teachers were needed for a large number of children.[24] In such schools, ragged children were cleaned up and socialized to march in single file and instantly obey the schoolmaster: as one observer approvingly noted, 'the whole machinery moves, as it were, of itself – no noise, – no bustle, – no disorder of any kind.'[25] These schools were perfectly suited to prepare boys for life in the factory or the military.

But a coalition of reformers – the Catholic Church, Protestant political economists, and philanthropic ladies – objected to the operation of this system in Ireland. In part, they were trying to assert their own authority over Irish children, but they also objected to the institutionalization of children, calling the poor law a 'cold, hard cruel machine.'[26] While the district schools and reformatories treated children as a mass, reformers advocated 'individuation.' This is a very interesting concept which may seem somewhat anachronistic, but it is actually related to Victorian concepts of the self-reliant individual. Reformers believed that the authority children were subject to must help them gain autonomy and self-will, rather than function as cogs in a machine. This idea had several sources, including the Romantic idea of childhood, and continental reformers; Mary Carpenter, who founded 'ragged schools' for street boys in England, was an influential advocate of this view.[27] In this light, the workhouse system seemed to be the worst example of regimentation undermining children's individuality. Arthur P. Moore, an Irish MP, claimed that the workhouse system 'destroyed the self reliance and self respect of the children.' He complained that the children wore coarse uniforms, shared beds, ate off a common plate, or off the table, and drank out of cans chained to the table.[28] They literally had nothing to claim as their own.

The focus on individuality united religious and non-religious thinkers alike. Evangelicals, of course, stressed individual self-examination and salvation. But those who rejected their faith retained a high moral seriousness which required a belief in individual agency and judgement. For instance, poor law activist Frances Power Cobbe, who lost her Anglican faith and became a theist, declared, 'God has made all rational free agents for virtue.'[29] This stress upon the individuation of children was also found in the Irish Catholic Church.[30]

It may seem strange to think of the Catholic Church as criticizing the institutional upbringing of children, because when we think of the Irish Catholic Church, what comes to mind are its great institutions, its own orphanages, and schools. However, in mid-nineteenth-century Ireland, the Church was just beginning to rebuild itself after the years of the penal laws, when it had not been able to control property, so it did not have the funds to establish institutions right away. The Church worried that state or privately controlled institutions would force children to be Protestants. Indeed, by law, all deserted children whose religion was unknown had to be raised in the religion of the state, that is, Protestantism, although statistically, an Irish deserted baby was likely to belong to the majority religion. Even before the New Poor Law, the Protestant orphan society had been founded to ensure that orphans did not end up with Catholic nurses or in Catholic homes. It boarded out the children to Protestant families, which apparently worked very well.[31] Emulating the enemy, Catholics wanted to board out the children to save their souls from Protestantism and place them under the appropriate authority of Catholic foster parents.

Because the Catholic Church needed resources, it allowed women, often heiresses, to begin new Catholic charitable and educational institutions which could compete with Protestant organizations.[32] These women insisted on treating children in a family setting. For instance, Margaret Aylward founded the St. Brigid's orphanage in 1857 in order to rescue 37 orphaned children, born Protestant but raised as Catholic by their nurses, from being returned to the workhouse and Protestantism. However, she was determined to avoid institutionalizing these children, and instead, boarded them out in country Catholic homes. When the Protestant mother of one of her charges tried to reclaim her child, one of her officials apparently arranged for the child to be abducted and hidden away. Margaret Aylward was actually imprisoned for refusing to reveal who had abducted the child.[33]

The Catholic Church argued that the individual soul had to be regarded as innate and irreducible in order to ensure salvation.[34] Hence, the Catholic institutions, such as reformatories for young boys or girls, tried to 'individuate' their charges, and they believed that government institutions did not. A letter to the nationalist *Freeman* newspaper opposed the establishment of reformatory schools in Irish poor law workhouses on the grounds that in these institutions 'the family principle is ignored; individualization is ignored; the separation of religions is ignored.'[35] Of course, the Catholic Church also objected to district schools because they would be controlled by the Protestant state, not the Catholic Church.[36]

The Catholic Church and its advocates also began to use the poor law in general, and the call for boarding out in particular, as a weapon in its struggle against the British state – and in its competition with Irish nationalists for political leadership. The Dublin *Evening Post* denounced the poor law as an 'utter disgrace to civilization, and an outrage against Christianity.' The Catholic bishops had circulated a petition throughout the churches calling for poor law reform, an extension of outdoor relief, protection of Catholic rights, and the boarding out of orphaned and deserted children.[37] Archbishop Cullen upheld the sanctity of the family over the power of the state.[38] While the workhouse was generally accepted as a test for the able-bodied male, critics of the workhouse argued that it was an improper place to rear children, because it treated children as criminals when their poverty was no fault of their own.[39] A newspaper editorial opined, 'It is unnatural that children should be crowded together without mothers to care for them, without anyone to love them. It is like breeding birds in thousands by heating the eggs in the oven.'[40] Jeremiah Dowling lamented, 'It is impossible to look upon an orphan infant in a workhouse without thinking what a hard stepmother the workhouse must be to the little creature.' He went on, 'It would be just as humane to think of rearing these infants by machinery, as to commit them to the hands of the female paupers who were compelled to take care of them.'[41]

Mainstream Protestant opinion, however, feared placing orphan children in Catholic hands. In 1861, one author opposed taking children from the workhouse, where they were 'under the direct control of officials responsible to the State and to the ratepayers.' He feared that they would be more subject to Catholic control by being placed in the hands of Catholic peasants or in convents, or under the hands of Catholic ladies such as Margaret Woodlock. While boarding out may work in Scotland, 'our peasantry, unfortunately, are of a much lower class than the Scotch.'[42] Sir Richard O'Donnell, chairman of the Newport board of guardians, claimed that children entered the workhouse with 'ringworm, perhaps itch, every frightful skin disease,' but in the institution 'they become cleanly, nice, orderly little children, so that you would feel it quite a pleasure to have them running about you.' Outside the workhouse, in the cabins, 'they would learn everything that civilized people would desire them not to learn, while everything you could desire for poor people's children to learn, they do receive and have in the workhouse.'[43]

The largely Protestant reformers of the Dublin Statistical Society, however, did advocate boarding out. Many of them were academics at the Protestant Anglo-Irish bastion of Trinity College, but they believed that Ireland's crime and unrest could be traced back to bad education and an inadequate poor law system.[44] They belonged to the larger social science movement which wished to 'humanize political economy and the state,' stressing the family as the 'source of social virtue.' These reformers based their authority to pronounce on families to the logic of political economy and the validity of statistics. Orphans could be helped without dramatically interfering in the laws of political economy.[45]

These political economists advocated the patriarchal family as the ideal. For W. Neilson Hancock, the poor law deprived children of a mother's care, and even more, a father's control.[46] Hancock, a professor at Trinity College, began his career as a strict laissez-faire advocate but soon began to argue for more mercy and flexibility in the Irish poor law to prevent nationalist unrest and protect children. Another member of the Dublin Statistical Society admitted that 'we are a conquered and an alienated people,' but believed the Irish must become a 'mighty confederation of rational free agents' following the principles of political economy and rejecting sectarianism.[47] John Kells Ingram argued that 'the regulations of a poor law ought to be founded either on the facts of individual human nature, or on the relations and mutual duties of the members of a human family.'[48] The society's support of boarding out, with its focus on the need for individual attention in the family, enabled the political economists of the Statistical Society to join together on this issue with the Catholic Church, Irish nationalists and middle-class female social reformers.

Many of the female reformers advocating boarding out were members of the Social Science Association, which provided a link to the Dublin Statistical Society. Protestant women like Louisa Twining, part of the Twining tea fortune, and Frances Power Cobbe, an Anglo-Irish philosopher who was close to educational reformer Mary Carpenter, had ties to elites in both Ireland and England, and went back and forth between the two. They had political clout due to these family connections, and some testified in Parliamentary enquiries in the poor law.[49] They wanted to visit the poor in workhouses, but the guardians often blocked them, fearing the interference of 'ladies.'[50] These women became interested in boarding out in part as a reaction to a scandal concerning refractory girls in the South Dublin workhouse, whose riotous behaviour they blamed on an institutional upbringing.[51] Many female philanthropists had tried to create their own institutions to 'reform' girls and women, such as orphanages and Magdalen homes, which could be as regimented as any district schools. But philanthropists often found that these institutions were difficult to sustain financially, and did not succeed in reforming the girls.[52] As a result, they advocated boarding out.

Although these particular 'lady reformers' did not overtly challenge the conventional family, they believed that women must exercise autonomy as free individuals, and this trait must be cultivated in girls. Perhaps motivated by their own search for meaning and autonomy, they believed that girls must be allowed to make moral choices and be responsible for their actions.[53] The ladies were especially concerned that girls should learn how to be good servants, which required the inculcation of domestic skills in a home, rather than an institution. They also believed that female authority in the workhouse needed careful exercise. Ordinary matrons, who were from a working-class or lower-middle-class background, were held to be inadequate to supervise children. Instead, they argued for the need to have a 'woman of education and refinement – in other words, a lady.' They vigorously campaigned for the extension of boarding out, and volunteered to help supervise the children.[54]

By 1860, the Irish Poor Law Commissioners had actually allowed the boarding out of pauper orphans but only up to age five, justifying this change of policy out of concern for infant mortality; they refused to admit the inadequacies of workhouse schools for education and training of children.[55] In 1871, the commissioners allowed the boarding out of children up to the age of ten, but with reluctance, for they believed that the Irish workhouse school advantaged pauper children by providing them with education, food and medical care, and isolating them from contaminating slums. In fact, they compared it to a boarding school to which 'parents in a better class of life send their children from home for the purpose of a more systematic course of education and discipline.' For gentlemen of the upper class, it was common for boy children to be taken away from their mothers and sent away to boarding schools at the age of seven or eight; so they found it hard to understand why widows would not want to give up their children to district schools, or why it would not be acceptable for orphans to be sent there.[56] For these gentlemen, the institution could substitute for the father as the most appropriate form of domestic authority.

And it was true that problems could arise with boarding out, especially concerning the need to supervise children and their foster parents closely. In Cork, the Board of Guardians tried boarding out because one quarter of the babies admitted to the workhouse died in a year. But their relieving officer was supposed to inspect 73 boarded out children each month, often lodged with far flung rural families, which he could not and did not do. Given the low rates of pay for boarding out, only the poorest women would take on the children, and as a result, several died.[57] Nonetheless, by 1873, only 14 per cent of the boarded out children died. In contrast, in Tralee, where guardians refused to put boarded out children to nurse, 46 out of 47 orphan and deserted children admitted to workhouse in 1862–1872 died.[58]

Boarding out also raised interesting questions about maternal love: was it just a matter of providing food?[59] Did nurses become attached to their foster children as to their biological children? Was it better to have love in meagre conditions, or to be fed and clothed in an institution with no love? A baby-farming scandal in England in 1871 had brought these issues to public attention, when a number of children died with a wet nurse.[60] These issues came to Sligo, a town in the northwest of Ireland, in 1873.[61] There, the guardians tried to board children with nurses to keep them out of the workhouse. But the nurses were paid badly, and chosen from reason of patronage or connections from the poor of Sligo's back alleys. While the overall mortality of children sent out to nurse was under 10 per cent, one case of death from neglect horrified Sligo public opinion. Dr Roughan, the inspector from the central board, found an emaciated baby named Mary Feeney lying on the bare boards of a cradle with no bedding, not even straw, and an empty bottle. Three other children huddled under a thin blanket on a bedstead, which was the only furniture in the filthy house. Although Dr Roughan warned the relieving officer that the child needed help, nothing was done, and she was found dead, starved, a few days later. The other children were taken from the nurse, Ann Harte, and put back in the workhouse.[62] When she later visited the workhouse, one of her former fosterlings 'began to cry, and hid away from her.'[63] Outraged, the guardians demanded that all the nurses bring the boarded out children to the workhouse and give them up. But many of the children and nurses were very attached to each other.

> The children and their nurses commenced to cry frantically, and the master entered the room with a troop of little children screaming in a most discordant style. It was with difficulty the women could be

prevented from rushing in and carrying off the children by force, as they seemed under the impression, that a dreadful fate was in store for the innocents.[64]

Mary McKendrick wrote to the guardians begging to have her fosterling restored to her,

I cared for him with as much caution as if he were my own, as I got dotingly fond of him and [he] slept with myself and husband since I got possession of him....If the board be kind enough to restore him to me I will support him myself, as I feel much distressed at parting with him as I have no family of my own.[65]

As guardian Simpson declared, 'Dicken's stories are nothing to this.' For some, the Sligo scandal undermined the cause of boarding out, but for others, it was an example of the heartlessness of the poor law and the need for reform.[66]

The 1870s also witnessed a tremendous controversy over women's authority in the poor law. When the Irish Poor Law Commissioners had finally extended boarding out in 1871, they indignantly refuted the notion that they might be responding to 'female writers' who denounced the workhouse.[67] The controversy had begun in 1870 when poor law officials such as Alexander Doyle stymied Miss Adelaide Preusser's efforts to board out London pauper children in her Lake District neighbourhood.[68] In response, Preusser gathered signatures from over three thousand ladies, petitioning the Poor Law Board that ladies be legally empowered to cooperate with poor law authorities and made responsible for pauper children 'in the same way as a Guardian or Trustee is for his ward.'[69] The ladies, therefore, wanted both legal recognition for the kinship relation they wished to establish with the children, as overseers of boarding out, and also a legal recognition of their relationship with the Poor Law Board. This initiative also represented an important step in women's political life, as a deputation of the ladies – the first to be received by government officials – met with the Poor Law Board to present their petition. They were received favourably by George Goschen, the President of the Board, and the Board officially allowed pauper children to be boarded out in country districts away from their home unions.[70]

However, in 1871 poor law officials and reformers campaigned against outdoor relief, trying to make the poor law stricter.[71] As a result, more pauper children ended up in the workhouse, leading to medical concerns over the excessive mortality of pauper children in workhouses.[72] Poor law officials and their supporters, however, insisted that children would be better off in well-run workhouses than in dirty homes, as inspector R. Basil Cane insisted when he found boarded out children clothed in rags, with skin diseases, and in homes with illegitimate children.[73]

Mrs Jane Senior, the first woman to be appointed as a British poor law inspector, was charged by the Poor Law Board to assess whether boarding out or pauper schools were better for children. She found that girls turned out badly in district schools, and that boarding out was the only answer. Mrs Senior found also many allies such as John Kells Ingram of the Dublin Statistical Society. He argued that the Irish poor law must be placed in the same relation to the state as the English poor law. The English commissioners had allowed boarding out, and many boards of guardians had accepted it; this practice did not require Parliamentary approval. Ingram complained that Irish children were unfairly disadvantaged because the commissioners still resisted the boarding out of older children, and left less initiative to local guardians.[74]

In response, a poor law inspector, Edward Tufnell, sarcastically dismissed the authority of ladies, denouncing Mrs Senior as the author of 'several sensational letters to the newspapers' and asked, 'of what use is a lady's inspection' of the medical condition of the children. Like many who wrote about the poor at the time, Tufnell both argued that poor children were tainted by 'hereditary pauperism' which explained their bad physical condition and that district schools could remove the pauper taint (according to a Lamarckian philosophy). Boarding out was not a satisfactory alternative, because it violated the poor law principles that children must be kept separate from adults, that they must not receive outdoor relief, and that they must be trained in a combination of academics and industry. He idealistically believed that only large institutions could provide an excellent education for pauper boys and girls. Although small schools were family-like, one bad individual master or mistress could corrupt them, and the standard and variety of education would be limited – the boys were trained in the already overstocked trades of shoemakers and tailors. He believed that a loose, voluntary, impermanent association of ladies could not properly oversee boarded out children. Boarded out children were vulnerable to sexual abuse, and ladies should not be concerned with such matters. Ladies simply did not have the proper authority.[75] Instead, children should be raised in institutions and inspected by male experts.

But the ladies believed that district schools destroyed children's individuality. As Florence Hill observed, visitors to district schools were pleased by the neatness and order of

> many hundreds of children, dressed alike, acting in unison, and rendering instant obedience to the word of command; but ... we are constrained to ask how will individuality of character develop itself from this complete subject to the will of others, which leaves open no temptation to wrong

and annihilates the choice of right? Yet, without such individuality, how can moral beauty or strength exist?[76]

The philanthropic ladies believed that this system turned children, especially girls, into automatons who could not function outside the institution.

Anti-Catholicism also lay behind some of the antagonism to the district schools and workhouses. Mary Carpenter acknowledged that if she instituted 'a system of steady repression and order,' as in Catholic reformatories, her ragged school students would be better scholars, but she had 'no confidence in the slavish obedience they produce and the hypocrisy which I have generally found inseparable from Catholic influence.'[77] Hannah Archer found it 'strange that Englishmen of the present day, who are, many of them, intent on resisting all approaches to Romanism, should have hit upon a scheme for the education of pauper children [that is, district schools], which so nearly resembles the monastic system in its unnatural influences.'[78] Of course, they were not acknowledging the work of Catholic reformers such as Margaret Aylward and Ellen Woodlock, who tried to individuate their charges, and who also denounced the poor law as a cold machine.[79]

Part of the difference between the Senior and Tufnell camps also lay in their approach to the role of surveillance in social welfare. A baby-farming scandal had just erupted, exposing the perils of commercial boarding out, when several infants had died in the home of a foster mother. As Behlmer notes, poor law officials believed that the solution was inspection by experts.[80] But the reign of the Benthamite experts had eroded in mid-century Britain, when civil service reformers shunted aside visionary middle-class reformers such as Edwin Chadwick in favour of generally educated gentlemen who might take a more measured approach and cooperate with local elites.[81] Given the elevated social connections of Mrs Jane Senior and her cohort (after all, she was the daughter-in-law of Nassau Senior, pioneer of the New Poor Law), she could be a formidable adversary to the Benthamite experts.

In response to Tufnell, boarding out advocates asserted that only ladies could provide the proper surveillance over boarded out children. This idea originated in Thomas Chalmers' notion that voluntary philanthropists and church workers could solve the problems of the poor with precisely administered charity. The home, not the institution, was to be the basis of society. Ladies were supposed to have special qualities which enabled them to oversee boarding out correctly, from picking the nurses to inspecting the children. As Joanna Hill asserted at a meeting of boarding out advocates, the poor law

> Union chills, numbs, unbeautifies the work of charity. We have to restore the bloom which rates brush off; and of course, as all tenderness and delicacy finds its truest development in the English gentlewoman, she,

preeminently she, is to be the bond that is to knit hearts together outside and inside the Union, and her work begins with taking the oversight of this pauper orphan.[82]

As Belfast feminist Isabella Tod argued,

> The State was composed of men and women, and had both masculine and feminine duties. The masculine guardians represented the State in the function of providing the money – the raw material, as it were, of shelter, food, clothing and teaching. The ladies, now occupying a recognised place as feminine guardians, must represent the State in the function of seeing that money properly used, and in doing so seeing also that the wants of the heart and the soul are supplied likewise.[83]

As time passed, there was increasing recognition that for boarding out to succeed, voluntary committees of ladies would not suffice; a more formal governmental role must be established. Because they were voluntary, ladies' committees could be ephemeral; ladies might go off and travel, neglecting their duties; they might simply tire of the job and abandon the children.[84] Furthermore, they were not accountable if they failed in their jobs. In 1877, the Local Government Board (which now had responsibility for the poor law) transferred the duties of inspecting boarded out children, formerly carried out by voluntary committees, to parochial, medical, and relieving officers.[85] However, eventually a lady inspector of boarded out children was appointed.

In Ireland, advocates of boarding out continued to believe that only ladies' committees could make the system work, since the scandals showed that relieving officers could not be trusted to ensure the health and welfare of orphaned and deserted children.[86] Irish women followed the English lead and established ladies' committees to help supervise boarding out in the 1870s, and were often welcomed by guardians because they lifted the burden of inspection outside the workhouse, but did not interfere with its inner workings. Irish women were not able to be poor law guardians, however, until 1896, much later than the first English female poor law guardian who was elected in 1875. By 1898, ladies committees acquired official legal recognition, and lady inspectors of boarded out children were hired as well.[87] The 1916 novel *The Amazing Philanthropists*, by Susanne Day, gives some insight into the politics of domestic authority exercised by such ladies in Ireland. Mrs Blake was

> one of those tireless, energetic, capable, practical women...who has brought the Boarding-Out of Children to a fine art, she can rule a Committee with a rod of iron, check a babbler into silence, coax speech from stuttering nerves, and explode in a blaze of righteous anger when

meanness, or stupidity, or selfishness, or jobbery sneak into the room. She is not good at debate, and rarely speaks in the Board Room, but she is a tower of strength.[88]

This novel also elucidates the conflicts between ladies such as Mrs Blake – whose authority derived from their Protestant, Anglo-Irish status – and the local authorities of Catholic guardians, who now dominated the poor law.

Although advocates of boarding out often emphasized that it would allow children to be raised as individuals, with affection, rather than submerged in the mass of the workhouse, later advocates of boarding out in Ireland also had more practical reasons. Aside from its cheapness – it cost less to board a child out than raise it in an institution – children raised in homes might solve the problem of agricultural labour in Ireland. They would also be raised just like the children of the peasantry, and not get ideas above their station. In particular, the ladies had always advocated that girls be boarded out, so they could learn how to run a home and be better servants. But apparently people often applied to adopt older children merely because they wanted to hire out a young servant or farm labourer they would not have to pay; and the guardians liked this system because they did not have to give an allowance.[89]

Boarding out could also be a means of undermining the domestic authority of natural parents. Officials and lady visitors often wanted to remove children from unsuitable families with their bad influences. In one example from the North Dublin Union, 'the nurse, an excellent woman, had to return the little girl to the Union, on account of the mother, a most disreputable woman, following the children to the National School she attended, and to the nurse's house.' As a result, the St. Brigid's Association did not allow mothers of boarded out children to know where their children were. They could visit them at the office under supervision, but not go to their homes.[90] The Vice-Regal Commission of 1906 also recommended that the children of unmarried mothers be taken away from them a year and after and boarded out.[91]

Advocates continually called for the extension of the system, but the institutional inertia was too great. S. Shannon Milin called for the creation of a Children's Bureau in the government largely to be in the hands of women, with full powers to board out children and to approve or disapprove sending children to industrial schools.[92] But this was not to be. By 1909, 72 per cent of poor children remained in workhouses instead of being boarded out. Repeated scandals about boarding out, and the seeming impossibility of adequate inspection, led Bishop Gilloolly of Sligo to turn away from his earlier advocacy of boarding out to assert that, instead, children should be placed in district or industrial schools.[93] On independence, of course, the Catholic Church acquired much of authority over children, and preferred large institutions over which it had greater control. By the twentieth century, many Irish children were institutionalized in large, sometimes abusive institutions.

Conclusion

The plight of poor Irish orphans raises complicated questions about domestic authority. Boarding out reveals the tensions in the phrase, 'domestic authority' – the domestic connotes home, warmth, and affection but authority implies institutions and laws. Poor law officials envisioned authority over children which was accountable and disciplined, structured through schedules and buildings, which would turn them into self-reliant individuals. In Ireland, they believed this authority was properly vested in the state. The ladies, Protestant political economists, and the Catholic Church believed that this system treated children like cogs in the machine. They wanted to increase the autonomy and individuality of children, but they were also claiming authority in the state. For Irish political economists, the plight of the orphan child justified their claims for greater Irish autonomy in the running of the poor law, as a way of preserving the empire by gaining the consent of free agents to it. For the Catholic Church, the orphan child enabled it to defend the family against the state, but also assert its own role as defender and eventually supervisor of children and families; and of course, to eventually rebuild its own powerful regimented institutions even before Ireland became independent. For philanthropic ladies, protecting poor children gave them a way into the workhouse, and justified establishing power structures, such as local committees overseeing boarding out, both within and outside of the poor law system. Philanthropic ladies had domestic influence as ladies, but they also had authority as mistresses of servants, and great clout when they were Catholic heiresses or members of well-connected Protestant Anglo-Irish families. Such women eventually moved from the unpaid philanthropic to a professional role in the poor law system, aiding in the institutionalization of children as they did so.

Finally, the debate over Irish orphans and boarding out contributed to a larger debate over the relationship of the family and the state. English boarding out advocate Florence Hill influentially redefined orphaned and deserted pauper children as 'Children of the State.' By doing so, she established the precedent that the state was responsible for their maintenance, but that institutional solutions were not the answer. She argued that for pauper children, 'Food, clothing, and shelter, may be paid for by the State; but the love, watchfulness and sympathy which are equally essential to a child's welfare should be the far more precious contribution of the foster parent.'[94] Boarding out enabled these social reformers to advocate an increased state role without the mass institutions which often accompanied it. However, in the long run, the institutional authority of the poor law overrode the domestic influence of philanthropic ladies and the domestic authority of poor parents, and only a few children were rescued from poor law institutions.

Notes

1. T. Brodie (1859) *The Report of Terence Brodie, Poor Law Inspector to the Commissioners for the Administering the Laws for the Relief of the Poor in Ireland, Upon an Investigation Held by Him into the Condition of the Children in the Cork Workhouse, and the Sanitary State of That Institution, Together with the Minutes of Evidence Taken During Said Investigation* (Cork), pp. 3–70; J. Arnott (1859) *The Investigation into the Condition of the Children in the Cork Workhouse with an Analysis of the Evidence* (Cork), pp. 1–55.
2. In *Discipline and Punish*, Foucault demonstrates how in carceral institutions such as prisons and schools, the individual would be identified as a unique personality – or even dysfunctional personality – marked, and recorded. He would then be subject to the discipline of the institution, the rewards and penalties intended to ensure that he 'becomes the principle of his own subjection.' In his later work, Foucault began to think about the problem of the liberal individual, and how liberalism was 'anxious to have the respect of legal subjects and to ensure the free enterprise of individuals.' M. Foucault (2003) ' "*Omnes Et Singulatim*": Toward a Critique of Political Reason,' in P. Rabinow and N. Rose (eds) *The Essential Works of Foucault, 1954–1984* (New York: New Press), p. 183; M. Foucault, 'The Birth of Biopolitics,' in P. Rabinow and N. Rose (eds) *The Essential Works of Foucault, 1954–1984* (New York: New Press), p. 202.
3. M. Poovey (2002) 'The Liberal Civil Subject and the Social in Eighteenth-Century British Moral Philosophy,' *Public Culture*, 14, p. 139. C. Gordon (1991) 'Government Rationality: An Introduction,' in G. Burchell, C. Gordon, and P. Miller (eds) *The Foucault Effect: Studies in Governmentality* (Chicago: University of Chicago Press), p. 38; P. Joyce (2003) *The Rule of Freedom* (New York: Verso), p. 1; L. Goodlad (2003) *Victorian Literature and the Victorian State: Character and Governance in a Liberal Society* (Baltimore: Johns Hopkins University Press), p. 43.
4. T. Holt (1991) *The Problem of Freedom: Race, Labor, and Politics in Jamaica and Britain, 1832–1938* (Baltimore: Johns Hopkins University Press), pp. 179–82; C. Hall (2002) *Civilizing Subjects* (Chicago: University of Chicago Press), pp. 116–18. This argument changed later and they were not seen as capable of self-government.
5. J. S. Mill (1962 [1859]) 'On Liberty,' in M. Warnock (ed.) *Utilitarianism* (New York: New American Library), p. 134.
6. I. Pinchbeck (1981 [1930]) *Women Workers and the Industrial Revolution, 1750–1850* (London: Virago), p. 199; A. Clark (1995) *The Struggle for the Breeches: Gender and the Making of the British Working Class* (Berkeley: University of California Press), p. 216.
7. Nancy Armstrong, quoted in J. Sterne (2003) 'Bureaumentality,' in J. Z. Bratich, J. Packer, and C. McCarthy (eds) *Foucault, Cultural Studies, and Governmentality* (Albany: State University of New York Press), p. 115.
8. H. Martineau (1833) *Poor Laws and Paupers Illustrated*, 2 vols (London: Charles Fox), II, p. 11.
9. S. J. Connolly (1979) 'Illegitimacy and Pre-Nuptial Pregnancy in Ireland before 1864: The Evidence of Some Catholic Parish Registers,' *Irish Economic and Social History*, 6, p. 8.

10. Anon. (1834) 'Introduction of Poor Laws into Ireland,' *Edinburgh Review*, 59, p. 241.
11. Commissioners for Inquiring into the Condition of the Poorer Classes of Ireland (1836) 'Poor Laws in Ireland – Third Report of the Commissioners for Inquiring into the Condition of the Poorer Classes of Ireland,' *London and Westminster Review*, 25, p. 346; Anon. (1831) 'Poor Law for Ireland,' *Quarterly Review*, 44, p. 515; Anon. (1846) 'Letters to the Right Honourable Lord John Russell, on the Expediency of Enlarging the Irish Poor-Law, to the Full Extent of the Poor-Law of England,' *Edinburgh Review*, 84, p. 267.
12. J. Robins (1980) *Lost Children: A Study of Charity Children in Ireland, 1700–1900* (Dublin: Institute of Public Administration), pp. 157–60.
13. Ibid.
14. Anon. (1837) *Remarks on the Application of the Workhouse System with Other Modes of Relief to the Irish Poor, by an Assistant Commissioner* (London), p. 18.
15. E. Chadwick (1864) 'Poor Law Administration, Its Chief Principles and Their Results in England and Ireland as Compared with Scotland,' *Journal of the Statistical Society of London*, 27, pp. 492–504.
16. F. Hill (1868) *Children of the State: the Training of Juvenile Paupers*, 1st edn (London), p. 12; F. P. Cobbe (1864) 'The Philosophy of the Poor Laws and the Report of the Committee on Poor Relief,' *Fraser's Magazine*, 70, p. 376.
17. V. Crossman (1994), *Local Government in Nineteenth-century Ireland* (Belfast: Institute of Irish Studies), pp. 46–52.
18. Anon. (1842) *Inquiry into the Treatment, Condition, and Mortality, of Infant Children, in the Workhouse of the North Dublin Union* (Dublin), p. 18.
19. L. Abrams (1998) *The Orphan Country: Children of Scotland's Broken Homes from 1845 to the Present Day* (Edinburgh: John Donald Publishers), p. 42; J. J. Henley (1870) 'Report on the Boarding out of Pauper Children in Scotland,' *Parliamentary Papers*, 71, p. 29; H. J. MacDonald (1996) 'Boarding-out and the Scottish Poor Law, 1845–1914,' *Scottish Historical Review*, 25, pp. 197–220.
20. Robins, *Lost Children*, p. 173.
21. Hill, *Children of the State*, 1st edn, p. 7, quoting [James Phillips Kay] (1841) *Report to the Secretary of the State for the Home Department, from the Poor Law Commissioners, on the Training of Pauper Children* (London), p. 191.
22. N. J. Smelser (1991) *Social Paralysis and Social Change: British Working-Class Education in the Nineteenth Century* (Berkeley: University of California Press), p. 116.
23. J. P. Kay-Shuttleworth (1841) *The Training of Pauper Children in England during the Fourth Decade of the Nineteenth Century* (London), p. 17.
24. Goodlad, *Victorian Literature and the Victorian State*, p. 52.
25. Anon. (Jun. 1854) 'Reformatory and Ragged Schools,' *Irish Quarterly Review*, 2, p. 425.
26. L. Twining (1858), *Workhouse and Women's Work* (London), p. 24; Anon. 'Reformatory and Ragged Schools,' p. 425.
27. H. Cunningham (1991) *The Children of the Poor: Representations of Childhood since the Seventeenth Century* (Oxford: Blackwell), pp. 85–112.
28. A. J. Moore (1878) *Children in Irish Workhouses* (London: Cornelius Buck), p. 1.
29. F. P. Cobbe (1895) *Life of Frances Power Cobbe by Herself*, 2 vols (Boston), I, p. 106.
30. For this tension, see also I. Hunter (1996) 'Assembling the School,' in A. Barry, T. Osborne, and N. Rose (eds) *Foucault and Political Reason: Liberalism,*

Neo-Liberalism and Rationalities of Government (Chicago: University of Chicago Press), p. 161.

31. M. Smedley (1875) *Boarding-out and Pauper Schools Especially for Girls, Being a Reprint of the Principal Reports on Pauper Education in the Blue Book for 1873–4* (London), p. xii.

32. M. P. Magrey (1998) *The Transforming Power of the Nuns: Women, Religion and Cultural Change in Ireland, 1750–1900* (New York: Oxford University Press), p. 100.

33. J. Prunty (1999) *Margaret Aylward 1810–1889: Lady of Charity, Sister of Faith* (Dublin: Four Courts Press), p. 57.

34. For an interesting French angle on Catholicism and the self see Jan Goldstein (2000) 'Mutations of the Self in Old Regime and Postrevolutionary France,' in Lorraine Daston (ed.) *Biographies of Scientific Objects* (Chicago: University of Chicago Press), p. 97.

35. Anon. (Jan. 1859) 'A Glance at Irish Charitable Institutions,' *Irish Quarterly Review*, 8, p. li; P. J. Murray (1861) 'On the Irish Catholic Reformatory Schools,' *Transactions of the National Association for the Promotion of Social Science* (London), pp. 461–4.

36. J. Kelly, Letter to Bishop Gilloolly, 23 Aug. 1858, Elphin Diocesan Archives, B 1/4/1 (1) f. 4.

37. Clippings from *Nation*, 19 May 1860; *Freeman*, 25 Apr. 1861, in Larcom Collection, National Library of Ireland, Manuscripts division, Mss. 7780; E. R. Norman (1965), *The Catholic Church and Ireland in the Age of Rebellion* (London: Longmans), p. 73.

38. Select Committee on Poor Relief [Ireland] (1861) 'Proceedings,' *Parliamentary Papers*, 10, p. 177.

39. In private, however, Catholic workhouse chaplains were divided on whether boarding out was a good idea; half of those Gilloolly surveyed believed that it would be too difficult to provide enough oversight against abuses in foster families, box marked Section III C. Workhouses/Reforms.

40. M. S. O'Shaughnessy (Apr. 1862) 'Some Remarks Upon Mrs. Hannah Archer's Scheme for Befriending Orphan Pauper Girls,' *Journal of the Dublin Statistical Society*, 3, p. 150, quoting *Dublin Daily Express* (6 Sept. 1861).

41. J. Dowling (1872) *The Irish Poor Laws and Poor-Houses* (Dublin), p. 15.

42. Anon. (1861) 'The Irish Poor-Laws,' *Dublin University Magazine*, 57, pp. 63–70.

43. Select Committee on Poor Relief [Ireland] (1861), *Proceedings*, p. 281.

44. M. E. Daly (1997) *The Spirit of Earnest Inquiry: The Statistical and Social Inquiry Society of Ireland, 1847–1997* (Dublin: Statistical and Social Inquiry Society of Ireland), pp. 29–30.

45. E. J. Yeo (1996) *The Contest for Social Science: Relations and Representations of Gender and Class* (London: Rivers Oram Press), p. 131; Joyce, *Rule of Freedom*, p. 118.

46. W. N. Hancock (Apr. 1855) 'The Workhouse as a Mode of Relief for Widows and Orphans,' *Journal of the Dublin Statistical Society*, p. 84.

47. A Member of the Statistical and Social Inquiry Society of Ireland (1865) *The Real Wants of the Irish People* (Dublin), p. 12.

48. John Kells Ingram, quoted in W. N. Hancock (1880) *On the Anomalous Differences in the Poor-Laws of Ireland and of England Being an Address to the Trades' Union Congress, at the Meeting in Dublin, 15 Sept. 1880* (Dublin: R.D. Webb and Son), p. 5.

49. L. Twining (1880) *Recollections of Workhouse Visiting and Management During 25 Years* (London: Kegan Paul), pp. 15–21.

50. *Dublin Daily Express* (20 Sept. 1861) in Larcom Ms. 7782, National Library, Manuscripts, Ireland; South Dublin Union Board of Guardians Minute Books, 21 Aug. 1861, 19 Sept. 1861, National Archives, Ireland; Anon. (1862) 'Cork Union – Ladies' Visiting Committee,' *Journal of the Workhouse Visiting Society*, 1, p. 572; F. Taylor (1867) *Irish Homes and Irish Hearts* (London: Longmans), p. 154.

51. A. Clark (2005), 'Wild Workhouse Girls and the Liberal Imperial State in Nineteenth-Century Ireland,' *Journal of Social History*, 39 (2), pp. 389–410.

52. H. Archer (1869) *To the Rescue* (London: Simpkin, Marshall & Co.), p. 4; Select Committee on Relief of the Poor (1861) 'Report,' *Parliamentary Papers*, 9, p. 550.

53. For instance, Frances Power Cobbe was well known for her essay celebrating unmarried women and their vocations; see F. P. Cobbe (1862) 'What Shall We Do with Our Old Maids,' *Fraser's Magazine*, 66, p. 607. See also Twining, *Workhouse and Women's Work*, p. 30.

54. F. Hill (1889) *Children of the State: the Training of Juvenile Paupers*, 2nd edn (London: Macmillan & Co.), pp. 111–16; Lady Visitor (1864) 'Society for Visiting the South Dublin Workhouse,' *Journal of the Workhouse Visiting Society*, 2, pp. 143–7.

55. Anon. (1862) 'Copy of a Letter Addressed to the Chief Secretary for Ireland, or Any Other Member of Government, by the Dublin College of Physicians, on the Physical Effects of Rearing Children in Workhouses,' *Parliamentary Papers*, 49, p. 15; Robins, *Lost Children*, p. 272.

56. *Annual Report of the Commissioners for Administering the Laws for Relief of the Poor in Ireland* (1871) (London), p. 13.

57. Incoming Letters from Poor Law Commissioners Rathdown, 11 July 1871, National Archives of Ireland, Dublin. BG 137 BC 3; Incoming Letters from Poor Law Commissioners, entries for 24 Feb. 1863, 2, 8 Jun. 1863, Cork Archives Institute, Cork, BG 69 BC18; W. d'Esterre Parker (1870) *The Irish Infant Poor in Workhouses, and Those Sent to Nurse in Peasants' Cottages* (Cork, [read at National Association for Promotion of Social Science, 1869]), pp. 5–6.

58. Anon. (1873) 'Annual Report of the Local Government Board for Ireland,' *Parliamentary Papers*, 24, pp. 15, 84; Anon. (1878–1879) 'Infants in Workhouses (Ireland),' *Parliamentary Papers*, 61, p. 299.

59. See the interesting dissertation by Anne Heubel, 'The Paradox of Motherhood' (University of Minnesota History Department, PhD, 2004).

60. M. Arnot (1994) 'Infant Death, Child Care and the State: the Baby-Farming Scandal and the First Infant Life Protection Legislation of 1872,' *Continuity and Change*, 9, pp. 271–311.

61. 'Annual Report of the Local Government Board for Ireland,' (1873), *Parliamentary Papers*, 24, p. 84.

62. Ibid., p. 85; Sligo Board of Guardians Minute Books, 27 Jan. 1873, Sligo County Library, Sligo, f. 155.

63. Editorial on 'Workhouse Children,' *Sligo Champion*, 15 Feb. 1873.

64. 'Poor Law Articles,' *Sligo Champion*, 11 Jan. 1873, Editorial, 6 Feb. 1878.

65. 'Board of Guardians Meeting,' *Sligo Champion*, 22 Feb. 1873.

66. 'Poor Law Articles Sligo,' *Sligo Chronicle*, 1 Feb. 1873, reprint of article from *Dublin Evening Post*.

67. 'Annual Report of the Commissioners for Administering the Laws for Relief of the Poor in Ireland,' (1871) (Dublin), p. 13.

68. G. K. Behlmer (1998) *Friends of the Family: The English Home and Its Guardians, 1850–1940* (Stanford: Stanford University Press), p. 285.

69. A. Preusser (1883) *Boarding out Pauper Children. A Reprint of the Memorial of Ladies and Subsequent Orders, Observations, and Forms Issued by the Poor Law Board, to Which Is Appended Suggestions by a Lady, Forming Complete Instructions for Carrying out the System*, 3rd edn (London).
70. Hill, *Children of the State*, 2nd edn, p. 185; Behlmer, *Friends of the Family*, p. 285.
71. M. MacKinnon (1987) 'English Poor Law Policy and the Crusade against Outre-lief,' *Journal of Economic History*, 47, p. 605; R. Humphreys (1995) *Sin, Organized Charity and the Poor Law in Victorian England* (Basingstoke: Palgrave Macmillan), p. 53.
72. Clipping from *Lancet*, 24 Aug. 1878, p. 259, in Poor Law Correspondence, PRO, MH 32/8.
73. Cane, 4 Dec. 1869, to Guardians of Garstang union, in R. Basil Cane, District Inspector, Correspondence with Poor Law Commissioners, PRO, MH 32/9.
74. J. K. Ingram (1875) 'The Organization of Charity and the Education of the Children of the State,' *Journal of the Statistical and Social Inquiry Society of Ireland*, 48, pp. 449–70; J. K. Ingram (1876) 'Additional Facts and Arguments on the Boarding out of Pauper Children,' *Journal of the Dublin Statistical Society*, 6, pp. 503–23.
75. E. C. Tufnell (1875) *Observations on the Report of Mrs. Senior to the Local Government Board as to the Effect on Girls of the System of Education at Pauper Schools* (London: Stationary Office), pp. 1–19; see also L. Murdoch (2006) *Imagined Orphans: Poor Families, Child Welfare, and Contested Citizenship in London* (New Brunswick, NJ: Rutgers University Press).
76. Hill, *Children of the State*, p. 72.
77. Cobbe, *Life of Frances Power Cobbe by Herself*, p. 258.
78. 'Select Committee on Relief of the Poor' (1861) *Parliamentary Papers*, 9, p. 511; Archer, *To the Rescue*, p. 5.
79. E. Woodlock and S. Atkinson (1861) 'The Irish Poor in Workhouses,' *Transactions of the National Association for the Promotion of Social Science* (London), pp. 645–52.
80. Behlmer, *Friends of the Family*, p. 272.
81. Goodlad, *Victorian Literature and the Victorian State*, p. 122.
82. *Report of a Drawing-Room Conference on Boarding-out Pauper Children* (1876), p. 46.
83. I. Tod (1878) 'Boarding out Pauper Children,' *Englishwoman's Review*, 11, p. 404.
84. Tufnell, *Observations on the Report of Mrs. Senior to the Local Government Board as to the Effect on Girls of the System of Education at Pauper Schools*, 19; Miss M. H. Mason, 'General Report,' to Local Government Board (11 Feb. 1887), PRO MH/32/92.
85. F. Hill (1883), *The Boarding-out System. Discussion in the Plymouth Court of Guardians, on the Boarding-out System, Which Was Followed by Its Unanimous Adoption. London* (London), p. 6.
86. Moore, *Children in Irish Workhouses*, p. 10; Marion Mulhall, 'Boarded out Children,' *New Ireland Review*, 6 (Mar. 1896), p. 136.
87. D. Assistant Clerk O'Sullivan, Wexford Union (1906), *Handbook of the Law Relating to the Boarding-out and Hiring-out of Pauper Children in Ireland*, Public Record Office Northern Ireland, Belfast, BG 17/BE/2.
88. S. R. Day (1916) *The Amazing Philanthropists: Being Extracts from the Letters of Lester Martin, P.L.G. [Poor Law Guardian]* (London: Sidgwick & Jackson), p. 129.
89. O'Sullivan, *Handbook of the Law Relating to the Boarding-out and Hiring-out of Pauper Children in Ireland*.
90. Dublin Women's Suffrage and Local Government Association (1900) *Papers Read at a Conference of Women Poor Law Guardians and Other Ladies* (Dublin).

91. Poor Law Reform Commission [Ireland] (1906) *Report of the Vice-Regal Commission on Poor Law Reform in Ireland* (Dublin), I, p. 183.

92. S. S. Millin (1909) 'The Duty of the State towards the Pauper Children of Ireland,' *Journal of the Dublin Statistical Society*, 12, p. 260.

93. P. Irwin, Letter to Bishop Laurence Gilloolly, 29 Sept. 1890, G. Morris, Letter to Bishop Laurence Gilloolly, 22 Mar. 1886, Bishop Gilloolly Collection, Elphin Diocesan Archives, B 1/5/2 (5) ff. 453, 422.

94. Hill, *Children of the State: the Training of Juvenile Paupers*, p. 235.

4
Fatherhood and Family Shame: Masculinity, Welfare and the Workhouse in Late Nineteenth-Century England[1]

Megan Doolittle

> ...I got a pocketful of horse beans...I put them on a shovel and toasted them over the fire. They weren't all that ripe, but the kiddies scrambled for them. In the rush one was shoved up the babby's nose instead of her mouth. She started to blather, she wouldn't stop, so in the end I carried her to the doctor.... The horse bean had started to chit! That cost a shilling. The missus was hopping mad when she heard: 'You let those kiddies do what they likes! You'll 'ave us in the workhus yet![2]

This story was told by George Hewins, a building labourer from Stratford on Avon, about looking after his four young children circa 1910, during a period when he was unemployed and his wife was out working. The children were often hungry, so this was a good opportunity for a snack of broad beans, which he had filched from a bag outside a shop selling them for pig food. In their very small home, things easily got out of hand but he was never the strict disciplinarian, using his storytelling gifts to keep them in order:

> I'd tell them anything to keep them quiet. We had a houseful! They got a bit out of hand sometimes, but not one of the knowed the weight o'mine. I never tapped them. The missus did that – with the slipper. She let them know who was boss.[3]

In this case, things went very wrong not only for the baby, but for the household economy where every shilling was precious and every financial crisis threatened the destruction of family life by entering the dreaded workhouse.

In this anecdote, we can trace the themes that will be explored in this chapter about authority, masculinity, shame and the shaping of welfare subjects. The chapter begins by looking at ways that masculinity and domestic authority were negotiated in the context of interdependent family relationships. It then turns to the relationships between domestic masculinities and welfare interactions between families and welfare providers. The particular effects on masculinity and domestic authority of the institution of the workhouse and of the shame associated with pauperism are then examined. It concludes with a discussion of working-class strategies of engagement and resistance to forms of welfare which undermined men's sense of being recognised and respected as full, adult male citizens.

It is important to acknowledge that welfare and families were (and are) both complex sets of relations and each has extensive histories as well as very diverse sets of practices and meanings. Welfare is used here in its broadest sense as including policies, practices and structures of feeling which were designed to ameliorate or improve social life. Welfare in this period had widely varied origins, scope and implementations with often contradictory as well as reinforcing effects on those defined as its subjects. Families are understood in this context as a set of processes and practices which involved identifiable but flexible and porous relationships which can be traced through social structures such as the household and kinship networks. In this period, families deployed a very wide range of strategies and responses to welfare in diverse circumstances.[4]

At the heart of social debates about welfare we can find questions of gendered domestic authority and its fluid nature within the economies of poor families. Keeping clear of the harsh and shaming regimes of the workhouse was a significant struggle for working-class men in sustaining a robust gendered identity as the provider and head of a household. Providing for a dependent wife and children and exercising authority over them had long been a significant marker of adult masculinity and continued to be so during this period despite the many changes in nineteenth-century labour markets and family strategies.[5] However, this identity sat uneasily with the interdependent nature of family life for the poor, who relied on resources from every available source when poverty struck. There was thus a profound disjunction between these fluid and interdependent relationships and the more bounded model of the household headed by a male breadwinner that was not only a goal for the respectable working class, but was deeply engrained in the thinking of policy makers and philanthropists. The poor law system acknowledged both the interdependencies of the poor and this dominant ideal, seeking to discipline husbands and fathers through the threat of the workhouse and the loss of autonomy and authority it entailed. Resistance and demands for changes to the Poor Laws were rooted in these experiences.

The particular period and location chosen for discussion is England[6] in the late nineteenth and early twentieth centuries because, in this period, new ideas about welfare and its place in the social order were emerging while older regimes were also being questioned. In particular, the Poor Law was increasingly seen as problematic and fragmented as its basic premise of less eligibility (that poor relief should always be less than what those on the lowest incomes could obtain elsewhere, and therefore was only available to the completely destitute) was impossible to sustain across all its provisions.[7] At a wider level, relationships between the state, the nation and families were being reshaped around questions of 'national efficiency'[8] which focused on how to improve the physical health and strength of the poor, as demonstrated by the 1904 Report of the Interdepartmental Committee on Physical Deterioration.[9] Poverty itself was being actively examined and redefined in the great surveys of Booth (1902–3) and Rowntree (1901).[10] Working-class political demands for change were also making themselves felt through the extensions to the franchise, burgeoning working-class organisations including unions and socialist groups, and also, from 1894, through representation in local government and poor law boards.[11] Citizenship itself was being reimagined in terms of the need for a healthy and educated population, able to exercise democratic rights and responsibilities.[12] This required more extensive forms of welfare to be provided, whether by the state or through voluntary impulses.[13]

This chapter focuses on a small number of autobiographical examples to tease out the meanings of welfare encounters through the lens of fatherhood and masculinity. These sources provide us with some of the very few direct articulations of working-class experiences of poverty, although they do require careful interpretation.[14] Of particular importance were the difficulties that autobiographers experienced in exposing what was shameful in their past, and thus times when they were in their worst straits were not easy to narrate.[15] Many male writers resolved this by omitting most aspects of their family lives altogether particularly in adulthood, being far more likely to write about poverty experienced when they were children.[16] The shameful aspects of being poor were keenly felt, as we shall see, but these could be more easily expressed when related to the writer's parents rather than themselves. Oral history accounts have been more fruitful in including accounts of family life in adulthood, such as George Hewins' above who told stories of his childhood and young adulthood to his family when he was a very old man.[17] This method gives opportunities for listeners to ask about the low points in their subject's life, and for the speaker to construct stories about painful emotions in ways which make it possible to admit stigma and shame, often through the use of empathy and humour, as Hewins demonstrated.[18]

As often noted, the time of writing or telling a life story is significant in shaping what is included (and absent) and how the story is told.[19] The examples used in this chapter were all narrated after the First World War and were very much coloured by the social changes and political impulses of the period when they were written. In particular, the higher standard of living for many working-class families meant that by the time of creating their narratives, many working-class men had achieved the respectability of the breadwinner model with its more bounded gender roles. On the other hand, many autobiographers had been personally affected by the traumas of the Great War as soldiers or as the fathers of soldiers, and some were to face the threat of inter-war unemployment and the hated means test. Looking back at the 'bad old days' gave writers like Hewins the space to express difficult and conflicting feelings about their younger lives. Memories were thus necessarily coloured by a writer's social, political and emotional context at the time of telling; when Hewins was interviewed as a very old man in the 1970s, his stories of his younger years were so radically different from his contemporary experience that their sting had largely faded except, tellingly, the shame of his grandmother's pauper funeral which he admitted he had never before revealed.[20]

Writers and storytellers also found ways of revealing the shame of poverty through a commitment to reforms in welfare policy, in the tradition of the 'condition of England' novel. By exposing their own experiences, writers hoped to draw attention to social inequality and its iniquities in order to bring about change.[21] This agenda necessarily structured and coloured their accounts, but also enabled them to find a way to articulate hidden aspects of their lives, providing political explanations for the ways that masculine identities relating to domestic authority were difficult to sustain. Many writers expressed an overtly political agenda relating to poverty as we shall see below. Many also deliberately and frequently included anecdotes about subverting authority – treading a fine line between illegality and survival, as exemplified by Hewins' theft of a handful of beans for his hungry children. As August argues, this low-level, day-to-day resistance can also be seen as a political stance, particularly in constructing a narrative which gave the writer a sense of agency in potentially shameful circumstances.[22]

The theme of shame and anger dominates these accounts of poverty and pauperism. Scheff argued that shame is the paramount social emotion. It has the effect of dividing people from each other and breaking social bonds, with the normal response to social shame being an increase in social alienation which turns inwards on the individual, or outward resentment and conflict.[23] On the other hand, Scheff argues that the acknowledgement of shame strengthens social bonds, as 'the glue that holds relationships and societies together, [while] unacknowledged shame [is] the force that tears them apart'.[24] He also identifies Sennett and Cobb's research in *The Hidden Injuries of Class* as showing that shame and social-economic dependence are intertwined with shame used as a central tool in disciplining workers in the modern American context.[25] Workers saw themselves as individually responsible for their lower class position, not least because of their experience of schooling when they were consistently shamed and silenced. It is not difficult to see that pauperism, a deeply shaming identity, was overtly designed to discipline the poor in similar ways. Writers who experienced it found it easier to write about it in the context of class oppression rather than individual failure, but ambivalences about personal responsibility could be difficult to avoid. Carolyn Steedman has also explored the more uncomfortable ways that autobiographers can use their narratives to 'hurt' others by telling their stories of bitterness and envy.[26] In the following narratives of poverty and survival we can find these various effects of social shame in the context of poverty and masculinity.

Interdependence and masculinity

The deeply ambiguous nature of relations of authority between men, women and children in working-class families can only be understood in the context of the interdependent relationships which poor families relied upon for survival in this period. The necessity to pool all resources of a household, whether material, financial or social, was a characteristic of many working-class families, where the earnings of children and wives, income from lodgers, help from brothers, sisters, aunts and uncles, neighbours and workplace friends were all drawn upon at times of difficulty.[27] The assertion of an independent adult manhood by a husband and father was not always easy to maintain in these circumstances, and the tensions particularly between husbands and wives were often acute. The many family secrets and silences which needed to be maintained to support viable masculinities were a significant sign of these tensions, which could and did erupt into violence.[28]

There were two central aspects of adult masculinity which underpinned men's authority in domestic life which were difficult to sustain: the breadwinner or provider role, and the position as the head of the household. Being the breadwinner for a family of dependents was a central aspect of adult masculine identities, but in poor families breadwinning was rarely the sole province of the man of the family.[29] The decline of craft-based employment for men, which was well advanced by the late nineteenth century, also undermined masculine identities rooted in craft traditions.[30] The highly variable and changing labour markets for women and young people meant that earnings from other family members could be the norm, such as in textile areas. Where there was little waged work for married women, less visible occupations were found to supplement family incomes, such as taking in lodgers, laundry and other work which could be done at home. The growing earning power of young women outside domestic service in offices, shops and light industrial sectors and the concerns about the greater availability of casual work for 'juvenile' workers, young men working outside the apprenticeship system brought opportunities for earning for young people without former levels of adult control.[31] While men's earnings were significantly higher than women's and young people's, and those in regular skilled employment might be able to 'keep' a wife and children, for most men this was difficult to achieve and even harder to sustain over the whole life course.

If breadwinning was a difficult basis from which to assert authority, there were further tensions around who controlled the day-to-day use of family resources, very often the province of wives. Men, boys and girls were often called upon to help with domestic work, including caring for babies, as George Hewins demonstrated above, but it was widely acknowledged that women had the crucial role of managing of the household, and they could exercise considerable control over the behaviour and life-chances of every-one within it.[32] As we saw in the Hewins family, it was his wife who kept everyone in order, at least within their home. Men's dependence on others would extend beyond the ties of wife and children as families drew upon kin relationships for resources of all kinds, frequently negotiated through women's social networks. A small inheritance from an uncle, the labour of nieces, nephews or grandchildren, exchanges of food or clothing, having a relative to 'speak for you' to get a job – these could make a world of dif-ference.[33] But they could also complicate and disrupt authority relations by undermining the position of the husband and father as provider, protector and breadwinner.

Such complex arrangements of care and survival were thus characterised by a fluidity of authority, unlike the dominant family paradigm for the respectable working class, which also underpinned the standpoint of most welfare providers and policy makers. This was based on a fairly rigid set of hierarchical divisions between a father and husband as provider, a mother and wife who managed household resources and children who respected and obeyed their parents. This model placed a husband and father at its apex, and was predicated on a masculinity which looked back to the early modern idea that marriage and children announced a man's entry into full adulthood and an adult masculine identity which included the exercise of authority over others through the establishment of a separate household.[34] As its head, he also gained a set of public duties and identities as the only independent individual who could fully engage with civil society and the public world. It could be argued that it was the authority he commanded over all other members of the household which gave men this status and without a household of some kind to rule over, a man could not be a pub-lic person.[35] As McCormack has pointed out, citizenship in the polity was reliant on successfully establishing domestic responsibilities in ways which were explicitly defined as masculine throughout the process of reforms to the franchise in the nineteenth century.[36] This was recognised in legal terms; husbands and fathers had long-established common law and legislated rights to represent and determine family life with few formal restrictions.[37] A sub-text of authority based on Christian teaching can also be traced, with the language of God the father permeating social discourse.[38]

The position of the head of the household had always been particularly difficult for labouring men to establish or sustain, and claims to citizenship rights had been closely tied to ownership or control over land and property for centuries. Working-class men's political campaigns for the vote had been premised on 'the respectable working man', someone who successfully demonstrated his capacity for citizenship through his role as the provider and protector of dependents. Thus widespread social values of self-help, thrift and independence were reworked as political tools by working-class activists, looking back to the Chartists and forwards to the Labour Party. This argument for an extension of the franchise based on manhood defined in these terms resonated at many social levels, and had been largely accepted by the end of the nineteenth century.[39] At the same time, there were growing political and social demands by women across all classes for recognition as independent adults who exercised authority within families, thus requiring political rights to fulfil the demands of motherhood and household management. These arguments were difficult to reconcile, and debates raged within the labour movement between those fighting for manhood suffrage and those embracing women's demands for the vote.[40]

This model of adult masculinity based on providing for and heading a household was very much current throughout the nineteenth and early twentieth centuries, although for families of all classes, the realities and uncertainties of life meant that many would not easily fit into such ideals. Relationships between genders and generations were thus never equal in these families, but for the poorest, authority and power were particularly fluid and contestable.

Welfare and masculinity

In the field of welfare, tensions of authority and masculinity could be particularly acute. When times were hard and working-class families turned to welfare and charity for assistance, the interactions and relationships between families and welfare providers were necessarily inflected by questions of age and gender. Questions of domestic authority and masculinity within families were thus brought to the surface in these encounters. The one form of assistance which was modelled on the provider and head of the household ideal was the friendly society, a collective association with many social and political functions as well as being a source of welfare benefits. Friendly societies were often modelled on male solidarities symbolically linked to ties of blood reflected in rituals of belonging and loyalty, such as parades and initiation ceremonies. They drew on languages of family as well as class solidarities and local bonds.[41] They were a central marker of self-help and independence for labouring men, and as such, they were called upon as models of working-class self-help and respectability in the fight for widening the franchise.[42] Membership of friendly societies was overwhelmingly male and directly related to paid labour, reinforcing masculine roles of protecting and providing for dependents.[43] The small amounts saved through these societies were seen as the first call on a man's wage packet before handing over housekeeping money to his wife. Most families insured the male breadwinner against their own illness, injury or disability, not other members of the family. This indicated, and helped to reinforce, the place of husbands and fathers as providers and the rest of the family as dependents on his labour, rather than welfare subjects in their own right.[44] Benefits were explicitly connected with the paid employment of an individual man (although a small number of employed women were also contributors), in marked contrast to the Poor Law and many forms of charity which rigorously examined the family as a whole.[45] In practice, friendly societies had complex and variable ways of assessing family need, but the channel for assistance remained the working man.[46] Claiming benefits was not seen as shameful, but as a right earned through foresight and thrift. In the friendly society model, the welfare subject was the respectable husband and father, the provider and protector of his dependent wife, children and his parents in their old age.

Other forms of welfare were much less likely to engage with a male head of household. Charity of various kinds was often directly targeted at women, children or the elderly, and thus family survival strategies called for particular gender or age positions to be deployed in encounters with charitable donors. For example, children would often be sent to collect donated food because they were seen by the philanthropic as more deserving. We can see how a desperately poor family negotiated these opportunities in the autobiographical example of Arthur Harding, who was interviewed by Raphael Samuel in the 1970s. His father had always bullied him, but by the time Arthur was old enough to be useful to the family his father had become a violent alcoholic and was losing his sight.

> The people in charge of the Mission gave him a ticket to go round the restaurants to see what they would give him in leavings. I used to go round with him. I used to carry the bag for him. It was a Saturday job which I detested – cadging for food: I would sooner have pinched it.[47]

Arthur's presence was clearly necessary to obtain charity, but to have to do it in the company of his father was clearly a particularly shaming experience for him, despite his frequently being hungry and the high quality of the food from this source. This anecdote emphasises his contempt for his father, a theme which recurs throughout the rest of his story.

> I had no respect for my father – no feeling at all. He wasn't really an invalid. It is true his sight became bad – in the end he went completely blind and got a pension – but that was only through neglect and ignorance. By the time I was nine or ten he had become a confirmed part of the casual poor, depending upon alms from the rich, and remained so for the rest of his life. A few years later we threw him out of the house and he went to live with a sister.[48]

Barbara Fox's idea of a 'dialectic of exposure' in working-class fiction is useful in interpreting Harding's account. By revealing shameful experiences Arthur is able to claim both authenticity for his story and his personal integrity as the teller of that story.[49] In turn this hateful episode in his life is used to establish his adult identity as a man who would (and did) steal rather than beg. But he also indicates the long-term effect on his father when he adds to this story that his father grew to fear him: once Arthur was older and began to use violence to make his way in the world, his father called him 'the big fellow'.[50] We can see here that deploying children to obtain welfare could have its costs not only for the children concerned but also for their fathers who could find their masculine identities being undermined in quite profound ways.

Wives would often be the ones to deal with a range of welfare encounters in their homes, including the many middle-class philanthropic visitors.[51] Arthur Harding's mother, disabled after a road accident, was well versed in obtaining charity, insisting that the children be clean and well behaved in front of the philanthropic women they dealt with. Breakfast was available to children at the local mission, but they had to go to Sunday school both morning and afternoon, something they would never have done otherwise.[52] Harding did not express the same kind of anger with these strategies, saving his disrespect for those who doled out charity rather than his mother. His older sister, known by everyone as Mighty, was the main earner of the family selling lemons at the market. She had the most difficult task of dealing with shops where they always owed money. His mother was the one who arranged things so that Mighty could work for the family: 'My mother came to some arrangement with the school inspector. They didn't want to summon her, my mother being a cripple, so they made this special arrangement – twice a week she went to school and the other days she had off.'[53] Thus the Harding family demonstrated a complex set of arrangements which shifted over the life cycle and according to the health and strength of its members, although eventually these arrangements broke down as Arthur left to live on the streets and his father was turned out of their home by Mighty; interdependence had its limits. Their use of many different kinds of welfare provision (and minor criminality) shows how norms of gender and age were actively used and negotiated to bring resources to the family and individuals within it, an example of the agency of poor families in their engagements and negotiations with welfare which Linda Gordon explored in an American context.[54] Assumptions and values about domestic authority in this family rarely conformed to the expectations of welfare providers, even when attempts were made to appear to conform to such expectations. Yet the failure of Harding's father to conform at least minimally to the model of independent breadwinner and the material consequences of hunger and deprivation were portrayed by Arthur as the root of his family's many troubles.

The growing engagements with questions of child education and welfare by the state, both nationally and locally, had the greatest potential to challenge and destabilise the domestic roles of fathers. Those who were concerned about the poor and particularly those engaged in welfare, philanthropy and social policy questions, found the blurring of authority within poor families deeply problematic.[55] The maintenance of social order, as they understood it, was threatened by a range of economic and social strategies which poor people were obliged to use in order to survive. In such circumstances, it was not always clear who should be targeted as welfare subjects: husbands and fathers as the formal head of household; or wives as managers of the household economy and carers for young children; or children themselves as future citizens.

One response to these tensions was to define the welfare subject as a person or group who lived outside a recognised family, and therefore was without a father or husband whose authority could be challenged. Paternalism was also a way of framing welfare relationships of this kind. Both philanthropy and state welfare could be understood as a form of substitute fatherhood, providing the protection, care and material aid for the fatherless and powerless, placing the provider and protector in a position of power and authority over the dependent recipient.[56] Anna Clark explores this relationship in the context of Irish orphans in this volume (Chapter 3). Another striking example might be the concerns about young children working on the streets, vividly portrayed by journalists such as Mayhew as being inappropriately adult. The rescue missions of Dr Barnardo and others were to some extent premised on the assumption that such children did not have parents at all, and could thus be removed from the street into an institution without any interference. In practice, this sometimes proved to be incorrect, as Barnardo found when he faced hostile parents in court.[57]

In cases such as this, tensions between state and fathers of poor families were partly contained by the widespread use of the generic term of 'parent' when developing policy concerning children, an approach still widely used today. In many ways parents did share responsibilities, and as we have seen, there was much blurring of authority, as Pooley explores in this volume (Chapter 10) where both mothers and fathers actively engaged with educational authorities. But by using the neutral term 'parent', policy could be more easily shifted away from being directed at fathers to being negotiated with mothers when it was implemented on the ground. Many day-to-day welfare encounters were between mothers and the middle-class women who implemented philanthropic ideas and projects throughout the nineteenth century.[58] As Clark demonstrates in this volume (Chapter 3), women had some difficulty in establishing their authority in such encounters, but gradually moved into professional welfare roles. By feminising the welfare relationship, the underlying conflicts of authority between welfare and families could be mediated and thus minimise their emergence into public discourse. Potentially conflictual situations could be understood as maternal and nurturing when they occurred between women whose mutual concerns, however differently understood, could find some common ground in the territories of domestic life and motherhood.

But there were also more direct ways that parental rights and the authority of fathers were being challenged. For example, the establishment of industrial schools in the mid-nineteenth century to incarcerate children found begging, destitute or deemed to be beyond parental (or Poor Law) control meant that fathers and mothers could be coerced into giving up their children on the grounds that they had failed to protect and provide for them.[59] One example of this kind of intervention can be seen in the childhood of Sam Shaw, who was born in 1884.[60]

Sam was the sixth child of eight, and was physically abused by his father until his younger brother became the focus of his father's violence. His father lost his sight and stopped working when Sam was seven, and shortly afterwards was taken away to a mental hospital. The family was broken up and Sam was sent to live with an aunt and uncle, one of many temporary homes. Once his father came out of hospital, Sam went back to his parents who sent him out to sell matches on the street with his older sister, the family's main source of income. Finally, the family went on the tramp; he was sent to the workhouse, and then to a cottage home. He expressed a mixture of feelings about this:

> Family life, however poor, possesses the family ties of love. Pauperism cuts into the human love ties and mercilessly rips them asunder. On arriving at Erdington we were separated from one another. . . . I forgot the past and all its troubles.[61]

He puts the pain of separation into an impersonal voice here rather than something he felt himself, thereby deflecting the more shameful aspects of his family life. Whether he experienced his family as a loving one he does not reveal to us, although he frequently mentions elsewhere in his autobiography how important his brothers and sisters were to him in his childhood. After about a year, the family came back together without his older siblings and travelled to London where Sam found a match-selling pitch at Victoria. After a few months, he was arrested and sent to an industrial school. He was not yet 11 years old.[62] His family were appalled to lose his earnings, but he remembered the relative security of industrial school as a welcome relief. He lived in institutions until he was an adult, seeing his parents only once in that time.

Sam was brought up in a complete and recognisable family, but one whose father had failed to provide for his children and this had been made visible through Sam's very public role as a breadwinner. It was this which enabled welfare authorities to successfully challenge his father's authority. It also deeply affected Sam, who longed for a father-figure, often mentioning other men who had fulfilled this role at different times in his life. Like Arthur Harding, he bitterly resented his father's failings: 'His attitude towards me robbed me of the joy of hero-worship which every child has towards his father whom he generally looks up to as a big, big father supreme over all other fathers.'[63]

Another key area which directly challenged domestic authority relations was the growth of child protection policies and institutions.[64] It is clear, however, that it was often mothers, not fathers, who were principally targeted by child protection agencies.[65] We can see how complex such encounters could be in the case of Annie Barnes who was the eldest of 12 children, 6 of whom survived childhood.[66] Her mother died when she was aged 23, and she stayed at home to look after the rest. When she left home to get married her father remarried, but she was very concerned about her younger siblings who she left behind and eventually called in the National Society for the Prevention of Cruelty to Children (NSPCC) who took her stepmother to court for neglecting them. It is interesting to note that it was the mother, not the father, who was prosecuted, perhaps because they felt it was the mother's role to care for the children and not the father's responsibility. But also as a stepmother, she was an 'outsider' and it might have been easier for family and neighbours to blame her when things went badly. Annie herself had an ambivalent view of her father's responsibility. She said, 'My father didn't care about us kids. He kept us and that was it.'[67] And she repeated again: 'Our old man didn't care about us kids. We worked there and lived upstairs, that was all.'[68] While these statements affirm the centrality of the breadwinner role and her father's ability to provide, they also show deep anger that his emotional engagement and concern for her and her siblings was so limited. While the NSPCC may not have thought it was his fault that they were neglected, in her eyes he had a moral responsibility which he had failed. The guilt and shame of her siblings being very publicly shown to be neglected was clearly something which still rankled even at the age of 92. In Annie's narrative, the division of responsibility in her family may have reflected the dominant welfare paradigm of masculine provider, but it was seen as woefully inadequate in the context of the more complex and interdependent arrangements of poor families.

Entering the workhouse

There was one core welfare institution which was not a novel intervention: the New Poor Law, which since 1834 had explicit powers to break up a family if they were destitute.[69] The workhouse system was the symbolic as well as physical means for cutting off day-to-day relationships between family members as a punishment and deterrent to those who sought assistance from the state. The workhouse was a celibate institution deliberately policing the sexual and reproductive practices of families to prevent further paupers being born or recruited through 'moral contamination'. The workhouse system deliberately used shame not only to discipline its inhabitants, but also to divide communities. To submit to the workhouse, to wear its uniform and to have its shadow cast across a family's history was to lose any claims for respectability among neighbours, friends and family for the majority of the working class, not only at the time of incarceration but for their lifetime, and their children's lifetimes as well.

George Hewins argued about this with his wife. One of his jobs was to repair the local workhouse roof, and while there he saw the children of a workmate living there.

> Who should I see but Hilda Rowe and Violet. They'd had their hair chopped off, weared long Holland pinnas with big red letters: STRATFORD-ON-AVON WORKHOUSE.... those red letters haunted me all day... when I got home I told the missus but she said: 'It's to *distinguish* em.'
>
> 'Oo from?'
>
> 'From kiddies oo's Dad's workin! Ow would you like our George took for a pauper?'
>
> 'Teddy Rowe *was* workin' I said, 'till e went to the Infirmary.' He'd got T.B. They took you to the Infirmary to die.
>
> I was angry: 'There's no need for them red letters! The pauper kids is distinguished alright! You can spot em straight away... when they marches out a-night [from school back to the workhouse], the other kiddies is callin "Workhus brats!" after em.'...
>
> I could see she didn't think the same as me. She was wrong, the Guardians was wrong, and all of us, letting it happen. Why was you punished for being poor?
>
> 'Why do they part husbands and wives in the workhus, mother an kiddies, tell me that? Some sent one way, some t'other, according? It's cruel!'
>
> 'Shut up, George,' said the missus.'[70]

Hewins was one of many autobiographers who railed against the workhouse and its regimes. While the humiliations of the workhouse affected all who entered, it had particularly devastating impacts on masculine identities. To be deprived of civil rights, to be incarcerated, to be cold, hungry and uncomfortable were not unfamiliar experiences to many working-class men. But what the workhouse deprived them of was their wives and children, their position as the head of their household and their standing in the world as providers and protectors. To expose themselves and their dependents to shame as well as deprivation was what was so bitterly felt.

To explore the workings of the Poor Law on domestic authority, we turn to another example, the story Frank Steele told in his autobiography about his family's struggles with poverty and the poor law.[71] He was born in the 1860s and his autobiography was written around 1919, by which time he had emigrated with his wife and two sons to North America. It followed many of the conventions of the genre of working-class autobiographies, including a polemic about the punitive treatment of his father and himself by the poor law authorities.

Frank Steele's parents held a rather ambiguous class position. He describes his father as a 'gentleman' and 'a bit of a snob', and his mother as coming from a well-off family.[72] When in work, his father was employed as a draper, then a salesman, but seemed unable to stay in work for very long, especially after his sight began to fail. His mother was 20 years younger, and had worked as a barmaid. His childhood in Hackney, East London, was characterised by short periods of respectable poverty between longer periods of severe deprivation. This included times when his father was in debtor's prison, other times when the family received outdoor relief, and a period of four years spent in the workhouse. He had an older brother, who (unlike Frank) was sent to dame school and then to boarding school, supported by a local charity. He had two younger brothers, both of whom died in infancy. The family had very few contacts with wider kin networks, perhaps because they were much poorer than most of their relations.

When poverty finally reached a crisis point, the family was initially rescued by his mother's sister, who bought them a mangle to bring in some much-needed income. This enterprise disrupted the clear divisions of gender and generation which they had struggled to maintain: Frank and his brother looked after the baby, while his father turned the mangle and delivered laundry. He did so in the evenings: 'Such was my mother's unwillingness to have my father publicly identified with the mangling trade.'[73] His wife was attempting to minimise his exposure to shame; not only did he have to rely on his wife's earnings, but was obliged to assist her in a highly feminised area of work in a public way. Tensions arose leading to rows and even swearing by his father, shocking to his children who had never heard their parents argue or use course language before.

The family was finally forced to go into the workhouse for several years. They emerged from its clutches through the efforts of this same aunt, who brought his mother out and established a small cookshop. After a year they had earned enough to bring Frank and his father out to join them and re-establish a home life together. His older brother returned home from school to begin earning, as did Frank who from the age of 12 began to work his own way out of poverty. After one more short-lived business venture, his father no longer pretended to work: 'no longer worrying about "getting something to do" '.[74]

The results of his father's inability to provide for his family were profound. Frank expressed a great affection and love for his father, but it is clear that he could not respect him. He felt that the demands made upon his father were unreasonable:

> There runs through all our false social consciousness a pervading and prevailing inference and implication conventionally applicable to a man placed as he was: some absurd axiomatic fiction about 'standing up' and 'being a man' – showing what is 'in him' (deuced little when he is at starving point!), and rot of that kinds, that stirs me to anger against its parrot-like enunciators.[75]

Despite his sympathy, the shame of his father's failure permeates his account. Before the cataclysm, he describes his home life as revolving around his father's return from work each day. His mother would prepare their tea by firelight, only lighting candles when his father arrived home, which would be followed by storytelling, jokes and reading out bits of the newspaper.[76] This echoes John Gillis' insights about the role of gendered rituals of the threshold which served to emphasise the home as a wife's domain, where men's coming and going was marked by welcoming and leave-taking each day.[77] Steele goes on to contrast this ordered vision of domestic life with the degradation of the rituals of entering the workhouse:

> It struck me with a distinct feeling of outrage on my father's dignity that he could be (by a man who, though larger, was so palpably inferior to himself) ordered to go here and there – to do this and do that. To take a bath, for instance. 'Everybody takes a bath fust thing here,' the old fellow explained. It was doubly an outrage when my father had to strip before us boys. We all bathed together in a big tank that would perhaps have held twenty.[78]

Steele articulates here the humiliations incurred in marking the transition from independence to pauperism. The bath marked the stripping away of his father's former life as the head of his family and the emergence from the bath into the new, humiliating role of pauper. It exposed him to his son, and everyone else, as a failure as a man and a father.

> Then – horror upon horrors!.... when I saw our dear old Dad arrayed in the ugly brown cloth coat with brass buttons, which I had seen often in the streets and learned to despise as something wholly alien and remote from our family outlook or concerns, my young mind was simply ablaze with the sense of accumulated abasement and indignity. I shall never forget it![79]

As we saw with Hewins, the workhouse uniform provoked the deepest shame, representing a public and inescapable display of the family's descent into the abyss. For Steele's family, it was a shock from which they never really recovered:

> My experiences of that day were burned into my brain as with a branding-iron. And though my father has now been dead for over a third of a century, my ears tingle and the blood rises hot in my face on his behalf as I write.[80]

His father never spoke of this episode in their lives again. In this narrative, Scheff's outlines of the social meanings of shame emerge very clearly. The workhouse experience finally undermined any claim his father could make to an adequate masculine identity and his reaction was to withdraw into himself, a process of social alienation in Scheff's terms. The workhouse also drove his family apart from each other and from their wider social networks with the notable exception of his aunt. But by sharing this shame with his readers, Steele found a way to build a sense of shared injustice by demanding change in the poor laws, and refusing to accept the alienation that silence would entail. Steele's autobiography thus falls within the longstanding themes of anti-poor law discourses, including the fiction of Dickens and many other first-hand accounts, in which issues of shame could be explicitly articulated as part of the history of working-class resistance.

However, his experience of pauperisation was not a common one, even for the very poor. The proportion of families incarcerated in workhouses compared with other kinds of paupers was very small, variously estimated at 4–10 per cent by the end of the nineteenth century.[81] Its punishing regimes and in particular its disruption of familial authority relations could thus be seen as a successful deterrent. We have seen throughout this chapter some of the many strategies which families drew on to avoid the workhouse, including drawing on kinship, charity, philanthropy, crime and even other kinds of incarceration such as industrial schools. Given their very limited choices, some destitute men even deserted their families rather than face the workhouse. George Lloyd (born around 1850) wrote about the time after his mother had died after giving birth to her seventh child:

> My father was terribly depressed at the loss of Mother and work getting slack he was nearly demented. Then one day [he went] down the docks looking for work. A ship was going out minus a carpenter. So Father jumped aboard. She was bound for the West Indies. We children waited up all night. But no father returned.[82]

His grandparents had to send the children to the workhouse, and some years later when George's father returned, 'He went to the Poor Law authorities right away to get us children. He paid for their keep which they eagerly took and had him arrested for deserting us. Which everyone said was an injustice. However, he had one month in Cardiff jail.'[83] When he emerged from prison he found George, offered to take him to London and look after him, but George (aged about 13) refused to leave the family who had taken him in when he was homeless, given him work as a miner and treated him as 'family'. This led to a long break from his father, brothers and sisters. He could not easily set aside the resentment at being abandoned, the hardships of life without a father, and the shame of being sent to the workhouse.

For some, respectability had long been abandoned as a goal, and for these families the workhouse was treated as just another resource.[84] Poor Law officials were constantly attempting to restrict the ways that families and individuals would move in and out of workhouses to suit their own needs and desires. Charlie Chaplin remembered his mother taking him out of the workhouse school for a day so they could see each other outside of the normal three monthly visiting times, a process which involved days of bureaucratic procedures of checking out and readmission.[85] Sam Shaw remembered using the casual wards as 'bed and breakfast' each night as his family walked from Birmingham to London to improve their fortunes.[86] In the desperate straits of these families, social shame was of little use as a deterrent.

But in most circumstances, the workhouse represented the most drastic form of state intervention in family life, challenging the core elements of masculinity and adulthood as a way of disciplining poor families into submission to the most rigorous hardships, both inside and outside its grim walls. Pauperism for the able-bodied man was always coloured by the assumption that it was the result of a failure of individual character rather than social circumstances, and this was the basis for the shame which was attached to it. Failure came at a very high cost to a man and his family, not only in terms of his inner sense of who he was, but also in the display of outward signs of humiliation: the uniform, the social stigma demonstrated by the taunts suffered by his children, and the withdrawal of the rights of citizenship.

Turn of the century reforms

Working-class men and women had actively opposed the humiliations of the New Poor Law since its inception in 1834 both politically through the labour and socialist movements and through developing alternative forms of welfare such as friendly societies. Working-class men and women became eligible for office as Poor Law Guardians in 1896 and began to press for reform from within. For example, Percy Wall wrote about his father who was an active trade unionist and Labour Representation Committee member, and was elected as Guardian in Fulham, London in 1904, contributing evidence to the Poor Law enquiry of 1909.[87] Percy remembered, 'My father often raged inwardly at his inability to help where he would, when satisfied in his own mind of genuine hardship.'[88] His father successfully campaigned for old couples in the Fulham workhouse to be able to live together, a provision available from 1896 but not always implemented.

His mother and aunt had spent some time in a workhouse as children after their father (his grandfather) died leaving them penniless. He remembered his aunt being deeply affected by this experience:

> She was not suited to any form of institutional life. Probably the experience of her childhood remained predominant and all the ameliorations in the way of furnishings, heat and light, ample and varied food regularly supplied, could not soften the impact of institutionalism. Aunt was a natural rebel: she could impose discipline and routine but could not endure it.[89]

And his mother also:

> The early life of my mother had not fit her for the struggle on which she was now engaged.... She must soon have learned how to make a little go a long way. She was never guilty of waste.... The effort was praiseworthy, if not the skill.[90]

His father's commitment to Poor Law reform sprang from not only his knowledge of the damaging effects of the workhouse on these sisters, but also his own family's frequently perilous state as his own health deteriorated. He found it increasingly difficult to provide for them, only avoiding the workhouse himself by calling on relatives and comrades for assistance.

Attempts to reform the Poor Law were gathering strength by the turn of the century, driven by socialists and the trade union movement, who demanded justice, not charity or pauperism.[91] Feminists demanded greater recognition and support for wives and mothers in managing poverty rather than the breaking up of families, most strikingly seen in the work of the Women's Cooperative Guild.[92] Women guardians (elected from 1875) were also noted for their efforts to de-stigmatise and redefine poverty.[93] For example, Hannah Mitchell reported that her (female) predecessor as Poor Law Guardian had successfully campaigned to abolish workhouse dress for children in Ashton under Lyne by 1904. Their efforts were reinforced by wider concerns about the ill effects of institutional life on children, being recast as future citizens of the nation.[94] By the end of the nineteenth century, workhouses had lost many of their original functions to more specialised institutions such as schools, hospitals, asylums for the mentally ill and homes for the elderly. The de-pauperisation of these institutions was slow and uneven, but, for example, those receiving free medical treatment through the poor law system gradually regained rights of family life, and also from 1885 no longer lost the franchise.[95] The Royal Commission on the Poor Law of 1909 recognised these changes, and to a large extent welcomed them.

The question which most deeply troubled the Commission was how to manage the able-bodied pauper, that is, those men (and a few women) who were fit enough for the labour market but who were still destitute, unable or unwilling to provide for themselves and their dependents. The Minority Report, with its origins in Fabian ideas about the role of the state and welfare, marked the growing importance of the concept of unemployment as a structural rather than an individual failing.[96] Under their proposals for dismantling the Poor Law, the existing requirement of the able-bodied to work would be transformed into a requirement to *seek* work. Benefits were to be based on the individual as a worker, who was assumed to be a head of household with dependents, much like the Friendly Society model. In these ways, masculinity based on the breadwinner model could be protected, not undermined, and the social shame associated with pauperisation could be removed.

Conclusion

In this chapter, stories of shame, anger and resistance have been used to explore the tensions surrounding domestic authority and masculinity in families which struggled for survival in the face of poverty. The interdependent relationships of support and care in such families challenged two touchstones of adult masculinity: the role of provider for dependents and the position of head of household. Multiple sources of income and support for poor families could undermine a husband and father's position while the vital work of a wife in managing scarce resources further blurred questions of domestic authority. The wider context of working-class demands for employment rights and the suffrage demonstrated a desire to resolve these tensions as the labour movement focused on measures which would enable men to successfully assert these two roles. The dominant model of family life of clear, hierarchical distinctions between the places of men, women and children for both respectable working-class families and middle-class philanthropists thus sat uncomfortably with the day-to-day exigencies of life for the poor.

It is in the encounters between those in need and the many sources of welfare to which they resorted that these domestic and political tensions became visible. Many forms of charity required families to deploy women and children to access their resources, thus bypassing questions of men's responsibilities and failings. Both philanthropy and the growing number of state providers tended to use women to work with the poor, further diffus-ing and feminising the welfare relationship. Welfare was also concentrated on those who, it was assumed, had no father or husband to support and protect them, even where this was patently not the case. Thus welfare sub-jects were constructed around norms of feminine (and young) helplessness which confirmed the dominant model of family authority relations rather than challenging it overtly.

On the other hand, the Poor Laws were directly aimed at disciplining the poor through the pauperisation of men who were forced to turn to its provision to keep their families alive, explicitly removing rights to family life and citizenship, challenging men's domestic authority and social stand-ing. The shame which accompanied pauperism was deliberately generated through such measures as the wearing of uniforms, not only by husbands and fathers deemed to have failed as men, but also their children whose lives were blighted by their experiences in the workhouse system and the social shaming that persisted afterwards. Thus it is not surprising that the Poor Law was widely hated by the working classes, and formed the focus of day-to-day acts of resistance and wider political action which became more intense by the late nineteenth and early twentieth centuries. As Poor Law provi-sion fragmented and diversified and as working-class Guardians worked for reforms from the inside, other forms of state welfare began to emerge. One of the long-term results was to be the shaping of benefits around the model of Friendly Societies which supported dominant ideals of family authority rather than challenging and undermining men's positions as husbands and fathers.

Thus, the relationships between families and welfare in this period were being shaped by acute tensions about men's authority within families and ideas about the rights and responsibilities associated with adult masculin-ity. As welfare regimes and the assumptions behind them were contested, disrupted and subverted, the blurring of authority which had long been a necessary feature of life for the poor became more visible and prob-lematic. Solutions which would reassert and strengthen families along normative lines were constantly being sought, but as we still see today, rarely completely achieved.

Notes

1. I would like to thank Katherine Holden, Leonore Davidoff, Janet Fink, Jane McCarthy, the editors and readers of this volume, and those who heard ver-sions of this as a conference paper, all of whom made important comments and suggestions towards this chapter.
2. A. Hewins (ed.) (1982) *The Dillen: Memories of a Man of Stratford-upon-Avon* (Oxford: Oxford University Press).
3. Ibid., p. 93.

4. L. Davidoff, M. Doolittle, K. Holden and J. Fink (1998) *The Family Story: Blood, Contract and Intimacy, 1830–1960* (London: Longman), ch. 4.

5. S. Rose (1992) *Limited Livelihoods: Gender and Class in Nineteenth-Century England* (London: Routledge), pp. 138–48. See also Creighton's discussion of these changes in C. Creighton (1996) 'The Rise of the Male Breadwinner Family: a Reappraisal', *Comparative Studies in Society and History* 38(2), pp. 310–37.

6. There were significant differences in welfare provision in Scotland, Ireland and, to a lesser extent, Wales which are beyond the scope of this chapter.

7. Thus, for example, provision for the sick began to focus on higher standards of medical care and the disqualifications associated with pauperism were removed from those entering workhouse infirmaries in 1885. P. Thane (1996) *Foundations of the Welfare State* (London: Longman), pp. 31–7. See also M. Daunton (2007) *Wealth and Welfare: An Economic and Social History of Britain 1851–1951* (Oxford: Oxford University Press), pp. 527–32.

8. L. H. Lees (1998) *The Solidarities of Strangers: The English Poor Laws and the People, 1700–1948* (Cambridge: Cambridge University Press), p. 318; H. Hendrick (2003) *Child Welfare: Historical Dimensions, Contemporary Debate* (Bristol: Policy Press), p. 69.

9. Report of the Interdepartmental Committee on Physical Deterioration, 1904, Cd. 2175, 2210 and 2186 Vol. xxxi.

10. C. Booth (1902–3) *Life and Labour of the People in London* (London: Macmillan); B. S. Rowntree (1901) *Poverty, A Study of Town Life* (London: Macmillan).

11. Lees, *The Solidarities of Strangers*, ch. 9.

12. Hendrick discusses this in the context of child welfare: Hendrick, *Child Welfare*, pp. 19–20.

13. D. Vincent (1991) *Poor Citizens: The State and the Poor in Twentieth Century Britain* (London and New York: Longman), pp. 24–5.

14. For example, R. Gagnier (1991) *Subjectivities: A History of Self-Representation in Britain 1832–1920* (New York: Oxford University Press); J. Peneff (1990) 'Myths in Life Stories', in R. Samuel and P. Thompson (eds) *The Myths We Live By* (London: Routledge). See also the discussion about autobiography as a source by Jane Hamlett (Chapter 5) in this volume.

15. Peneff discusses the silencing effect of shame in shaping life stories: Peneff, 'Myths in Life Stories'.

16. In the middle-class autobiographies analysed by Donna Loftus, few contain details of their adult family life: D. Loftus (2005) 'The Self in Society: Middle-Class Men and Autobiography', in D. Amigoni (ed.) *Life Writing and Victorian Culture: The Nineteenth Century* (Aldershot: Ashgate), pp. 67–86. The same can be found in working-class autobiographies: M. Doolittle (1996) 'Missing Fathers: Assembling a History of Fatherhood in Mid-Nineteenth-Century England' (PhD Thesis, University of Essex), p. 176.

17. These taped conversations were then edited by his daughter-in-law: Hewins, *The Dillen*, pp. v, 178.

18. See Lees, *The Solidarities of Strangers*, ch. 9.

19. J. Burnett, D. Vincent and D. Mayall (1984) *The Autobiography of the Working Class: An Annotated Critical Bibliography* (Hassocks: Harvester Press), p. x.

20. Hewins, *The Dillen*, p. ix.

21. D. Vincent (1981) *Bread, Knowledge and Freedom: a Study of Nineteenth-Century Working Class Autobiography* (London and New York: Methuen), p. 23. For a discussion of popular literatures and poverty, see P. Joyce (1991) *Visions of the People:*

Industrial England and the Question of Class 1848–1914 (Cambridge: Cambridge University Press), pp. 294–300.

22. A. August (2001) 'A Culture of Consolation? Rethinking Politics in Working-Class London, 1870–1914', *Historical Research* 74(183), pp. 202–4.

23. T. J. Scheff (2000) 'Shame and the Social Bond: A Sociological Theory', *Sociological Theory* 18(1), p. 84.

24. Ibid., p. 98.

25. R. Sennett and J. Cobb (1973) *The Hidden Injuries of Class* (New York: Vintage Books), pp. 45–9, quoted in T. J. Scheff, 'Shame and the Social Bond', p. 96. Carolyn Steedman also refers to this research and its silencing of working class women's experience. C. Steedman (1986). *Landscape for a Good Woman: a Story of Two Lives* (London: Virago), p. 113.

26. C. Steedman (1992) 'History and Autobiography: Different Pasts', in C. Steedman (ed.), *Past Tenses: Essays on Writing, Autobiography and History* (London: Rivers Oram), p. 43.

27. See, for example, W. Seccombe (1993) *Weathering the Storm: Working Class Families from the Industrial Revolution to the Fertility Decline* (London and New York: Verso); E. Roberts (1984) *A Woman's Place: An Oral History of Working-Class Women 1890–1940* (Oxford: Basil Blackwell); E. Ross (1993) *Love & Toil: Motherhood in Outcast London 1870–1918* (Oxford: Oxford University Press); A. Davin (1996) *Growing Up Poor: Home, School and Street in London 1870–1914* (London: Rivers Oram Press).

28. S. D'Cruze (1998) *Crimes of Outrage: Sex, Violence and Victorian Working Women* (London: UCL Press), ch. 4.

29. C. Creighton, 'The Rise of the Male Breadwinner Family'.

30. P. Joyce (1993) 'Work', in F. M. L. Thompson (ed.) *The Cambridge Social History of Britain 1750–1950. Vol. 2: People and Their Environment* (Cambridge: Cambridge University Press), pp. 149–56.

31. J. Harris (1972) *Unemployment and Politics: A Study in English Social Policy 1886–1914* (Oxford: Clarendon Press), p. 31; J. Burnett (1994) *Idle Hands: The Experience of Unemployment, 1790–1990* (London and New York: Routledge), pp. 172–4.

32. For a discussion of this division in poor London families, see E. Ross, *Love and Toil*, pp. 78–81.

33. Davidoff *et al.*, *The Family Story*, p. 121.

34. For the early modern period, see A. Shepard (2003) *Meanings of Manhood in Early Modern England* (Oxford: Oxford University Press). For the early nineteenth century, see A. Clark (1995) *The Struggle for the Breeches: Gender and the Making of the British Working Class* (Berkley, Los Angeles and London: University of California Press); For the middle class in the nineteenth century, see J. Tosh (1999) *A Man's Place: Masculinity and the Middle-Class Home in Victorian England* (New Haven and London: Yale University Press).

35. M. Doolittle, 'Missing Fathers', pp. 87–97; C. Pateman (1989) *The Disorder of Women* (Cambridge: Polity Press), pp. 183–4.

36. M. McCormack (2007) ' "Married Men and the Fathers of Families": Fatherhoood and Franchise Reform in Britain', in T. L. Broughton and H. Rogers (eds) *Gender and Fatherhood in the Nineteenth Century* (Basingstoke: Palgrave Macmillan).

37. M. L. Shanley (1989) *Feminism, Marriage and the Law in Victorian England, 1850–1895* (New York: Princeton University Press).

38. For example, J. Tosh, *A Man's Place*, p. 90.

39. K. McClelland (2000) 'England's Greatness, the Working Man', in C. Hall, K. McClelland and J. Rendall (eds) *Defining the Victorian Nation: Class, Race, Gender and the Reform Act of 1867* (Cambridge: Cambridge University Press).

40. S. S. Holton (1986) *Feminism and Democracy: Women's Suffrage and Reform Politics* (Cambridge: Cambridge University Press), ch. 3.

41. D. Weinbren (2002) '"Imagined Families": Research on Friendly Societies', *Mitteilungsblatt des Institutus fur die Geschichte der sozialen Bewegungen* 27, pp. 129–31; S. Cordery (2003) *British Friendly Societies 1750–1914* (Basingstoke and New York: Palgrave Macmillan), p. 39.

42. K. McClelland (2000) 'England's Greatness, the Working Man', pp. 93–4.

43. P. Thane (1991) 'Visions of Gender in the Making of the British Welfare State: The Case of Women in the British Labour Party and Social Policy, 1906–1945', in G. Bock and P. Thane (eds) *Maternity and Gender Politics: Women and the Rise of the European Welfare States, 1880s–1950s* (London and New York: Routledge), pp. 27–9.

44. M. Levine-Clark (2006) 'The Gendered Economy of Family Liability: Intergenerational Relationships and Poor Law Relief in England's Black Country 1871–1911', *Journal of British Studies* 45(1), pp. 72–89.

45. But on the blurring between charity and mutual aid in this period, see D. Weinbren (2007) 'Supporting Self–Help: Charity, Mutuality and Reciprocity in Nineteenth-Century Britain', in P. Bridgen and B. Harris (eds) *Charity and Mutual Aid in Europe and North America Since 1800* (New York: Routledge).

46. S. D'Cruze and J. Turnbull (1995) 'Fellowship and Family: Oddfellows' Lodges in Preston and Lancaster, c.1830–1890', *Urban History* 22(1), pp. 46–7.

47. A. Harding with R. Samuel (1981) *East End Underworld: Chapters in the Life of Arthur Harding* (London: Routledge & Kegan Paul), p. 29.

48. Ibid., p. 30.

49. P. Fox (1994) *Class Fictions: Shame and Resistance in the British Working-Class Novel, 1890–1945* (Durham and London: Duke University Press), p. 93.

50. A. Harding with R. Samuel, *East End Underworld*, p. 28–9.

51. E. Ross (1990), 'Hungry Children: Housewives and London Charity, 1870–1918', in P. Mandler (ed.) *The Uses of Charity: The Poor on Relief in the Nineteenth-Century Metropolis* (Philadelphia: University of Pennsylvania Press), pp. 161–96.

52. A. Harding with R. Samuel, *East End Underworld*, p. 27.

53. Ibid., p. 31.

54. L. Gordon (1988) *Heroes of Their Own Lives: the Politics and History of Family Violence, Boston, 1860–1960* (New York: Viking).

55. See Siân Pooley's chapter (Chapter 10) in this volume.

56. This position had long been held by the monarch in wardship relationships; see M. Doolittle, 'Missing Fathers', p. 35.

57. Barnardo was taken to court twice by parents who wanted their children returned to them. In one case which went to the House of Lords, the mother of an illegitimate child (who had then married) was successful in having her son returned to her and her husband's care. *Barnardo v. McHugh* [1891] A.C. 388. See also L. Murdoch (2006) *Imagined Orphans. Poor Families, Child Welfare and Contested Citizenship in London* (New Brunswick, New Jersey and London: Rutgers University Press). For a discussion of the ways Barnardo used photography and other representations of orphan children, see S. Koven (2006) *Slumming: Sexual and Social Politics in Victorian London* (Princeton and Oxford: Princeton University Press), ch. 2.

58. E. Ross (2007) *Slum Travellers: Ladies and London Poverty, 1860–1920* (Berkeley: University of California Press); H. Rogers (2006) 'Women and Liberty' in P, Mandler (ed.) *Liberty and Authority in Victorian Britain* (Oxford: Oxford University Press), pp. 125–55.

59. H. Hendrick (2003) *Child Welfare*, pp. 84–6.

60. S. Shaw (1946) *Guttersnipe* (London: Sampson Low, Marson & Co.) This is a written memoir, published just after the Second World War just as Beveridge's welfare state was coming into being.

61. Ibid., pp. 27–8.

62. Ibid., p. 35.

63. Ibid., p. 5. It is interesting that both Harding and Shaw were involved in right-wing politics in the interwar period, Harding joining Moseley's fascists and Shaw working as a public speaker for right-wing causes.

64. H. Hendrick, *Child Welfare*, ch. 2; G. Behlmer (1998) *Friends of the Family: The English Home and its Guardians, 1850–1940* (Stanford: Stanford University Press). See also Chapter 10 in this volume.

65. M. Arnot (1994) 'Infant Death, Child Care and the State: The Baby Farming Scandal and the First Infant Life Protection Legislation of 1872', *Continuity and Change* 9, pp. 271–311.

66. A. Barnes (1980) *Tough Annie: From Suffragette to Stepney Councillor* (London: Stepney Books Publications). This text was produced through interviewing Annie as part of a local history project in 1979.

67. Ibid., p. 21.

68. Ibid., p. 23.

69. L. H. Lees, *The Solidarities of Strangers*; M. MacKinnon (1987) 'English Poor Law Policy and the Crusade Against Outrelief', *Journal of Economic History*, 47, pp. 603–25; M. A. Crowther (1981) *The Workhouse System 1834–1929: The History of an English Social Institution* (London: Batsford Academic and Educational Ltd); F. Driver (1993) *Power and Pauperism: The Workhouse System, 1834–1884* (Cambridge: Cambridge University Press).

70. Hewins, *The Dillen*, pp. 72–3.

71. F. Steele (1939) *Ditcher's Row: A Tale of the Older Charity* (London: Sidgwick & Jackson).

72. Ibid., pp. 10, 26.

73. Ibid., p. 70.

74. Ibid., p. 234.

75. Ibid., pp. 72–3.

76. Ibid., p. 41.

77. J. R. Gillis (1996) *A World of Their Own Making: Myth, Ritual, and the Quest for Family Values* (New York: Basic Books), pp. 193–5.

78. Steele, *Ditcher's Row*, p. 79.

79. Ibid.

80. Ibid., pp. 79–80.

81. For a discussion of the counting of workhouse inmates, see Crowther, *The Workhouse System*, pp. 226–35.

82. G. Lloyd (n.d.) *The Autobiography of 'Georgie Brawd'*, p. 6. This was an unpublished memoir.

83. Ibid., p. 22.

84. L. H. Lees (1990) 'Survival of the Unit: Welfare Policies and Family Maintenance in Nineteenth-Century London', in P. Mandler (ed.) *The Uses of Charity:*

The Poor on Relief in the Nineteenth-Century Metropolis (Philadelphia: University of Pennsylvania Press), pp. 68–91.

85. C. Chaplin (1964) *My Autobiography* (London: the Bodley Head), p. 21.
86. Shaw, *Guttersnipe*, p. 29.
87. P. Wall (n.d.) *Hour at Eve*, unpublished ms, p. 17.
88. Ibid., p. 19.
89. Ibid., p. 25.
90. Ibid., p. 68.
91. Lees, *The Solidarities of Strangers*, pp. 305–8.
92. As demonstrated in M. Llewellyn Davies (ed.) (1977) *Life as We Have Known It by Co-operative Working Women* (London: Virago).
93. H. Mitchell (1984) *The Hard Way Up: The Autobiography of Hannah Mitchell, Suffragette and Rebel* (London: Virago), p. 122.
94. Hendrick, *Child Welfare*, ch. 2; see also Chapter 3 in this volume.
95. Thane, *Foundations of the Welfare State*, p. 35.
96. B. Webb and S. Webb (1909) *The Break-Up of the Poor Law: Being Part One of the Minority Report of the Poor Law Commission* (London: Longmans, Green and Co.); I. Gazeley and P. Thane (1998) 'Patterns of Visibility: Unemployment in Britain during the Nineteenth and Twentieth Centuries', in G. Lewis (ed.) *Forming Nation, Framing Welfare* (London and New York: Routledge), pp. 182–226.

Part III
Domesticity

5
'Tiresome trips downstairs': Middle-Class Domestic Space and Family Relationships in England, 1850–1910

Jane Hamlett

Beryl Lee Booker, a gentleman's daughter who grew up in London and Leicestershire in the second half of the nineteenth century, described her childhood as punctuated by 'tiresome trips downstairs,' visits to the drawing room from the nursery that upset her 'after tea plans.'[1] Like most middle-class children in the second half of the nineteenth century, Lee Booker's home was organised according to the nursery system. The children were sequestered in a nursery, usually at the top of the house, under the care of a nurse. The organisation of domestic space and material culture in middle-class homes had a crucial impact on authority practices in the home. Although the arrangement of the home differed from family to family, the relatively rigid use of domestic space in the nineteenth century encouraged the construction of intimacies and distances. Access to parents was often limited to a couple of hours a day at best, and children spent the majority of their time in the nursery. Parental authority was exercised through the control of access to the drawing room, study, bedroom and dressing room. Relationships with favoured children were fostered through intimate time spent together in parental personal space, from which other siblings were excluded. Children often cherished time in parental space, closely identifying with material cultures that contributed to the formation of their own gendered identities. The analysis of domestic space also reveals how domestic authority was mediated through wider relationships in the household, demonstrating the limits of parental power. The division of the house into areas for parents, children and servants created spaces in which servants and children interacted beyond parental eyes. Nannies and nurse-maids, constantly sequestered in the nursery with the children, wielded the ultimate power. Spatial division shielded these relationships from parental knowledge, which could sometimes allow for abuse. In upper middle-class homes with a large servant presence, children were likely to seek out liminal spaces in the home, such as attics and outhouses, beyond adult authorities. Here, children were able to adopt behaviour that would have been considered unacceptable in adult space. But domestic authority practices learned in the home were also recreated through play, in the construction of sibling hierarchies and imaginative worlds. In addition, this chapter will discuss accounts of doll play which also reveal how space and material culture could be used to subvert conventional structures of adult gendered authority.

Approaches to domestic authority in the nineteenth-century middle-class family have focused on parental roles and responsibilities. Much ink has been spilt over the nature of these authorities, and their temporal specificity. David Roberts defines the early Victorian upper-class paterfamilias in terms of three features: remoteness, sovereignty and benevolence.[2] Davidoff and Hall, who examine the middle class before 1850, also see fathers as figures of strong paternal authority, but emphasise their loving side.[3] The rise of interest in the history of masculinity has inspired detailed analyses of nineteenth-century fatherhood, most notably by John Tosh who argues that 'fatherhood encompassed every variant from the almost invisible breadwinner to the accessible and attentive playmate.'[4] Eleanor Gordon and Gwyneth Nair's study of the nineteenth-century Glasgow middle-classes also stresses a spectrum of motherly behaviour: 'what it meant to be a mother differed according to material circumstances and culture of the middle-class woman as well as the stage of the family cycle.'[5] They downplay the classic image of the Victorian mother who deserted her children for the pleasures of the drawing room, emphasising women's investment in their children, and their careful plans for their education and entertainment. These works have all contributed to the complicated picture of authority and love through which we now understand the nineteenth-century family, which is additionally also increasingly nuanced by attention to locality, as Chapter 10 in this volume emphasises. It is virtually impossible to construct a single narrative of change in family life that encompasses the variance of experience in this, or indeed any, period.[6] Yet this emphasis on diversity and difference can detract from our understanding of what was distinctive about nineteenth-century family life. Rather than creating a new single narrative of nineteenth-century family experience, this chapter approaches the family from a new perspective, through the study of domestic space and material culture.[7] Domestic authority is considered from the point of view of the spatial and material practices through which it was constituted: revealing the web of power relations between parents, children and servants within the walls of the middle-class home.

Authority practices beyond typical relationships within the nuclear family have received less attention, although Leonore Davidoff, Megan Doolittle,

Janet Fink and Katharine Holden have drawn attention to the need to chart different kinds of intimacy in the home, looking at lodgers, domestic servants and single women.[8] Gordon and Nair have recently pointed out that many homes did not contain conventional nuclear families.[9] Teresa McBride notes that, 'contacts with servants helped to shape children's attitudes towards class status and behaviour. While servants were learning to be deferential to their employers, children were acquiring either a paternalistic benevolence or disdainful suspicion toward their lower-class employees.'[10] But there have been few detailed studies of servant relationships in the household that rival Tim Meldrum's nuanced exploration of the lives and power relations of seventeenth-century London servants.[11] Davidoff's study of nineteenth-century sibling relationships stands alone in its discussion of how the life experiences of William and Helen Gladstone were deeply influenced by their brother–sister relationship.[12] The analysis of how domestic authority was constituted in domestic space allows us to view children's position within the family as a structural whole, rather than focusing on a particular aspect or single relationship in family life. Domestic space reveals the limitations of parental authority, and how it was mediated through servants. The study of spaces that children occupied alone also helps us understand how sibling relationships were formed, and how authority was learned, practised and negotiated. The organisation of the domestic interior also reveals how wider ideas of authority and hierarchy in nineteenth-century society such as class and gender were inculcated in the home. Material culture often carried specifically gendered meanings, and the division of space between servants and family was designed to reinforce the divide between the middle- and working-classes. Although, as will be shown, domestic practices negotiated and resisted these hierarchies as much as they reinforced them.

Uncovering nineteenth-century childhood experience is difficult. Most histories of childhood have been written from the adult's perspective: as sources have often been written and compiled by adults, some historians have found that 'the voice of the child is more or less absent.'[13] Very few children's letters or diaries survive and those that do are likely to have been written under adult supervision. In the absence of a large number of children's diaries I have used accounts of childhood experience in autobiography as the source for this chapter. Autobiography is shaped by its time of writing, and is about engagement with the issues of the present as much as past behaviour.[14] Many autobiographers, writing in the mid-twentieth century, grappled with new concerns over potential psychological damage caused by the separation of children from their parents. Dora Montefiore's reflections on her childhood experiences are typical, she writes, 'When I look back at those happy sheltered days of what I suppose was more or less typical Victorian home life, I note the vast difference that separates the psychology of parents, children and domestic staff from that of the twentieth century.'[15]

But although autobiography was for some time considered less than trustworthy, historians now accept it as a valid source.[16] Autobiographies were more likely to be written by certain types of people: writers or poets, or those with successful public careers. All published autobiography was filtered through editors. Nevertheless, read with an awareness of the circumstances in which they were written and sensitivity to the layering effects of age and memory, autobiographies are a rich source of historical information. Kate Flint's study of nineteenth-century readers has shown that by examining a large number of such texts, it is possible to construct complex arguments that show a range of possible views or behaviours, rather than drawing conclusions for a class or gender group as a whole from a single account.[17]

The research for this chapter draws on a sample of 80 autobiographies from an initial survey (which covered 200 texts). The criterion for the selection of these accounts was that they included a commentary of reasonable length on the childhood home. The writing of autobiography was a clearly gendered practice. While women have produced more autobiographies that deal exclusively with childhood, I have only found four male counterparts. In order to produce a balanced account of male and female experiences for this chapter, I have therefore included more male accounts in the sample. Approximately, 30 per cent of the texts selected here have been written by women. For the purposes of this chapter I have defined the term 'middle class' broadly. The survey includes 8 families from the minor gentry, 12 families from the business and mercantile sector, 11 families of Anglican and Nonconformist ministers and 20 other professional families. The sample also represents a wide range of geographical regions: 23 childhood homes were located in central London, 10 in suburban London, 14 in urban areas outside the metropolis and 19 in rural areas. In this chapter I will examine early childhood experience, from birth until about seven years of age. More autobiographies emerge from the upper middle classes than the lower. While acknowledging the bias of these representations, where possible this chapter contrasts the experiences of different kinds of middle-class homes.

Nineteenth-century middle-class families shared distinctive spatial practices that had important consequences for family relations. The nursery system was in common use amongst the British middle classes during the second half of the nineteenth century. While Annmarie Adams has argued that after 1870 the nursery system became the dominant mode of family spatial organisation, this chronology can be questioned.[18] Nurseries had been designed and represented before 1850.[19] Nursery wall papers were manufactured from the 1850s.[20] The nursery was certainly a feature of the aristocratic house plan much earlier in the century.[21] A survey of room names in homes of the London middling sort in the seventeenth and eighteenth centuries shows that the word 'nursery' has been used to describe rooms used for children since at least 1590,[22] although it is unclear to what extent the social practices associated with the space were similar to its use in the nineteenth century. Just under half of the autobiographies made a clear reference to the nursery as a physical space.[23] Those accounts that did refer to the nursery, rather than being clustered in the post-1870 period, were more or less equally spaced throughout.[24] Only those at the margins of the lower middle class do not mention a nanny or nursemaid.[25] These conclusions are reinforced by Theresa McBride's study of the nineteenth-century census: she argues that the nanny-cum-housemaid was the most commonly employed servant.[26] Figure 5.1 shows an idealised image of a carefully decorated day nursery, from Jane Ellen Panton's best-selling advice manual, *Nooks and Corners*, published in 1889. The amount of space available for nursery facilities depended on house size and wealth. J. J. Stevenson's *House Architecture*, published in 1880, stated that 'a complete nursery suite includes a day-nursery, one or two night nurseries, with space for a bed for a nurse and cribs for the children, a scullery and a water-closet.'[27] Many middle-class homes would have been too small to have a nursery suite on this scale, and the nursery quarters would have consisted of a day nursery and a night nursery or even a single room.

Within the nursery, children were required to operate within previously set physical limits. This sense of physical restriction led some autobiographers to employ military metaphors to describe their nursery existence. William Aubrey Darlington, son of an academic and later a journalist, writes of the 'permanent strength' of his East Dulwich nursery and refers to the giving of 'rations.'[28] Sonia Keppel, whose family lived in semi-aristocratic style, describes her nursery thus: 'My day-nursery was a white-painted fortress, my nurse the garrison-commander; my sister's French governess a spirited captain of the guard... At first, the fortress floor controlled all my movements, and any expedition outside it was tacitly on parole.'[29] The physical restriction to the nursery prompted both Keppel and Mary Carbery to try to escape.[30] Both girls, when very young, attempted to leave the home (although both were eventually retrieved from their journeys and returned home), evincing a desire to move beyond it. But the restriction of the nursery could also be interpreted as security. One writer described her nursery as filled with 'nest-like warmth.'[31]

The decoration of the nursery could be literally didactic. By the 1850s, cups, bowls and plates decorated with themes for children had appeared on the market; such goods would often bear moral mottoes such as 'never speak to deceive nor listen to betray.'[32] *A Book with Seven Seals*, written about the 1850s, describes a small girl being filled with terror on the receipt of a sampler featuring a didactic motto 'Thou God Seest Me.'[33] But such visible didacticism was not always a source of terror. Robert Graves and his sister

Figure 5.1 Illustration showing an empty nursery from J. E. Panton (1884) *Nooks and Corners* (London: Ward and Downey)

rather priggishly entered into the spirit of things by voluntarily decorating their nursery with instructive notices. Graves wrote:

> We learned to be strong moralists and spent a great deal of our time on self-examination and good resolutions. My sister Rosaleen put up a printed notice in her corner of the nursery – it might just as well have been put up by me: 'I must not say bang bust or pig bucket, for it is rude.'[34]

Moral didacticism did not always work. Kendon retrospectively remarks that he completely missed the moral purpose of one picture that was displayed in his nursery. The image showed a dog stealing from a boy engrossed in a frivolous magazine: 'I never saw the significance of the name of the paper; but we did not see the boy as a boy, nor follow out the consequences of his neglect.'[35] Figure 5.2, a photograph of the children of the Garsten family posed in their London nursery, demonstrates the gendered behaviours that were encouraged in these spaces. The eldest girl of the family is shown diligently bent over her needlework; a younger girl holds a doll, while the boys of the family are posed more freely, although one is posed with a book. This photograph seems to show an idealised version of nursery behaviour: these children may have behaved very differently when adults were not present.

The nursery, then, was a distinctive space in which children first experienced middle-class home life. Through its material culture children learned their first lessons about social identity and morality. However, the most

Figure 5.2 The nursery of the home of the Garsten family in London, Greater Manchester County Record Office, Documentary Photography Archive, 2357/143

important aspect of the nursery may have been its spatial relationship with the rest of the home that contributed to the formation of relationships in the wider family. Autobiographies suggest that the rigid spatial organisation of the Victorian middle-class home, which segregated parents and children and brought them together at different times of the day, was crucial to the creation of family intimacies. Of course, internal spatial relations were not uniform in every home. Complete solitude was a rare experience for anyone, although more possible in the rambling gentry manor than the small terraced house. The degree of separation created by typical Victorian family structure varied from family to family. A. C. Deane, the son of a barrister at Lincoln's Inn, recalls frequently playing in the drawing room.[36] But generally, when the family could afford to employ a nurse or nursemaid, children spent a large amount of their time away from their parents in the nursery.

Parental authority was exercised by permitting or restricting access to adult domestic spaces. The primary space in the home for adult socialisation was the drawing room. This was usually considered the domain of the woman of the house. The drawing room was used for public entertaining and family interactions, and was the setting for the daily five o'clock tea. The issue of access to the drawing room figures frequently in autobiographies. This was a form of power that was not always exercised judiciously: some children were singled out for greater intimacy and so granted more spatial access. Beryl Lee Booker comments on her sister: 'we were jealous of her. She was pretty and petite, and Mummy had her down to the drawing-room far more often than she had us.'[37] Mothers could control their relationships with their children by proscribing access to the drawing room. In some families children were frequently present in the drawing room. Dora Montefiore, who grew up in the 1850s and 1860s, at Kenley Manor in Surrey, recalls spending the 'children's hour' from six to seven each evening in the drawing room.[38] This practice was not repeated everywhere, and children might visit the drawing room for as little as five minutes a week.[39] Lee Booker certainly found such compelled attendance annoying.[40] The controlling of children's entry into the drawing room was an important factor in building relationships between children: children were clearly aware of the potential for favouritism to be exercised through this mechanism, and it is clear from accounts such as Booker's that this aspect of family life could be much resented.

Yet adult space was not always sacrosanct: the varied uses of the study show that it could be penetrated, and could host different kinds of authority. The study has been described as a secluded area of the home where a man could achieve distance from the rest of his family. John Tosh has written,

> The 'study' as it was usually called, was not so much sited *within* the home, as carved out *from* the home. Reserved for the husband's exclusive use and often out of bounds for the rest of the family, it conformed to the principle of separate spheres by removing his work from the domestic atmosphere.[41]

The study was certainly a place where paternal authority was meted out. Carola Oman, the daughter of an Oxford don, recalls being lectured to and taught accounts in the study.[42] Vicar's daughter Noel Streatfield also recalls the forbidding aspect of her father's study, and the fact that no portraits of women were displayed there. Although Streatfield was reprimanded in the study, her autobiography shows that she was unmoved by the telling off.[43] But the study was also the site for the negotiation of relations between father and child. It should be noted that the study as a place of refuge is represented equally strongly in female autobiography. One writer recalls how her fractious sister was pacified by being taken into her father's den,[44] and another remembers how she would take refuge with her father in his study from her mother's antagonism.[45] Male autobiographies more frequently discuss the formative influence of their fathers' library on their education,[46] yet this may be a product of the more general preoccupation with education that such works tend to emphasise. Some accounts, particularly those from the end of the period, do not portray the library or study as an exclusively male space at all. Clare Leighton, growing up in the 1900s, describes the study in 'Vallombrosa,' the family home in St John's Wood, as the territory of both her father and her mother who were writers.[47] Horace Collins, the son of a Maida Vale-based architect, also writes of how during the 1890s, the family library, supposedly his father's sanctum, was frequently invaded by the entire family in the evenings, forcing the father to retreat with his book to his bedroom.[48]

The granting of access to parents' personal spaces built warmth and intimacy between particular children. This practice could strengthen bonds with chosen children, cementing favouritism. In the case of upper middle-class fathers, the dressing room was a key site for this. Dressing rooms were small rooms, attached to the master bedroom, used primarily for male dressing. Children, male and female, were often allowed into the father's dressing room early in the morning.[49] Separation and the control of children's access to parents allowed the privileging of some children over others and facilitating the building of special relationships with chosen children. Beryl Lee Booker, who lived on Elgin Avenue in Maida Vale in the 1890s, recalls how as her father's favourite she was allowed privileged access to his dressing room in the mornings: she describes its messiness with affection.[50] Booker also notes that her siblings were not allowed access to this space in the same way, and she links her trips to the dressing room with her position as her father's favourite child. Brian Lunn, the child of Sir Henry Lunn, the famous business man and Nonconformist, was brought up at Harrow Hill in the 1890s. He recalls how just before he was sent to school at age nine, his parents primed him for this important experience in their personal domains:

> mother told me in the drawing-room how I had come into the world, an interview which left me with a slight sense of having been reprimanded.

Father told me in his dressing-room, where I often used to talk to him while he shaved, not to allow any master to play with my person.'[51]

Lunn's comments show how the special atmosphere in these different spaces made different kinds of intimacy possible between mother and son and between father and son.

Notions of gendered authority were also conveyed through the material culture of the home. In upper middle-class homes, smoking rooms, billiard rooms, studies and libraries were allocated to men, whereas boudoirs, drawing rooms and morning rooms were seen as a female terrain. These spaces had distinctive material cultures: male spaces tended to be furnished in heavy furniture with dark and sombre colours, whereas female spaces were lighter and often heavily ornamented.[52] Children could cherish their time in adult space, paying close attention to its material culture and drawing away from it a sense of their own identity and position within an adult gendered hierarchy. Sonia Keppel found the spaces belonging to her father and her mother equally alluring: 'Sensually, I loved the smell of Mamma's room, with its flower smells, and a certain elusive smell, like fresh green sap, that came from herself. And the smell of Papa's room (hair oil and tobacco), next door. And I loved their thrilling intimacy, generously extended to me.'[53] Keppel notes, 'each morning I visited Mama's room, where, enchantedly, I played with all the lovely things she had worn the night before.'[54] Keppel's family, who, if not extremely wealthy, were of aristocratic origin, may represent upper-class social practice. But similar accounts emerge from lower down the social scale. The author of *Tempestuous Petticoat* was fascinated by her mother's dressing table, and made regular trips to her mother's bedroom to steal her face cream: 'My fingers strayed upon my mother's hair-curlers, and suddenly I wondered whether part of her power over her admirers lay in the beauty of her yellow curls.'[55] But the bedroom did not always foster warmth. Booker was repelled by the exquisite femininity of her mother's bedroom; instead her description of the material culture of the room expresses rebellion and discontent:

Mother rustled and glittered round her beautiful bedroom. Often she would be ill, and then perhaps we could be allowed to creep down at teatime to see her lying in beautiful embroidered sheets ... But we mustn't touch her, or jog the bed, or fidget.[56]

Children's early experiences of these spaces were closely connected to their understanding of what it meant to belong to one sex or the other. Gendered space in the home taught children how to understand and imagine themselves as gendered. Male memoirs frequently recall a fascination with smoking paraphernalia. Lindsay W. Brown recalled playing with the ends of cigars in the family billiard room.[57] Smoking in the home in this period was accompanied by a distinctive and often exotic material culture. Hubert Nicholson was fascinated by the smoking room in his godfather's house: 'The smoking-room was like an excavated Egyptian tomb, with odds and ends of science and art from far countries.'[58] Thomas Beecham recalls his father smoking in a 'remote den' on the top floor of his home:

> There he would put on a cap of Turkish design crowned with a long flowing tassel, and a richly coloured jacket decorated with gold-braided stripes and silver buttons. On the rare occasions when I was admitted to this holy of holies I would gaze upon this gorgeous spectacle with rapture while my sire puffed away in placid and silent content, absorbed in reflections which I felt were of world-shaking import.[59]

While the control of access to certain areas could reinforce parental authority in the home, the division of space between parents, children and servants also effectively limited that authority. Of course, how this operated depended on how many servants were present in the home: the average servant employing household included one or two servants,[60] although upper middle-class houses might contain five or six and lower middle-class households might not be able to afford any help at all. But where there was a significant servant presence in the home, this had an important effect on the organisation of domestic space and the practice and operation of domestic authorities. While the nursery was usually on the second to upper floor of the middle-class home, the servants' rooms would usually be located at the top of the house and the kitchen, their main place of work, in the basement. Despite this spatial separation children and servants often had a close relationship. A house with an unusual layout might lead to greater contact between the two groups. C. Reilly, an architect's son who lived in London and was born in 1874, noted the consequences of the unusual layout of his home: 'It meant, too, that we were cut off from our parents and from the only lavatory by a couple of servants' rooms...it meant in our early days [we] were at the mercy of the servants.'[61]

The spatial configuration of the home was such that children might have different points of spatial contact with the servants to their parents. Leighton recalls how the children knew far more about the servants' clandestine assignations than their parents, because the back gate was clearly visible from the nursery window.[62] In *Four to Fourteen*, the servants took pity on the children, who were fed a spartan diet by their parents, and gave them jam on the sly,[63] and when the parents were away for the evening the children went down to the kitchen where they joined in the servants' laughter as one of the footmen dressed in drag.[64] Similarly, in *A Book with Seven Seals*, which describes the life of two sisters who grew up in a Chelsea vicarage, the children dress in the clothes of the grandmother and aunt, and go and parade before the servants in the kitchen, imitating their relatives for the servants' amusement.[65] Such illicit interactions between servants and children were not always benign. H. J. Bruce recalls how, unknown to his parents, the servants would dress up as ghosts and invade the nursery, terrifying the six-year olds.[66]

From a child's perspective, the most important servant was the nanny or nurse who was an ever-present force in the life of her charge.[67] Usually sleeping in the nursery with the children, nannies and children shared the same space constantly. Jonathan Gathorne-Hardy's popular account of the British nanny presents the nanny as an upper-class ideal, a matronly figure who has been with the family her entire life and is retained in old age.[68] Theresa McBride's wide-ranging census survey sets up a different picture that is more accurate for the middle class in this period. She suggests that in the middle-class home it was common for the nursemaid to be the only servant of the house; nursemaids were often young and untrained, and there was a high turnover.[69] Children would have spent some time with parents, and nannies would have had occasional time off, but the bulk of their existence was spent in the same physical space. Nannies were generally responsible for the physical care of the children. Although mothers varied in their willingness to perform some childcare tasks, nannies frequently performed the lion's share of the work. The practice of having a specialised nanny was distinctively British.[70] Such constant contact often meant that a strong bond of love was formed between nanny and child. Autobiographical descriptions of these carers are frequently glowing.[71] Mary Cholmondeley, the daughter of a vicar from Hodnet in Shropshire, describes her nanny as 'the source of all comfort.'[72] The author of *Four to Fourteen* openly states that she loves her nanny, Ann, more than her mother and was devastated when her mother dismissed Ann.[73] The extent of the attachment of children to their nannies is sometimes shown by the introduction of the nanny into the autobiographical narrative before either of the parents.[74]

While nannies are accused of being too strict, their constant power over children in space beyond parental eyes could be a licence for abuse, again revealing the limits of parental authority in domestic space. Booker writes: 'We lived upstairs in a different world, and were at the mercy of our nurses.'[75] She goes on to describe the nanny's physical abuse of the children. Eventually, the nanny was dismissed, but the parents only discovered her behaviour because she made the mistake of hitting one of the children with an umbrella in the street, thus revealing herself to the local vicar who contacted the children's father.[76] Doubtless the abuse would have continued in private, had the abuser not revealed herself in public space. Mary Carbery, the daughter of an ex-army officer who was brought up in a Hertfordshire country home in the late 1860s and 1870s, felt unable to report her governesses' violence to her parents.[77]

In its three-way division between spaces for servants, children and parents, the middle-class home was designed to reinforce not just the hierarchy of authority within the family, but a hierarchy of class. However, the closeness of nanny and charge could transcend the class division that the spatial segregation of the middle-class home set up. Theresa McBride argues that middle- and upper-class children learned the ideals of class and status in the home through their contact with servants.[78] To a certain extent, autobiographies bear this out. Servants are not granted central places in autobiographical narratives, and discussions of servants' rooms are rare. In contrast, the importance of the nanny is often signalled by an early mention of her in the narrative, sometimes before parents, and the reproduction of photos of her with the text, which tended to be reserved for family members only. Cholmondeley, rather than identifying with her nanny's working-class origins, promotes her nanny to middle-class status by imbuing her with key moral qualities that were seen to betoken lady-like behaviour: 'Ninny [sic] was in the best sense a lady, well-bred, incapable of a coarse word of a mean and self-seeking action, respectful in manner and self-respecting, refined and dignified.'[79] Cholmondeley's description of her nanny's possessions reinforces her definition of her nanny as 'refined,' as she has books and a collection of fine china and knows its value.[80] Of course, this was not the case for every family. Booker had the opposite reaction to her nanny's china collection, which she criticised as cheap, using it to underline the differences of class and culture between herself and her nanny.[81]

The reach of adult authority in the home depended on the presence of adults in domestic space. In lower middle-class families where there was not enough money for a nurse, children were more frequently left to their own devices. Mary Ann Hughes' family, at first dependent on her father's fluctuating income from work as a stockbroker and later left with few funds on his death, were too poor to employ even one servant.[82] A room in their East London home was dedicated to their sole use, and called 'the study,' presumably because it was expected that it would be used for homework.[83] It was here that Mary Ann Hughes and her brothers pursued childhood games, free from adult intervention. Upper middle-class children like Booker had to work harder to find spaces free from parental interference. Booker and her brother Chas, who taking over an attic, attempted to set up a 'gambling hell,' which they had learned about from penny dreadfuls: 'Here, swearing horribly as we thought, we played nap, old maid and other games of skill or chance while we consumed home-made elderberry wine of disgusting inkiness... We tried also, but failed, to acquire the tobacco chewing habit.'[84] Children often colonised liminal spaces in and around the home, such as attics, outhouses and the garden through play. Figure 5.3 shows two small boys at 'Frondeg,' in Weston-super-Mare, who have taken over an attic space to create a 'museum' where they are engaged in laying out an elaborate collection of natural history specimens. This evocative photograph was probably produced with adult connivance – the boys may have been more messy when away from the eye of the camera.

Figure 5.3   Photograph of 'Museum' at Frondeg, Greater Manchester County Record Office, Documentary Photography Archive, 1642/30, 1/U12/25

Although free from adult interference, these child-only spaces saw the establishment of intimacies and practices of authority between siblings. Mary Ann Hughes, for example, was often excluded from the children's room by her male siblings.[85] In secret nursery games in the Powys family household, in the vicarage at Shirley in the 1880s, John Cooper Powys (the eldest male sibling) led his brothers and sisters in the role of parish clergyman, in imitation of his father.[86] Power relationships between siblings were mediated through material objects. Many men recall having a strong interest in collecting, particularly objects relating to natural history such as eggs.[87] Several men associated the practice of collecting with their mothers, rather than seeing themselves as engaging in masculine practice. E. L. Grant Watson recalls how his mother stimulated his interest in natural history by taking him to the zoo in Regent's Park which was near their home, and by going out collecting with him: 'my mother and I would compete, taking opposite sides of the road, scrutinising the fence and the tree stumps.'[88] While domineering males could assert control over family collections,[89] brothers and sisters could collect together, as Paley Marshall recalls.[90] More often, collections were a keen source of competition between siblings, indicating that sisters did not willingly adopt subordinate roles. Oman remembers how she was encouraged to collect crests in competition with her sister who collected stamps.[91] Booker describes how when her brother arrived home from school with butterfly collecting paraphernalia she took up photography in response.[92]

Finally, the material culture of childhood offered girls in particular the opportunity to recreate but also to resist the hierarchical values of the social world around them. Social historians of the nineteenth century have viewed toys as gendered. Davidoff and Hall note that 'while boys were given hoops, balls and other toys associated with physical activities, girls played with dolls, dolls' houses, needlebooks and miniature workbaskets.'[93] An examination of nineteenth-century English prescriptive literature confirms that dolls were thought to awake the desire for motherhood in young girls.[94] Figure 5.4 shows a late nineteenth-century photograph from the album of the Shaw Storey family of Bursledon. We cannot tell from the image whether the dolls shown here are collector's items or would have been used in play. However, the dolls clearly communicate contemporary ideas of class and of race. Dolls do generally seem to have belonged to girls, and few boys admit to playing with them. Booker, predictably, 'loathed' dolls.[95] But many girls built emotional worlds around them. *A Book with Seven Seals* recalls Mary Ann's joy on being given a doll.[96] Brothers could intervene in doll play and manipulate their sisters' belief in their dolls. Mary Carbery remembers how two boys who were staying with the family buried her doll and her

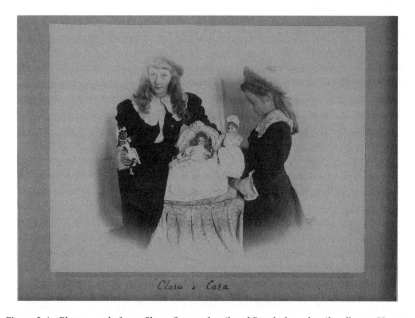

Figure 5.4 Photograph from Shaw Storey family of Bursledon, family album, Hampshire Record Office, 58A01/1.

'frantic' response when she heard that it was buried.[97] Parents could also intervene. Mary Paley Marshall tells of how her religious father burned their dolls, believing that the children had begun to treat them as idols.[98] Dolls could also be confiscated as punishment.[99] But the relationships between girls and dolls were also a source of strength. Doll play allowed the creation of a secret world ordered by the girls in which they could play out their fantasies. To a certain extent doll play did imitate life, but girls did not necessarily chose the conventional female roles that dolls were thought to encourage. A fascinating example of this is Carbery's detailed account of her doll play with her sister. The girls played at being mothers, but they chose to adopt the role of widows, giving them the power to punish and discipline their children in an accepted role, yet avoiding subjection to male authority.[100]

By exploring domestic space and material culture, this chapter has shown new ways in which domestic authorities were constructed and exercised in the nineteenth-century middle-class home. Historians have scrutinised nineteenth-century fatherhood and motherhood, generating a spectrum of parental authorities that reveals a diverse range of experiences. But an examination of the exercise of these authorities in domestic space reveals that nineteenth-century middle-class families shared distinctive spatial practices that had important consequences for family relations.

The nursery system was a common feature in middle-class homes where there were young children. The nursery was clearly defined, spatially and materially. It restricted children's movements and taught them their first ideas of moral order and social identity. Most importantly, however, the nursery separated children from adult spaces in the middle-class home. Controlled entry into adult spaces reinforced the authority of adults over children in the home, creating both intimacies and distances between parents and children. Domestic space enables us to see how the family operates as a whole, rather than focusing on a single relationship. The father shielding his daughter in the study might be a response to an over-dominant mother; the child privileged by access to professional or personal spaces of fatherhood could generate sibling rivalry. There are many examples of fathers and mothers allowing some children but not others into their personal spaces. Such spatial practices magnified favouritism within the family, cementing intimacies with favoured pets and furthering ruptures with disaffected progeny. Domestic authority was also communicated more subtly, through the material culture of gender that often suffused parents' personal spaces, and in spaces where servants held sway. Many children were inspired by the gilded femininity of their mother's chamber or the exotic orientalism of their father's smoking room, and worked these ideas into their own sense of gendered identity. Not every child was influenced in this way, however: the ever recalcitrant Booker positively rebelling against the cloying femininity of her mother's personal space.

Spatial practices also reveal the limits of parental authority in the home: as space was divided between parents, servants and children, children and servants often met beyond parental eyes. Children might have secret knowledge of servant assignations, and vice versa. Behaviour that would have been unacceptable in the drawing room could be indulged in the kitchen. Of course, such experience was influenced by the extent of servant presence in the home: the experience of lower middle-class children in homes with one or no servants was very different to that of upper middle-class children in homes with five or six servants. While the inferior spaces designated to the servants and their dark and unknown quality provided many children with their first notions of class, the extreme spatial closeness of the nanny and the loving relationship this often created could mitigate a child's sense of difference between itself and the 'lower' orders. Finally, perhaps the most interesting spaces are those in which children escaped adult supervision and played out their own versions of nineteenth-century domestic authority. Wider spaces in the home were transformed through the imagination and through the material culture of childhood. Here the early foundations of sibling relationships were laid, early rivalries established. Although the toys given to children clearly carried the gendered values of a patriarchal adult world, the way in which toys were used in play did not always reflect these ideals. The study of domestic space shows us how domestic authority was lived out in practice, and sharpens our awareness of its definition and limitations.

Notes

1. B. Lee Booker (1937) *Yesterday's Child 1890–1909* (London: Long), p. 72.
2. D. Roberts (1978) 'The Paterfamilias of the Victorian Governing Classes' in A. S. Wohl (ed.) *The Victorian Family: Structure and Stresses* (London: Croom Helm), p. 59.
3. L. Davidoff and C. Hall (1987), *Family Fortunes: Men and Women of the English Middle Class 1780–1850* (London: Hutchinson), p. 329.
4. J. Tosh (1999) *A Man's Place: Masculinity and the Middle-Class Home in Victorian England* (New Haven and London: Yale University Press), p. 195. For recent confirmation of this position, see E. Gordon and G. Nair (2003) *Public Lives: Women, Family and Society in Victorian Britain* (New Haven and London: Yale University Press), p. 63.
5. Ibid., p. 145.
6. N. Tadmor (2000) *Family and Friends in Eighteenth-Century England: Household, Kinship and Patronage* (Cambridge: Cambridge University Press).
7. There has been little work on the British material culture of childhood, but studies of American material culture suggest that this is a potentially fruitful field of research. See K. Calvert (1992) *Children in the House: The Material Culture of Early Childhood 1600–1900* (Boston: North Eastern University Press); and M. Formanek-Brunell (1993) *Made to Play House: Dolls and the Commercialisation of American Girlhood 1830–1930* (New Haven and London: Yale University Press).

 8. L. Davidoff, M. Doolittle, J. Fink and K. Holden (1999) *The Family Story: Blood, Contract and Intimacy* (Harlow: Longman), p. 13.
 9. Gordon and Nair, *Public Lives*, p. 46.
10. T. McBride (1978) ' "As the Twig is Bent": The Victorian Nanny' in *The Victorian Family: Structure and Stresses*, p. 53.
11. T. Meldrum (2000) *Domestic Service and Gender 1660–1750: Life and Work in the London Household* (Harlow: Longman). T. McBride (1976) *The Domestic Revolution: The Modernisation of Household Service in England and France 1820–1920* (London: Croom Helm) is currently the fullest available survey for nineteenth-century Britain. See also Judy Giles' discussion in this volume (Chapter 9) of the emotional texture and spatial organisation of twentieth-century domestic service.
12. Leonore Davidoff (2005) 'Kinship as a Categorical Concept: A Case Study of Nineteenth Century English Siblings,' *Journal of Social History*, 39: 411–428.
13. H. Hendrick (1997) *Children, Childhood and English Society 1880–1990* (Cambridge: Cambridge University Press), p. 3.
14. M. Freeman (1993) *Rewriting the Self: History, Memory, Narrative* (London: Routledge), pp. 51–2.
15. D. B. Montefiore (1927) *From a Victorian to a Modern* (London: E. Archer), p. 18.
16. For a full discussion of the merits of autobiography as a source in relation to current historiographical practice, see J. P. Roos (1994) 'The True Life Revisited: Autobiography and Referentiality after the "Posts",' *Auto/Biography*, 3(1): 1–16. For a consideration of the construction of accounts of childhood in autobiography, see R. N. Coe (1984) *When the Grass was Taller: Autobiography and the Experience of Childhood* (New Haven and London: Yale University Press), passim.
17. K. Flint (1993) *The Woman Reader 1837–1914* (Oxford: Oxford University Press), pp. 187–249.
18. A. Adams (1996) *Architecture in the Family Way: Doctors, Houses and Women 1870–1900* (Montreal and London: McGill University Press), p. 138.
19. For images of the nursery before 1850, see P. Thornton (1984) *Authentic Décor: The Domestic Interior 1620–1920* (London: Wiedenfield and Nicholson), p. 205; C. Saumarez Smith (1993) *Eighteenth-Century Decoration: Design and the Domestic Interior in England* (London: Wiedenfield and Nicholson), p. 325; C. Gere (1989) *Nineteenth-Century Decoration: The Art of the Interior* (London: Wiedenfield and Nicholson), p. 168.
20. C. White (1984) *The World of the Nursery* (London: Herbert), p. 60.
21. J. Franklin (1981) *The Gentleman's Country House and Its Plan 1835–1914* (London: Routledge and Kegan Paul), p. 80.
22. J. Hamlett, Geffrye Museum Report 3, July 2004.
23. This is not an indication that the other homes did not contain nurseries. It may simply be because writers chose to describe other spaces in the home.
24. Sixty-two percent of the accounts from the period 1850–1859 mentioned a nursery, 45 percent from the following decade and roughly 50 percent of the accounts from the following periods with the exception of the period 1880–1889, which mentioned slightly fewer.
25. E. Thomas (1938) *The Childhood of Edward Thomas: A Fragment of Autobiography* (London: Faber); M. V. Hughes (1991) *A London Family 1870–1900* (Oxford: Oxford University Press); L. Knight (1965) *The Magic of a Line: The Autobiography of Laura Knight* (London: William Kimber).
26. McBride, ' "As the twig is bent",' p. 45.

27. J. J. Stevenson (1880) *House Architecture* (London: Macmillan), Vol. 2, p. 70.
28. W. A. Darlington (1947) *I Do What I Like* (London: MacDonald & Co.), p. 27.
29. S. Keppel (1958) *Edwardian Daughter* (London: Arrow Books), p. 8.
30. M. Carbery (1941) *Happy World: The Story of a Victorian Childhood* (London: Longmans & Co.), p. 30.
31. Montefiore, *From a Victorian to a Modern*, p. 12.
32. White, *The World of the Nursery*, p. 48.
33. A. M. Douton (1974) *A Book with Seven Seals: A Victorian Childhood* (London: Chatto and Windus), p. 52.
34. R. Graves (1929) *Goodbye to All That: An Autobiography* (London: Jonathan Cape), p. 28.
35. F. Kendon (1930) *The Small Years* (Cambridge: Cambridge University Press), p. 60.
36. A. C. Deane (1945) *Time Remembered* (London: Faber & Faber), p. 8.
37. Booker, *Yesterday's Child*, p. 46.
38. Montefiore, *From a Victorian to a Modern*, p. 12.
39. Booker, *Yesterday's Child*, p. 72.
40. Ibid.
41. Tosh, *A Man's Place*, p. 60.
42. Carola Oman (1976) *An Oxford Childhood* (London: Hodder and Stoughton), p. 113.
43. N. Streatfield (1963) *A Vicarage Family* (London: Collins), p. 10.
44. Douton, *A Book with Seven Seals*, p. 196.
45. Olive Haweis (1939) *Four to Fourteen* (London: Robert Hale), pp. 26–7.
46. J. Marriott (1946) *Memories of Four Score Years: The Autobiography of the late Sir John Marriott* (London: Blackie & Sons), p. 16; E. Parry (1932) *My Own Way: An Autobiography* (London: Cassell & Co.), p. 31.
47. C. Leighton (1948) *Tempestuous Petticoat: The Story of an Invincible Victorian* (London: Victor Gollancz), p. 13.
48. H. Collins (1941) *My Best Riches: Story of a Stone Rolling Round the World and the Stage* (London: Eyre and Spottiswood), p. 33.
49. O. Berkeley Hill (1939) *All Too Human: An Unconventional Autobiography* (London: Peter Davies), p. 3; W. Leaf (1932) *Walter Leaf 1852–1927 Some Chapters of Autobiography, With a Memoir by C. M. Leaf* (London: John Murray), p. 20.
50. Booker, *Yesterday's Child*, p. 63.
51. B. Lunn (1948) *Switchback* (London: Eyre and Spottiswood), p. 21.
52. H. J. Jennings (1902) *Our Homes, and How to Beautify Them* (London: Harrison and Sons), p. 173.
53. Keppel, *Edwardian Daughter*, p. 13.
54. Ibid.
55. Leighton, *Tempestuous Petticoat*, p. 182.
56. Ibid., pp. 71–2.
57. L. W. Brown (1933) *Suivez Raison and I.T. or a Chap's Chequered Career An Autobiography* (London: Watts & Co.), p. 10.
58. H. Nicholson (1941) *Half My Days and Nights* (William Heinemann, London), p. 12.
59. T. Beecham (1944) *A Mingled Chime: Leaves from an Autobiography* (London: Hutchinson & Co.), p. 9.
60. McBride, *The Domestic Revolution*, pp. 19–20.

61. C. H. Reilly (1938) *Scaffolding in the Sky: A Semi-Architectural Autobiography* (London: Routledge & Sons), p. 6.
62. Leighton, *Tempestuous Petticoat*, p. 59.
63. *Four to Fourteen*, p. 99.
64. Ibid., p. 100.
65. Douton, *A Book with Seven Seals*, pp. 82–3.
66. H. J. Bruce (1946) *Silken Dalliance* (London: Constable), pp. 11–12.
67. In later childhood the nanny might be replaced by a governess. For a full account, see K. Hughes (1993) *The Victorian Governess* (London: Hambledon), passim.
68. J. Gathorne-Hardy (1993) *The Rise and Fall of the British Nanny* (London: Hodder and Stoughton), p. 20.
69. McBride, ' "As the twig is bent",' pp. 49–50.
70. P. Robertson (1991) 'Home as Nest: Middle Class Childhood in Nineteenth-Century Europe' in L. de Mause (ed.) *The History of Childhood: The Untold Story of Child Abuse* (London: Bellew), p. 424.
71. Douton, *A Book with Seven Seals*, p. 20; Carbery, *Happy World*, p. 39.
72. M. Cholmondeley (1918) *Under One Roof: A Family Record* (London: John Murray), p. 58.
73. Haweis, *Four to Fourteen*, p. 79.
74. H. Redwood (1948) *Bristol Fashion* (London: Latimer House), p. 21.
75. Booker, *Yesterday's Child*, p. 23.
76. Ibid., p. 27.
77. Carbery. *Happy World*, pp. 192–93.
78. McBride, ' "As the twig is bent",' p. 53.
79. Cholmondeley, *Under One Roof*, p. 61.
80. Ibid.,
81. Booker, *Yesterday's Child*, p. 80.
82. Hughes, *A London Family*, p. 4.
83. Ibid.
84. Booker, *Yesterday's Child*, p. 44.
85. Hughes, *A London Family*, p. 39.
86. L. Powys (1937) *The Joy of It* (London: Chapman and Hall), p. 35.
87. References to boys collecting include A. A. Milne, *It's Too Late Now: The Autobiography of a Writer* (London: Methuen & Co.), p. 43; Edward Thomas (1938) *The Childhood of Edward Thomas: A Fragment of Autobiography* (London: Faber and Faber), p. 96; D. Munro (1941) *It Passed Too Quickly: An Autobiography* (London: Methuen & Sons), p. 21.
88. E. L. Grant Watson (1946) *But To What Purpose: The Autobiography of a Contemporary* (London: Cresset Press), p. 10. Also see P. Neame (1947) *Playing with Strife: The Autobiography of a Soldier* (London: George G. Harrop & Co.), p. 16; O. Lodge (1931) *Past Years: An Autobiography* (London: Hodder and Stoughton), p. 32.
89. M. B. Reckitt (1941) *As It Happened: An Autobiography* (London: J.M. Dent & Sons), p. 11.
90. M. Paley Marshall (1947) *What I Remember* (Cambridge: Cambridge University Press), p. 1.
91. Oman, *An Oxford Childhood*, p. 113.
92. Booker, *Yesterday's Child*, p. 44.
93. Davidoff and Hall, *Family Fortunes*, p. 344.

94. W. H. Cremer Junior (1873) *The Toys of Little Folks of All Ages and Countries or the Toy Kingdom* (London: W. H. Cremer Jun.), p. 50.
95. Booker, *Yesterday's Child*, p. 20.
96. Douton, *A Book with Seven Seals*, p. 52.
97. Carbery, *Happy World*, p. 23.
98. Marshall, *What I Remember*, p. 5.
99. Carbery, *Happy World*, p. 192.
100. Ibid., p. 129.

6
Love and Authority in Mid-Twentieth-Century Marriages: Sharing and Caring

Simon Szreter and Kate Fisher

Introduction

This chapter explores oral history evidence as a basis to discuss how the gendered politics of domestic authority were perceived as central to the contested meanings of love in marriage among both middle- and working-classes during the middle decades of the twentieth century. The oral history evidence comes from a set of interviews conducted by the two authors in Blackburn, Lancashire, and in Harpenden, Hertfordshire, as part of a project primarily addressing sexuality and birth control in marriage among the generation born during the first three decades of the twentieth century. These two locations were chosen as representing contrasting northern, working-class and affluent, southern middle-class communities. Working-class and middle-class persons of each sex were interviewed in both locations. The great majority of interviewees had married during either the 1930s or the 1940s (for further details, see the Appendix at the end of the chapter).

What did love mean to the respondents in the context of their marriages? Interviewees were asked about what, in their opinion, made for happy and unhappy marriages, good and bad husbands and wives, and what, in their personal experience, had been good and bad about their own marriages.

During the course of the respondents' lifetimes, the themes of love, marriage and sex have all, of course, been the subject of intense intellectual, academic and public, mass media debate. It is generally agreed that there have been extremely significant social and cultural changes in the course of the twentieth century. Indeed, there is something of a consensus that from the late nineteenth century through to the mid-twentieth century there occurred the rise of the 'companionate marriage' as ideal and then practice.[1] Championship of the companionate ideal initially took the form of an ideological reaction to Victorian patriarchy among progressive and radical sections of the elite and then became an evangelising social movement during the interwar and immediate postwar decades, when middle-class sexologists, pioneering marriage and sex guidance counsellors, birth controllers and, eventually, even clerics and the medical profession spread the word to the lower-classes.[2] As the chapter by Alana Harris (Chapter 7) in this volume suggests, 'companionate marriage' was a complex entity, amenable to becoming a resource in both sacred and secular conceptions of marital norms. It was the Americans, Judge Ben E. Lindsey and Wainwright Evans, who are often credited with coining the term or giving it currency, as the title of their 1927 book.[3] As its most recent historian, Marcus Collins, states, 'The keywords of companionship were intimacy and equality' and, as Davidoff *et al.* have written, the companionate model 'was based upon the idea of an exclusive emotionally and sexually intimate relationship...It was a powerful ideal, which stressed the importance of romantic love, sexual attraction and mutual interests, while disguising realities of gendered inequalities of power and access to resources.'[4]

In embracing and engaging with the thesis of the rise of the companionate marriage model in Britain, c.1880–1980, historians and sociologists have endorsed a view of twentieth-century change in marriage behaviour and practice, which largely reproduces an account of the changes which the contemporary proponents of these ideals for marriage hoped to bring about. This is, perhaps, not surprising, since so much of the best, accessible sources of historical evidence with which to study the history of the family, love, sex and marriage during the twentieth century were either directly created by apologists for the companionate marriage or by those working within this self-consciously progressive intellectual agenda.[5]

The interviewees' views and recollections reflect these public debates in various ways and it would be extraordinary and a matter of methodological concern if they did not. However, the oral history testimony also provides an independent historical primary source. It affords the opportunity to explore how a number of diverse individuals, who lived through the period when the companionate marriage model was supposedly on the rise but who were not themselves public proponents of it, view these matters of central concern to their own marriages.

A crucial preliminary point that emerges from listening to the respondents is that, contrary to an implied assumption of the thesis of the rise of companionate marriage, interviewees were very aware that love has no singular meaning – it takes many different forms. However, among all these different kinds of love, there is a considerable consensus that there is one kind that is particularly important for the long-term success and happiness of a marriage. This is not the romantic excitement of 'being in love', nor does it relate directly to the quality of the sexual relationship – two aspects emphasised as important by the companionate marriage ideology. It is, rather, the prosaic, persistent process of working at love in the marriage.

This chapter focuses on exploring what respondents mean by this process of working at marital love. Most respondents believe that loving should involve sharing with the partner the emotional concerns and the joys of the marriage and the family's fortunes. This notion of sharing certainly corresponds to the two 'keywords' identified by Collins as defining the companionate model – intimacy and equality. However, the interviewees also emphasise that there is something else, just as important as 'sharing' for the success and happiness of their marriages. This is 'caring for' or 'looking after' each other and the family. As we shall see, there can be a tension between caring and sharing. In fact, trying to achieve a satisfactory practical balance between sharing and caring was for many the key to a 'loving' marriage. However, combining caring with sharing was a far from straightforward matter, with much potential for misunderstanding or dissatisfaction between spouses. There was no magic formula since it depended on the circumstances, personalities and expectations brought to each marriage. Respondents depict marriages in which a great diversity of arrangements, with respect to caring and sharing, were negotiated with varying degrees of success.

Sharing

So, first, what do respondents say about sharing? They certainly talked about the significance to them of 'sharing' and doing things together:

And what do you think is the most important thing in a good marriage?

Elizabeth   Sharing love, sharing everything, an' working together, if yer both work at it, there nothing go wrong love, . . .[6]
As I say, we done everything together. We used to do the shopping together, and whatever we done in the house we done together. And we always used to help one another whenever we could in different, different ways.[7]

Husbands who routinely handed over their wage packets to their wives – receiving something back for their own leisure – were certainly represented as good providers. But this did not necessarily amount to full sharing in the household's economic decisions. That required a husband also giving his full time and attention, as well as his income. For instance, actively sharing together in choosing how to spend the money for the family and the home:

. . . he'd give me his last ha'penny. We worked together, we put our wages together, paid our way before we did anything and then er we saved a bit, he had a bit, he used to hang back before he got any spending money you see, but that were all, all together and we used to go when we'd saved up enough and wanted something, we'd go off and, and enjoy that er that shopping, you know...[8]

Sharing shopping and consumer choices and pleasures was considered an especially important, practical locus for 'emotional sharing' by working-class respondents. Agreeing together what priorities to spend on, with what little disposable income they had, was a very significant activity. Faced with an ever-increasing range of consumer goods, which could both ease the housework burdens of the wife and improve the amenities of the home for all members of the family, such choices were also clearly understood as expressions of love and of caring for each other's needs.

Thus, Dora told a story of her husband's D-I-Y (do-it-yourself) feats which emphasised to the full how extensively he loved her by caring for her and the home in this way – making domestic improvements because of the pleasure it gave his wife, extending even, in Dora's case, to doing similar things for her mother, as well.

Dora ...when we had our cottage in Radlett, we was sitting there one morning and he said, 'You love this, don't you?' And I said, 'Oh yeah, I've always loved the cottage.' And he said, 'You wanted some beams, didn't you Dory?' And I said, Oh yeah, they'd look lovely.' So he said, 'Come on, get your coat, I'm going over to, erm, MFI, no, erm Jewson's in the village' and erm I said, 'What you going to do?' He said, 'Never mind what I'm going to do. Come on.' We got in the car and we drove to Jewson's and he walked in and he saw some Canadian, but he didn't want to put cheap beams up. He wanted them to look like good beams with the, erm, steel holding them up, you know. And big, bit nuts in it you, and he, er, erm he said, when we got them home he said, 'Help me to clear away', he said. Mind you, we always helped one another to do anything. Even we done a little bit of painting, I was always with him and he used to call me his mate really [laughs] and er, erm, we, he put these up and, er it was about one o' clock when we was finished and he sat in the dining area and he said, 'What do you think of it?' I said, 'Oh Ted [pseud], it's lovely.' And he said, 'Yeah, I think it's lovely'. So he said, 'Come on, let's get to bed.' So we run up to bed and we was up at six o'clock in the morning. [laughs] We were both sitting there, 'Ain't it lovely?' 'Yeah', he said, 'next week I'm doing it in the other room.'
...
Dora He was lovely. He was. I am not kidding you. And he kept my mum's just the same. My mum used to say to everybody, 'I've got a lovely brother-in-law, er son-in-law.' He was.[9]

In telling this story Dora emphasises how her husband not only demonstrated his caring love for her in a sharing way but also directly affirmed the importance of her own wishes and desires through discussing with her what they were doing together.

Sharing choices together over discretionary consumer spending was the point of intersection, where the female role of 'caring' for the household and improving its facilities met with the male role of providing income. Respondents such as Dora could express an almost sensual pleasure at the memory of how their shared activities with their partners in this respect could achieve a loving outcome for their family.

Eileen brought out the importance to a working-class wife and mother of this aspect of love from a partner in an inverse way. She bluntly observed that she didn't put any store by her husband's protestations of love because they only happened in bed. By contrast, he didn't consult with her over saving and spending on important consumer items, buying himself a motor bike and then a car. This forced her to go out charring to make some pocket money to be able to afford the things she wanted for the house:

Did you ever tell your husband you loved him?

Eileen   Yes! any time! 'e said 'e loved me, I didn't believe though but 'e said so.

Why didn't you believe him?

Eileen   In bed 'e used to tell me, I don't know...I don't know [pause]
...

Did you have a happy marriage?

Eileen   [pause]

What makes you wave your hand, unsurely?

Eileen   Yes and no.

Yes and no?.

Eileen   Yes and no, ya know. We, we, never fell out or anything, 'e'd only about £7 a week yer know when we married. There was five of us and of course as time went on we 'ad more, and course when 'e went to Thews [the name of an employer in the Blackburn area] it got more. I didn't get 'is wage then, so I went on, I went on 'ome 'elp, cos I'd no money and I kept me wage to meself, so I used to buy little ornaments and things for the 'ouse and all sorts of things...yeah, 'e bought a car...'e 'ad a motor bike at first.[10]

As this extract exemplifies, while many individuals valued sharing as an important aspect of love in marriage, concern for sharing was, however, also something which could cause much dispute and conflict. Respondents did not necessarily get from their partners the degree of sharing that they wanted, nor did they necessarily agree over what was to be shared and how.

There were a number of potential pressure points, where the idea of sharing could create tensions and disputes. First, sharing the task of income-earning for the household, for instance. Husbands could be very sensitive about their wives expressing an interest in going out to work, as a possible affront to their pride and manhood and as putting them in the improper position of 'having to make their own tea':

> *Sarah* ...this was my husband's idea, if his mother didn't work, I shouldn't work, see? [chuckle] That was my husband's idea.
>
> ...
>
> *So did you ever have arguments about your work?*
>
> *Sarah* Oh yes, he didn't like me working, oh, he didn't like me working.... 'I'm not going out to work and coming home, making my own tea!', uh, that sort of a thing. 'My mother never went out!'[11]

A second common point of tension, especially for working-class couples, focused around the use of the husband's earned income and whether or not this was put entirely at the disposal of both partners for their shared and equal deliberation on how to spend it (as also exemplified in the extract from Eileen, above):

> if you tucked anything in your back pocket you were robbing the family, you see, you know. But I were more or less I think a home loving. If I got a woman I I kept her, like you know, I looked after her.[12]

Another aspect of this was the extent to which husbands did or did not go to the pub or club on their own and whether they used a part of the family's precious income on their own personal leisure activities. This certainly appears repeatedly as a major issue among most female and male working-class interviewees, both those drawn from the north in Blackburn and from the south in Hertfordshire or London. Ed, who was born in Blackburn but worked in the south and in London during the 1930s in the early years of his marriage before returning to his home town, drew a distinction in these terms between himself and men who hadn't adjusted to marriage and were still trying to live the life of a single man:

> *Ed* They were fond of their beer too much, neglected their homes.
>
> *In what way, what, neglected in what way?*
>
> *Ed* Well, they'd spend their money on beer and the rest on theirself. *Yeah.*
>
> *Ed* And didn't give it to the'r home. Wanted to live a life of their, a single man, then they couldn't do it, you can't do it if your married, can you?[13]

For many wives this was such a bone of contention because a husband who spent too much money and time on his beer and cigarettes in the pub was also simultaneously stepping heavily on a third highly sensitive area of contention, which was the extent to which the couple shared any leisure time together.

> *So when your husband was in the pub a lot of the time, did you ever consider leaving him?*
>
> Pam   [pause] No. I went once to the pub, opened the door, and see him sitting surrounded with other fellas and they're singing their heads off, and I just come out and shut the door, I didn't think much to that.
> . . .
> Pam   And I thought that's the life he likes, he liked that life best, yeah he did. He never got married, not really. [pause][14]

However, it was certainly not the case, as in the simplistic version of the companionate model, that very many respondents expressed the wish to share intimately all their thoughts and activities together. There were in fact just two middle-class respondents who happily presented their marriage as having been quite dominated by an equal and shared mutual interest in something with their partner, which was exclusionary of all others, even their children. In one case, opera was the focus of the couple's passion;[15] and in the other case, it was their sexual relationship with each other.[16]

Equally, there were one or two working-class respondents who articulated a similar view that an ideal married life meant social exclusiveness for the couple concerned:

> *so what was really good about your marriage?*
>
> Marian   We . . . both talked things over together and we both, all, we never went out without, he, he, he wouldn't go out, he, we never had no mates, we always went out together and the only time he went out when he went to library, he liked reading, he were a good reader and he liked, he used to go library for books, but he weren't ever so long before he come back. . . . and if, if he fancied a drink he'd have one in house, he wouldn't go for a drink with hiself in pub . . .

But this testimony was unusual. What most middle-class and working-class respondents said they wanted in relation to their partner and their leisure activities was not exclusiveness but a balance of enjoying some interests and pursuits together – especially those related closely to children and family life – along with some personal freedom and independence.

So what do you think is the most important thing in a happy marriage?

Hugh   Give and take . . .

. . .

Angela   We don't like to be apart.

. . .

Angela . . .   But I belong to different things and he does, you know, we're not, sort of, not doing anything, we have a good variety of friends and family, of course, yes.

. . .

Angela   Having lots of friends, having different interests, not being selfish . . .[17] Mostly we went out together but um when er when he was in different concert parties, he was in some that I wasn't in, he'd go to them. He er he would join the choir, that was right, at the church, well, I wasn't in the choir so he'd have one night out a week at the choir practice, you see. There were things like that . . .[18]

Indeed, the importance of some balancing individual autonomy and freedom within the marriage relationship was expressed whimsically by Emily:

What is it you miss about married life?

Emily   Oh, the companionship.

And what are the advantages of not being married?

Emily   Well you can please yourself, huh, yeah [pause] ya haven't to ask.[19]

One of the complaints from a number of female respondents was that they had to do more than 'ask' – they felt their husbands had spoiled their experience of 'sharing' because of a claustrophobic possessiveness, which had been too insistent on exclusive 'togetherness':

Marilyn   Well when we went away on holiday I hadn't to speak or be friendly wi' anybody else that were in hotel um he er he used to say 'Come on' like he wouldn't' bother with anybody else, like he were, he were such a jealous somehow.[20]

At first glance, confirmation in the oral testimony of an emphasis on the importance for love of sharing as an ideal may appear to look like a simple confirmation of the validity of the rise of companionate marriage thesis. However, what many respondents say is that the aspiration of sharing was also the source of dynamic tension and of difficulties in their marriages. A number of respondents affirm that they wanted to share and saw this as important for love but also that this could cause dispute and conflict, misunderstanding and disappointment.

Caring

If we now turn to examine what respondents say about love in marriage as 'caring', 'providing' and 'looking after' each other, we can begin to see how these values could be at variance sometimes with those of 'sharing'. Although respondents talked a lot about the desirability of sharing and many valued doing things together and talking to each other, this does not mean that they shunned or rejected a marriage model of segregated and distinctive gender roles and sought instead one in which everything was shared and discussed together. The aspiration to share was balanced against an appreciation that the realities of most marriages required husbands and wives to each perform to the best of their abilities quite different and specialised roles. The tension between sharing and not sharing in marriage was resolved for many by representing what a husband and wife each separately contributed and took responsibility for in the marriage as a matter of 'caring for' or 'looking after' each other – what they each separately provided for the family and its needs. All recognised that it was of great importance that each spouse satisfactorily provided for the family in the highly gendered way which was the conventional norm for men and women. It was important that a husband was dependable in bringing in the family's income:

> *Catherine* My husband, I don't think he did much, he might have changed the odd nappy but he wasn't the most domesticated of men, you know [laughs]. He kept working and bringing in enough money to feed us, that's right,...[21]

Wives, correspondingly, were deemed to exhibit their caring contribution primarily as good home-makers, looking after the family home and nurturing the children:

> *And what do you think is important in a good mother?*
>
> *Clare* Looking after the children and cooking for 'em and washing fer'em.[22]
>
> *And what's the most important thing to make you a good wife?*
>
> *Maud* I don't know, I suppose looking after them and eh, ya know, all the work and keep the house clean and tidy and the cooking an' all that, looking after them really.[23]
>
> ..... *what do you think makes a, makes for a good wife?*
>
> *Ed* She's got to be a good housekeeper, hasn't she. Good cook, understand you, I don't know what else I could say....
>
> ...
>
> *Ed* Oh aye, yeah...love of children I should say.[24]

In normal circumstances, with both partners alive and healthy, how to combine these highly distinctive, gendered roles with the desirability of sharing as equals constitutes a central, unstable dynamic and focus of contention in the meaning of love in marriage for most respondents. Neither male nor female respondents were comfortable with the subversion of their conventional, gendered 'providing' role or with conceding control over it to the other partner.

It required a concession on the part of the husband over something in his control – the income from his job – in order for genuine sharing of spending and saving to occur. This was much appreciated by wives as symbolising both sharing and caring when husbands did offer this concession; and it could be resented when they didn't, as we have seen.

Equally, female respondents could be quite protective of their own area of jurisdiction. Managing the children in the household on a daily basis was usually acknowledged to be a mother's principal area of responsibility, which a husband respected if for no other reason than that a hard-working husband was out of the house for many hours of the day, no matter how much he was considered a loving father:

Dora Ted left it to me. Ted said, 'I'll leave it to you because I'm not here'.[25]

Real, full involvement and emotional sharing of all aspects of children's upbringing by the husband required a significant concession from the wife in an area of her recognised control. Women didn't necessarily want such 'interference', as Maria described it:

What about bringing up your daughter, did, what did, what was his role in that?

Maria Oh, he never interfered a lot, not with bringing Jane [pseud] up. No, he wasn't a kind of a strict man.[26]

Penny, for instance, was very careful to manage her partner's contribution to the childcare:

You were the disciplinarian?

Penny Yes.

. . .

Peggy Day in and day out. I was, they they were my, that that was my job. And and I thought well, I'm with them and I know what they can do and what they can't do. Um, and I know what I can give them and what I couldn't give them so um, and I didn't want him saying oh no, you're not going to do that, you can't do that, you know and then there'd be er, mummy, daddy daddy won't let us do this and there'd be trouble that way so in that respect I was the boss then.

...

Why didn't you want him disciplining them?

Penny   Because I thought he him, er, he would er, he would be heavy, too heavy-handed, if he hit them or something. Um, when we started having, when we were having the children, we [made] an agreement, you know, when they were old enough to be smacked, I said to him, um, how I want it to happen.

...

Penny   And it it it did work, um...

So he was, he carried that deal out?

Penny   Oh yes, yes, oh yes...[27]

For Penny, as for many mothers, as regards the children, 'I was the boss'; and she saw it as one of the most important things in her marriage that 'as far as the children were concerned, he agreed with... how I wanted to bring them up.'[28]

Despite the well-rehearsed feminist ideological denunciation of housework as an unpaid exploitative chore, respondents did not necessarily subscribe to this view. Indeed, some expressed quite the diametrically opposite view:

Lyn   Well, I've told [you] I loved doing the housework, which I did.[29]

Many female respondents proudly portrayed the burdens and responsibilities of such caring work which they discharged for their families and partners as integral to their own positive power and authority within the marriage relationship. Women do not necessarily see themselves in a dependent position as mere unpaid 'carers'. Caring is a very positive concept, closely related to love. Caring was used by women to express and assert their personal power and authority over their children, over child-rearing and over their husband.

And what do you think is the most important thing to be a good wife?

Elizabeth   Well, looking after 'im, yer know, cookin' fer 'em, and showing that yer care, yer know, yeah, I do love, and 'e knows that anyhow, don't yer love?

Peter   Yeah.[30]

Pride in their own capacity to care and to love matched that of a husband's pride in his breadwinning. Women did not want others caring for their loved ones, just as men didn't want anybody helping them to earn the family's income. Women could be intensely competitive in this respect towards other women:

> Penny I just wanted to to get married to look after him. Umm.
>
> Penny I, I thought I could have looked after him better than, you know, than his mother, his mother was looking after him. I mean that's, that's what you, what you always hope. I could cook, his mother couldn't cook. I mean if she boiled water she'd let it burn.[31]

Loving as 'caring' work done for husbands and children is not just drudgery for women but also constitutes their proud identity and, with it, their primary claims to power and authority, not just in practical matters in the home but much more widely. Significantly, it was one of the male interviewees who expressed, in a most telling way, the kind of high status and authority that he considered to be due to a good wife and mother because of the emotional caring work which was such a central part of female loving in marriage:

> Alf This is how it should be I think. After all, I've always said I've always said that the, the main thing about a, any family in my opinion is not, not so much the bloke who's supposed to be the breadwinner. It's not, it's the mum, it's the mother. She's the figurehead of that family, I don't care what anybody says...
>
> Heather Mm
>
> Alf ...no matter how good the bloke is and how clever he is, might be bringing the money in. A kingpin is, if the kids get hurt at school they, they come running, you know, they don't go running for their dad. In the Army with blokes that were grovelling on the ground, they're being shelled, they don't ask for their dad they're calling out for their mum. Always, it's always the same.
>
> Heather Oh yeah.
>
> Alf That's why I think [?] that's what it all bases down to.
>
> Heather Oh yeah.
>
> Alf And if you get a relationship like that, it's nothing better, I don't think, it's marvellous.[32]

And Dennis from Harpenden concurred:

> *Did you ever have differences of opinion on how to bring the children up?*
>
> Dennis No! No! There again we were one, two as one, I mean I acknowledged that Angie [pseudo] was the er most essential...
>
> ...

... she was the main stay of the home I mean, er I gave her my wages and she, she got a tin and she put so much in each one as she had it and then what was left over, she'd do with as she wishes.[33]

Consequently, female interviewees did not necessarily want a 'domesticated' man for a husband, and were often quite happy to acknowledge that their husband was not at all domesticated:

Did you ever want your husband to do more work in the house?

Elma   No, no. That's something I never asked. No, I don't believe in a man being a slave in the house, no.[34]

When women said they would have appreciated more help around the house or commented negatively on how little their husbands did, they did not want husbands to do this in place of their primary role as breadwinners. Nor did they want husbands who would encroach on their domestic authority. They wanted some handy assistance, on their own terms. Lorna described approvingly how careful her partner was to defer to her greater talents in the household, when giving her some assistance:

Lorna   I did all the housework – he never. He would when he was on shift work and I was working. He'd er, especially when it was er 2 till 10, he, he tried to do, he'd do the housework, and he said to me 'Do you know, you know cock, it neither looks like it's been done like you do it when I do it'. But he'd er he'd done it, and I were pleased he'd done it. And he had to mention it, you know, well 'It'll have to do... [until] you've done it, it'll have to do till next time round.' But he did try, we, we did actually pull together which you must do.[35]

Taking care of the garden and D-I-Y were the two commonly 'sub-let', self-contained areas of domestic work, where men's input was typically allowed, expected and appreciated, relieving his wife of a set of responsibilities in these demarcated areas of physical work.

Was there anything he would do around the house?

Kathleen   Well, he'd do all the decorating, um. Didn't ever have to worry about that, I never used to say, 'oh, I wish you'd do it', he did it, that was that. And he did the gardening, and um, I never did really any gardening...' Cos we had a big garden over there.[36]

So in the home what were your husband's duties?

Maud Well, e's help with anything, but e did all the paint and decorating and everything like that and all the gardening, so I think that was enough.[37]

For many female respondents these two areas were 'enough' in two senses. They were seen as a fair contribution; and they did not amount to any encroachment on a wife's authority and control over the rest of the home and over the children.

Thus, the difficult art of combining caring with sharing was at the core of what respondents say about working at love in the context of marriage. It was something that they represent as having been subject to much negotiation, adaptation and conflict along the way.

It was because the health of a loving marriage was perceived by respondents as intimately related to the balanced ecology of reciprocal roles, combining husband's primary earning contribution and wife's practical household management, that periods of male unemployment (such as the periods of short time experienced in Blackburn in the 1920s and 1930s) could be recalled as especially disruptive, not simply of the family's standard of living, but – very revealingly – of the loving relationship itself:

Sarah ...we were on three days a week for years we were on three days a week, he was on three days a week. I did all my own sewing, all [chuckle] my own everything, and uh, I learned how to manage my money, the hard way, I really did, and love nearly went out of the window, because [chuckle] money is really, its, its, um, its the centre of everything, if you haven't got it,...[38]

This was the same respondent whose 'husband's idea [was] if his mother didn't work, I shouldn't work'. The husband's short-time was perceived as generating such serious problems, not just in the family's finances, but in the loving relationship, because the normal balance of caring and power broke down, with the husband's identity as provider challenged by his inability to provide an adequate flow of money, while the wife continued to struggle with all her caring duties, though with far less money to manage on.

Now you say, there was a stage at which love went out the window, tell me about that.

Sarah Well, you know, you never had any money. You never had any money, you never did, you couldn't do anything, and...I had my two children...your money was spoken-for before you got it...on three days a week, oh [sigh]. And there was no [chuckle], no social...couldn't go there for that, and if you didn't have it in your purse, you didn't have it and you did without. [pause] Yeah, what can I say about it? You had rows, you had rows, something and nothing, because you were tensed up all the time...[39]

It would have taken exceptional resources of sympathy and communication between the spouses to cope with this relentless pressure on their living standards and the disruption to their normal roles and identities. Wives like Sarah found that, even with husbands who they felt, overall, were good partners and with whom they could be amicable in their later lives, they were too tensed up to both talk over and share the burdens when they were under such chronic strains:

Sarah   ...my house keeping money didn't stretch to what it should, what I, I, wanted it, uh, I just had to do without. And its, its, awful doing without, you know, when you've not got two ha'pennies to rub together, it really is.

...

I, I, I was irritable, very short-tempered, just a short fuse. And uh, I couldn't, I couldn't tell him as I hadn't any money, I couldn't, you know, I couldn't have. It was just something I, I, I couldn't, I couldn't approach him about money. [pause] But uh, he was, he was um, [pause] basically a, a good man. [pause] [sigh] And a clever chap who, um, who should have been, should have been better off than he was.[40]

...

And why did you think that leaving would help?

Sarah   It didn't help, I knew, I knew jolly well it wouldn't help, I had {chuckle} enough sense for that {giggle}. I knew it wouldn't help. No, it uh, {chuckle} it was just, [pause] lack of understanding, lack of communication.

So you felt that he wasn't, that he didn't understand?

Sarah   [pause] He didn't, never wanted to talk. He never, he never wanted to talk, ...don't want to know, no, he wouldn't talk, no he wouldn't, and, I, I suppose I didn't help either. But we were quite amicable, in our later years you know, we, we sort of settled down and uh, uh forgot about all those, all the rows that we used {giggle} to have.

So what was it that made you unhappy in the earlier days?

Sarah   Lack of money. Lack of money.

And what was it about him that made you cross?

Sarah   Didn't want to know, ...he left it to me

For the middle-classes, inadequacy of the husband in performing his primary role as income-earner could also be a major issue;

Gay... there were a lot of rows about money umm well I suppose not rows, me complaining about umm

So what would happen in these rows?

Gay {sighs} he'd borrow from his father {pause} and his father kept a little book, he used to put down all the money he lent him, God...oh! it was terrible [pause]

...

Oh dear, it was dreadful but anyway, I stuck it for eighteen, no seventeen years, and umm, oh dear, he had, if I tell you that he had twenty three jobs in the eighteen years we were together, umm, I never knew from one minute to the next y'know if he'd be out of a job or not.[41]

Where a middle-class husband fell down on this primary income-providing role, it was equally likely to be interpreted as a failure in the loving relationship by both sides, not simply as a financial inconvenience:

Pru Um, I regretted, now this I shouldn't really be saying I suppose but I regretted marrying my husband almost before we were, we were on our honeymoon because I found he'd been borrowing money from my relations.[42]

Pru's husband's lack of probity with money ultimately resulted in suspension from his employment as a bank official. His public fall from grace and loss of social identity as a male breadwinner produced a form of emasculation. A marriage, in which sexual expression and mutual satisfaction had never previously been a problem now became a marriage without sex or love.

And how did the relationship with your husband, as it got worse, how did that affect your sex life with your husband?

Pru No, it completely stopped. We didn't h...have any more.

And when did it completely stop?

Pru Well, after all this business, he'd been embezzling his mother's money.

So, was that, was it your decision to stop, or was it his, was it mutual?

Pru I don't know, I didn't have the chance. He was a person that used to, if, if he was in trouble he'd go to bed. He was a bit odd like that.

And what about many years after the um all this this scandal with his mother's money, did you, did your sex life resume again or did it stop then forever?

Pru Stopped all together.

And how did you feel about that?

Pru   Well, we were just, I tried, I tried to be pleasant and that but he didn't give me the chance, he was just as, because don't forget, you see he was in an awkward position, he was suspended from the bank.

Umm. And what about, what about years after that, what about when you, when the children had left home and things like that, did things change?

Pru   Um, no, I don't think there was any change.[43]

In both working-class Sarah's and middle-class Pru's cases, the sense that she and her husband had failed to share the burden of their predicament was an upsetting aspect of the memory of the difficulties in the relationship. In one case 'he wouldn't talk' and 'left it to me' and, in the other, 'he just went to bed'.

Genuinely, egalitarian sharing of roles was not in fact an explicit aim of any of the individuals interviewed, whether middle or working class. All accepted that husbands and wives performed quite distinct roles and neither side found it easy to concede ground and to have their own gender's 'traditional' area of authority and control diminished. Most respondents portrayed marriages in which sharing took place and was negotiated in the context of expectations of quite strongly polarised caring roles, according to gender.

Caring for each other quite definitely carried two meanings simultaneously. Individuals cared for their partners and families with their breadwinning and their housekeeping but it was also important that these gendered activities were interpreted as signifying their caring for each other in the emotional sense. When husbands just brought in the weekly wage and promptly disappeared down the pub or just left their wives to it in times of difficulty, this was not caring in that second, emotional sense. Respondents principally used the terms 'sharing' or 'working together' to talk about the importance of this second aspect of caring and of love in marriage. It was important to many that caring for each other in reciprocal and complementary ways was combined with a sense of sharing, while carefully respecting the other partner's domain of authority. Loving marriages involved maintaining a delicate balance of combining caring with sharing.

Conclusion

According to the thesis of the rise of companionate marriage and the mutualist ideal of 'modern love', the first half of the twentieth century, culminating in the 1960s and 1970s, witnessed a profound cultural reaction against a previous dominant model, the Victorian patriarchal marriage of 'separate spheres', with its highly gendered marriage roles of independent, male breadwinner and dependent, domesticated female carer. It is certainly possible to see the oral history evidence as providing general support for the thesis that there has been a very active debate, played out not only by ideologists but also in ordinary people's aspirations and daily lives, over gendered roles in marriage and how this relates to love. The oral history testimony does not, however, support the notion of the middle-classes leading the way and the working-classes following towards an agreed single destination in which love, sex and marriage are fused in a gender-egalitarian companionate ideal. Rather, it reflects a lot of conflict and confusion around a contemporary debate over gender roles and how to combine caring with sharing for those of both classes marrying during the 1930s and 1940s.

The oral history evidence indicates that husbands and wives in this generation entertained differing notions of precisely how to achieve an arrangement which balanced caring and sharing. While there seems to have been general agreement among most interviewees that outright patriarchal authority within marriage was not desirable, and that some kind of 'sharing' was to be preferred, it was not clear to many of them how to arrange this 'sharing'. For there to be a more genuinely equal sharing and working side-by-side in marriage, it is not only men who would have to relinquish some of their authority and power, but so, too, would women. This tension and potential conflict between the long-established, highly valued and necessary gendered roles of 'providing' for the family, and the mutualist ideals of sharing together, appears as a central feature of the experience of love in marriage in these oral history interviews. Yet it is rather overlooked by the thesis of the rise of companionate marriage, which focuses primarily on sharing, implying that there is no tension between sharing and caring. It sets up a stark opposition between the supposedly segregated conjugal roles of the past, which were held still to characterise the traditional, 'patriarchal', working-classes, and the joint, shared roles of the future, pioneered by the suburban, privatised, 'egalitarian', middle-classes.[44]

The oral testimony respondents of both classes in this generation recognised that caring for each other in different and reciprocal ways, with husbands and wives bringing quite distinct capabilities and skills into a marriage, had been a very important and necessary part of their experience. How much authority a husband should still have and in relation to what; how much sharing there could be in the many practical matters of the household; and how each of these related to emotional sharing, companionship and love were all central themes of concern. It is not so much that joint roles were replacing segregated ones during the mid-twentieth century decades. Rather, most respondents, regardless of class, constructed their understanding of love in their marriages as revolving around the difficult practical problems of combining aspirations for both sharing and caring.

Marriage partners seem to have negotiated, with varying degrees of success and satisfaction, a wide diversity of arrangements for sharing responsibilities, activities and emotions. Consequently, in discussing how to achieve successful, happy and loving marriages – and what tends to wreck them – most respondents pay rather less attention to ideas of romanticised companionship and sexual love and much more to the importance of practicalities about working together, sharing aims, dividing up responsibilities fairly. This may for some have been to do with the timing of their reflections, coming towards the end of their lives when romantic love had been eclipsed by the practicalities of marriage. Nonetheless, for a generation where roles and rules were in flux and debate, achieving and maintaining agreement with each other over aims and responsibilities was a crucial practical problem. As Leonore Davidoff has observed, studying sibling households in the nineteenth century, continually 'having to negotiate who was in charge of what, could make life a constant source of frustration'.[45]

As to the key term, 'companionship' itself, it is worth noting that the term (or any of its derivatives) was used surprisingly little by respondents. Less than one in five of the interviewees used the term at all – and none of them used it extensively. If anything working-class respondents were more likely to use the term than middle-class interviewees. Second, and even more undermining for any thesis that companionship was an important new idea, which was supposedly widely adopted and was changing the rules of love and sex in marriage, is the fact that among the minority of respondents who did use the term, some clearly differentiated companionship from 'love'. For instance, Clare, when talking about the difference between the love she had experienced with her first husband and the mere 'companionship' with her second husband,

Clare   One was love and the other one was companionship.

And what's, what was the difference between love and companionship?

. . .

Clare   Well, you live for one another, live for one another, and wherever you went you both went together, there was no him going off in the pub and or anything like that, no if he went out an 'ad a drink at the club, he always used to take me with 'im.

And what was different then with your other husband did you spend more time apart?

Clare   Well, me second husband, he didn't used to go out like that, he was more as I say companionship, and I met him at work, I knew 'im before he was at work because he used to live in the next street, um, no it's not like the love that you have, yer first love, as I say it was companionship more than anything.[46]

In the new circumstances of a society of supposedly equal male and female citizens (constitutionally, at least, in voting terms since 1928), the objective conditions of child-bearing and the practical opportunities for income-earning had nevertheless remained patently unequal with respect to gender throughout the respondents' working lives. As noted above, Davidoff *et al.* have written of the rise of the companionate model stressing 'romantic love, sexual attraction and mutual interests, while disguising the realities of gendered inequalities'. Most of these interviewees do not seem to have been taken in by the disguise. They were only too well aware of the gendered differences in their roles and capabilities. To establish and maintain a happy marriage serving each other's mutual but different interests required much goodwill, compromise and 'give and take'. Loving marriage – where it existed – was not a story of romantic companionship but understood to be a working partnership with a finely negotiated balance of sharing and caring.

Appendix: Descriptive summary of the oral history sample of interviewees

The collection of oral histories took place between 1998 and 2001 and was funded by an ESRC grant to Simon Szreter, Grant Number R000236621. Kate Fisher was the project's Research Officer. Any names of respondents appearing have been changed. An interpretation of the qualitative evidence will be presented at length in K. Fisher and S. Szreter, *Private Lives: Sex, Love and Marriage in English Society 1918–1967* (Oxford 2010). See also K. Fisher and S. Szreter, (2003) and K. Fisher (2006).

The study was conducted in two contrasting communities – Blackburn, Lancashire, and Harpenden, Hertfordshire. Both middle- and working-class persons were interviewed in each location. A total of 88 married men and women were interviewed using open-ended semi-structured interviews. The 57 women and 31 men interviewed were all born between 1901 and 1931 (90 per cent were born between 1905 and 1924). Most respondents were first married between 1930 and 1950. Most of those interviewed were widows or widowers who had been married once, although nine couples were also interviewed together. The interviews were conducted either by Kate Fisher or by Simon Szreter (and a few by James Mark), usually involving multiple visits and generating three to five hours of taped material for each interviewee, which was then transcribed.

The child-bearing characteristics of each of the two groups of interviewees do not exhibit any unexpected features. Marriages producing two births was the most common pattern, as would be expected for these marriage cohorts, and there was a slight tendency for those marrying after 1940 to have produced a greater number of births per marriage than those marrying before 1940, which conforms with the national pattern of higher marital fertility after the Second World War.

In Blackburn, 38 working-class individuals were interviewed. They were predominantly lifelong local residents of the city. All but four were born in

Lancashire and as many as 63 per cent (24) were born in Blackburn itself. Of the Blackburn middle-class group of 12 respondents, 5 were born and bred in Blackburn and had lived in the area all their lives, and most others, though not born in Blackburn, had spent all their marriages in the region – mostly in Lancashire itself.

By contrast all of the 22 middle-class Harpenden interviewees had moved place of residence not just once but at least twice in their lives and most of them had moved several times. Geographical and social mobility has been increasingly characteristic of the middle-classes throughout the twentieth century, especially among the 'new' middle class of the south and these interviewees were typical of this general pattern of the southern, and metropolitan middle classes (McKibbin 1998, pp. 90–105). Despite their diverse birth places all over Britain, 17 had lived either in Hertfordshire or in the extra-metropolitan Home Counties throughout all or virtually all of their married lives. Of the 16 Harpenden working-class interviewees, all but 3 had resided locally in or near Harpenden throughout all of their marriages (although only 5 were actually born in Hertfordshire). The other three had all brought up their families in inner London, before moving to the Harpenden area after their children left home.

Notes

1. J. Finch and P. Summerfield (1991), 'Social Reconstruction and the Emergence of Companionate Marriage, 1945–1959', in D. Clark, ed., *Marriage, Domestic Life and Social Change* (London: Routledge); J. Reibstein and M. Richards (1992), *Sexual Arrangements. Marriage, Monogamy and Affairs* (London: Heinemann), ch. 1; L. Davidoff, M. Doolittle, J. Fink and K. Holden (1999), *The Family Story. Blood, Contract and Intimacy, 1830–1960* (London: Longman). The most recent proponent of the thesis, Marcus Collins, also claims that companionate marriage is now in decline. He argues that since achieving its apogee in the 1960s and 1970s, this model of 'mutualism' in marriage has been increasingly subject to both feminist critique and exposure of the tensions it contains – the unreachably high expectations of finding a perfect partner. According to Collins, companionate mutualism has been in process of being superseded since the 1970s by a new emphasis on individual autonomy, rather than interdependence, as previously. M. Collins (2003), *Modern Love. An Intimate History of Men and Women in Twentieth-Century Britain* (London: Atlantic Books).
2. Collins, *Modern Love*, chs 1–2, 4; Hera Cook (2004), *The Long Sexual Revolution. English Women, Sex and Contraception 1900–1975* (Oxford: Oxford University Press), Part II.
3. B. E. Lindsey and W. Evans (1927), *The Companionate Marriage* (New York: Boni & Liverwright).
4. Davidoff *et al.*, *The Family Story*, p. 190; Collins, *Modern Love*, p. 93.
5. Thus Lesley Hall has researched the texts and lives of a number of the leading intellectual figures of the late nineteenth and early twentieth centuries; see L. A. Hall (2004), entries for William Acton, F. W. Stella Browne, Eustace Chesser, Margaret Shurmer Sibthorp, Marie Stopes, Charlotte Carmichael Stopes,

Alice Vickery, Helen Wilson, and Helena Wright, in *The Oxford Dictionary of National Biography* (Oxford: Oxford University Press). Ross McKibbin has provided an illuminating introduction for a new edition of the classic ideological statement of the virtues of companionate marriage, Marie Stopes' *Married Love*, published in 1918: R. McKibbin (2004), 'Introduction' to Marie Stopes, *Married Love* (Oxford: Oxford University Press); Hera Cook's *The Long Sexual Revolution* has mounted a systematic examination of sex and marriage guidance manuals; Marcus Collins' *Modern Love* (ch. 4) has investigated the social pathology case-work files of the National Marriage Guidance Council, 1929–1965, dealing with the very poor in London, and has surveyed the published views of postwar marriage guidance counsellors and psychotherapists.

6. Elizabeth (and Peter) msf/kf/bl/#26. See appendix to this chapter for further details of the oral histories drawn on and cited here.
7. Bryan msf/kf/ht/#25.
8. Lorna msf/kf/bl/25.
9. Dora msf/srss/ht/#38.
10. Eileen msf/kf/bl/#12.
11. Sarah msf/kf/bl#30.
12. Colin msf/kf/bl/#36.
13. Ed msf/ssrs/bl/#23.
14. Pam msf/kf/ht/#19.
15. Emma msf/kf/ht#37.
16. Roger msf/kf/ht#10.
17. Hugh and Angela msf/kf/ht#18.
18. Lyn msf/kf/bl/#1.
19. Emily msf/kf/bl#13.
20. Marilyn msf/kfbl#7.
21. Catherine msf/kf/ht/#1.
22. Clare msf/kf/ht#8.
23. Maud msf/kf/bl/#18.
24. Ed msf/ssrs/bl/#23.
25. Dora msf/srss/ht#38.
26. Maria msf/kf/bl#8.
27. Penny msf/srss/ht#20.
28. Penny msf/srss/ht#20.
29. Lyn msf/kf/bl/#1.
30. Peter and Elizabeth msf/kf/bl/#26.
31. Penny msf/kf/ht/#20.
32. Alf and Heather msf/kf/ht/#14.
33. Dennis msf/kf/ht#15.
34. Elma msf/jm/bl/#42.
35. Lorna msf/kf/bl/#25.
36. Catherine msf/kf/ht/#1.
37. Maud msf/kf/bl/#18.
38. Sarah msf/kf/bl#30.
39. Ibid.
40. Ibid.
41. Gay msf/kf/ht/#13.
42. Pru msf/kf/ht/#12.
43. Pru msf/kf/ht/#12.

44. Collins, *Modern Love*, ch. 4, seems content to reproduce such dichotomies, actively seeking (p. 252, n. 44) to downplay the extent to which contemporary sociological research by E. Bott (1957) and by Young and Willmott (1957) might have indicated a rather less straightforward relationship between social class, patriarchy and segregated or joint networks of kin and friendship; E. Bott (1957), *Family and Social Network* (London: Tavistock; second edition with preface by Max Gluckman 1971); M. Young and P. Willmott (1957), *Family and Kinship in East London* (London: Routledge and Kegan Paul).
45. L. Davidoff (2010), Provisional title: *Thicker than Water: Sisters and Brothers in Society 1780–1920* (Oxford: Oxford University Press).
46. Clare msf/kf/ht/#8.

7
'A paradise on earth, a foretaste of heaven': English Catholic Understandings of Domesticity and Marriage, 1945–1965

Alana Harris

Introduction

In a sermon delivered to the Catholics of northern England in 1945 which explicitly addressed issues such as the breakdown of family life and the spiritual priorities for post-war renewal, Bishop Marshall of the Salford diocese held before his flock a comprehensive model for familial relations:

> Catholic fathers can endeavour to follow the footsteps of St Joseph by the purity of their lives, by their vigilance and self-sacrifice. Catholic mothers can imitate the Mother of Jesus by their example, their modesty, their resignation and perfect faith. Catholic children can strive to be pious and obedient as the Child Jesus was. The whole family, father, mother and children, can unite daily in the service of God by family prayers. Thus Catholic homes can be preserved from the many dangers around them and, like the Holy Family, they can serve as models for many homesteads.[1]

Whilst this ideal was modulated through a distinctively Catholic rhetoric of the Holy Family, and one that had been vigorously promoted since Pope Leo XIII instituted a feast day in 1892 to commemorate the holy home in Nazareth, men and women within post-war England were *also* searching for models to inform and interrogate changing understandings of marriage, parenthood and domestic roles. For as Edward Griffith, co-founder of the National Marriage Guidance Council (NMGC), wrote in anticipation of the end of the war, 'the home, and all it stands for, must be the pivot of our social reconstruction'.[2] Whilst much of the historiography of twentieth-century British society specifically acknowledges the importance of changing perceptions of family and domesticity during the post-war period, particularly the rise of the 'companionate model' of marriage and shifting understandings of femininity and maternity, there has been very little exploration of the continuing role of Christianity in informing these ideals.[3] Nor have the detailed treatments of women's work,[4] the intersections between socialization, psychology and maternity,[5] and the nature of male insecurities in the wake of the war,[6] included a consideration of religion, as well as gender, which might thereby problematize traditional understandings of the public and private spheres.[7] This lacuna in the historiography is even more pronounced in respect of Roman Catholicism – for Christianity has been treated as synonymous with the established Church of England, reinforced by misconceptions about the specificity of a homogeneous Catholicism confined to the 'ghetto'.[8] By utilizing the Catholic conceptual framework of the Holy Family as a lens to focus attention on the personalities and pious activities of the mother and (foster) father of Christ, and the ways in which these informed diverse understandings of maternity and paternity within Catholic homes, I hope to highlight the broader societal shifts in understandings of marriage and domesticity in post-war England and the complexity of these religiously informed ideals circulating within the public arena. This model also requires a consideration of both masculinity and femininity when considering the intricacies of domestic power and gender politics within familial life[9] – integrating an analysis of gender and spirituality in ways that have so far been little examined by twentieth-century historians.

Focusing particularly on archival and oral history material from the Catholic Diocese of Salford,[10] this chapter will commence with a consideration of multifaceted and sometimes conflicting constructions of Catholic marriage available in the post-war period, and the ways in which this spectrum of opinion might contrast with, or complement, the companionate marriage ideal developing in broader British society. The second section will examine the shifting understandings of women as homemakers and mothers in the late 1940s and early 1950s, and illustrate the potentially powerful (though circumscribed) forms of autonomy and authority available to women inside and beyond the household. It will argue that these models of maternity were reified through devotion to the Virgin Mary and reinforced through the broader societal emphasis on mothers' formative spiritual and psychological influence on children. The third section will extend the recent work of historians of masculinity through exploring the ambiguities and instabilities manifest in male identities as father and breadwinner throughout the 1950s,[11] arguing that similar concerns for Catholics were formulated against the foil of Marian devotion and through the cult of St Joseph. Whilst heavenly ideals and divine paragons informed the rhetoric of English Catholics' understandings of marriage and parenthood, and by implication their conceptions of authority and morality beyond the hearth and outside the home, their domestic arrangements and self-understandings were equally conditioned by temporal preoccupations and the constraints of earthly application in post-war Britain.

Models of Catholic marriage – complementary and companionate ideals

First popularized as a concept upon the publication of Ben Lindsey's and Wainwright Evans' sensational tract earlier in the century,[12] the growing currency of the 'powerful ideal' of the companionate marriage in the period after the Second World War, with its attendant stresses on 'the importance of romantic love, sexual attraction and mutual interests', has long been recognized by historians of gender and the family.[13] Indeed, Janet Finch and Penny Summerfield have gone so far as to describe this model of marriage as 'the most distinctive feature of domestic life during the period'.[14] Whilst historians of twentieth-century British history have further developed this concept to speak of a 'set of ideas' about marriage,[15] very few studies have examined the changing intellectual underpinnings surrounding this renegotiation of the roles and responsibilities of spouses within marriage or, as Simon Szreter and Kate Fisher have explored in Chapter 6, its application within the domestic arrangements of British men and women. Nor has the role of a persistent and rich Christian discourse informing aspects of these ideals, ranging from the complementary but distinct roles of husbands and wives through to a conception of marriage as involving 'teamwork' and an implied breakdown in demarcated roles,[16] been recognized. Given the importance of religion, particularly evangelicalism, in the formulation of gender, marital and domestic ideals in the nineteenth century, such a consideration seems important when evaluating the changes and continuities in the tenor and context of these debates into the twentieth century.[17] Moreover, in view of the clerical backgrounds of Herbert Gray and David Mace, founders of the NMGC in 1938, and the explicit role of other religious commentators in the public debates about the increasing state interrogation and regulation of the family, this silence is surprising.[18] This chapter concentrates on this neglected dimension of the origins and shifting meanings of models of domestic authority in the twentieth century and their interrogation and integration into the everyday, married lives of practising Catholics in Manchester in the post-war period.[19]

Representative of the type of considerations involved in the increasingly heated discussions in Catholic circles about what 'partnership' and 'equality' in marriage might require was an instructional pamphlet by an Oxford Dominican in 1952. Rightly noting the broader societal ambiguity surrounding these terms, Dom Vann pontificated,

> ...you hear a great deal nowadays about the equality of the sexes: there is a great danger here. If you are trying to defend women from the

degradation of being treated as a chattel . . . then of course you are wholly right. . . . But be careful: if by equality you mean an obliteration of the differences between the sexes you will end by destroying the integrity of both. For the whole idea and purpose of the difference is that the two together are complementary.[20]

Such an attempt to clarify the 'correct' Catholic perspective on the marriage partnership is illustrative of the increasing renegotiation of the composition of this relationship in rhetorical terms and fears about the associated interrogation of longstanding and established understandings of domestic agency and authority. As Valerie Sanders' chapter (Chapter 11) also explores, these constructions were evolving throughout the nineteenth century and were founded in metaphorical and familial conceptions of God as father, Mary as mother and Jesus as elder brother with the parallel earthly 'household of faith' expected to emulate this divine hierarchy.[21] Whilst the rhetorical categories for these domestic arrangements remained constant for Catholics into the twentieth century, their gendered content and societal context required their reorientation and remodelling to address a profoundly changed Britain following both world wars.

The kind of tensions which such a prescriptive tract sought to address may be gleaned from an Advent sermon in 1945 by the Bishop of Salford which began by tracing the genealogy of the family from Adam and Eve through to the Christmas home in Nazareth to admonish:

The good Catholic mother must remember that her husband is the head of the home, and no matter how she may be provoked, she should not utter bitter words of reproach or disrespect in the presence of her children. The father has a right to expect reverence, obedience and love in his home, but he should take every precaution to render himself worthy of such veneration.[22]

Written against the backdrop of traumatized men returning from the front, and some women relinquishing the financial independence gained from war-work, the insistent tenor of this pastoral advice initially suggests a desire to reiterate norms in the face of an increasing instability in the Catholic, and indeed wider societal understanding of 'the husband [as] the head, [and] the wife . . . the heart of the home'.[23] Nevertheless, what emerged within the remainder of this pastoral instruction delivered from all Manchester pulpits was an increasingly complex understanding of the marital relationship, in which

The Christian home . . . should be a place where man and wife are united in mutual support and tender love. It should be a refuge in affliction, a shelter from the uncharitableness, the sorrows, and the quarrels of the world. Such a home can be found only where God is the acknowledged head of the home, and where husband and wife are permanently united in the service of each other...[24]

Although articulated within a distinctively Catholic rhetoric of the Holy Family, and drawing upon elements of the traditional theology of sacramental marriage, Bishop Marshall's description of the Christian home and the complementary roles of husband and wife within it also acknowledged many of the characteristics of the companionate model of marriage circulating within mainstream non-Catholic culture in its tacit endorsement of domestic co-operation, spousal reciprocity and familial cohesion.[25] As an example of the Catholic rhetoric about family stability and expectations of fulfilment within marriage encountered within countless marriage preparation pamphlets, his overly earnest prescriptions should be contextualized against the backdrop of the Royal Commission on Marriage and Divorce and fears about the 'divorce epidemic' which peaked at 60,000 marriage breakdowns in 1946–47.[26] In a collective submission on this issue to the Royal Commission, the Catholic Bishops of England and Wales naïvely (and disingenuously) stated the 'simple point' that:

> ...it is historical fact that the attitude of people outside the Church has changed considerably during the last hundred years or so. It is not Catholics who have changed their ideas, but others...[27]

But, in fact, Catholic understandings and expectations of marriage were also clearly changing, prompting both emphatic, defensive restatements of the traditional 'ends' of marriage and, from the other end of the spectrum of Catholic opinion, reactive reinterpretations of Catholic experiences of married life, including a greater emphasis on the importance of a healthy sexual relationship, in keeping with more socially progressive, middle-class conceptions.[28]

Additionally, the Church was also becoming proactive in responding to these trends, through the establishment of bodies such as the London-based Catholic Marriage Advisory Council in 1942, and its first equivalent in Manchester through the Church of the Holy Name in 1947.[29] The range of responses to these 'new patterns of family life' was made palpably clear in a memo written by the instigator of the innovative Mancunian marriage course, Father Waterhouse. In a slightly self-serving and congratulatory report to his Bishop on this important initiative, the Jesuit priest commenced with a discussion of the 'well-meaning' but 'Protestant' agenda of the NMGC under its chairman Reverend Herbert Gray, disparaging the 'tinge of hedonism' in its 'talk of "harmony"...about the happiness of partners and about the welfare of the nation, but not about pleasing God'.[30] He then proceeded to denounce the Catholic Marriage Advisory

Council, which was a rival to his parish-based programme, for 'following the fashion in social work instead of leading it'.[31] He was emphatic in his diagnosis that

> the Catholic Marriage Advisory Council has cramped itself from the start by taking the non-Catholic Marriage Guidance Council as its model. It has merely baptised its principles and methods to get rid of the twin evils of contraceptive teaching and permission for divorce, but by not drawing its inspiration primarily from Catholic sources it has missed an opportunity to start some really constructive and positive work to restore family life on Catholic lines... [through] dedication to the Holy Family and St Thomas More, together with an appeal for prayers...[32]

This priestly polemic may be critiqued for its misapprehension of the continuing emphasis on marriage stability which *was* advocated by the (non-Catholic) NMGC, at least in the 1950s,[33] and for its overestimation of a Catholic consensus on the 'evil' of contraception evidenced, for example, in Mass Observation's 'Little Kinsey' findings that over half the practising Catholics surveyed were in favour of some form of (undefined) 'birth control'.[34] Nevertheless, this clerical commentator did correctly identify the increasing re-appreciation in Catholic circles that a renewed appeal to a sacralized family life might yield 'constructive' and 'positive' models of the modern marriage. The creative and heterogeneous interpretations that arose from a sanctified understanding of married life, and its social consequences beyond the home, are well identified in Tim Madden's long-running cartoon strip 'How's the family?' which featured weekly in the (then) liberal *Catholic Herald* newspaper. Gently parodying the quirks and absurdities of everyday domesticity within this idealized middle-class Catholic family, the 1952 offerings showed 'Dad' helping with the after-dinner dishes and the tidying, actively involved in entertaining the children, and kneeling with his family by the hearth, under a portrait of Mary, to attempt to put into practice the conviction of the prominent, itinerant Catholic evangelist Father Patrick Peyton, an equivalent to Billy Graham,[35] that 'the family that prays together stays together' (Figure 7.1).[36] In addition to this slogan, popularized through his rallies which attracted a cumulative attendance of a million English Catholics in 1952, Father Peyton also reiterated his conviction that 'if enough families pray, they can save the world'; for 'a world at prayer is a world at peace'.[37] Drawing upon a distinctive arsenal of Catholic resources and heavenly personages to inform its vision of post-war reconstruction, English Catholic social teaching paralleled broader Christian thinking about the family as a microcosm of a well-ordered polis.[38] There was even an unexpected correspondence with the contemporaneous opinions of secular pundits such as the sexologist Eustace Chesser who, despite

Figure 7.1 Tim Madden (1965) *How's the Family? Cartoons from the Catholic Herald* (London: Burns and Oates), n.p. [Reproduced with permission from Bodleian Library, University of Oxford]

markedly different objectives, concurred that 'the ideal marriage is an ideal community in miniature'.[39]

The blessed Virgin Mary – modern homemaker and 1950s mother

Outlining his agenda to provide a 'noviceship for marriage' in the Holy Name pre-nuptial course, Father Waterhouse identified his foremost objective as 'preparing [couples] adequately for the task of training the children who will be theirs later',[40] which was founded in the conviction that

> The family is the unit which God planned for society and the more we try to split it, the more we produce an unstable and unnatural social order in which not only is the State in difficulties but the Church herself cannot work effectively.[41]

Advocating 'preventatives' rather than palliatives, maternity and child welfare featured prominently in this Jesuit initiative and in many ways this emphasis echoes an acknowledged broader societal preoccupation in the post-war period with women's domestic roles and the appropriate socialization of 'youth'. For Catholics, this powerful and prevalent emphasis on women's vocations as homemakers and mothers could be articulated, and indeed extended, through appeal to the Virgin Mary – who was both a model and an intercessory aid, as in centuries past, for the attainment of these ideals.[42] In a representative instructional pamphlet, recommending recourse to her 'who is an example to us all' in 'these times...when there are many vexed questions about what is right and proper in a woman',[43] Reverend J. Nutt took great pains to illustrate the continuing relevance of the Christian witness to the sorts of questions facing Catholics in 1948. Refracting controversies about the 'new women' and the glamorous housewife through the lens of Marian devotion, he addressed the wearing of makeup through an instructional analogy:

> Do not think within yourselves that times have changed so that it is sheer sentimentalism to put forward Mary as the ideal... When Our Lady walked through the streets of Jerusalem, she met with all the varieties of women that are to be found in any modern city. With their airs and graces, their trinkets, their bleached hair, rouge and lipstick, they went mincing by the gentle maid... Yesterday, to-day and the same for ever, she is the woman who finds favour in the sight of God, and also in the sight of men.[44]

Father Nutt's emphatic insistence on a particular understanding of Mary's femininity suggests increasing tensions about the interpretation of femininity in wider British society and the need to provide a potent counter-image in order to dissuade Catholic women from adapting to these social mores. Numerous Catholic manuals for young women addressed the issue of makeup and the appropriate balance between attractiveness, fashionable dress and proper Catholic behaviour.[45] In a similar vein, the Bishop of Salford in a sermon to the Union of Catholic Mothers had recourse to Mary as the one who offered 'the true norms and right ideals' of 'delicacy and modesty', allowing present-day youth to escape from the 'contagion' of the 'popular vision and corrupted public standards'.[46] However, in an article in the Young Christian Workers' (YCW) magazine in 1948 on the formation of female leaders within the Movement, chaplain Louis Hanlon advocated the need to make the 'idea' of Our Lady relevant to the modern working girl through reconstructing the 'vision in blue and white who blushes if she whistles or smokes a cigarette' so that

> Sanctity instead of being something queer and abstract becomes something tangible... The things God asked of her were human things, human joys and sorrows: to have a baby, love It, educate It and suffer because of It. He asked her to employ her body, hands, will and intelligence on quite normal human activities; to bend her back, scrub the floor, to wash clothes, to look after a home.[47]

Within all these instructional commentaries, mirroring more secular publications, there is an insistence that the 'modern girl', against the foil of her 'Victorian' counterpart, should strive after a femininity that encompassed both emotional maturity and intellectual independence.[48]

Whilst some of these examples and instructional commentaries could be seen as constraining and conservative, these same Catholic resources might also offer, paradoxically, a means for reconceptualizing models of femininity and the rethinking of domestic roles so that household responsibilities might be renegotiated and shared. In a bulletin to lay leaders of the 'Girls YCW', its clerical author urged 'working girls of the world' to abandon the stars of Hollywood and reappreciate the 'Star of Heaven' who is 'a hundred per cent girl, full of every quality that you could ever admire in a girl' and like the reader in sharing 'all the worry that can come to any working-class girl and mother':

> Worry of a mother with nothing but a bit of straw for her new-born child. Worry of sudden evacuation, State control, looking for a house, unemployment, poverty and want.[49]

Advocating a quite powerful and potentially radical reconceptualization of Mary (and motherhood), the bulletin urged its female readers to appreciate that Mary

> Formed the body of Jesus within her, bought Him forth to the light of day, and trained Him up to perfect manhood, as her task is to form Christ within us, so that we may think like Christ, speak like Christ, and act like Christ.

Advocating a similar equality of male and female discipleship, and also informed by leftist political principles, the chair of the prominent Catholic feminist organization, St Joan's Alliance, drew upon Catholic teaching to challenge traditional divisions of domestic labour. Reacting to an ongoing correspondence in May 1952 within the *Catholic Herald* on the need for greater domestic training in Catholic schools, Phyllis Challoner stressed the desirability of moving the debate beyond practicalities to principle, and advanced that

> 'Home-making' is a wider thing than skill in domestic work, and we maintain that a training in accordance with their talents for both boys and girls, with a training of both equally in the whole subject of home-making, will result in a comradeship in and out of the home that will solve more questions than how to satisfy a husband's pangs of hunger.[50]

At a time in which there was an extraordinary premium on maternity and homemaking to address birth-rate anxieties,[51] and a valorized domesticity to encourage middle-class women to embrace housework following the demise of domestic servants, these examples illustrate dimensions within Catholic teaching which might offer resources for dealing with the difficulties and stresses of domesticity. Marriage and household maintenance were sanctified and, through appeal to a 'holy ideal', Catholic women were offered not only reassurance but also the means for a potential reconfiguration of maternal roles and responsibilities. Moreover, there were also alternative models of femininity available within Catholic discourse with which to celebrate the single state and work outside the home. For example in his Catholic Truth Society pamphlet, clearly indicating its audience by its title, *To Those Getting Married* (1946), Walter Jewell used the example of two girlfriends, one called to a religious order and the other to marriage, to celebrate the single (religious) life as well as to elevate matrimony as a vocation and channel of God's grace.[52] This same theme was taken up by Bishop Marshall addressing the many thousands of Mancunian Catholics gathered for the Whit walk in 1948. Remarking that 'the social position of women is, from the Christian point of view, very imperfectly set forth in the expression "Woman belongs in the home"', Bishop Marshall was a most unlikely radical in urging the 'most emancipated woman of to-day' to realize the 'influence and freedom of action' offered by the church through history in the example of women like St Brigid. Through making reference to this saint of the early Irish church, he held before his audience the cult of a powerful religious woman, known for her independence of mind and her capable administration of a number of religious houses. Further contending that 'never has the official church countenanced the "Kitchen theory" of womanhood', he continued to observe that whilst

> Luther wishes to confine her ambitions to wash-tubs and baby-linen; and the Koran quite takes it for granted that, outside marriage, she has neither value nor importance – the truth is that her own unique influence is intended to reach everywhere.[53]

Ecumenical and inter-religious scruples aside, this use of Catholic resources to support women's agency outside marriage, and beyond domestic confines, offered some alternatives to the overwhelming societal prioritization upon marriage and maternity in the post-war period.

In addition to these intriguing and shifting understandings of women's role as homemakers, historians have long recognized the overwhelming emphasis in the wider 1950s British culture on a maternalist rhetoric[54] and the state-endorsement of 'the greatest of all jobs' to encourage women to move out of some areas of the labour market back into the home. As the spokesman for an emerging social policy which sought to emphasize the scientific professionalism of good homemaking in a context of continued rationing, and the heroism of motherhood after their war-work, Field Marshall Sir William Slim utilized a home service broadcast in 1952 to praise women 'who set the standard in all the really important things – in truthfulness, honesty, decency, self-sacrifice and honour'. He went so far as to attest that 'the economy of the country was based on her shopping basket'.[55] Catholic mothers were equally exhorted to the realization that that 'the hand that rocks the cradle not only rules but saves the world'.[56]

Perhaps mindful of the widespread influence of parenting manuals like those of Bowlby[57] and Winnicott[58] and the increasing influence of popular Freudianism (discussed by Deborah Thom's chapter in this volume), the Westminster Cathedral chaplain, writing in anticipation of the official 'Marian Year' of 1954, acknowledged that it was self-evident that Catholics relied on Mary, as Christ did, for 'a family must have a mother. It does not need modern psychology to tell us that.'[59] In his devotional reflection, he then proceeded to remind his readers that

> We should not forget Mary as a human mother. If we picture her as 'a queen most womanly', we must see her too with her back aching, her eyes tired, her fingers cracked with washing. We must see her in anxiety, in poverty, in aridity.[60]

Similarly seeking to make Mary 'everywoman', but moving beyond the arduous labour and trials of such maternity, another commentator reflected,

> Mary had all the rights of a mother over her Son. She had the joy of the Child's first smile, the delights of His first steps when He began to walk, the tender satisfaction of hearing His first uttered syllable...the loving and intimate union of a mother suckling her child.[61]

This impulse in Catholic devotional and educational literature, as well as animating and informing a simple but highly engaged theology of the Incarnation, also facilitated an intensely personalized relationship with Mary, and the expression of Catholic spirituality in an everyday context. The ways in which this relationship with Mary were mapped onto familial models, and gave potency to her status and power as an agent and intercessor for that generation of Mancunian Catholics born immediately after the war, is well illustrated by retired Deputy Head Teacher Peter Kerr (b. 1944, Fairfield) when asked about the place of Marian devotion in his life:

> PK: There's a tale told about an old Irish woman who was in church one Sunday night and she was saying the rosary. And Jesus appeared to her and said 'Excuse me Bridie'. And she said 'Shush, I'm talking to your mother'. Now I think that sort of idea – I can see this in real life. If our boys want anything, they don't ask me. They ask their mother. They ask their mother. And Mary is the intercessor – yeah, certainly. ... it's clear, to me at any rate, that you have the Trinity and above all others, then, there's Mary. No doubts whatsoever. The power behind the throne if you like. And the exemplar.[62]

Whilst on the one hand offering women a potent role model and vicarious respect and deference, the expectations born of comparison with this heavenly ideal might also be onerous. Exasperated and gentle resistance to overly sentimentalized and one-sided expectations of women, such as those outlined in the July 1951 edition of *Novena* under the heading 'Three Grades of Catholic Mothers', prompted correspondence from a Yorkshire women asking for 'Grades A, B, C of Catholics Fathers' and 'Catholic Children', and another from Cheshire protesting: 'Three *grades* of Catholic Mothers! Makes us sound like eggs!'[63] Similarly, the strain that an increasing societal emphasis on women's primary 'responsibility for the family's emotional and psychological, as well as material well-being'[64] could impose is well articulated by an anonymous Catholic laywoman, who wrote about her prayers while 'resting on my knees, trying to pray and recover from a long day'. This self-titled 'Catholic mother' intimately recounted her 'troubles' asking,

> Mary, what would you have done if there were electric toasters in your day and they didn't work and the toast was burned and the coffee wasn't good, and everyone left the house in a huff? Was St Joseph every surely [surly?] and short tempered on an early morning after a late night?...Just give me the help I need to take things as they come, please, Mary.[65]

Despite her tiredness and frustrations, little alleviated by the assistance of newly available consumer appliances, 'Catholic Mother' nevertheless clearly derived much personal satisfaction, and an unassailable (almost celestial) authority within the household – not to mention an accessible emotional resource to enable her to fulfil her charge. Within this worldview, maternal and household duties were 'sanctified' and, in the words of another devotional pamphlet, 'the love of Heaven [brought] to the humblest homes of earth'.[66] For, as a Father Greenstock reflected in his 1951 'Talks to Catholics Parents' which focused on the model of the Holy Family, motherhood was a 'public' role, best realized through their formation of children 'into the likeness of Christ,'[67] and which would create 'saints, not merely for the priesthood...but also in the workshop, the docks [and] the factories'[68]

The Virgin Mary, when conjured as a human mother in these prescriptive tracts, could be made to respond to many of the temporal concerns and the general conservatism of post-war society with its emphasis on an absorbing maternity and valorized domesticity. Nevertheless, as these examples from Catholic commentaries circulating during the late 1940s and early 1950s also illustrate, Mary's personal biography and a sanctified femininity might also complicate these models – offering to women (and indeed to men, as the next section will explore) ideals breaking the confines of the kitchen and reaching into the heavenly realm. Moreover, the mutability, flexibility and potency of this maternal model continued in Catholic circles well after the Second World War, which becomes markedly apparent if we compare the 1952 'Catholic Mother' with her contemporary, Mancunian counterpart,

Mary Howarth. Born in Trafford Park in 1967 to Irish parents, and juggling parental responsibilities with paid employment, she explains her devotion to Mary as vested in a shared maternity:

> MH: It's being a mother as well. I think she's [laughs]. I think sometimes, [laughs], yeah, because I work full time as well and trying to balance being that and doing every –. I think sometimes – I mean, I do chat to her. Most days I'll have a chat with her and say 'You were a mother yourself, just…' [laughs]. Cause you know what its like – you've got that many balls in the air sometimes, just trying to keep them all going, so yeah.[69]

When asked how 'having a chat to Our Lady' in 'bed or the bath' helped, Mary reflected,

> MH: I suppose I've got that much going on sometimes I can always have a chat with her and say 'Ah, what do I do now?' And I've probably known what I should do, but after having the chat…I don't know. Maybe a couple of hours it becomes clear – 'Alright, well I sort it out, I prioritize, that needs to be done first, and that'. You know, work it like that.[70]

Whether as a sympathetic ear for domestic complaints, an aid to patience or a project manager assisting with prioritization, devotion to Our Lady had the potential to elevate certain constructions of the feminine, enabling some women then, and now, to negotiate personal difficulties and to access the divine outside institutional constraints and clerical control.

The holy couple and Catholic masculinity

Paternity too was becoming increasingly contested in the post-war period, and the industry and input of fathers in the creation of saints within the family and wider society more widely appreciated. As the historian of masculinity, Lynn Segal has observed, in the 1950s 'the man's place was also in the home' with men domesticated in the popular consciousness in the return from the battlefield to the bungalow.[71] The emergence of the welfare state model, with implications for understandings of the breadwinner's role and the family wage,[72] as well as improvements in leisure time and growing affluence as the decade progressed,[73] meant that the roles of husbands and fathers and their involvement around the house were shifting and changing.[74] As Szreter and Fisher have also explored in Chapter 6, conflict and anxiety could result around a male identity which was more home-based, if not house-trained. In the midst of these changes, it is perhaps telling that Catholic devotional literature exhorted wives to understand and support their husbands in 'the moments of failure and abjection' when 'the rational schemes of the male and all his work of building and all his ambitions tend to come tumbling down'.[75] After a shattering and brutal war, and a peace that initially brought acute housing shortages, employment dislocation, and the continuance of food rationing, men as well as women were unsure about their role in the household and anxious about their ability to provide for their families. Understandably, devotional practices that articulated a strong message of a stable, robust masculinity, as well as a sentimental spirituality and self-fulfilment to be found in the family, were designed to address a pressing contemporary need. Exemplary of these trends were the rosary crusades of Father Patrick Peyton who, to a crowd of 100,000 Catholics gathered in Wembley Stadium in 1952, endorsed a virile and self-consciously masculine Marian piety in which 'the family, in its proper character, [is] a little kingdom of God',[76] with 'the husband [as] God's representative'.[77] Reports of the crusades pointedly concentrated, for example, on the tenacious piety of father of five, Mr Charles Elliot, who walked 30 miles in the pouring rain to be present.[78] Much was also made of observations by Catholic[79] and indeed non-Catholic commentators such as the Anglican Rector, Canon Bryan Green of Birmingham, who confessed himself 'very impressed by the number of men' at the rallies.[80] Peyton's promotional material gave prominence to photographs of the regimented thousands of male-only volunteers collecting rosary pledges in Newcastle,[81] and reporters spoke of the enormous presence of 'shirt-sleeved fathers – some pushing prams'.[82] Male spirituality was also highlighted in speaking of the effects of

Figure 7.2 A Durham miner leading his family in the rosary. Reproduced from 'Crusader for Prayer', *Picture Post*, 26 July 1952, p. 5 [with permission of Getty Images]

the crusade, with photos of a Durham miner clutching his rosary featured in *Picture Post*,[83] reports of an increasing number of boys carrying their rosary beads at school,[84] and jubilation on the conversion of the Middlesbrough football star, Wilf Mannion (Figure 7.2).[85]

This reaffirmation of male authority within the domestic sphere, and ostensibly over matters spiritual, was enshrined in devotions like the enthronement ceremonies of the Sacred Heart in the home over which the father and the priest presided.[86] Similarly, the practice of the family rosary was advocated by laymen like Lawrence Rossiter, who commended the practice to his fellow fathers as a quick 'ten minute' cure for paternal problems and the world's 'black paganism'.[87] In fact, for some Catholic men such as Nora Walsh's (b. 1933, Galway) husband, leading the family rosary was a way of expressing fatherly care and a Catholic identity independent of church attendance:

> NW: My husband was Catholic but he wasn't a wonderful Catholic.... he would go, you know, for special occasions or when they were having First Communion ... But he would say the rosary with them and he'd always insist. We used to go to the bedroom and say it there.... they'd all be up stairs and I had six children and, well, some of them didn't know, they'd hardly know their prayers, like the younger ones. But he'd always say the rosary, which was good. That was a good thing.[88]

These trends were counter to the dominant strain in the devotional literature, dating well back into the nineteenth century as Sanders' chapter (Chapter 11) illustrates, which voiced the commonplace assessment that spiritually 'it is the woman who indisputably reigns'.[89] They also provided a counterpoint to the numerous secular parenting manuals which evidenced a 'tendency to see successful childrearing in terms of constant mothering render[ing] the father relatively unimportant' (see also discussions by Siân Pooley and Deborah Thom in this volume of the historical development of parental advice manuals).[90] The 'legions of men' publicly participating in the huge processions to the shrine of Walsingham,[91] or to the little-known pre-Reformation shrine of Willesden for the Marian year in 1954,[92] illustrate the tensions apparent in the 1950s within these highly complex understandings of gender roles and responsibilities – for on the one hand these were proud and public male assertions of masculine power and authority, but nevertheless in service and deference to Our Lady. The 'true Catholic husband' was reminded to view his wife as 'a reflection of Mary of Nazareth' and as such manifest devotion to both women by love, respect and 'never utter[ing] an unseemly word' in her presence.[93] Indeed, this was a perspective expressly articulated by father of five Francis Leigh (b. 1928, Eccles), who had earlier confessed to having a 'crush' on the Virgin Mary, and who spoke in emotional terms about her centrality to his faith and his associated understanding of marital roles:

AH: And Our Lady? You talk about praying the rosary – how important is Mary in your faith?

FL: Well very much so actually, because of – every woman, to me all my life, has been on a pedestal. Because most of them are mothers you might say – except the single ones, that's understandable – but I've still got the greatest respect. And I've had it all my life. Every woman, irrespective of what people say about her... You find your own views. I mean, I would say there's 80 per cent of women have got two jobs, men I think they're only 5 per cent. And that alone is an admiration that I have for women that, you know, they do it.[94]

This self-conscious reflection on marital expectations and duties and the insistence within other commentaries on appropriate 'manly' conduct suggest that the position of husbands, their place in the domestic sphere and the nature of their interactions with their wives were undergoing intense scrutiny and some redefinition.

As a way of providing further substance to these expectations of Catholic masculinity, beyond being a foil to Marian femininity, the Holy Family analogy also proffered St Joseph as a model for the right behaviour of Catholic husbands, workers and fathers – explicitly promoted as a cult by Pope Pius IX in 1847 and 1870,[95] but gaining widespread popularity into the twentieth century.[96] Priests composed prayers for 'family devotion to St Joseph', such as the following illustrative example which opened with the exclamation:

St Joseph! Obtain for fathers courage to endure all that is demanded of them. Let them see in every wife and mother an image of Mary, the Mother of God, that they may show forth towards them the spirit of reverence and of chivalry. Give them fidelity to their married life, blessing to their labours and grace to guide those entrusted to their care.[97]

After extolling the sacrifices yet blessings of domestic life, this prayer then considered

the anxiety about daily food, the maintenance of home... [and] the spirit of the world... [which] bring worse danger to our children than did the dagger of Herod to the Holy Innocents.[98]

The prayer closed with a salutation to the 'Father of Christ esteemed' as a father 'to those Thy Foster son redeemed', whose intercession would aid fathers to 'stand out before their children as models of faithfulness to God and of strict fulfilment of duty'.[99] This somewhat unorthodox Trinitarian theology offered a construction of masculinity that was not only strong and stable, but also intimate and domestic. The imaginative possibilities stimulated by this devotion were articulated by the 'baby-boomer' Peter Kerr, who followed on from speaking about Mary to express an admiration for the marital commitment and conjugal fidelity of the foster father of Christ:

> PK: And I would go perhaps a little bit against everything else and put St Joseph up there as well. But then that's partly to do with the fact that... to take somebody as your wife knowing that they are carrying a child and not knowing whose it was... that's faith. Dear me. I don't have a faith like that. That is a quantum leap from the ordinary.[100]

In her writings the mystic, sculptor and best-selling Catholic author of the 1950s, Caryll Houselander, also concurred with such an assessment. She dismissed the 'grey-bearded statue' of St Joseph as quite misrepresenting his character, which should rather be recognized as that of a just, strong man who trusted in God, accepted hardship and danger and renounced himself to protect the little and weak.[101] It was not surprising therefore that in the popular Catholic culture of the period, St Joseph was invoked as both a model for and a means of procuring 'good husbands', as lightly parodied in a *Catholic Herald* cartoon in which a bride's nuptials were attributed to sustained prayer to St Joseph, who might not always be reliable in supplying a 'good catch' (Figure 7.3).

As a provider, the Catholic male was also expected to emulate 'the guardian of the Holy Family [who] could not fail them, say, through bodily indisposition, ... [as] the breadwinner for the Bread who had come down from Heaven'.[102] Portrayed within such literature as a stoic, silent type,[103] St Joseph's role as a model worker – to inspire the Catholic working class and to counter communist ideal types[104] – was endorsed through the establishment of his feast day on 1 May 1955 by Pope Pius XII and explored through

Figure 7.3 Tim Madden (1965), *How's the Family?* (London: Burns and Oates), n.p. [Reproduced with permission from Bodleian Library, University of Oxford]

Figure 7.4   'St Joseph the Workman', *Catholic Times*, 6 May 1955, p. 9 [Reproduced with permission from Bodleian Library, University of Oxford]

cartoons in the Catholic press paralleling his profession with modern-day, blue-collar workers (Figure 7.4). Nevertheless, within this period of a more ambiguous domesticity, the emphasis on duty and dependence was softened by an added emphasis on the foster fatherhood of Joseph, depicted in this poignant vignette about the child Jesus:

> Before He had sat in the midst of the doctors he sat on Joseph's knee and at it. And can we doubt that he was any more sparing with His questions than He was with those who were not likely to have the answers? Christ added to His experimental knowledge in the ordinary way. And surely in this case the mother did not occupy the whole scene.[105]

Other writers of more psychologically influenced parenting manuals also deplored those who ignored or diminished the father's role in the education of his children. One such clerical pamphleteer instructed fathers to patience and interest in school work and conversation, deploring the confinement of the paternal role to discipline or as a fearful 'ogre' because 'many of the more difficult problems of adolescence would never arise at all if there existed more confidence between the child and father'.[106] The male educative and formative role extended to setting an explicit example in religion to counter the insults of those who assert that 'religion is a thing for silly women and not meant for men'.[107] These exhortations to exemplary personal, social, religious and moral standards inevitably also made explicit reference to restrain from excessive drinking;[108] a vice specifically targeted in Peyton's parables of marriages saved through the displacement of the pub by the routine of the evening rosary.[109] Peyton was not alone in articulating the clergy's blithe expectation that 'no father could [pray] ... night after night and be a bad man'.[110]

These examples all demonstrate the concern of some Catholic educators to stress that, in his appropriate involvement in domestic life and spiritual socialization, 'the [Catholic] father is just as important as the mother in this matter'.[111] As such, they illustrate the increasing ambiguity within the period surrounding gender relations and the division of familial responsibilities. Discussing the considerable changes in contemporary married life and the renegotiation of relationships between husband and wife, the *Royal Commission on Population* (1949) attributed the loss of male status within the family and the end of 'unrestricted childbearing' to emerging models of marriage which stressed collaboration and concern for maternal health and well-being.[112] Identifying similar changes in domestic authority and women's working patterns, but divergent in its sharp condemnation of these developments, Pope Pius XII in a late-1940s address to newly weds identified modern life's tendency 'to make women the equal of men' and sought to differentiate between the equality of the spouses in the life of grace whilst maintaining that 'in the life of the family, the wife is subject to her husband and that by her free consent'.[113] The need to restate vigorously these domestic hierarchies is perhaps illustrative of the extent to which previously operational family structures were now being critiqued. Indeed, 1960s sociologists like Willmott and Goldthorpe were to reflect contemporaneously on the ways in which men from relatively affluent working-class backgrounds were more actively involved in home life and parenting in a way that their fathers had not been.[114] Nevertheless, as Chapter 6 also argues, conventional gendered divisions of labour and the distribution of economic power were not disturbed fundamentally by these trends, and rather there were increased demands imposed on women by the companionate model of marriage – requiring them to be 'more comradely wives, more devoted mothers of more children, more satisfying and satisfied sexual partners and more professional homemakers'.[115] Two decades on from the war, a self-consciously 'modern' pamphlet prepared for newly weds by the Catholic Marriage Advisory Council was keen to acknowledge women's increasing independence, candid in the provision of physiological information for love-making, and careful to avoid any language of superiority in stressing that 'husbands and wives share spheres of authority and spheres of love in the family' and that 'these will vary with personalities and situations'.[116] Nevertheless, in a section entitled 'authority and freedom', it recycled the old adage that 'man is the head; woman is the heart' – suggesting, in the final analysis, that the renegotiation of gender roles and understandings of authority within and beyond the family continued to be unresolved, at least in Catholic circles, well into the 1960s and 1970s.

Conclusion

In a widely circulating pamphlet published by the Catholic Truth Society in the 1940s and entitled *Married Life*, Catholics were exhorted to 'obey the laws of marriage', particularly those enunciated by the church on birth control, so that 'your wedded life will be what the Creator of marriage intended it to be, "a paradise on earth, a foretaste of heaven"'.[117] This aphorism illustrates perfectly the sacralized understandings of the family, parenthood and domesticity integral to Catholic interpretations of married life which have been discussed in this chapter. Moreover, it provides an example of the continuing role of Christian discourse in post-war conceptualizations and conversations about the companionate marriage and family stability within, and indeed beyond, religious circles in broader British society in ways that have been little examined by historians to date. As an initial contribution to this exploration of the intersections of gender and religion in the post-war period, this discussion has illustrated the various ways in which the Virgin Mary was used as both an ideal and an intercessory aid for Catholic women, renegotiating shifting understandings of modern femininity, their role as homemakers, and the pleasures and pressures of maternity. Similarly, the biographies of the mother and father of Christ also served as a source of inspiration and instruction for Catholic men, who were being urged to become more involved in domestic life and felt insecure about their identities and capacities as modern parents and sole breadwinners. Finally, the designation of married life as a 'paradise on earth, a foretaste of heaven' also encapsulates one of the continuing thematic contentions of this chapter – that Catholic teaching in the post-war period explicitly understood the family, as expressed by Father Peyton, as the 'atom of civilization' and a means for the realization of the kingdom. This necessarily complicates the theoretical constructs of the public and private spheres within gender historiography, for Catholic husbands and wives understood their relationships within the home, and engagement with wider British society, as an elaboration of the ideals and values encountered around the sacralized hearth or dining table. Therefore, Catholic mothers might pray to Mary for patience with husbands and against the perils of burnt breakfast toast, but they should also see their calling as supporting the economy and the formation of workers for the factories. Similarly, St Joseph might be proffered to Catholics as a paragon of the steady, reliable breadwinner, but he was also represented as a faithful, supportive husband and involved father with the inquisitive Christ-child on his knee.

In this consideration of the spectrum of ideals surrounding Catholic marriage and parenthood in the post-war period, this chapter has also argued that the politics of the family and associated constructions of gender were becoming increasingly contested through the decade. It has illustrated that lay Catholics and clerical commentators were directly engaging with these manifold societal and civic shifts in wider English society and in doing so, they were utilizing and repackaging traditional resources from a rich repository of devotional spirituality and sacramental theology. In considering the politics and constructions of domestic authority within the English family in the 1950s, the historian of gender and intellectual culture is therefore required not only to direct attention to the space beyond the hearth and outside the home, but also to look afresh at the 'secular', and thereby discern the continuing operation of the 'sacred' in the formulation and application of these ideals.

Notes

1. Burnley, Salford Diocesan Archive (hereafter SDA), File: Box 226 Marshall Papers – Pastorals, p. 8: 'An Advent Pastoral Letter on the Christian Family', Bishop Henry Vincent Marshall, 19 November 1945.
2. E. Griffith (ed.) (1944) *The Road to Maturity* (London: V. Gollancz), p. 14.
3. This is attributable to the virtually unquestioned acceptance of the secularization thesis within most historical and sociological accounts of twentieth-century Britain, which broadly postulates the waning influence of Christianity and its public importance with the onset of industrialization and the impact of the Enlightenment. For a highly influential revisionist interpretation illustrating the continuing influence of Christianity in constructions of gender and family relations until the 1960s, see C. Brown (2001) *The Death of Christian Britain: Understanding Secularization 1800–2000* (London: Routledge); and idem (2006) *Religion and Society in the Twentieth-Century* (Harlow: Longman). For a contrasting and inter-disciplinary reinterpretation of secularization, the role of Christianity in British culture, and the intersections between religion and gender, see J. Garnett, M. Grimley, A. Harris, W. Whyte and S. Williams (eds) (2007) *Redefining Christian Britain: Post-1945 Perspectives* (London: SCM Press).
4. S. Todd (2005) *Young Women, Work and Family in England, 1918–1950* (Oxford: Oxford University Press); S. Rose (2003) *Which People's War? National Identity and Citizenship in Wartime Britain 1939–1945* (Oxford: Oxford University Press); and P. Summerfield (2000) 'Women and War in the Twentieth-Century' in J. Purvis (ed.), *Women's History: Britain 1850–1945. An Introduction* (London: Routledge), 307–32.
5. D. Riley (1993) *War in the Nursery: Theories of the Child and the Mother* (London: Virago).
6. L. Hall (1991) *Hidden Anxieties: Male Sexuality, 1900–1950* (Cambridge: Polity Press), pp. 75–82.
7. See S. Morgan (2002) *Women, Religion and Feminism in Britain, 1750–1900* (New York: Palgrave Macmillan), p. 10. For a discussion of the literature surrounding 'separate spheres' theory, see the 'Introduction' to this volume.
8. M. P. Hornsby-Smith (1988) 'Into the Mainstream: Recent Transformations in British Catholicism' in T. M. Gannon (ed.), *World Catholicism in Transition* (New York: Macmillan), 218–31; K. Aspden (2002) *Fortress Church: The English Roman Catholic Bishops and Politics 1903–63* (Leominster: Gracewing); and on Catholic spirituality, see M. Heimann (1995) *Catholic Devotion in Victorian England* (Oxford: Clarendon Press); and idem (1996) 'Devotional Stereotypes in

English Catholicism, 1850–1914' in F. Tallett and N. Atkin (eds), *Catholicism in Britain and France since 1789* (London: Hambledon Press), 13–25.

9. See particularly M. Roper and J. Tosh (eds) (1991) *Manful Assertions: Masculinities in Britain since 1800* (London: Routledge), pp. 1–7; and L. Davidoff, M. Doolittle, J. Fink and K. Holden (eds) (1999) *The Family Story: Blood, Contract and Intimacy 1830–1960* (London: Longman), pp. 135–57.

10. The Salford Diocese encompasses the urban centres of Manchester and Salford as well as other large urban centres such as Blackburn and Burnley. For a broader consideration of themes but briefly touched upon in this chapter, such as the 'secularization thesis' and the incorporation of religious history into twentieth-century British historiography, see A. Harris, 'Transformations in English Catholic Spirituality and Popular Religion, 1945–80' (DPhil, Faculty of History, University of Oxford, 2008).

11. See C. Creighton (1996) 'The Rise of the Male Breadwinner Family: A Reappraisal', *Comparative Study for Society and History* 38(1), 310–37. For a helpful summary of contemporary scholarship on masculinity, see M. Francis (2002) 'The Domestication of the Male? Recent Research on Nineteenth- and Twentieth-Century British Masculinity', *Historical Journal* 45(3), 637–52.

12. B. B. Lindsey and W. Evans (1927) *The Companionate Marriage* (New York: Boni and Liveright).

13. Davidoff (et al.), *The Family Story*, p. 190.

14. J. Finch and P. Summerfield (1991) 'Social Reconstruction and the Emergence of Companionate Marriage, 1945–59' in D. Clark (ed.), *Marriage, Domestic Life and Social Change: Writings for Jacqueline Burgoyne* (London: Routledge), p. 7.

15. Ibid. See also A. Giddens (1992) *The Transformation of Intimacy: Sexuality, Love and Eroticism in Modern Societies* (Cambridge: Polity Press); J. Lewis (2001) 'Marriage' in I. Zweiniger-Bargielowska (ed.), *Women in Twentieth-Century Britain* (Harlow: Longman), pp. 69–85; and M. Collins (2003) *Modern Love: An Intimate History of Men and Women in Twentieth-Century Britain* (London: Atlantic).

16. Finch and Summerfield, 'Companionate Marriage', p. 7.

17. L. Davidoff and C. Hall (2002) *Family Fortunes: Men and Women of the English Middle Class, 1780–1850*, rev. edn (London: Routledge); J. Tosh (1999) *A Man's Place: Masculinity and the Middle-Class Home in Victorian England* (London: Yale University Press); S. Williams (1999) *Religious Belief and Popular Culture in Southwark c.1880–1939* (Oxford: Oxford University Press); and Brown, *The Death of Christian Britain*.

18. For a detailed study of the range of publications of Griffith, Mace and Gray, but one that fails to closely examine the differing religious perspectives underpinning the diverse stances they adopt on marriage, see J. Lewis (1990) 'Public Institution and Private Relationship: Marriage and Marriage Guidance, 1920–1968', *Twentieth Century British History* 1(3), 233–63. See also H. Cook (2004) *The Long Sexual Revolution: English Women, Sex and Contraception, 1800–1975* (Oxford: Oxford University Press), p. 343, who, in her comprehensive survey of twentieth-century sex manuals, reports that 'many... [authors] had a substantial religious commitment', 28 per cent were active Christians and nearly a tenth of the total were 'actually ministers'. Nevertheless, she goes on to assert that 'the nature of this commitment different widely and it has no consistent impact on the manuals'.

19. Nineteen in-depth and semi-structured interviews were recorded and transcribed encompassing three generations of Catholic men and women (1945–90)

from parishes in Crumpsall and Trafford Park as part of my doctoral research – see note 10.

20. G. Vann (1952) *Eve and the Gryphon* (London: Blackfriars Publications), p. 29.
21. A. Taves (1986) *Household of Faith: Roman Catholic Devotions in Mid-Nineteenth-Century America* (Notre Dame: University of Notre Dame), p. 48; Heimann, *Catholic Devotion in Victorian England*; and N. Christie (ed.) (2002) *Households of Faith: Family, Gender and Community in Canada, 1760–1969* (Montreal: McGill-Queen's Press).
22. SDA, File: Box 226, Marshall Papers – Pastorals, p. 4: 'An Advent Pastoral Letter on the Christian Family', Bishop Henry Vincent Marshall, 19 November 1945.
23. M. MacMahon (1948) *Nazareth: A Book of Counsel and Prayer for the Married* (Dublin: Eason and Son), p. 7.
24. SDA, File: Box 226, Marshall Papers – Pastorals, p. 3: 'An Advent Pastoral Letter on the Christian Family', Bishop Henry Vincent Marshall, 19 November 1945.
25. Finch and Summerfield, 'Companionate Marriage', p. 7; M. Richards and B. J. Elliot, 'Sex and Marriage in the 1960s and 1970s' in Clark (ed.), *Marriage, Domestic Life and Social Change*, pp. 33–4.
26. R. McKibbin (2000) *Classes and Cultures: England 1918–1951* (Oxford: Oxford University Press), p. 303; M. Abbott (2003) *Family Affairs: A History of the Family in 20th Century England* (London: Routledge), pp. 110–12; Lewis, 'Marriage', pp. 78–9.
27. Reporter, 'Divorce Wrecks Nation's Family Life: Bishops Issue a Grave Warning', *The Catholic Times*, 4 July 1953, p. 6.
28. For example, M. de la Bédoyère (1954) *Living Christianity* (London: Burns and Oates), pp. 128–9.
29. SDA, File: Box 226, Marshall Papers – Pastorals, p. 6: 'An Advent Pastoral Letter on Christian Marriage', Bishop Henry Vincent Marshall, 19 November 1948.
30. SDA, File: Box 186, Catholic Societies, Folder No 8 Catholic Marriage Advisory Council, p. 1: 'Some Notes on Marriage Guidance', Fr H. Waterhouse SJ for George Andrew Beck, 2 June 1947.
31. Ibid., pp. 2, 5.
32. Ibid., p. 2.
33. On the shift within the NMGC from guidance to counselling, and from regulation of a public institution to recognition of marriage as a private relationship, see Lewis, 'Public Institution and Private Relationship', p. 257.
34. L. Stanley (1995) *Sex Surveyed, 1949–1994: From Mass Observation's 'Little Kinsey' to the National Survey and the Hite Reports* (London: Taylor and Francis), pp. 98–9. For further discussion of the shifting understandings of the place of sex within marriage, sex education and birth control, well before the wide-scale tumult of the *Humanae Vitae* encyclical in 1968, see Harris, 'Transformations in English Catholic Spirituality', chapter 3.
35. See A. Harris and M. Spence (2007) ' "Disturbing the Complacency of Religion?": The Evangelical Crusades of Dr Billy Graham and Father Patrick Peyton in England, 1951–54', *Twentieth Century British History* 18(2), 481–513.
36. T. Madden (1965) *How's the Family? Cartoons in the Catholic Herald* (London: Burns and Oates), n.p.
37. P. Peyton (1954) *Ear of God* (London: Burns and Oates), p. xv. For a more detailed discussion of the immensely popular visiting religious evangelists spearheading a religious revival in Britain in the 1950s, see Brown, *Death of Christian*

Britain, pp. 170–5; A. Hastings (2001) *A History of English Christianity 1920–2000* (London: SCM Press); P. Pasture (2004) 'Christendom and the Legacy of the Sixties: Between the Secular City and the Age of Aquarius', *Revue D'Historie Ecclesiastique* 99(1), 82–116.

38. E.g. J. Fitzsimons, 'The Family and the Nation: Reflections on Some Recent Statistics', *The Tablet*, 8 September, 1951, pp. 152–3 and Bishop of Southwell, 'Faith and Freedom', *The Sunday Times*, 3 August, 1952, p. 6.

39. E. Chesser (1946) *Marriage and Freedom* (London: Rich and Cowan Medical Publications), pp. 15, 144.

40. SDA, File: Box 186, Catholic Societies, Folder No 8 Catholic Marriage Advisory Council, p. 5: 'Some Notes on Marriage Guidance', Fr H. Waterhouse SJ for George Andrew Beck, 2 June 1947.

41. Ibid., p. 3.

42. See e.g., M. Warner (2000) *Alone of All Her Sex: The Myth and Cult of the Virgin Mary* (London: Vintage).

43. J. A. P. Nutt (1948) *Talks for the Month of May* (London: Burns and Oates), p. 14.

44. Ibid.

45. For example, Medical Woman (1930) *'Into their Company': A Book for a Modern Girl on Love and Marriage* (London: Burns, Oates and Washbourne), p. xiv and the follow-up Catholic Woman Doctor (1939) *Growing Up: A Book for Girls* (London: Burns and Oates), pp. 35, 40–3.

46. SDA, File: 021 Bishop Marshall Sermon Notes Seal, p. 1: 'Sermon Notes – Union of Catholic Mothers', Bishop Henry Vincent Marshall, 194(–).

47. L. Hanlon (1948) 'Our Lady and the Formation of Leaders', *New Life* 1(5), 99–100.

48. Compare Griffith (ed.), *Road to Maturity*, pp. 220–1 and the Catholic advice pamphlet by M. T. St Clair (1942) *The Vice of To-Day* (Limerick: City Printing), p. 47.

49. YCW, File: Occasional Publications, p. 5: 'Girl Mother', May 1948, *YCW Girl Leaders' Bulletin and Campaign Programme*.

50. P. C. Challoner, 'Domestic Science: Homemaking', *Catholic Herald*, 23 May 1952, p. 2.

51. P. Summerfield (1994) 'Women in Britain since 1945: Companionate Marriage and the Double Burden' in J. Obelkevich and P. Catterall (eds), *Understanding Post-War British Society* (London: Routledge), pp. 60–2.

52. W. Jewell (1946) *To Those Getting Married* (London: Catholic Truth Society), p. 2.

53. SDA, File: Box 200 Marshall Papers 1941–1948 Ad Clerum and Other Papers, 200/236, p. 5: 'The Authorised Official Programme of the Catholic ANNUAL Procession', 1948.

54. Summerfield, 'Women and War', p. 326, and discussion of the Beveridge report in P. Hennessy (2006) *Having it So Good: Britain in the Fifties* (London: Allen Lane), p. 123.

55. 'Housewives do Greatest of all Jobs, says C.I.G.S.' *Daily Telegraph and Morning Post*, 7 June 1952, p. 5. See also W. Slim (1957) *Courage and Other Broadcasts* (London: Cassell), pp. 57–63.

56. M. E. Yates, 'The Catholic Mother in the Modern World', *The Catholic Times*, 1 October 1954, p. 7.

57. J. Bowlby (1951) *Maternal Care and Mental Health* (Geneva: World Health Organization); and idem (1953) *Childcare and the Growth of Love* (London: Penguin).

58. D. W. Winnicott (1957) *The Child and the Family: First Relationships* (London: Tavistock).
59. M. Hollings, 'Every Year a Marian Year', *The Tablet*, 5 December 1953, p. 539.
60. Ibid.
61. T. Holland (1954) 'Everyman's Mariology: Mother of God', *Catholic Gazette* 45(2), 39.
62. Interview with Peter Kerr, 7 August 2007 at St Antony's Trafford Park, Recording STE 003 at 29.46–31.04.
63. Letters to the Editor, *Novena*, October 1951, p. 146.
64. S. D'Cruze, 'Women and the Family' in Purvis (ed.), *Women's History*, p. 77.
65. 'Catholic Mother', 'Talking to Mary', *The Catholic Times*, 18 July 1952, p. 7.
66. Rev R. J. Roche OP, *Mother Most Admirable* (Dublin: Irish Rosary Publications, n.d.), p. 7.
67. D. Greenstock (1951) *Christopher's Talks to Catholic Parents* (London: Burns and Oates), p. 59.
68. Ibid., p. xi.
69. Interview with Mary Howarth, 7 August 2007 at St Anthony's Trafford Park, Recording STE 007 at 16.20–16.45.
70. Ibid., Recording STE 007 at 16.53–17.20.
71. L. Segal (1988) 'Look Back in Anger: Men in the Fifties' in R. Chapman and J. Rutherford (eds), *Male Order: Unwrapping Masculinity* (London: Lawrence and Wishard), pp. 68–96.
72. See, for example, J. Keating (1998) 'Faith and Community Threatened? Roman Catholic Reponses to the Welfare State, Materialism and Social Mobility, 1945–62', *Twentieth Century British History* 9(1), 86–108.
73. On affluence, consumption, leisure and D-I-Y, see A. H. Halsey and J. Webb (eds) (2000) *Twentieth-Century British Social Trends* (Basingstoke: Macmillan), ch. 18; J. Hill (ed.) (2002) *Sport, Leisure and Culture in Twentieth-Century Britain* (Basingstoke: Palgrave).
74. See also S. de Caigny (2005) 'Catholicism and the Domestic Sphere: Working-Class Women in Inter-War Flanders', *Home Cultures* 2(1), 1–24.
75. Vann, *Eve and the Gryphon*, p. 32.
76. Peyton, *Ear of God*, p. 112.
77. 'Famous Football Ground Scene of Rosary Rally', *Catholic Times*, 20 June 1952, p. 12.
78. '35,000 at Another Great Rosary Rally', *Catholic Times*, 16 May 1952, p. 1.
79. See, for example, the comment of the Auxiliary of Birmingham, Bishop Bright, who in a speech to the Catholic Young Men's Society declared, 'This is a man's Crusade' yet one not confined to Catholic families only – see 'Wembley Plans Growing for Crusade', *Catholic Herald*, 6 June 1952, p. 6.
80. North Easton, Massachusetts, Archives Holy Cross Family Ministries (hereafter AHCFM), File: 01-13-02-04-00 Lancaster, p. 17, 'One of the Greatest Religious Crusades', 1952.
81. AHCFM, File: 01-13-03-04-00 Durham, p. 12, 'Record of the Family Rosary Crusade', Paul Grant, 1952,
82. 'Rosary Crusade Rings Capital', *Catholic Herald*, 11 July 1952, p. 1.
83. 'Crusader for Prayer', *Picture* Post, 26 July 1952, pp. 4–5.
84. 'Record of the Family Rosary Crusade', pp. 18–19.
85. 'One of the Greatest Religious Crusades', p. 13.

86. See J. Chinnici (2004) 'The Catholic Community at Prayer, 1926–1976' in J. O'Toole (ed.), *Habits of Devotion: Catholic Religious Practice in Twentieth-Century America* (Ithaca: Cornell University Press), p. 71, who describes this devotion, but also explores the gender ambiguities encountered within it, for the domestic arena was traditionally acknowledged as a sphere for feminine spiritual agency.

87. L. Rossiter, 'Rosary Solves Father's Problems', *Catholic Times*, 4 July 1952, p. 7.

88. Interview with Nora Walsh, 17 September 2007 at St Anne's Crumpsall, Recording STE 022 at 54.12–54.58.

89. Vann, *Eve and the Gryphon*, p. 30.

90. Finch and Summerfield, 'Companionate Marriage', p. 12.

91. See, for example, the description of the 'tired young men' who had carried the cross in pilgrimage to Walsingham and the Union of Catholic Mothers leading the procession and carrying a statue of Our Lady – 'Our Lady of Walsingham: Impressions of a Pilgrim', *The Tablet*, 24 July 1948, p. 56.

92. The event centred around a lay male speaker (Mr Alan Ryde), and involved 2000 men from Catholic organizations around the country, supplemented by the Knights of Columba who acted as stewards – London, Archives Archdiocese of Westminster (AAW), File: Griffin Coronation of Our Lady of Willesden, 3 October 1954, pp. 1–2, 'The Coronation of Our Lady of Willesden – Report', Mgr Derek Worlock, 26 July 1954. For a description of this ceremony, see 'At Wembley', *The Tablet*, 9 October 1954, p. 345.

93. SDA, File: Box 215 Marshall Papers (Folder 1935–6), p. 9: 'Christian Marriage and the Christian Home: A Lenten Pastoral Letter', Bishop Henry Vincent Marshall, 29 January 1940.

94. Interview with Francis Leigh, 15 September 2007 at St Anne's Crumpsall, Recording STE 016 at 16.49–17.37.

95. Taves, *Household of Faith*, p. 39.

96. On the earlier popularity of St Joseph as a model for the contemplative life, see R. Faesen (2007) 'The Great Silence of Saint Joseph: Devotion to Saint Joseph and the 17th Century Crisis of Mysticism in the Jesuit Order' in H. Laugerud and L. K. Skinnebach (eds), *Instruments of Devotion: The Practices and Objects of Religious Piety from the Late Middle Ages to the 20th Century* (Langelandsgade: Aarhus University Press), pp. 73–92.

97. MacMahon, *Nazareth*, p. 249.

98. Ibid.

99. Ibid., p. 250.

100. Interview with Peter Kerr, 7 August 2007 at St Antony's Trafford Park, Recording STE 003 at 31.05–31.32. For a similar devotional reflection, see M. Joseph, 'I Think of Joseph . . . A Christmas Meditation for Husbands and Fathers', *Novena*, December 1968, pp. 17–19.

101. C. Houselander (1949) *The Passion of the Infant Christ* (London: Sheed and Ward), p. 101.

102. M. Oliver (1949) *Fair as the Moon: Mary, Purest of Creatures* (Dublin: M. H. Gill and Son), p. 98.

103. See Peyton, *Ear of God*, p. 48 and Nutt, *Talks for the Month of May*, p. 55.

104. See the model bidding prayers circulated by Bishop Holland in the Salford diocese in 1968 which were directed towards workers injured 'in fields, factories, mines and laboratories' advocating a 'gentle yet strong influence in the world of industry'.: SDA, File: Box 220 Marshall – Beck – Holland, Beck Papers,

Holland Papers 1956–, 12/68, n.p., 'Prayer for those in Industry', Bishop Thomas Holland, 2 May 1968.

105. Oliver, *Mary*, p. 98.
106. Greenstock, *Christopher's Talks*, p. 114; and P. Rorke (1960) *Through Parents to Christ* (Billinge: Birchley Hall Press), p. 11. On the specific role advocated for fathers in the sexual education of their sons, particularly discussion of masturbation, see Greenstock, *Christopher's Talks*, p. 232; C. C. Martindale (1931) *The Difficult Commandment: Notes on Self-Control Especially for Young Men* (London: Manresa Press); J. Leycester King (1944) *Sex Enlightenment and the Catholic* (London: Burns and Oates), p. 56; and Rorke, *Through Parents to Christ*, p. 33.
107. Greenstock, *Christopher's Talks*, p. 115.
108. Ibid., p. 117.
109. AHCFM, File: 01-13-03-04-00 Durham, p. 33, 'Record of the Family Rosary Crusade', Paul Grant, 1952.
110. AHCFM, File: 01-13-02-02-00 Lancaster, p. 1, 'Quotes from Father Peyton's Speeches', 1951.
111. Greenstock, *Christopher's Talks*, p. 16, speaking specifically of mixed marriages and the tendency to excuse adherence to Catholic teaching on the grounds that the mother is the primary spiritual influence.
112. Royal Commission on Population Report (1949) (London: His Majesty's Stationery Office), pp. 40–1, 137–51, 220; and P. Thane (1999) 'Population Politics in Post-War British Culture' in B. Conekin, F. Mort and C. Waters (eds), *Moments of Modernity: Reconstructing Britain 1945–1964* (London: Rivers Oram Press), pp. 114–33.
113. 'Address of His Holiness Pope Pius XII to the Newly Wed', Appendix 1 in MacMahon, *Nazareth*, p. 273.
114. See M. Young and P. Willmott (1957) *Family and Kinship in East London* (London: Routledge and Kegan Paul), pp. 10; 13–15; and J. Goldthorpe, D. Lockwood, F. Bechhofer and J. Platt (1969) *The Affluent Worker in the Class Structure* (London: Cambridge University Press), pp. 104–5; for a detailed consideration, see F. Mort (1999) 'Symbolic Fathers and Sons in Post-war Britain', *Journal of British Studies* 38(3), 353–84.
115. Finch and Summerfield, 'Companionate Marriage', p. 15.
116. Catholic Marriage Advisory Council (1963) *Beginning Your Marriage* (London: CMAC), p. 56.
117. Catholic Truth Society (c. 1940s, undated) *Married Life: A Word of Friendly Advice to the Wise* (London: Catholic Truth Society), p. 4.

Part IV
Domestic Service

8
Domestic Servants as Poachers of Print: Reading, Authority and Resistance in Late Victorian Britain

Margaret Beetham

> Useful books for a servant are a Bible and Prayer Book, a Dictionary, some cheap domestic weekly or worthy paper, and recipes.[1]

The huge growth in popular print in the second half of the nineteenth century meant that books and serials of all kinds (magazines, newspapers, penny novelettes) saturated the middle-class home and became crucial to its management. Print became the medium for advice on how to exercise domestic authority and the management of print in the home (who should read what, where and when) was defined as part of the mistresses' task. The anonymous author of the pamphlet in the Bodleian Library from whom I quote above was among those eager to ensure the proper use of print. If even domestic servants might now be able to read, the mistress must ensure that what they read was 'useful'. In this chapter I explore the politics of domestic reading and particularly the reading of domestics, that is of servants, in the late nineteenth-century middle-class household in Britain. The servant reading a book or magazine was a figure who produced conflicting tensions and anxieties. In the first part of the chapter I describe the context of these anxieties and suggest some theoretical models which may be useful. In the second half I read a variety of evidence and debates in relation to these historical and theoretical concerns. My general argument is that the reading of printed texts by servants presented itself as a knot or tangle in the webs of power and resistance which characterised domestic authority in the period.

Everyone a reader? Domesticity and the mass press in the late Victorian period

> The great point for us, at the present moment to observe, is that the whole civilised world has acquired a taste for reading: and that it has become for all classes the universal and the favourite amusement.[2]

185

... Don't read 'silly sensational stories' in 'poisonous publications which are brought to the back door in gentleman's houses'.[3]

Contemporaries and later historians alike accept that by the latter part of Victoria's reign, Britain had become a literate society. Walter Besant, the prolific novelist, journalist and commentator, put it like this in 1899:

> reading which has always been the amusement of the cultivated class has now become the principal amusement of every class; all along the line from peer to chimney sweep we are reading. Some of us are said to be reading rubbish. That may be; but it is certainly less mischievous to be reading rubbish than to be drinking in bars or playing with street rowdies.[4]

Besant here was articulating a view generally held at the end of the century that Britain now boasted a 'free press' and a population in which reading was a general source of entertainment as well as information. The last of the notorious Taxes on Knowledge, which had kept the price of print, especially newspapers, prohibitively high, had been repealed by the 1860s and the Board Schools, set up by the 1870 Education Act, had made Britain for the first time a truly literate population, or so commentators and print entrepreneurs alike believed. The publisher, George Newnes, for example, claimed that by the 1890s there were 'no illiterates' in England.[5] Later scholars, including David Vincent, have argued that the Board Schools did not have quite the dramatic effect assumed by contemporaries but they agree that by the 1890s most people in Britain could, and probably did, read.[6]

Moreover, the growth of the popular press since the 1840s ensured that by the end of the century, the British working class had at their disposal a cheap mass press and in particular a range of affordable weekly and monthly papers.[7] However, by the 1890s Besant's determinedly optimistic stance was looking rather old-fashioned and 'early Victorian'. Most contemporary commentators lamented that all the advances of the nineteenth century had produced a people who only read 'rubbish'. In his magisterial and still definitive work on the growth of the British reading public, Richard Altick concludes that late Victorians had 'recognised that ... the reading habit was contributing nothing to cultural improvement'.[8] Altick does not take as his typical late nineteenth-century reader the chimney sweep, whom Besant obviously chose as an extreme and shocking figure. Instead, Altick refers to the recurrent tropes of

> the cook in the kitchen who let the joint burn as she pored over the *Family Herald* and the mill hand sat on his doorstep of a Sunday morning, smoking his pipe and reviewing the week's outrages in the *Illustrated Police News*.[9]

The figure of the cook letting the joint burn as she reads the *Family Herald*, the domestic servant who neglects her work because she is 'reading rubbish' or because her Board School education has given her inflated ideas of herself, haunts the pages of such middle-class publications as *Punch*.[10] For *Punch* the cook should not be reading at all but attending to the joint. However, if she must read, why not something more suitable to her situation, as suggested in my opening quotation? To middle-class commentators, the reading cook was not a cause for the celebration of mass literacy, as was Besant's chimney sweep. Instead, she was a sign of the collapse of domestic authority and the proper hierarchies of home. I use the female pronoun deliberately, for whereas the chimney sweep was an aggressively masculine figure, the cook was almost certainly female and her gender is an important element of the story. I would argue that it is at least as important as class.

Leaving aside for a moment the question of whether the cook did read, and if so whether she read the *Family Herald*, questions to which I shall return, I want to address briefly the cultural anxiety which Altick so brilliantly describes. In the figure of the reading cook are concentrated a number of different nineteenth-century concerns. First, she can be understood as one manifestation of what middle-class Victorians called 'The Servant Problem'. Having at least one servant was an indicator of being middle class and it was in the domestic sphere and in the relationship of mistress to servant that class relations were worked out at the most intimate and inescapable level. No wonder there was a boom in advice literature which dealt among other topics with the proper exercise of authority by the mistress over her domestic servant or servants. Beeton's *Book of Household Management*, for example, which came out in volume form first in 1861 but went through numerous editions and reprints before 1903, assumed that the engaging and treatment of servants was an important part of domestic management. The pages on servants were reprinted as separate pamphlets. Magazines addressed to middle-class women regularly addressed the questions of the management of servants, sometimes with wit and humour, more often in tones of indignation and despair at the impossibility of finding 'good servants' and at the difficulties of the proper exercise of authority over them. Jane Carlyle, the wife of Thomas Carlyle, ran a household which was hardly typical but her letters make clear that she shared with her less remarkable contemporaries the problems of managing her servants.[11] Though as Judy Giles has suggested in this volume (Chapter 9), middle-class women endlessly read about servants, the ways in which the reading of servants entered into the exercise of domestic authority is more difficult to evidence.

What is clear, however, is that the figure of the reading servant embodied another set of nineteenth-century middle-class anxieties about class relations and the exercise of authority, which centred not on how to manage servants but on the control of reading. Historians of the press have characterised the early Victorian period as marked by power struggles over working-class access to print. These were fought out in the political and pub-lic arena, through legislation (what radicals called 'The Taxes on Knowledge') and through forms of resistance which included overtly illegal practices, such as the publications of the unstamped press.[12] Late Victorians were proud that the press in Britain was now 'free', indeed took it as a mark of progress. A 'free press' meant, of course, one controlled by the market rather than by legislation. However, as I have already suggested, the development of the market and the 'freedom of the press' produced a new set of anxieties about the abuses of such freedom and its impact on class relationships.

Edward Salmon was one of several commentators who attempted to survey and write about the problem of this new reading public produced by the Board Schools. In an article on working-class reading, one of three published in *The Nineteenth Century*, he lamented that

> An important constituent in the mental food – or rather poison – of the people is the penny novelette... Crime and love are the essential ingredients and the influence exercised over the feminine reader, often unenlightened by any close contact with the classes whom the novelist pretends to portray, crystallises into an irremovable dislike of the upper strata of society. The same dish is served up again and again and the surprising thing is that the readers do not tire of [it].[13]

This concern that the people were reading poisonous publications rather than improving works was typical and so was the easy move from 'the people' to 'the feminine reader'. Women readers were assumed to be less rational and more susceptible to the insidious poison of trashy publications than men of the same class. This was because anxieties about the deleterious effects of popular reading were often directed particularly at those groups who were perceived to be least able to make rational judgements, namely women but also the young and the working class in general. Domestic ser-vants, who typically were young working-class woman, embodied a group triply at risk – at least in the eyes of those concerned that indiscriminate readers might be seduced by the penny novelettes and cheap papers which Salmon described.

These groups (women, the young and the working class) were, of course, precisely those targeted by the new entrepreneurs of print who saw in them potential untapped markets. It is significant, as I have argued elsewhere, that Harmsworth, whose publishing empire was one of those which came to dominate the cheap magazine press in the first half of the twentieth cen-tury, established his empire in the 1890s by producing magazines like *Forget Me Not, Home Sweet Home* and *Home Chat* which were aimed specifically at working-class women.[14]

If women were seen as particularly likely to be affected by reading rubbish, women were also posited as part of the solution. With the end of punitive taxation as a form of control of print, authority over the what, the how and the where of reading had come to be increasingly vested in the home and with the mistress who managed the domestic space. This was in part related to the powerful trend, which persisted through the century, of valorising the home as *the* place in which reading ought to take place. Besant was in this mainstream tradition of thinking when he argued that even if men (his readers are clearly assumed to be male) were reading rubbish, at least they were not in bars or roaming the streets. Making home attractive so that men wanted to be there rather than on the street or in bars was an important part of the task of the woman, whatever her class and there was plenty of advice produced by publishers instructing her in how to do it.

Nor was this only a matter of advice. The material practices of the publishing industry were shaped by and in turn shaped the discourses which connected the domestic with reading. When *The Daily Telegraph* heralded the arrival of the penny newspaper in 1856, it made it possible for middle-class men to afford to buy their own copy.[15] This meant that even the newspaper, that most public of print forms, could now be read in the domestic space rather than in a public house, club or coffee house. Not surprisingly, therefore, much of the periodical literature produced from the 1850s onwards emphasised that it was designed to be read at home, even if the content might be sensational. Magazines designated as 'family' reading ranged from the cheap *Family Herald*, through the slightly dearer *Family Friend*, to the late nineteenth-century sumptuously illustrated *Hearth and Home*, reputed to be Victoria's favourite magazine. It is significant that when Dickens launched his own journal in 1850 he chose to call it *Household Words*, a title which gives no indication of content but tells everything about the way domesticity was central to the material and discursive practices of reading.

Of course, Reading Rooms and clubs continued to be important, especially those in the newly opened Public Libraries. However, the model for healthy reading, particularly by women and children, was neither the public consumption of shared print nor the solitary devouring of potentially poisonous text. Rather it was 'family reading', for it was 'the reading aloud of some good standard work' in the domestic circle which, it was argued, particularly delighted 'the feminine members of the family'.[16] Like eating together, reading together was thought to enhance the ties of the domestic realm.

Not only was the domestic the site for reading, it was increasingly the subject. Not just the idea of home but the practices of everyday domestic life were increasingly constructed in and through printed texts. From its earliest manifestations, the novel as a form had targeted women readers and focused on the domestic scene. Richardson's *Pamela*, published in 1740, was the story of a young servant who marries her master, a narrative worked and reworked throughout the nineteenth century. These narratives of master/servant seductions and resistance represented various scenarios of the relationship between reading and writing and domestic authority which deserve further treatment in their own right. My point here is that *Pamela* combined exciting narrative with advice on how to run a household. A century later, the story telling and the domestic advice had separated into two different strands of book publication, novels and novelettes on one hand and advice literature on the other, though the two continued to be held together in women's magazines.

By the end of the nineteenth century both strands (domestic fiction and domestic advice) had become hugely important in the publishing industry with hundreds of books and periodicals of all kinds not only designed to be read in the home but also *about* the home. The launch of Beeton's *Englishwoman's Domestic Magazine* at tuppence per month in 1852 pioneered the middle-class magazine which claimed to help women in their task of 'making home happy', as Beeton put it. A book like Beeton's *Book of Household Management* (a spin-off from the journal) constituted not just domestic reading but a powerful intervention into the everyday exercise of domestic authority, a point to which I will return. As Beeton and others argued in print, the task of the mistress, therefore, included not only ensuring her household's proper consumption of food but also ensuring the proper consumption of texts, particularly by children and servants. Charlotte Yonge, for example, in her advice book, *Womankind*, assumed that relationships with servants would be an important part of womanliness and that providing servants' reading was the task of the mistress:

> [By servants] in general, either a religious book, or a good, rather exciting, story are the best liked – the present amount of cultivation generally appreciates these, but not often history, travels, or tales connected with unfamiliar scenes – and it is best to give such tales, or the perilous cheap literature will supply the appetite for something interesting and not innocent.[18]

The reading of the servants in the kitchen, those working-class women embedded in the middle-class household, was seen as important to the moral and intellectual health of the entire household. No wonder that advice books for both mistresses and servants constantly warned against allowing 'rubbish' to be brought into the kitchen. No wonder that the Society for Promoting Christian Knowledge (SPCK) included in its advice to domestic servants, besides the need to be thrifty and to say your prayers, the warning, 'Don't read silly sensational stories in poisonous publications which are brought to the back door in gentlemen's houses'.[19]

This warning is exemplary not least in its deployment of the trope of poison. Threading through much of the advice and discussion on reading in the period was an assumption that ingestion of texts and ingestion of food were analogous and linked activities. Sometimes the link between reading and eating was enacted explicitly and even materially in texts. The growing importance of recipe books and advice on menus and cooking in women's magazines meant that reading and writing entered into the practices of choosing and preparing food and even of 'dining', if we take that word to mean the social habits of eating which (according to Mrs Beeton) distinguished the civilised from the savage.[20] Reading for moral improvement and eating healthy food in socially appropriate ways were explicitly linked in advice books like Henry Southgate's *What Every Lady Would Like to Know Concerning Domestic Management and Expenditure*. Along with a great deal of advice on domestic matters, Henry Southgate offered for each day of the year an uplifting quotation and an appropriate menu with recipes. December 12th, for example, the day on which I am writing this page, begins with a quotation from Rev. James Fordyce's sermons (a favourite source), 'Works of ingenuity and elegance are particularly becoming and the study of them ought to enter into female education as much as possible.' Beneath this is the suggested menu for the day, Stuffed Carp, Roast Sucking Pig and Vegetables, together with recipes.[21]

More usually the links between reading and eating remained implicit and metaphoric. That cultural anxiety which I have described persistently represented popular reading matter as poisonous, disgusting or addictive and the methods of reading deployed, particularly by young working-class women, were not those of polite 'dining'. Rather these unsuitable texts were described as being 'gobbled', or devoured as stimulants rather than as nourishing food. In seeking to combat these fears, publishers who supplied cheap reading constantly claimed that their publications were 'healthy', as did Newnes, for example, when he started his tuppenny weekly *Tit-Bits* in 1892 and Harmsworth, later Lord Northcliffe when he launched his publishing empire in the 1890s with cheap magazines aimed at women.

The analogy between the ingestion of food and the ingestion of texts, though particularly evident in the late nineteenth century, was not original. Francis Bacon's distinction between those books to be tasted, those to be chewed and those to be digested has entered into the language. Anglicans would have been used to hearing and indeed praying every year on the Second Sunday in Advent that they might 'read, mark, learn and inwardly digest' holy writ. Certainly, the late nineteenth-century deployment of these tropes was pervasive and represented, I have argued, anxieties which were historically specific. However, the widespread nature of these analogies should alert us to some aspects of the relationship of reading and authority which persist across historical periods. Reading depends not only having been taught to read but also on certain material conditions (access to print as well as space and light by which to read). However, these do not of themselves define reading or explain its significance. By analogy, books or journals are undeniably material objects – the 'same' book may appear in very different formats (hard back or paper back) – nonetheless, their significance is not only material.

Reading involves the psychological as well as the physical and social.[22] Reading, like eating, involves the taking into the self of what is other, which then becomes part of the self. It is a mysterious process. Both reading and eating are potentially dangerous (we may indeed be poisoned) but also have the potential to change us. Especially since the invention of silent reading, the processes involved in making sense of a story or article or joke are not easily accessible to measurement. For the historian of reading this presents problems. We may find out what someone read in 1882 (though even this is not always easy) but how they made sense of what they read, *how* they read is a far more slippery historical enquiry.

These aspects of reading not only make it difficult to measure; they also make it difficult to control. This opens out a set of problems important not only in historical enquiry but also in literary theory, where there has been much discussion of reading over the past two or three decades. Put briefly, there is a paradox here. On one hand print is authoritative. The advice book carried into the Victorian home an alternate authority to the one already there; the author, as the word indicates, has authority, the words come from the same root. A text like Beeton's, sometimes called the Bible of domestic management, was an authority. However, the authority of the author is never absolute. Readers always make their own sense of the text in ways which neither the author nor other authorities can completely control. This underpins Roland Barthes' discussion of the death of the author as a source of absolute authority over the reader.[23] It is also the point of theoretical work on the power and importance of readers in the work of theorists as far removed from each other as Stanley Fish, who developed the idea of reading communities, and second-wave feminists like Judith Fetterley who stressed the power of readers to read against the grain and resist authorial intention.[24] Such debates suggest that reading always involves negotiations of meaning between text and reader.

It is not my purpose here to enter into a theoretical discussion on 'the Death of the Author' or on what constitutes a 'readerly' text. I simply want to point out that this structure of authorial authority and readerly power, if not readerly resistance, is built into the practice of reading. It accounts, of course, for the anxiety of all authorities, whether the State, the Church, teachers or parents to control access to reading; who can read, what is read and how it is read. The anxiety about domestic reading in late nineteenth-century Britain can be seen as part of a long history of debates around control of access to the information, knowledge and pleasure which reading can give. It took a different and historically specific form to our early twenty-first-century concerns but there are structural continuities as well as discontinuities.

One nineteenth-century writer who understood very well the complexities presented by ideas of authority in relation to reading, including the reading of domestic servants, was Wilkie Collins. His 1862 novel, *The Moonstone*, is not only a powerful examination of Britain's imperial and class system as exemplified in the domestic life of one upper-class family; it also explores the question of authoritative texts and independent readers through the character of the family's butler, Betteridge, who is also one of the narrators of the story. Betteridge refers to his copy of *Robinson Crusoe* in all circumstances. It is his authority, his Bible. Collins may be making some satiric references to the way the Bible was sometimes used as a kind of oracle but the questions he raises of how to read and understand a text are crucial to the way his own novel works. Betteridge may treat *Robinson Crusoe* as authoritative but his readings are idiosyncratic. He reads it in his own way and for his own purposes, certainly not in ways which would be obvious to another reader or be endorsed by any other authority. Collins may be laughing at the reader in the text but he is also pointing up the way no author can control the way his text is read.

This sophisticated self-referentiality, a kind of post-modernism *avant la lettre*, should not blind us to the historical specificity of this fictional account of a servant's reading habits. *Robinson Crusoe* was recommended by The Ladies Sanitary Association as an item in its list of appropriate reading for servants.[25] Collins' novel brings into sharp focus the ways in which class and gender shape relationships between masters/mistresses and servants, just as he addresses the relationship of the violence of Empire to the apparent order and tranquillity of English upper-class society in the 1860s. Betteridge's reading tactics in relation to *Robinson Crusoe* are thus both historically specific and point beyond the immediate, alerting us to the ways we as readers have to make our own sense of the partial and fragmented narratives through which *The Moonstone* is structured.

Collins' account of one servant's reading practice chimes with the theoretical work on popular reading undertaken by the twentieth-century French theologian and cultural historian, Michel de Certeau. De Certeau, in his studies of popular culture in contemporary France, argued that what he called 'the practices of everyday life' enabled the relatively powerless to exercise an endlessly creative and always fluid set of creative 'tactics'.[26] De Certeau suggests that for 'the binary set of production-consumption one would substitute its more general equivalent, writing-reading'.[27] Consumption and reading, he argues, can themselves become forms of production, places for the production of meaning and of the self. In reading,

> A different world (the reader's) slips into the author's place... this mutation makes the text habitable like a rented apartment. It transforms a another person's property for a moment... Renters make comparable changes in an apartment they furnish with their acts and memories.[28]

Confronting a later set of elite attacks on popular reading, de Certeau argued that in the practice of reading, the powerless are like poachers on the territory of the rich, taking what they can.[29] He writes:

> Far from being writers – founders of their own place... readers are travellers; they move across lands belonging to someone else, like nomads poaching their way across field they did not write, despoiling the wealth of Egypt to enjoy it themselves.[30]

Reading, like walking the streets, he argued, could become a place of small but important creative encounters, always conducted within the constraints laid out by street planners or authors of texts. Indeed, he argues that reading can effect 'a transformation of the social relationships that overdetermine [the reader's] relationship to the text'.[31]

I find this a useful theoretical framework in which to consider popular reading in this period. For a start, it gives me a way into reading the vast amount of advice literature about the control of domestic servants (including their reading) which was produced in the latter part of the nineteenth century. It is hard for us to know how to read these texts. Who are they for? Were they to be read by the mistress or to be read aloud by the mistress to the servant or to be read by the servant herself? Beeton's original volume (much of which was itself 'poached' from earlier sources) was certainly aimed at the mistress who could then decide her own tactics of use. However, later cheap editions of the recipe part of Beeton's *Book* or the extracts of those parts of the volume specifically about domestic service were almost certainly targeted at the servant herself. More importantly, how were these texts read? We clearly cannot take them simply as evidence of practice but the problem of how far they entered into and shaped practice as well as discourse is a vexed one. At one level, all readers are poachers in de Certeau's sense and middle-class women almost certainly behaved like poachers when confronted with an authoritative text like Beeton's *Book of Household Management* or the latest advice on domestic servants in their favourite periodical. That is, they took from it what they could, but always within the context of the strategies embodied in the text.

As I have suggested, late nineteenth-century discourses about the power of print shaped and were shaped by domestic authority in a wide range of ways. A comprehensive discussion of these is beyond the scope of a single chapter. In the rest of this chapter, therefore, I turn to look specifically at the question of domestic authority in relation to the reading of women in domestic service rather than on that of the Betteridges, the butlers and male servants of the late nineteenth century. Since male servants were paid more, it was only the wealthiest households who could afford to employ them. Households who could afford to employ indoor male servants were likely to have large domestic staff in contrast to the typical middle-class family where there would often be only one or at most two. There is some evidence that the reading of men in service differed from female servants and the experience of staff in a large household was very different from that of the solitary maid of all work or general servant. However, the vast majority of domestic servants were women and domestic service continued to be the most common occupation for women up to the First World War with 'almost one in three girls between the ages of fifteen and twenty classified as domestic servant'.[32] I, therefore, take the reading of women domestic servants as a key question in relation to domestic authority and one which requires a sophisticated understanding of both the historically specific and the theoretical questions raised by the available material from the late nineteenth-century period. Drawing on de Certeau's discussion of reading as poaching, I focus on the 'tactics' of servants in relation to reading printed texts. Did servants 'poach' what they could from the riches of middle-class print culture in the period? What were their tactics and how were they constrained by the strategies of authority both inside and outside the domestic space?

Domestic reading; domestics reading

Plotting the tactics of the relatively powerless is difficult and that difficulty is compounded when we come to the tactics of the most marginal, like the maid on her own in the basement of a house. This difficulty is made even worse when that elusive practice, private reading, is the subject. Scholars like Jonathan Rose have helped to open up our knowledge of working-class reading enormously and his opening chapter shows how even into the twentieth century servants who confessed to enjoy reading were regarded as not fit for their job.[33] However, even Rose can find comparatively little to say about the reading of domestic servants, given that service was the major source of employment for working-class women. There are some sources available to us. The body of journalistic discussion and survey material on reading (more or less anecdotal) which I have already mentioned, statistical evidence from publishers' records (though unfortunately not independently audited figures), biographies and autobiographies of middle- and working-class people, letters, diaries and fictional accounts can each give us some clues, but we ourselves have to become 'poachers of print', taking what we can.

Such evidence as there is on servant's reading is largely negative – negative in two different senses. First, servants' reading is rarely or never mentioned in most sources. How to interpret this absence is the first difficulty. Was it that, like servants themselves, it was simply taken for granted in middle-class households? This seems unlikely because, secondly, and significantly, where reading by servants is mentioned, it is usually castigated, prohibited or strongly discouraged. It is not just 'poisonous publications' or sensational trash which is prohibited but often reading per se. The experience of Mrs Layton in her 'Memories of Seventy Years' for the Co-operative Guild Collection edited by Margaret Llewelyn Davies and published in 1931 can be taken as typical.

My mistress used to teach her children instead of sending them to school. I had often to mind the youngest child while the mother in the same room taught the two elder children to read. In this way I learnt how to spell and pronounce a good many words. After the baby came, the children went to school and as I had the principal care of the child, I had very little time to myself. If by chance I was seen reading, I was told that I ought to find something better to do, and generally speaking a job was found for me.[34]

The prohibition on women reading until their domestic work was done (which, of course, it never is) was internalised by many working-class women whether they had begun their working lives in service or not. Contemporary surveys like that undertaken by Lady Bell in Middlesburgh at the start of the new century showed that the women she interviewed generally read less than their men because their work was never done: they had no leisure at all.[35] While most of their homes did have some forms of books, magazines or papers, these women did not have even the level of personal spending money exercised by their men and few of them felt able to afford to buy a half-penny or penny paper for themselves.

Unlike these women in Middlesbrough, domestic servants were usually in houses where reading matter was all around them. Dusting the books was part of their job. Several writers, including George Eliot, complained that the maid did not dust the books properly, and the prolific journalist, collector of fairy tales and folk-lorist, Andrew Lang, assumed that the readers of his regular column in *Longman's Magazine* would enjoy his joke about the comic yet threatening figure of 'the maid' who tidies the study and so disturbs his train of thought.[36] Servants therefore did have some access to print and they probably sneaked a look at the books they were dusting or at the periodicals lying on the table in the drawing room as did Lavinia Swainbank when she had a brief period as a housemaid in a large house. Here for the first time she was 'treated as a human being' and given some time off in which she read voraciously in her employer's library.[37]

Most servants who wanted to read, therefore, were in houses where print was available and in most cases they were probably well able to read. However, in many cases they read in the face of prohibitions and discouragements. Such readers did poach not only in the sense that de Certeau suggested but also in the sense that they poached *time* to read when they should have been working, as did Mrs Layton, who read despite being told she ought to find something 'useful' to do. De Certeau describes such activity through the French slang term 'la perruque', which may be translated into English as 'doing a foreigner', that is the practice whereby workers 'borrow' time or tools from the employer to use for their own ends.[38] He sees this as part of the tactics of resistance to authority. Certainly, the prohibition on reading had the opposite effect from that intended in Mrs Layton's case:

The result of this treatment caused me to read when I ought to have been doing my work. I managed to do so when I went upstairs to make the beds etc. The servant next door lent me some trashy books that came out weekly. These books had tales that continued week by week and the tales were so arranged that they left off 'to be continued in our next' at a very exciting part of the story. This gave an impressionable girl a keen desire for the next chapter. After a while I became so fascinated with the tales that when the day came for the book to come out I had no peace of mind until I had been to the shop to get it and found some means to read it.[39]

However, she had so internalised the strictures on the penny novelettes as unhealthy and was so afraid of being dismissed that she gave up reading them, even though she passionately wanted to.

I don't quite know what made me give up reading the trashy things; I think it must have been thinking of my mother. I had heard my brother had been discharged from his employment for reading while he should have been at work and my mother was upset about it.[40]

Some servants with liberal employers were bold enough to ask if they could borrow books, as did Margaret Powell. Liberal though she was, Powell's mistress was astonished and exclaimed, 'I didn't know you read'. Powell wrote that 'They knew you breathed and you slept and you worked but they did not know you read.... You could almost see them reporting you to their friends: "Margaret's a good cook but unfortunately she reads. Books, you know" '.[41] Occasionally, a servant would write to one of the women's magazines taken by her mistress. One calling herself 'A General Servant' wrote to Annie Swan's advice column in *Woman at Home* in 1896, advocating 'more love between mistress and maid' because

I feel quite disgusted with mistress and maid sometimes, hearing of such petty squabbles when a kind word from one side would soon set matters straight. I am a servant myself and I know the trouble a mistress has with a servant coming fresh in the house where all is strange. I came to my present home after I lost both my parents at the early age of sixteen ... My master and mistress are God-fearing people and have been like father and mother to me.[42]

Annie Swan, the editor of this six-penny middle-class monthly, was pleased to receive a letter from a servant with 'something sensible and interesting to say'. However, reading this and other similar letters from the position of the early twenty-first century it is difficult to know how to read them when they are clearly such highly mediated texts, mediated first through the filters of the mistress' authority and then through the filter of editorial policy. What we can take from them is that servants in some households were expected, perhaps encouraged, to read those journals which the mistress regarded as suitable. A. J. Lee suggests that it was common practice for a paper like *The Morning Post* taken in large households to be read 'by gentlemen and gentlemen's gentlemen, by ladies and by ladies' maids'.[43] Most of the advice books suggested a 'good magazine' as suitable reading matter.

Much of the advice on servants' reading, as I have already shown, was motivated by a desire to prevent servants reading unsuitable or poisonous texts as much as by any positive concern for good reading. But there were positive suggestions. Some organisations and authors provided very specific lists of books which the mistress was advised to provide for her servants.

> A useful present for parents or godparents to girls thinking of engaging in domestic service is The Girls' Little Book; A Book of Help and Counsel for Everyday Life at Home and School by Charlotte M. Yonge . . . Useful books for a servant are a Bible and Prayer Book, a Dictionary, some cheap domestic weekly or worthy paper, and recipes.[44]

The rather finely titled 'Mrs. Findlay's Tea-party of Duties of Mothers, Mistresses and Maids' published by the Ladies' Sanitary Association advised that '[Servants' reading may include] Chambers Tracts, Pilgrim's Progress, Adam Bede, The Old Curiosity Shop and Robinson Crusoe'.[45]

As I have suggested, such advice literature may not tell us much about what books, if any, mistresses did provide for their servants. However, given that there was a body of writing which gave both general and specific advice on provision of suitable books, we may take it that some servants would be given at least some of the texts suggested by publications like those from the Ladies' Sanitary Association. Some of these suggested texts (the recipe book, the Dictionary) were clearly intended to be practical and used for reference (though even these can offer the reader the opportunity for fantasy and exploration of meaning). However, others clearly gave space for those processes of 'poaching' or occupying the space of the text with personal memories which de Certeau describes. Of course, gift books or books bought by others are not necessarily read. However, in the absence of much hard evidence to the contrary these lists suggest a quite wide range of reading provided for servants including novels. Perhaps the most surprising suggestion is George Eliot's *Adam Bede* with its narrative of the seduction and abandonment of a servant girl by the upper-class man who owns the estate. This was a particularly powerful reworking of that persistent narrative trope of master/servant seduction and betrayal which was the staple of sensational serials.

There was thus some reading sanctioned by domestic authority in some households at least. What is not clear is how far any of these were for the servants' private reading. For private reading was only part of the story. Like many members of the working class, domestic servants would have had access to print through being read to by others. However, while Mayhew's costermongers enjoyed having one of their more literate number read aloud the exciting stories of wicked aristocrats seducing working-class maidens which characterised publications like *Reynolds News*, the domestic servant's experience was rather different.[46] The practice of reading aloud in the middle-class home included, but was by no means exhausted by, family prayers, with its Bible readings. Reading aloud of improving works while the female members of the family did needlework was well established in middle-class households like that of Florence Nightingale's. Servants would probably not have been included in such circles but might well have the experience of being read to at other times. Amy Cruse records that even in the bohemian household of Hubert Bland and Edith Nesbit, hardly a model of Victorian domestic virtue, the mistress read *Jessica's Last Prayer*, a text of Victorian religious sentimentality, to her maid.[47] Nesbit was apparently deeply moved but we don't know how the maid felt about it. Florence Nightingale described the family reading times as like 'lying on one's back with one's hands tied and having liquid poured down one's throat', a form of torture.[48] However, Nightingale unlike her servants was free to choose other kinds of reading for herself. And we don't know how the cook or housemaid might have responded, especially if – like Mrs Layton – she was hungry for print.

However, what is clear is that reading aloud did not just work one way nor was culture always trickled down from above. M. V. Hughes in her account of *A London Childhood in the 1870s* tells of how horrified her father was to discover the servants had been reading *Lloyds Paper* to her in the kitchen.[49] The role of nannies and servants in bringing up middle-class children and giving them access to culture, including popular culture, is too large a topic to enter into here but it is worth pointing out that Andrew Lang, who complained about the maid disturbing his writing, almost certainly owed his lifelong interest in folklore and fairy tale – so crucial to his literary work – to the Scottish nurse who had brought him up on traditional tales and songs.[50]

In addition to being read to and having gifts of improving works and despite warnings to the contrary, domestic servants certainly did buy and share with each other the cheap serials which Salmon and others regarded as so poisonous. Mrs Layton was typical in that regard. The traditional novelettes were supplemented in the 1890s by a new kind of cheap women's magazine, such as *Sweethearts*. Unlike the radical sensational literature of publications like *Reynolds News*, so loved by the costermongers, in which the seduction and betrayal of the working-class servant by an aristocrat is taken as a type of exploitative class relations, these tales tended to be of the type pioneered by Richardson's *Pamela*, stories in which the virtuous servant marries her aristocratic lover. For example, the penny magazine, *Sweethearts*, ran a complete short story in its second number in which Norah, a poor

Irish girl working as a servant in London, overcomes the machinations of her jealous upper-class rival to marry a Duke. The story is entitled 'A Lover of High Degree or How Norah Flynn became a Duchess, A Romantic Story of Unswerving Affection and Mad Passion'.[51] The author, Lorna O'Reilley, was billed as also having written 'A Splendid Crime, One Summer's Flirtation, Jilted, A Strange Wooing, Her Heart's Lord etc.etc.'

Salmon was right in thinking that these publications addressed class differences and the dangers of working women's seduction by employers and did so in stark, if repetitive, terms. Perhaps as Tania Modleski has argued about twentieth-century romances of the Mills and Boon type, they were popular with women because they asked the right questions, even though the answers they provided continued to leave readers unsatisfied.[52] For servants like the print-loving Mrs Layton, such tales were unsatisfactory but they were all that was available. As she says looking back from her old age, 'I often think how different my life might have been if I had had a good book lent to read and could have read it openly'.[53]

Finally, we do find evidence that there were some servants who, despite everything, took advantage of being in houses with books and journals to read widely and seriously. Amy Cruse reports that Mary Howitt, who with her husband, William, pioneered good quality periodicals for the artisan, had gone into the kitchen on a visit to a friend and found the cook reading not the *Family Herald* but *Essays and Reviews*, the controversial theological work.[54] Not many cooks perhaps read theology by choice but we may take Winifred Foley's account of her reading as exemplary if not typical. Foley was working for an elderly woman whose attic was full of books which the young maid borrowed on what she called her 'burglar' expeditions. Ironically, these were designed to allay her mistress' fears of lurking strangers but they enabled Foley if not to burgle, then certainly to carry out 'la perruque' as well as 'poaching' in de Certeau's sense. Finding an edition of *Uncle Tom's Cabin*, the anti-slavery novel by Harriet Beecher Stowe, she took it down to read.

> [My mistress] never gave me a minute's peace to read, so I hid it on a shelf in the kitchen cupboard: all my chores in there were done slapdash-quick so that I could poke my head in and have a read. The tap-tap of her stick across the yard warned me of her approach. One day I got so engrossed in the part where Eliza braved the frozen river with her little son in her arms, I was indeed deaf to the world around me, the scalding tears falling on a pile of plates already inadequately wiped. I came smartly back to earth with a stinging swish from her walking stick across my behind... My uncontrollable fit of crying against the cupboard door took my old mistress by surprise. She was quite contrite. I didn't bother to enlighten her on the cause of my tears – she might find me with my head stuck in the cupboard again![55]

Foley was remarkable, not least because she left an account of her life as a servant and because of her wonderfully sharp prose style. Was she unusual, too, in that her determination to read did not falter? Like Mrs Layton of the Co-operative Women's Guild, she found in her reading both feeling and a way of understanding her world. She furnished the text with her own imagination as de Certeau argues we all do as attentive readers. In turn the story gave her the potential in de Certeau's terms to effect 'a transformation of the social relationships that overdetermined [her] relation to texts'.[56] Winifred Foley crying because of the story of Eliza's escape from slavery seems a fitting place to end this brief account of domestic servants as poachers of print.

Notes

1. [Raynor, John?] (undated, possibly 1896) *Employers and Female Domestic Servants; their respective rights and responsibilities*, no publishing details, p. 30.
2. W. Besant (1899) *The Pen and the Book* (London: Thomas Burleigh), p. 30.
3. From *A Mistress's Counsel or A Few Words to Servants* (undated) quoted in F. Huggett (1977) *Life Below Stairs: Domestic Servants in England from Victorian Times* (Stevenage: Robin Clarke), p. 64.
4. Besant, *Pen and the Book*, p. 30.
5. H. Friederichs (1911) *The Life of Sir George Newnes* (London: Hodder and Stoughton) p. 121.
6. D. Vincent (1989) *Literacy and Popular Culture: England 1750–1914* (Cambridge: Cambridge University Press).
7. R. Altick (1957) *The English Common Reader: A Social History of the Mass Reading Public, 1800–1900* (Chicago: University of Chicago Press), passim and p. 364.
8. Ibid., p. 364.
9. Ibid.
10. D. Abbott (2002) *Good and Faithful: Representations of Domestic Servants in English Fiction 1870–1920* Unpublished PhD thesis, University of the West of England, passim.
11. See, for example, Carlyle, Alexander (ed.) (1903) *New Letters and Memorials of Jane Welsh Carlyle Vols. I and II* (London: John Lane), I, pp. 87, 102, II, pp. 37–9.
12. J. Wiener (1969) *The War of the Unstamped: The Movement to Repeal the British Newspaper Tax* (Ithaca and London: Cornell University Press).
13. Salmon, Edward G. (1886) 'What the Working Classes Read', *Nineteenth Century*, XX, 108–117, pp. 112–13.
14. R. Pound and G. Harmsworth (1959) *Northcliffe* (London: Cassell), p. 200, 202; M. Beetham (1996) *A Magazine of Her Own? Domesticity and Desire in the Woman's Magazine 1800–1914* (London: Routledge), pp. 122ff.
15. Altick, *English Common Reader*, pp. 354–5.
16. [Beeton, Isabella] (1861) *Beeton's Book of Household Management* (London: S.O. Beeton), p. 17.
17. *Englishwoman's Domestic Magazine* (1852) I, p. 1.
18. C. M. Yonge (1876) *Womankind* (London: Mozley and Smith), pp. 199–2000.
19. Quoted in Huggett, *Life Below Stairs*, p. 64.
20. Beeton's *Book of Household Management*, p. 905.

21. H. Southgate (1876) (4th edn) *Things a Lady Would Like to Know Concerning Domestic Management and Expenditure* (London and Edinburgh: William P. Nimmo), p. 350.
22. W. Ong (1982) *Orality and Literacy: The Technologies of the Word* (London: Methuen).
23. R. Barthes (1977) *Image, Music, Text*, trans. Stephen Heath (London: Fontana).
24. J. Fetterley (1978) *The Resisting Reader; A Feminist Approach to American Fiction* (Bloomington, Indiana University Press); S. Fish (1980) *Is there a Text in this Class; The Authority of Interpretive Communities* (Cambridge, MA: Harvard University Press).
25. Anon. (undated) *Mrs. Findlay's Tea Party of Duties of Mothers, Mistresses and Maids* (London: The Ladies' Sanitary Association), unnumbered page.
26. M. de Certeau (1984) *The Practice of Everyday Life*, trans. Randall, Steven (Berkeley and Los Angeles: University of California Press), pp. 36–9 and passim.
27. Ibid., p. xxi.
28. Ibid.
29. Ibid., pp. 165–76.
30. Ibid., p. 167.
31. Ibid., p. 173.
32. L. Davidoff and R. Hawthorn (1976) *A Day in the Life of a Victorian Domestic Servant* (London: George Allen and Unwin), p. 73 and passim.
33. J. Rose (2001) *The Intellectual Life of the British Working Class* (New Haven: Yale University Press), p. 24 and passim.
34. 'Memories of Seventy Years, by Mrs Layton', *Life as We have Known it* (1931, 1977) M. Llewellyn Davies (ed.) (London: Virago), p. 26.
35. Lady H. B. Bell (?1907?1911) *At the Works: A Study of a Manufacturing Town* (London: Thomas Nelson and Sons), pp. 207, 236, 241.
36. G. Haight (1954) *The Collected Letters of George Eliot* (Oxford, Oxford University Press) p. 535; *Longman's Magazine* (1899), XIII, pp. 659–60.
37. J. Burnett (1974) *Useful Toil: Autobiographies of Working People from the 1820s to the 1920s* (Harmondsworth: Penguin Books), p. 224.
38. Certeau, *The Practice of Everyday Life*, p. 29.
39. Davies, *Life as we Have Known It*, p. 26.
40. Ibid.
41. Quoted in Rose, *Intellectual Life of the British Working Class*, p. 25.
42. 'Over the Teacups with Annie S. Swan', *Woman at Home* (1896) VI, p. 631.
43. A. J. Lee (1976) *Origins of the Popular Press in England, 1855–1914* (London: Croom Helm), p. 38.
44. ?Raynor, *Employers and Female Domestic Servants*, pp. 23, 30.
45. *Mrs. Findlay's Tea-party* (unpaginated).
46. P. Quennell (ed.) (1984) *Mayhew's London* (London: Bracken Books), p. 65.
47. A. Cruse (1935, 1962) *The Victorians and Their Books* (London: George Allen and Unwin), pp. 80–1.
48. R. Strachey (1978) *The Cause; A Short History of the Women's Movement in Great Britain* (London: Virago), p. 402.
49. M. V. Hughes (1934, 1977) *A London Childhood of the 1870s* (Oxford: Oxford University Press), p. 73.
50. R. L. Green (1946) *Andrew Lang; A Critical Biography and Short Title Bibliography* (Leicester: Leicester University Press), p. 1. See the discussion of servant–child interactions in Chapter 5, this volume.

51. *Sweethearts*, 1, no. 2, 1898, reprinted in M. Beetham and K. Boardman (2001). *Victorian Women's Magazines: An Anthology* (Manchester: Manchester University Press), pp. 133–9.
52. T. Modleski (1984) *Loving with a Vengeance: Mass-produced Fantasies for Women* (Connecticut: Greenwood Press).
53. Davies, *Life as We Have Known It*, p. 26.
54. Cruse, *The Victorians and Their Books*, pp. 100–1.
55. 'Winifred Foley, "A Plebeian's Progress" ' in Burnett, *Useful Toil*, p. 231.
56. De Certeau, *The Practice of Everyday Life*, p. 173.

9
Authority, Dependence and Power in Accounts of Twentieth-Century Domestic Service

Judy Giles

In his collection, *London in the Thirties*, the photographer, Bill Brandt, includes a picture entitled 'Parlourmaid and underparlourmaid ready to serve dinner'.[1] This portrays two young women, dressed in maids' uniforms, standing by a table set with silver, crystal and flowers. The diners they will serve are not shown but we can deduce their class and status from the crystal glasses, the bone-handled cutlery, the silverware, the pictures on the walls and, of course, the servants themselves. The two women are part of the conspicuous consumption that is on display here. Positioned between the pictures and the elegant table settings, they belong to their employers as much as the tableware and pictures. Their matching uniforms, snowy white and starched, their rigid posture and their expressionless faces tell us something of, what Nigel Henderson calls, 'the uncompromising severity of the social caste system'.[2] This photograph offers us a glimpse into a forgotten way of life in which one set of people not only serve the needs of another, but remain invisible 'disappearing into darkened chambers, hurrying back to the kitchens or the courtyards, a blur on the edge of vision'.[3] I look at the parlourmaids in Brandt's photograph and I wonder what is going on behind those wooden faces, what they think, what stories they would tell, and how their sense of self is shaped by the conditions of their existence. Are they contemptuous, or deferential, hostile or filled with admiration for their employers – or a mixture of all? As Alison Light reminds us servants' experiences, whilst more varied and different than has ever been acknowledged, have remained silent and anonymous, '[s]ervants form the greatest part of that already silent majority – the labouring poor – who have for so long lived in the twilight zone of historical record. Their voices are rarely heard and their features seldom distinguished.'[4]

This is true of the inter-war period even as the range and forms of domestic service changed with changing social and economic conditions. Brandt's image of servants is the one that most readily springs to mind for most of us today. Films like *Gosford Park*, TV series like *Upstairs Downstairs* and the few memoirs of those who worked in the big houses of the period have confirmed his image of servants as the dominant one. This is a world in which 'the green baize door' separated servants from their employers, in which two different but parallel worlds co-existed:

> Chilford House was divided into two parts by the green baize swing-door which separated the kitchen regions from the abode of the Gentry. My life, of course, was centred on the inferior side of that door, and indeed I hardly went through it all the time I was there. Although I had nothing to do with 'them' on the other side, they were subject of so many intimate and derogatory comments in the servants' hall that there was not much I didn't know about them.
>
> (Dickens 1939: 111)

However, as the large households of the Victorian upper classes became increasingly more difficult to maintain, as new employment opportunities for working-class women became available, and as smaller 'servantless' houses were built for an aspiring lower middle class, new forms of relationship, played out in different spaces, emerged. Such spaces were no longer simply the large households of a previous era with the spatial markers and rituals that mitigated the intrusive aspects of living with what were virtual strangers (though as Margaret Beetham's exploration in this volume of late Victorian domestic service makes clear, even at its height, domestic service comprised an uncomfortable and contested set of social relations). Instead, the servantkeeping settings of the inter-war years increasingly included the suburban house and the town flat. The purpose of this chapter is to capture something of the flavour of these relationships in the first half of the twentieth century. Caught between a continuing desire for servant help and the tensions involved in a relationship with mechanisms for creating spatial and emotional distance compared to the past, maintaining authority became increasingly problematic for employers, particularly mistresses. In addition, the politics of domestic authority were shaped by wider challenges from the developing ideals of social democracy and citizenship. One of the purposes of this chapter is to probe the micro-politics of the middle-class household in which authority over servants was one of the few ways that middle-class women might assert a powerful identity at a specific historical moment when the characteristics of this servant population were changing rapidly. The intimacy of live-in domestic service once 'the green baize door' disappeared had the potential to produce relationships of great intensity – defensive, belligerent, affectionate and mutually dependent. Virginia Woolf, as Light has shown, despised and loved her servant, Nellie Boxall, in equal measure, hardly able to part with her but resenting Nellie's demands and capriciousness.[5] Thus, my attempt to understand the relationships created by domestic service at a specific historical moment has to be located in the wider context that is the emotional landscapes produced by the forms of dependency found in domestic service.[6]

Very few people born before the Second World War remained untouched by the discourses of domestic service, produced by a range of material and legal practices, upheld by certain forms of psychological power, and debated in a variety of, sometimes competing, languages, from the purely economic to those of fiction and the imagination.

Yet, one of the problems inherent in any attempt to reconstruct the historical specificity of mistress–servant relations is, of course, that the sources are fragmentary and incomplete. There are official pronouncements on domestic service as a desirable employment for young women, government reports, census data and social surveys but for the lived experience of the system, historians are reliant on autobiographical, fictional and oral accounts with all the flaws inherent in such sources. Nevertheless, these sources can yield rich insights into the psychic economy of servantkeeping: insights that illuminate not only the micro-politics of a system played out in the domestic spaces of middle-class life, but the emotional territories of a class system that interacted with gender in quite specific ways. These sources provide access into the ways in which domestic service was imagined and experienced by employers and employees but they also suggest how domestic service became a metaphor for wider anxieties about middle-class life, about deference, loyalty and authority in a changing world, and about the implications of social democratic forms of political organisation. The written sources explored here include Monica Dickens' comic account of service, *One Pair of Hands*, Celia Fremlin's *The Seven Chars of Chelsea*, Daphne Du Maurier's best-selling novel, *Rebecca*, and a short story by Agatha Christie.[7] These stories, all published in the late 1930s and early 1940s and all by women, testify to an intense curiosity on the part of women writers to explore the so-called 'servant problem'. The forms of writing in which servants feature vary from the Gothic imagination of Du Maurier, to the comic vignettes of Dickens, to the quasi social survey of Fremlin, to the detective fiction of Christie. Servants are either observed from the outside (Dickens and Fremlin) or imaginatively realised in ways that hint at profound anxieties and fear (Du Maurier and Christie). I have also juxtaposed these written fictions with the, albeit fragmentary, voices of ex-servants. These need to be approached with caution: they were collected long after the event when memories may have faded. Nevertheless, whilst I have tried to avoid imputing motives where I have no evidence, I think it is permissible to speculate judiciously from the language and tone used, as well as the incidents recalled. Before exploring the detail of these stories, however, it is important to locate domestic service and those who wrote about it in a specific historical context.

It is generally accepted that by the 1950s the practice of residential 'servantkeeping' had all but disappeared except in a few aristocratic households.[8]

The expansion of alternative occupational opportunities for working-class women in retailing, clerical and factory work is frequently cited as a major reason for the increasing shortage of female servants. As a result, the cost of keeping a servant rose, particularly after 1945, and demand decreased as middle-class households found themselves unable or less willing to incur this expenditure at a time when increasing taxation and a sharp rise in the cost of living were squeezing income.[9] However, despite being perceived as in crisis between 1918 and 1950, domestic service continued to be the largest employer of young women. Selina Todd argues that the persistence of domestic service as a major occupation for young women was the result of industrial and agricultural depression in the later 1920s and the 1930s.[10] Young women from rural and depressed industrial areas frequently sought work as domestic servants because there was little else in the locality: in 1929 the largest concentration of servantkeeping households was in the relatively affluent and urban South and Southeast whilst Wales had relatively fewer servants.[11] Equally, the provision of board and lodging and even, for some, the uniform were attractions.[12] As late as 1950 *The Lady*, a magazine targeted at upper middle-class women, carried advertisements for live-in maids-of-all-work, cooks and companions, and the debates that took place in Parliament and on the BBC in 1945 and 1946 assumed that domestic help of some kind, for some women, was necessary because 'if the difficulty of getting the housework done is not solved, women will not be able to make their contribution in the world'.[13] The decline of the Victorian household and the shift to non-residential help meant that the age profile of domestic servants changed dramatically between 1931 and 1951. In 1931, 639,057 young women between the ages of 14 and 24 were employed as domestic servants: by 1951 this had fallen to 108,919, a drop of 19 per cent.[14] Furthermore, the decline of large rural households, the reorganisation of space both in and outside the house which is explored by Jane Hamlett (Chapter 5) in this volume, and the replacement of carriages with motor cars meant that fewer servants were male. The relative disappearance of footmen, butlers, boot-boys, pantry boys, stablehands and coachmen, except in the most wealthy or socially elevated homes, meant that service became a female dominated occupation in the inter-war years.[15] Thus, the relationships between employer and employee in the inter-war middle-class home were almost always between women and were increasingly non-residential. After 1950 non-residential domestic help was increasingly undertaken by older married women who wanted to work part time: women like Doris whose story is recounted below.

Throughout the period in question there were constant discussions about what was frequently perceived as 'the servant problem'. Discussions about how the domestic work of middle-class homes could and should be organised were not new. As Carole Dyhouse argues, such debates were ferociously engaged in before and during the First World War.[16] The debate continued after the First World War as it became harder to attract young women to domestic service, particularly in areas where there were alternative forms of employment. In 1919 the *Report of the War Cabinet Committee on Women in Industry* noted that many women were unwilling to return to domestic service, having tasted greater freedom and higher wages during the war.[17] And in 1923 the Ministry of Labour published the *Report of the Committee Appointed to Enquire into the Present Conditions as to the Supply of Female Domestic Servants*, a report aimed at encouraging young women into domestic service.[18] The Labour Party produced a pamphlet entitled *What's Wrong with Domestic Service?* in 1930 that outlined some of the issues around domestic service such as low pay and long working hours, and all the social surveys of the period referred to the problematic conditions of domestic service.[19] The Central Committee on Women's Training and Employment (CCWTE) provided domestic service training schemes for unemployed working-class women in urban industrial areas from 1921 onwards and the Domestic Workers Union was set up in 1938 in an attempt to regulate wages and conditions of service. During the Second World War Ernest Bevin, then Minister of Labour and National Service, floated the possibility of setting up a National Service Orderly Corps to provide domestic help for private households as well as hospitals, nursing-homes and nurseries.[20] And in response to wartime anxieties about domestic service, Bevin commissioned a report, published in 1945, on the ways in which domestic employment might be organised in the post-war period.[21]

Without exception these initiatives focused on the need to improve the conditions of domestic service in order to encourage recruitment and in order to provide educated women with the domestic help that would free them to make 'their contribution in the world'.[22] What is notable about these official debates is the way in which the discussion and solutions focus on a particular mode of authority – the contractual relationship between employer and employee. It was believed that a rational system of incentives such as reasonable wages, training opportunities and decent working conditions would attract young women into domestic service. Violet Markham's *Report* saw the refusal of young working-class women to enter domestic service as a response to media caricatures and a general stigmatisation of servants rather than as the rational consequence of a changing economy and a sensible response to the psychological injuries of service.[23] Markham was in her seventies when she produced the *Report*. Her recommendations that domestic authority should be regulated by a contractual model of employment stem from her attempt to negotiate the tensions between her Victorian middle-class consciousness and a genuine wish to engage with the 'more egalitarian outlook of the present day'.[24] Women, like Markham, were dependent on their servants for the time and energy that enabled them to engage in non-domestic activities such as writing, painting or public service. However, the relationship between servants, particularly residential servants, and their mistresses was not, and never could be, simply that of employer and employee. For mistresses it involved sharing their homes with women of another class over whom they were expected to wield authority and, where the servant was young, moral guardianship. It meant allowing another person, not only to cook and clean, but to open doors, to draw the curtains, to fetch a book. It infantilised the mistress at the same time as expecting her to wield authority. For servants it meant cleaning someone else's home, cooking someone else's meals, looking after someone else's children for low wages; it could mean living in someone else's home and, as one servant put it, belonging 'body and soul to the mistress'.[25] For 14-year-old Winifred Foley it meant sleeping in the same bed as her 90-year-old employer.[26] Given the intimate nature of the one or two maid households that emerged in the inter-war period the emotional experience of domestic authority has remained shadowy, finding its expression, often as traces, in fiction and stories, whilst the official language of Reports, legal strictures and employment contracts attempts to ignore or conceal this in a drive to modernise an occupation that was not really susceptible to scientific rationalisation.

Roy Lewis and Angus Maude's survey of the middle classes, entitled *The English Middle Classes*, written in 1949, devotes a whole chapter to domestic service. Lewis and Maude believe that 'the amount of work done within the home by the middle class housewife is greater than that to be done by the working class wife with the same number of children'.[27] They argue that domestic help is necessary to ensure that middle-class standards of 'gracious' living do not fall or disappear all together. Rhetoric, like that used by Lewis and Maude, drew on well-established discourses of middle-class domesticity that produced powerful meanings about 'comfort', 'service' and 'place'. Since the eighteenth century a belief that the 'domestic organic community was the upholder of moral order in a chaotic external world' had placed the middle-class family as the arbiters of morality, taste and, increasingly, social status.[28] The middle-class home, separated geographically and figuratively from the dirt, disorder and chaos of city poverty or the decadence and frivolity of the aristocratic upper classes, had become the symbol of quintessential English values. Its physical comfort was matched by the order, harmony and restraint that characterised its household relations. According to this ideal, husbands, wives, children and servants knew their 'place' and willingly accepted the rights and responsibilities that were thus demanded.[29] The difficulties involved in recruiting and retaining servants that had continued since the end of the First World War were, to many middle-class observers, a clear example of the erosion of middle-class power. *The English Middle Classes* is one manifestation of the anxieties expressed by a threatened middle class who feared what a 'classless' society might mean for their domination of the intelligentsia, politics, business, the arts and industry, a domination that had been hard won over the previous century. It should not be surprising then that *The English Middle Classes* continued to propound the Victorian view that the middle-class home is the symbol and heart of civilised society and, as such, the traditional relations of master, mistress, husband, wife, child, servant should be supported, if necessary by the state in the form of tax relief, certainly by mistresses in their treatment of servants. After all the growth of a lower middle class drawn from the upper reaches of the working-class, the emergence of a mass culture in the form of the cinema, the radio, the dance-hall and 'pulp' fictions, and the possibility of owning a home in the suburbs for those who had once served in the homes of others, suggested to an embattled middle class that the working classes were no longer prepared to stay in their traditional 'place'.

The symbolic as well as the literal function of servants was to keep dirt, chaos and disorder ('the rough') at bay in order to sustain the ideal that middle-class domestic life was ordered, 'civilized' and 'gracious'.[30] A middle-class woman's role in the home was to supervise, teach and guide the invisible hands that kept 'the rough' firmly distinguished from 'the gracious' and 'clean'. To this end she was expected to wield a firm but kindly authority over her servants: as one household manual warned its readers,

A servant is quick to grasp the fact when her mistress is not versed in the arts of domestic science, and quicker still to take advantage of the ignorance thus displayed. She knows that there is no trained eye to detect flaws in her work; that a room half dusted will seldom evoke a protest; that a table carelessly or slovenly laid will as often as not pass unheeded. The mistress will be made to suffer in many little ways for her ignorance in respect to household duties until by bitter experience she will awaken to the realisation of the fact that knowledge is indeed power, and strive to learn what she should have known when she first began to reign as mistress of her own home.[31]

'To reign as mistress of her own home' was a position of, albeit limited, power for middle-class women who, even after the First World War, were still precluded from many public and professional offices. The legal limitations of this power are spelled out in the same household manual:

As all dealings with servants are mainly conducted by the wife, as superintendent of the domestic side of the home, the mistress is more often than not regarded as having supreme control over them. She it is who engages them, allots their various duties, provides for their outings and holidays, and dismisses them when their work is unsatisfactory. This is a typical instance of the wife acting as her husband's agent, for where husband and wife live together it is the husband who is the legal head of the servants of a household.[32]

Thus, the wife was the conduit through which a certain form of patriarchal authority was invested in the middle-class home. Wives represented the master's authority in the household, supervising all aspects of a servant's work, but having no independent legal authority over them. While, for many mistresses, this role created anxiety and was often time-consuming, it also offered opportunities for a measure of power. There are many recorded instances of the unpleasant ways in which this power manifested itself. Generic names like 'Peggy' or 'Mary Ann' were given to women on enter-ing service; a maid-of-all-work could be at the mercy of her mistress' bell, forced to respond immediately every time it rang; servants were not allowed to speak unless spoken to by their mistress; heavy workloads often made it impossible to take the limited time off allowed; servants were the first to be suspected or accused when anything went missing; young women in service were often not allowed 'callers' of either sex; and as one mistress is quoted as saying 'I pay my housemaid her wages, and I shall speak to her as I like'.[33] Even where the mistress was benevolent she still controlled the payment of wages and had the power to give or refuse a reference. Without 'a char-acter' servants were unlikely to find a similar job elsewhere. The growing willingness of women to stand up to their mistresses, deplored as 'rudeness', stemmed in part from the knowledge that there were other jobs available in shops and factories that did not require references. Fourteen-year-old Joyce Storey, for example, forced to wash the coal cellar floor, before beginning her afternoon off, fuelled with righteous rage, at what she perceived as her mistress' game-playing walked out on her employment. She quickly found alternative employment in a corset factory.[34]

If open anger was one response to the injustices of domestic service, covert resistance was another. Winifred Foley's account of her first job rep-resents the relationship between her and her 90-year-old employer as one characterised by duplicity and deception. Winifred soon discovered the joys of hoodwinking what she called the 'cantankerous old tartar', alter-ing the clocks, for example, in order to get more time in bed.[35] Pauline Charles became adept at pretending to be dusting or scrubbing when she had, in fact, been reading; the late Victorian battles over servants' reading explored by Margaret Beetham in this volume (Chapter 8) persisted into the mid-twentieth century. During the Second World War, when her mistress removed all the light bulbs and expected the servants to operate in the dark, Pauline managed on occasions to subvert this, and exerted her authority through the threat of leaving.[36] Domestic service often became an emo-tional war zone in which numerous battles of attrition and manipulation were fought between suspicious mistresses and resentful maids, between a sense perhaps of useless dependency and the servants' knowledge of this. Servants like Winifred and Pauline felt that the authority and privilege wielded by their mistresses justified certain deceptions. Indeed, it was pre-cisely such deceptions that enabled Winifred, Pauline, and countless others

like them, to maintain their self-esteem in situations that consistently functioned to diminish this. Defined by middle-class culture as duplicitous, rude,
lazy, or alternatively, deferential, silent, loyal, servants had few dignifying
identities to draw on. It is not surprising, therefore, that relations between
maids and mistresses produced structures of feeling that involved deeply felt
ideas about obligation, privacy, authority and 'place', and that these might
manifest themselves in contempt and deception, as well as condescension
and deference. As such the domestic organisation of the middle-class home
became the focus for, generally unacknowledged, but nevertheless fierce,
struggles around self-dignifying identities that were strongly inflected by
class. When people discussed the 'servant problem' they were nearly always
talking about other things – 'civilised standards' and 'comfort', 'service' and
'deference', and 'place'. In turn, these expressions of anxiety might hide a
fear of servants who knew too much about the intimate workings of the
households they served. The possibility of equal friendships in such circumstances remained utopian. Virginia Woolf comments in her diary that one
of the worst things about the London air raids in the First World War was
having to make conversation with the servants all night and Vanessa Bell
complained that although her servant, Grace, was 'extraordinarily nice...
she is, like all the uneducated, completely empty-headed really, and after
a bit gets terribly on one's nerves'.[37] Nevertheless, an almost obsessive
desire to know, to understand, to comprehend these apparently alien beings
permeates the writing produced by middle-class women in this period.[38]
It is noteworthy that three of the four narratives considered below involve
middle-class women disguising themselves as servants.

In 1940 Celia Fremlin published her survey into domestic service in which
she disguised herself as a servant in order to experience the conditions of
service (Fremlin 1940). Fremlin was the daughter of a Hertfordshire doctor.
She graduated from Oxford in 1936 with a degree in classics and little idea
about what she wanted to do. During her time at Oxford she had briefly
been a member of the Communist Party, leaving because she felt her friends
in the party talked 'what sounded like rubbish about working-class life'.[39]
She participated in and observed the daily life of cooks, maids of all work,
'chars', residential parlourmaids and waitresses in order to write about the
'peculiarities of the class structure of our society ... from the angle of domestic service'. Thus her purpose was avowedly political and originated in the
increasingly social democratic climate of 1930s universities. Fremlin was to
become an observer for Mass Observation, recruited as a result of *The Seven
Chars of Chelsea* by its founder, Tom Harrisson. Later she wrote *War Factory*, a Mass Observation study of morale among wartime women factory
workers (Fremlin 1943/87). *The Seven Chars of Chelsea* owes much to the
movement for social realism and documentary that characterised political
writing and film-making of the period. Fremlin, like George Orwell, Walter
Greenwood, Mass Observation and documentary filmmakers such as John

Grierson, was concerned to document the lives of working-class people in order to foster egalitarianism through a greater understanding of those lives. Her achievement was to appropriate the methods of social documentary and the language of egalitarianism in order to reveal the injustices of an institution that was of particular relevance to women.

The Seven Chars of Chelsea was written in 1940 when many believed that the 'people's war' heralded the prospect of a 'people's peace' in which the barriers of class and prejudice would be dismantled permanently. Fremlin's study of domestic service makes visible the class inequalities, the snobbery and the prejudices that were reproduced daily, not in the public spaces of work, politics, leisure and education, but at the very heart of private life – the middle-class home. Her belief that an unbridgeable gap separates mistresses and servants underpins her account, though it is stated far less offensively than in the asides of Woolf or Bell. Addressing women like Bell, Fremlin recognises that

> you would have no idea how to set about finding out from your charwoman what it feels like to live and work as she does. You would not know what questions to ask her, and she would not know how to answer them, not even what you were getting at. Deadlock would be reached in the second sentence.
>
> The trouble is that the two of you speak different languages; you think different thoughts; you live in different worlds. In a word, you belong to different classes in this British society of ours.
>
> (Fremlin 1940: 2)

However, despite her commitment to egalitarianism, what Fremlin's rhetoric failed to grasp was that the intensities produced by intimate dependency could create a heady mixture of hostility and need. However kindly the mistress, however enlightened the conditions of employment, whatever the contractual arrangements, for many working-class women domestic service would always be 'servitude' and for many middle-class women an intrusion into the privacy they valued so highly. Despite the quasi-socialist rhetoric of her case studies, Fremlin's dream of maid and mistress working harmoniously together represents a specifically liberal middle-class utopia in which 'all girls are of your own class' with 'the same cultural background and the same education'.[40] Working-class women had different aspirations, dreaming perhaps of a home of their own and the better material life offered by the promises of modernity.

Monica Dickens, on the other hand, writing about her experiences as a 'cook-general' has no overt political purpose. In 1939 Dickens, the great-granddaughter of Charles Dickens, also published an account of her time masquerading as a servant. Bored and dissatisfied with the 'crazy cyclone of gaiety' she had experienced in New York, and restless in a London 'which seemed flat and dull', Dickens, a debutante from an upper-class London family, decides to get a job doing the only thing for which her upbringing has fitted her – cooking.[41] *One Pair of Hands* consists of a number of comic vignettes of the various households in which Dickens works. Many of these are London flats where Dickens is employed as a 'cook-general' on a non-residential basis. In these employments she is also expected to clean and tidy up as well as cook and order food supplies from tradesmen. Even where she is employed on a non-residential basis she is expected to arrive at her workplace early enough to make breakfast, light fires and take early morning tea to her employers. Dickens provides evidence of the disdain with which employers could treat their servants: fingers permanently on the bell, querying every small expenditure on food or drink, cancelling time off because there were jobs they wanted done. But she also describes benevolent and kindly employers who show solicitude for their servants. Nevertheless, as Dickens recognises, servants were always treated as if they were a different species:

> It is a curious game that people like to play sometimes, drawing out the maid ... in order to get amusement out of the screamingly funny idea that she may have some sort of a human life of her own. Nice people like the Vaughans laugh with you, others laugh at you; but it comes to the same thing in the end.[42]

Dickens' account is interesting because, first, it provides evidence of the excessive workloads that, even non-residential, servants were expected to undertake. The modernisation of domestic service so that servants might live at home and come in on a daily basis as an employee does not, from the evidence here, appear to have reduced employers' expectations. At one point Dickens finds herself having to make beds, provide early morning tea, clean baths and boots, lay fires, dust and polish, and cook all the meals for a family of four plus a baby. On days when the family was dining in, Dickens would be expected to stay all evening until the meal was over and cleared up. She would then be expected to arrive early the next morning to cook breakfast and make tea. Second, Dickens' account relishes recounting some of the ways in which servants were happy to hoodwink even the most benevolent employer. Indeed, much of the humour in *One Pair of Hands* comes from Dickens' accounts of her minor victories over her employers, victories such as polishing off the left over puddings, surreptitiously using the best port instead of cooking port, hiding broken ornaments, or sweeping dirt under beds. On the other hand, Maud a maid of all work is laughed at for having 'a feudal feeling for the family': she is concerned that they should be 'kept in their place'. Maud disapproves of mistresses who are over-friendly and 'demean themselves' and would not dream of taking advantage in the way

Dickens does.[43] In the world of Dickens' servants, employers are not welcome in the kitchen which is seen as the private sanctum of the servants, and maids are seen by employers as lazy, stupid, pitiable, or an alien species who, even when they clearly belong to the same class like Dickens or work as a daily employee, are treated with a condescension that is mixed sometimes with pity, sometimes with contempt.

Dickens and Fremlin offer realist and empirical accounts of service, often focusing on the servant as a 'character'. Traditional deference like that shown by Maud in *One Pair of Hands* or Lydia in *The Seven Chars of Chelsea* is presented as outmoded and dangerously repressed in the modern world. *Rebecca* by Daphne Du Maurier (1938) and a short story 'The Perfect Maid' by Agatha Christie (1941) engage in different ways with the figure of the traditionally deferential and loyal, apparently 'perfect' servant. The narrative of *Rebecca* unfolds entirely through the memories, dreams and fantasies of the unnamed young woman who becomes the second wife of the wealthy Maxim de Winter. The novel focuses on the interior life of the narrator whose timidity and naivety constantly allow others to exploit her. She desperately desires the self-confidence and poise that she imagines of her predecessor, Rebecca. The dreams and aspirations of the narrator are as firmly located in a particular class situation as much as in the romantic. She yearns for her husband's love and is jealous of his first wife whose spectre constantly haunts her. But it is not just emotional security that she desires. It is also the social confidence and status that being mistress of Maxim's country house, Manderley, will bring. The narrator's insecurity is fuelled by the hostility she encounters from the sinister housekeeper, Mrs Danvers, who remains devoted to her dead mistress. Her inability to manage the Manderley servants becomes the public manifestation of her inner anxieties and timidity: she believes the servants, led by Mrs Danvers, despise her and is constantly making *gauche* mistakes in her dealings with them. It is hard for contemporary readers to register the narrator's difficulties with the servants in the same way that these might have struck middle-class women readers in the 1930s. It is only necessary to revisit the extract above from a household manual to realise that to be 'ruled' by one's servants smacked of 'lower-class' status and an immature inability to elicit the deference due to a certain social standing.

Moreover, when the narrator first meets the servants of Manderley she comments that 'they were the watching crowd about the block, and I the victim with my hands behind my back'.[44] Thus, the encounter between the servants and the mistress begins to take on, not only powerful psychological force, but also the status of a political struggle between the ruler and 'the mob'. It is not simply rendered, as mistress–servant relationships so often were, as trivial, comic, domestic matters, outside history and beyond politics. Even if this inscription is only temporarily achieved via the act of reading, it may, nevertheless, have offered Du Maurier's middle-class women readers the possibility of recognising their profoundest fears inscribed seriously and historically.[45] Deeply felt anxieties that servants who on the surface appeared deferential and respectful were, behind one's back, hostile, contemptuous, resentful and manipulative could find an outlet in the imaginary landscape of Du Maurier's novel. Mrs Danvers is described in the melodramatic terms of Gothic horror, 'someone tall and gaunt, dressed in deep black, whose prominent cheek-bones and great hollow eyes gave her a skull's face, parchment-white, set on a skeleton's frame'.[46] She terrifies the young narrator who creeps about the great house, frightened to do anything for herself, breaking things when she does, made childlike and dependent by the competence and power of this figure who carries an obsessive love for her predecessor. This is a nightmare vision of mistress–servant relations which is only dispelled by the narrator's growing independence and, suggestively, her loss of innocence as she lets go of her romantic yearnings and enters a mature marriage at the end of the novel. The text invites its readers to identify with either the childlike narrator or the sexually and socially accomplished Rebecca. The sinister figure of Mrs Danvers with her 'skull's face' and obsessive love for Rebecca embodies what those readers may have most feared about their servants and at the same time perhaps what they most desired.

In a very different vein is Agatha Christie's short story 'A Perfect Maid' published in 1941. In this story Miss Marple solves the mystery of a domestic theft purported to be the action of the maid, Gladys. 'A Perfect Maid' taps into a pervasive middle-class fear that servants were dishonest and, if not kept under constant surveillance, likely to steal from their mistresses. This concern is echoed in household manuals of the period where mistresses are advised to act with caution if they suspect their maids of stealing: 'you will be acting very rashly if you tell her to "pack her box" '.[47] Miss Lavinia in 'A Perfect Maid' acts rashly in dismissing Gladys when a brooch goes missing for Gladys is, of course, innocent. Miss Marple unravels the mystery which involves Miss Lavinia and her apparently invalid sister, Miss Emily, perpetrating a complex fraud, involving Miss Emily disguising herself as a replacement maid for Gladys (the Perfect Maid of the title), and stealing from the other residents of the flats in which they live. Miss Marple works all this out because, as she says, '... it did strike me that she [the Perfect Maid] was a little too good to be true'.[48] The story hinges on an understanding that would have been readily accepted by its middle-class readers that the 'perfect maid' does not exist. It also expects its readers to recognise the significance of dismissing a maid so rashly when servants are in short supply, and the disaster for Gladys of receiving a reference that refuses to comment on her honesty. In all this Christie speaks to the conventional wisdoms of her readers. Yet, at the same time, the story, perhaps unconsciously, suggests that in a small community where class positions are clearly defined and marked, in particular through the system of domestic service, it is possible for a middle-class woman (Miss Emily) to disguise herself as a maid 'with neat black hair, rosy cheeks, a plump figure discreetly arrayed in black with a white apron and cap' and to carry this deception off.[49] Moreover, it is not the expected servant who is a petty thief but the two middle-class sisters who, it transpires, are part of a network of organised crime. If the hierarchical world of the quintessential English village can be turned on its head, albeit only in the imagination, what does this hint about the stability of social divisions in a changing society? 'A Perfect Maid' follows the conventions of detective fiction while *Rebecca* is Gothic romance. Yet these generic distinctions can distract from the similar concerns being articulated, albeit with a different emphasis. 'A Perfect Maid', like *Rebecca*, creates a fictional landscape in which mistress–servant relations act as a metaphor for wider political concerns. The concerns articulated here are around the impossibility of knowing what is real, a fear that what appears benign may, in fact, be malevolent, and a recognition that evil is to be found, not only in an unfamiliar and dangerous, often urban, world, but also in the familiar, safe spaces of the private middle-class home and the rural village, so often, in this period, invoked as the essence of English national identity.

The gradual disappearance of middle-class women's supervisory role in the home left her increasingly bereft of that power which, however nebulous in practice, had defined her 'place' in the bourgeois home. From the 1950s onwards middle-class women found themselves running homes without the help of servants. Whilst this was in some ways a relief, it also proved burdensome to many educated women whose time became increasingly taken up with domestic chores.[50] It also removed a key marker of their classed identity as they lost their role as 'the mistress'. The 'people's war', the establishment of the welfare state and the emergence of a social democratic consensus led to the erosion of a culture in which deference and service had defined the relationships between classes. The class relationships of women played out in the middle-class home were crucial in this transition but are frequently overlooked in a historiography that focuses solely on documentary evidence. By 1955 few households employed residential servants and, although working-class women continued to cook, clean and care for children in institutions, they were increasingly absent from the middle-class home. Instead they found employment in jobs that echoed the demands of service: hairdressing, waitressing, retailing, cooking for restaurants and cafes. These jobs continued to offer low wages, little training, low status and frequently long hours. The middle-class subjectivities produced as a result of domestic service continued to treat such women with condescension and sometimes fear. Nevertheless, for better or worse, these relationships now took place in the public sphere of institutions, shops, offices and factories rather than behind the closed doors of the middle-class home. As such, the emotional relations of deference and obligation, authority and servility, dependence, love and resentment between women (and their manifestations as duplicity, loyalty and contempt) were played out in the public workplaces of the post-war world and as such were mediated by (or masked by) the rational languages of employment law.

Finally, mistress–servant relations also involved loyalty and affection, even where, as Light has shown, these also included possessiveness, spite and dislike.[51] Doris Arthurs born in 1908, left school at 14 and worked in various nursery and housemaid jobs before her marriage. Once married with a small child she worked as a non-residential 'char'. Doris recalls her relationship with her employer, Jessie, as one in which they were like sisters. Jessie, according to Doris, paid for a holiday, left her a legacy, and gave Doris clothes for her daughter. As Doris says, 'I shall never be out of her debt' but neither will Jessie who, after the death of her husband, 'couldn't have enough of my company'.[52] This is a story of mutual dependency and Doris' potential envy at Jessie's material wealth is perhaps partially assuaged by the pride she feels in having Jessie as a friend. Moreover, Doris is married and a mother, she and her husband rent one of the new council houses in Birmingham's outer suburbs and the social reforms of the 1940s offered people like her a new sense of dignity and respect. In these circumstances more equal relationships may have been possible. Hence, as I have suggested, if not made explicit until this point, it would be inaccurate to see mistress–servant relationships as simply the exploitation of one group of people by another. Servants, as Du Maurier's fictional creation suggests, wielded their own forms of emotional power deep within the invisible heart of the private sphere. Most importantly, as Doris reminds us, stories of affection and mutual dependence, if less recorded than those of hostility and struggle, do exist. However unequal the protagonists and whatever their circumstances, the relationships created by domestic service were never simply, to a greater or lesser degree, about wages, conditions of work, uniforms or generic names. These manifestations of the micro-politics of the domestic home also contained and frequently masked a range of deeply felt and sometimes contradictory emotions. This should remind us that history is not only about the factually verifiable events of the past but is also about the ephemerality of lived experience and emotion, traces of which can be found, as detailed here, in stories, memories, fiction and autobiographical writings.

Notes

1. Brandt, B. (1984), *London in the Thirties* (New York: Pantheon Books), no. 86.
2. Henderson in M. Haworth-Booth (1984), 'Introduction', *London in the Thirties* (New York: Pantheon Books).
3. A. Light (2007), *Mrs Woolf and the Servants* (London: Penguin), p. 1.
4. Ibid., p. xxi.
5. Ibid., pp. 163–221.
6. Ibid., p. xxii.
7. M. Dickens (1939), *One Pair of Hands* (London: M. Joseph Ltd); C. Fremlin (1940), *The Seven Chars of Chelsea* (London: Methuen and Co.); D. Du Maurier

(1938/1975), *Rebecca* (London: Pan Books); A. Christie (1941/1973), 'A Perfect Maid' in *Miss Marple's Final Cases* (London: Fontana).

8. P. Horn (1975), *The Rise and Fall of the Victorian Servant* (London: Gill and Macmillan); A. Jackson (1991), *The Middle Classes 1900–1950* (Nairn, Scotland: David St John); T. McBride (1976), *The Domestic Revolution* (London: Croom Helm); P. Taylor (1979), 'Daughters and Mothers – Maids and Mistresses: Domestic Service between the Wars', in Crichter and Clark (eds.), *Working Class Culture: Studies in History and Theory* (London: Hutchinson), pp. 121–39.
9. R. Lewis and Angus Maude (1973 [orig. published 1949]), *The English Middle Classes* (Bath: Cedric Chivers Ltd), pp. 150–75; Jackson, *The Middle Classes 1900–1950*, pp. 330–1.
10. S. Todd (2005), *Young Women, Work and Family in England, 1918–1950* (Oxford: Oxford University Press). According to the 1931 Census, 24 per cent of young women aged 14–24 were employed in domestic service (cited in Todd, *Young Women, Work and Family*, p. 23).
11. Jackson, *The Middle Classes 1900–1950*, p. 344.
12. Todd, *Young Women, Work and Family*, pp. 33–7.
13. *The Listener*, 1946, p. 466. See *The Lady* for 11 April 1940, 12 April 1945, 5 January 1950.
14. Cited in Todd, *Young Women, Work and Family*, p. 23.
15. Horn, *The Rise and Fall of the Victorian Servant*; Jackson, *The Middle Classes*; McBride, *The Domestic Revolution*; Taylor, *Daughters and Mothers*.
16. C. Dyhouse (1989), *Feminism and the Family in England, 1880–1939* (Oxford: Blackwell), pp. 107–44.
17. *Report of the War Cabinet Committee on Women in Industry* (1919), Cmd 135, xxi. 241, pp. 99–100.
18. *Report of the Committee Appointed to Enquire into the Present Conditions as to the Supply of Female Domestic Servants* (1923), London: HMSO, p. 12.
19. Labour Party (1930), *What's Wrong with Domestic Service?* (London: Labour Party); H. Llewellyn Smith (1934), *The New Survey of London Life and Labour* (London: P. S. King and Son), p. 468; D. Caradog-Jones (ed.) (1934), *The Social Survey of Merseyside* (London: Hodder and Stoughton), p. 311.
20. Bevin, Ernest to Brown, Ernest, 26 January 1943, Public Records Office Lab70.
21. V. Markham and F. Hancock (1945) *Report on the Post-War Organization of Domestic Employment*, Cmnd 6650 (London: Public Records Office).
22. *The Listener*, 1946, p. 466.
23. Markham and Hancock, *Report on the Post-War Organisation of Domestic Employment*, p. 7.
24. Ibid.
25. D. Spender (1984), *Time and Tide Wait For No Man* (London: Pandora), p. 218.
26. W. Foley (1986), *A Child In the Forest* (London: BBC, Ariel Books).
27. Lewis and Maude, *The English Middle Classes*, p. 206.
28. L. Davidoff, J. L'Esperance and H. Newby (1976), 'Landscape with Figures: Home and Community in English Society', in A. Oakley and J. Mitchell (eds), *The Rights and Wrongs of Women* (Harmondsworth: Penguin), p. 155.
29. L. Davidoff, and C. Hall (1987), *Family Fortunes: Men and Women of the English Middle Class, 1780–1850* (London: Hutchinson), pp. 151–3.
30. L. Davidoff (1974), 'Mastered for Life: Servant and Wife in Victorian England', *Journal of Social History* 7, pp. 406–428.

31. F. Jack and P. Preston (c. 1930), *The Woman's Book* (London: The Woman's Book Club), p. 36.
32. Ibid., p. 332.
33. Spender, *Time and Tide*, p. 217.
34. J. Storey (1987), *Our Joyce* (London: Virago), pp. 104–5.
35. Foley, *Child in the Forest*, pp. 132–9.
36. Pauline Charles, interview with Lindsey Murray-Twinn, April 1994.
37. H. Lee (1997), *Virginia Woolf* (London: Vintage), p. 356, cited in Light, *Mrs Woolf and the Servants*, p. 178.
38. As well as the texts referred to here, see also E. M. Delafield (1930/1984), *The Diary of a Provincial Lady* (London: Virago); J. Struther (1939/1991), *Mrs. Miniver* (London: Virago); L. Cooper (1936), *The New House* (London: Gollancz), amongst others.
39. Celia Fremlin, interview with Angus Calder, 17 March, 1980, University of Sussex, Mass Observation Archive.
40. Fremlin, *Seven Chars*, p. 177.
41. Dickens, One Pair of Hands, pp. 5–7.
42. Ibid., p. 214.
43. Ibid., p. 179.
44. Du Maurier, *Rebecca*, p. 72.
45. A similar reading of *Rebecca* was first published in J. Giles (2003), ' "A Little Strain with Servants": Gender, Modernity and Domesticity in Daphne Du Maurier's *Rebecca* and Celia Fremlin's *The Seven Chars of Chelsea*', *Literature and History*, 12(2), Autumn, pp. 36–50.
46. Du Maurier, *Rebecca*, p. 72.
47. 'A Barrister-at-law' (1936), *The Home Counsellor* (London: Odhams Press), p. 229.
48. Christie, 'A Perfect Maid', 102.
49. Ibid., p. 96.
50. H. Gavron (1966), *The Captive Wife* (London: Routledge & Kegan Paul); A. Oakley (1974), *The Sociology of Housework* (London: Martin Robertson).
51. Light, *Mrs Woolf and the Servants*.
52. Doris Arthurs, Interview, February 1987.

Part V
Parenting and Childhood

10
Child Care and Neglect: A Comparative Local Study of Late Nineteenth-Century Parental Authority[1]

Siân Pooley

The late nineteenth century was a period of pioneering state, institutional and philanthropic intervention in relationships between parents and their children. The political strategies adopted to justify this new 'public' authority over the 'private' family on a national scale have been the subject of much valuable research.[2] However, this study considers these developments from the opposite perspective: how was this intervention negotiated and contested at a local level, and to what extent was this also a period of change in the distribution of domestic authority within families? This chapter explores ideas of child care and neglect through a case study of two contrasting localities in England between 1860 and 1905.

Contemporary discussions of parent–child relations were pervaded by concerns about parental neglect of familial responsibilities. Extreme cases of physical and material negligence were increasingly addressed by the courts and by some philanthropic organisations, and these institutional responses to perceived neglect have been extensively studied.[3] However, parents' own ideas of their social, moral, religious and emotional responsibilities were also nascent and contested. The interaction between mothers, fathers, children, wider communities and extra-familial authorities in negotiating normative definitions of neglect and appropriate practices of care has been less frequently addressed.[4] In practical terms this is not surprising; the relative abundance of archived records of philanthropic organisations compared to those created by individual families makes this research more feasible, particularly prior to the availability of oral history accounts. However, instead of presuming that memories of the early twentieth century also apply to the previous 40 years, it is important to uncover sources that do provide evidence for Victorian familial relationships.

There is also a need to explore the interpretations and influence of the proliferating late nineteenth-century prescriptive and legislative discourses that advised on child-rearing. Philanthropic and didactic movements to reform motherhood have been studied extensively.[5] However, as Megan Doolittle's and Ginger Frost's chapters (Chapters 1 and 4) in this volume demonstrate, changing ideas about fatherhood and men's experiences of rearing children have only recently begun to be explored.[6] Moreover, it cannot simply be assumed that these nationally disseminated texts constructed a uniform, English culture of ideal parenthood or approved child-rearing practices. Case studies of child employment and education have shown that the roles of children did not follow a single national trajectory; most charitable activity was conducted at a district level, and local authorities maintained considerable autonomy in establishing bye-laws that were sensitive to local economic, social and political contexts.[7] Nevertheless, there are few studies of parent–child relations that highlight this diversity. As Deborah Thom's (Chapter 12) use of oral history testimonies suggests in this volume, the use of corporal punishment by mid-twentieth-century parents varied across the United Kingdom. It is thus important to focus on the ways in which these discourses were received by parents in specific localities, and their interaction with alternative understandings of parenthood and childhood.

This chapter uses an eclectic range of archival sources – particularly school log books, school attendance and poor law minutes, local newspaper reports and census enumerators' books – to provide an insight into the everyday dynamics of late nineteenth-century family relations in two contrasting localities.[8] The two study localities were both industrial communities, with very small professional middle classes, and with thriving Nonconformist cultures. The first locality, Auckland, was a coal-mining district in County Durham. This area has repeatedly been characterised as the epitome of patriarchal, insular communities built around male breadwinner households. There was very little formal female or child employment available and families were large. Although Liberal MPs were elected in Bishop Auckland borough from 1885, local government boards were dominated by the interests of laissez-faire ratepayers and urban reforms and social intervention were strongly resisted.[9] This contrasted with the Lancashire town of Burnley, where cotton weaving provided considerable opportunities for independent female and child wage-earning. In the 1901 census, more than one-third of married and widowed women recorded themselves as in paid employment, and 30 per cent of children aged 10–14 were in half-time employment. The average completed family size was relatively small here with many couples increasingly controlling their fertility from the 1870s. Liberal MPs were returned in 12 out of 13 elections between 1867 and 1905, but local government was the political opposite of Auckland. The town prided itself on its liberalism and social progressivism, and from the 1890s the Social Democratic Federation played an increasingly influential role in promoting pioneering welfare provision.[10]

These contrasting case studies are situated in the context of published prescriptive literature, such as household manuals and child-rearing tracts, which formed one source of advice that mothers and fathers were potentially conforming to, or rejecting, in raising their children. Instead of establishing a set age range for 'childhood', definitions of when parents ceased to be responsible for their offspring is made a central question in this research. Moreover, it is not claimed that either locality was in any way 'typical' of a national experience of parenting, but instead this research focuses upon the demographic, occupational and cultural contrasts between domestic relations in these two communities. This study explores these concepts of domestic authority over children on three levels, ranging from the models offered in nationally available published texts, to their interpretation in local literature, to the experience and negotiation of these relationships in everyday family life in Auckland and Burnley.

Models of parental authority

Inadequate parenthood was identified in many mid-nineteenth-century didactic texts and religious tracts as primarily the result of a failure on the part of mothers and fathers to exert their proper domestic authority. That most parents naturally loved their offspring was not doubted. Instead, it was the magnitude of parental responsibilities and the resulting difficulties that parents faced in establishing their authority that was represented as a threat to modern children. This attitude is obvious in many publications by the Society for Promoting Christian Knowledge, such as this extract from a tract published in 1871:

> However, what I want to think about at this time is not those who neglect their children, and care nothing that they should grow up God-less, wicked men, but those who really wish them well, love them, hope they will be good Christians, and at the same time are inclined to let them do very much what they choose, and to make their own wills their law.[11]

Aspects of this trope of the disordered household flouting gender- and age-specific domestic hierarchies had been represented for centuries in advice manuals.[12] However, what made nineteenth-century ideas about parent–child relations subtly different was that in addition to fathers' and mothers' divinely ordained domestic roles, parenthood was reimagined as a skill that had to be learnt, purchased and earned. A plethora of advice manuals, moralising stories and religious tracts were published all of which emphasised that while the birth of a child was a natural blessing, the rearing of a child was a skill that required intense devotion to duty to acquire. The early twentieth-century infant welfare movement was pioneering in focusing exclusively on scientific knowledge and the need to ensure that 'professional' advice

influenced practice. Nevertheless, literature from the 1840s onwards conceptualised the rearing of a child as a task that parents could only adequately
perform when assisted by didactic manuals, medical assistance, and, increasingly, specialist children's products. As Jane Hamlett's chapter (Chapter 5,
this volume) on middle-class domestic intimacy also suggests in respect to
nursery provision, there were thus important continuities in ideas about
child-rearing throughout the Victorian period.

This long-term perceived crisis in domestic care within 'ordinary' homes
was particularly powerful because of its universality. Neglect was not just
part of the suffering of the child of the drunken, wage-earning, irreligious
mother, but it could equally afflict the baby whose mother did not acquire
a scientific understanding of childhood illnesses, the scholar whose father
failed to exert himself in choosing a suitable school, or the child who suffered from 'moral leprosy from the Nursery' due to the inadequate selection
of servants.[13] One household medical text highlighted the ease with which
middle-class children could be made the victims of parental inadequacies:

> In daily practice we see so much harm that has resulted from ignorance
> and neglect. By this I do not mean to infer there has been intentional
> neglect, but from the want of knowledge on simple matters, which are
> of primary importance, attention has only been arrested when a disease
> or habit has become confirmed, or in the case of an acute illness, when
> the favourable time for treatment has passed, and thus what would have
> been a simple matter has developed into a grave condition.[14]

It was very rare for prescriptive literature to make any reference to the material, financial or time constraints that parents faced in raising their children.
Even in those texts aimed at working-class parents it was solely parental
ignorance, inattentiveness or obstinate immorality that were identified as
the causes of children's suffering. Although the pioneering social investigations of Booth, Collet and Rowntree were increasingly sensitive to problems
such as irregular employment or life-cycle poverty, these more sympathetic
attitudes to working-class livelihoods had little impact on child-rearing texts,
which were primarily published by middle-class female writers, male doctors and Christian charities. Instead, parenthood was conceived primarily
through a moral framework, in which ceaseless attention to the formation
of the habits of both sons and daughters was essential, and in which any
perceived lack of such devotion was unpardonable.

The increasing demands placed upon mothers have been widely recognised historiographically. However, prescriptive literature also emphasised
the importance of active paternal involvement, particularly when discussing
the rearing of older children and in texts that were published by explicitly Christian writers. In both tracts aimed at working-class parents and
in middle-class manuals the 'unspeakable responsibility that rests upon

parents' was shown to be enduring, with the importance of using their parental authority as an example to guide teenage sons and daughters to pure, pious and moral habits being emphasised.[15] Many texts explicitly addressed themselves to 'parents' rather than simply to the 'mother', and some included specific advice to encourage reluctant fathers to be more involved in family life.[16] It was suggested that the father should not simply be a figure of distant authority, but should be made 'keenly interested' in the progress of his children so as to 'become the mother's guide and support in her task'.[17] However, it is revealing to note that that the responsibilities of motherhood included inspiring their husbands to adopt this manly role, so as to avoid neglecting the children who were identified elsewhere in the same tracts as a shared responsibility.[18] Above all, the 'power of womanhood', which one manual proclaimed in its title would be celebrated through good parenting, was constructed from fragile and often contradictory foundations.[19]

Local interpretations of parental authority

These models of parental caring responsibilities were expressed in a wide range of nationally available publications and many of these were repeatedly reprinted, especially towards the end of this period. However, the ways in which these ideas were received and put into practice is far less clear. It is two aspects of this process of reinterpretation on which this study now focuses, exemplified first by the practicalities of child-minding, and second by understandings of economic care and neglect in Auckland and Burnley.

By 1900 ideas of neglected parental responsibilities were as prevalent in local newspapers as they were in nationally published child-rearing texts. Both Bishop Auckland and Burnley had bookshops that advertised these manuals, a local press that often republished extracts from literature idealising childhood, and fortnightly newspaper columns that provided advice on 'Health and the Household'. Moreover, in both localities newspapers and parish magazines regularly printed detailed reports of sermons, lectures and classes in which advice on domestic happiness was offered. Many of these expressed fears about mothers' and fathers' failure to bring their children up properly, but in neither locality was there any detailed discussion in the sampled newspapers of the practicalities of who should mind children or how they should be cared for.[20]

Where there was a striking difference in ideas about child-rearing is in the ways in which local governing authorities – most notably the Boards of Guardians of the Poor Law Unions, school attendance committees, elementary school managers and magistrates – interpreted caring responsibilities. National Poor Law and educational acts were highly permissive, so that these boards had considerable powers to shape and enforce national legislation in a way that made sense in their locality. Of course, the individuals who were on these boards did not necessarily share a single set of ideas, and disputes between board members about appropriate parenting responsibilities did occur. Nevertheless, the minutes of these authorities do suggest that quite different understandings of how working-class parents should rear their children were expressed in the two study localities.

Local government committees were expected to use bye-laws to specify the offences, processes and punishments through which parents were to be compelled to send children to school. Following the 1870 Education Act, Burnley immediately established a School Board committee that agreed the bye-laws to enforce attendance. By November 1871 a 'schedule' of all children aged 5–13 who lived in the textile town was established. Four 'visitors' were appointed to distribute posters and handbills, to issue written and oral notices of non-attendance, and to deliver summons to parents to appear before the Committee of the School Board on Saturday afternoon to explain their child's absence. Further summons to the Magistrate's court could then be issued, and fines of up to 5 shillings per week could be imposed.[21] This resulted in a plethora of warnings, and, in about one-sixth of these cases, in fines. In 1872 an average of almost 30 summonses to the School Board Committee were made per month and by 1896 the number of such summonses had more than doubled.[22] Both parents and school board officials repeatedly complained that they were overwhelmed by this process. The Attendance Committee admitted 'That, it is an everyday occurrence for respectable parents to be summoned to appear in a Police Court for no other reason than that their children have played truant.'[23] However, there does not seem to have been any attempt to reduce the rigour with which perceived parental neglect was punished.

This contrasted markedly with the situation in Bishop Auckland. Here local ratepayers refused to establish an independent school board and continued to fear 'throwing their money away'. Only the Poor Law Union and individual schools had responsibility for enforcing school attendance, so that as late as 1880 the Education Act was declared a 'dead letter' by local newspaper commentators in the coal-mining district.[24] Even following the appointment of a specific attendance officer, school teachers frequently complained that 'Parents seem quite regardless of threats as no power has been used to compel irregular children to attend.'[25] Only a handful of, often unsuccessful, prosecutions were made in 1880 and even by 1900 warnings to parents were infrequent.[26]

Attitudes to the financial responsibilities of caring for a large family were also very different in the two localities. In none of the national legislation relating to the costs of rearing and schooling children was it stipulated whether having a large number of children to raise justified receiving extra relief simply on the grounds of the additional costs incurred.[27] In Auckland having to rear a large number of children was repeatedly interpreted as a reasonable justification for requiring relief. Most schools either formally specified differential fees for the third or fourth child attending that school, or negotiated rates with individual parents as in this case in 1881:

> The Revd Canon Long visited the school this afternoon and made arrangements respecting the payment of school fees by four girls of one family: the fourth should be free, the third pay four pence a fortnight and the other two four pence each per week.[28]

While this system could cause practical difficulties – one exasperated schoolmaster wrote 'No other trade, I know of gives one article out of three free' and later modified the scheme in his school – it does seem to have been an interpretation that was widely adopted up to 1891.[29] Similarly, in criminal court cases where parents were accused of neglecting to control their children, magistrates seem to have sentenced families more leniently when parents made pleas such as that 'he had a large family and small wages'.[30] In all cases in this sample the demands of rearing a large family were treated sympathetically. This suggests that those with legal or legislative authority in Auckland did interpret ideas of familial poverty in such a way as to support parents with larger families to care for.

In Burnley quite different official interpretations of familial financial responsibilities were offered. No such provision was made in educational bye-laws for extra relief specifically for parents with large families; all schools seem to have set their rates purely according to the Standard to which the child was taught, and in no sampled court cases was a large family treated as a mitigating circumstance for parental neglect.[31] This difference in attitude cannot simply be interpreted as the result of greater financial stringency, since welfare provision was far more generous in Burnley than in Auckland. Local politics in Auckland were strongly conservative with ratepayers' voices being powerful, so that the Board of Guardians were repeatedly ordered to revise relief lists in order to reduce expenditure, and the school attendance officer was very reluctant to pay school fees. Although ratepayers in Burnley did voice concerns at their high rates, this does not seem to have prevented many parents successfully applying for relief. As one journalist in *The Burnley Gazette* wrote following a report that £130 had been spent on non-pauper school fees in six months,

> Now we are not the parties to complain at any reasonable expense to have poor children educated; we would any time rather pay schoolmasters than soldiers and policemen. Still the increase in the item is so great that it deserves close attention by the Guardians.[32]

Both Burnley ratepayers and parents grumbled at times about the rigorous implementation of compulsory elementary schooling, yet these complaints were not sufficiently powerful to influence policies.

Commercial ideas of care and neglect are a second area in which parental responsibilities were interpreted differently in the two localities. Just as nationally available prescriptive texts portrayed the maintenance of child health as a key area of maternal authority and expertise, commercial advertisements in Burnley vehemently portrayed the same message (Figure 10.1). A handful of health products aimed explicitly at children were promoted in 1860, but by 1880 readers of *The Burnley Gazette* were bombarded with advertisements claiming that their product was essential to good parenthood. Drawings of cherubic children complemented emotive language describing the impact of maternal neglect on the 'poor sufferer' in the 1890s and more than one-quarter of a double-page spread of the broadsheet newspaper was consumed with advertisements such as these by 1900 (Figure 10.2).[33] The following advert was placed weekly in prominent positions in *The Burnley Gazette* in 1900, often with subtle changes in the particular form of negligence practised by the mother:

Oh Dear Nurse you forgot to give Tudor Williams' Balsam of Honey to my children before they returned to bed ... No mother should neglect to keep this infallible Remedy in the house ready for any emergency ... Absolutely Pure, therefore best. Thousands of children die annually from Bronchitis, Whooping Cough and Croup ... It cures for one shilling when Pounds have been spent instead. Bottles 1s-4s 6d.[34]

This contrasted with advertising practices in the equivalent Auckland newspaper. This also contained pages of commercial advertisements but included only one small advert for children's medicine in 1880 and none at all in 1860 or 1900. The one advert that was placed – for 'Mrs Winslow's Soothing Syrup' – was also advertised in Burnley at the same date, but other products seem to have been targeted at a specific local market of concerned mothers. Moreover, it was not simply that the Auckland region was poorer and less commercially developed than Burnley, since many other luxury products that were not aimed at children were extensively advertised in these newspapers.

A similar, but slightly less marked, contrast was exhibited in the promotion of children's clothing, books, toys and entertainments. More than twice as many different advertisements for such products were aimed at parents in the Burnley weekly newspaper than in Auckland in each sampled date, with the disparity being increasingly marked by 1900. For instance, Thompson Brothers' children's clothing warehouse regularly placed advertisements in *The Burnley Gazette*, such as this:

EVERY MOTHER naturally desires to see her boys look smart, neat and stylish. To enable them to appear so, their clothing should be pretty and becoming. ... Will please the mothers. Will please the fathers. Will please the boys. Will please everybody.[35]

Figure 10.1 Extract from a page of advertisements for a range of children's medicines, published in *The Burnley Gazette and East Lancashire Advertise*, 26 November 1898. At this date an average of around five such advertisements was published each week

Figure 10.2 Advertisement for 'Scott's Emulsion', published in *The Burnley Gazette and East Lancashire Advertise*, 24 December 1898. 'Scott's Emulsion' was advertised in most editions of the Burnley newspaper in the late 1890s and early 1900s, with different illustrated and emotive stories of the curative powers of the medicine. It was not promoted to Auckland parents

What is particularly interesting is the constant prominence that is given in the Burnley advertisements to the consequences of the mother's failings. Not only would bad motherhood result in the suffering and even the death of her child, but the mother also had the power to shape the happiness of her husband through her treatment of their children, as the previous advertisement rather unsubtly emphasised. In the same way that neglecting to provide the proper remedies for childhood illnesses threatened the life of her child, a failure to care sufficiently to provide economic luxuries could undermine the well-being of the entire family. The relative prominence of these anxieties about child-rearing might appear to be surprising in Burnley, given that maternal paid employment was common in the textile town. It is thus important to consider the influence that these messages exerted on local understandings of parental responsibility and on the practice of child-rearing.

Practices of parental authority

It is at this third level – in terms of the practical negotiation of childcare responsibilities – that the most marked differences are visible in ideas of care and neglect in the two communities. Just as legislative, educational and commercial discourses reflected distinct local cultures, parents faced contrasting everyday issues in caring for their children. Two aspects of parental care, child-minding and medical care, will again be considered.

Practices of care in Burnley were firmly shaped by a culture of female and child employment. Evidence from a longitudinal 10 per cent sample of families from the Burnley census suggests that almost all teenage girls were employed in the textile industry and more than half of women without children continued to work there after marriage. Furthermore, many mothers, especially women in their thirties with only one or two young children, did not stop working as weavers, so that out of 308 households in the sample containing 3 or more children, 23 per cent of mothers were recorded in paid employment.[36] Relatives, particularly grandmothers and aunts, played a key role in taking care of children. This informal system of child care is often only apparent from newspaper reports of court cases, such as when the house of two mill workers was burgled, when it was stated that 'They have one child which is nursed by its grandmother, who also looked after the house.'[37] Similarly, an inquest following the death of a 16-week-old baby in 1900 reported that 'The child's mother had been in the habit of taking the child every morning to a house 200 yards away, where it was nursed.'[38] Where there was a slightly older child in the house (brothers too were often engaged to nurse), they were frequently left in charge, provided there was a relative or neighbour who could be called if necessary. For instance, in 1860 an eight-year-old girl was burnt to death when left alone in the house minding her younger brother, but her mother explained that

I and my husband go out to work, and we have always left our children in the house. My husband's sister lives near, and she has always been on the look out, but she could not constantly be with them. She washes at home.

What is particularly interesting in this case is that despite the fact that the parents and neighbours were clearly shocked by this domestic tragedy, they all maintained that the parents were in no way negligent to leave the children alone in the house. Evidence was given by a neighbour who stated that

The parents of the deceased went to the factory, and they had no other means of protecting their children during their absence. The child was well attended to during the whole of the time it lived.[39]

The form of these answers suggests that magistrates at the inquest were pressing to interpret the tragedy as the result of parental neglect, yet all concerned successfully maintained that this was not the case. A similar burning fatality occurred in 1900 when a nine-year-old girl, who had been left alone with her younger brother, died. Although it does not appear in this case that the mother was out working, even at this later date there is no evidence that allegations of inadequate parental care were made by neighbours or relatives.[40] Instead, these incidents were interpreted as family tragedies, but ones that were an unavoidable part of accepted childcare practices. Working parents maintained their own ideas of what parental neglect entailed, but in spite of the increasing moral condemnation of mothers' employment by some magistrates, doctors and parliamentary enquiries, they did not consider their child-minding practices to be negligent.[41]

As an alternative childcare strategy, the 'Babies' classes at public elementary schools in Burnley included infants as young as one year old. Many teachers recorded in their log books that they were constantly overwhelmed by the numbers of babies whose parents wished to enrol them. Moreover, some schools taught children all year round or only had very short holidays, so as not to leave children without minders. Some parents seem to have combined these forms of care; alternative child-minders, such as relatives, were used on Saturdays and in winter when they did not wish to send their young children to school in the cold and damp.[42]

The problems of how to mind children were far less pressing for parents in Auckland. Here employment opportunities even for unmarried women were scarce and very few mothers had employment outside the home. Interestingly, in the sample of newspapers studied, there were no descriptions of children being nursed by relatives, neighbours or lone older siblings without the mother's presence at home. Although schools again enrolled children into 'baby' classes, there are no references to children aged less than three years old attending school or to these classes being oversubscribed.[43]

This contrast in the social practices of care is visible in an activity as simple as getting children up in the morning. In Auckland and Burnley school teachers complained equally frequently about the lateness of their pupils and in some cases the same causes were identified, such as mothers requiring their child's help with too many household tasks or the distance the child had to travel. However, additionally in Burnley, parents often had to leave their children to get themselves up and dressed in the morning as the working day of mothers and fathers employed at the mills began at 6 a.m., whereas children did not need to be in school before 9 a.m. (although at least one infant school opened at 6.15 a.m.).

Cultures of child medical care also placed different responsibilities on parents. Not only were Burnley parents bombarded with adverts for children's medicines, but there does seem to have been an expectation that these were bought and used. Although there were only 18 cases of domestic accidents or fatalities reported in the sampled Burnley newspapers, in all cases one of the child's parents, usually the mother, was questioned about the medical care provided for the child. They often described how 'I ran off for the doctor immediately' or purchased drugs, such as 'emetics', to try to treat the child.[44] In the few instances where doctors were not called, their absence was stated and, in some cases, accusations of neglect were made against the mother.[45] In 14 similar incidents in Auckland, only on one occasion are details given of a mother trying to purchase medicine and then calling a doctor.[46] Other circumstantial details are given in these newspaper reports, and this difference cannot simply be explained by a shortage of doctors, since both localities made extensive use of medical provision in dealing with industrial accidents and certification. There is no evidence in the local sources studied that sons and daughters were considered to deserve, or in practice received, different standards of care. However, these contrasting practices and expectations of parental responsibilities do fit with the evidence from commercial discourses in each area.

What is particularly striking is that in both localities the authority to define caring practices as either appropriate or neglectful remained highly contested. School teachers repeatedly claimed that parents' inadequate domestic authority was responsible for their pupils' poor attendance, bad behaviour or lack of progress. Terms such as 'neglect', 'carelessness', 'idleness' and 'indifference' were frequently used by frustrated teachers to describe the attitudes of both mothers and fathers. However, occasional glimpses of parents' own justifications for what was interpreted as neglect make this picture of domestic authority more complex. In many cases the explanations offered certainly do not suggest a lack of concern for the child's welfare and, indeed, ideas of neglect were often used by working-class parents in very different contexts.

For instance, as elementary school boards and attendance committees were increasingly established and active in the period between 1870 and

1902, parents were constantly required to explain their children's absences from school. While teachers in both Auckland and Burnley frequently blamed their pupils' non-attendance on parental negligence, parents tended to argue that they were absent precisely because their child's well-being was endangered by schooling. A vast array of explanations were offered: the virulence of illnesses that parents believed to be 'contagious' in schools; unjust punishment by teachers; the damp and cold state of the school room or the journey there; or the inadequacy of the curriculum with parents stating, ' "I will not let him come any more, there would be more sense in teaching him arithmetic than bothering with such rubbish as Drawing".'[47]

Indeed, both mothers and fathers engaged in this form of frequent, voluntary interactions with their children's schools to ensure that their offspring were treated in a way that they perceived to be beneficial. One schoolmaster in 1887 was so perturbed by the 'evil' of visits by parents and other callers during lesson time that he published a notice asking people not to knock on the school door except during specified hours.[48] Indeed, what is particularly revealing is the frequency with which parental complaints forced schools into reforming their practices.[49] The provision of school facilities that parents perceived to be safe for their young children, the minimal and regulated use of corporal punishment, the establishment of sufficiently large schools in convenient locations, and the issuing of invitations to parents to visit schools at set times were often the direct results of parental complaints. In some voluntary schools in particular, parental financial authority was even increased by the introduction of free education in most elementary schools in 1891. Teachers then had to persuade parents to donate money rather than simply demanding the 'school pence' each Monday.[50] In 1900 one Auckland Church of England parish magazine published a plea for funding, stating that

> The enlargement of the School building is now really in hand. A large amount of money is required for it. We hear however so many complaints of the children being too small to walk to South Church or St Helen's, that we are sure parents will be willing to give something to help the work. Sixpence a fortnight is not very much, and in ten fortnights would make 5/ – from each house. Collectors are going round and all will have a chance of helping.[51]

In this way, perceptions of neglected responsibilities to children could be very powerful tools to be mobilised not only by local boards and charities against parents, but also by mothers and fathers to buttress their own parental authority outside the domestic sphere. Educational authorities could not simply accuse families of neglect or intervene in the care of children without actively engaging with the concerns of both mothers and fathers. Furthermore, evidence from school log books suggests that

child-rearing duties were far from rigidly gender-specific, with fathers intervening particularly frequently in Burnley. The ambiguity and flexibility of
these responsibilities meant that mothers and fathers could also blame their
spouse for failing to establish their proper domestic authority.

One particularly revealing case study of gendered ideas of parental medical
and material neglect was a prosecution brought by the Burnley branch of the
National Society for the Prevention of Cruelty to Children (NSPCC) in 1900
against a mother, Ellen Palmer, following the death of her only daughter.
The doctor had been called when the child fell ill, and the conflicting ideas
of childcare responsibilities expressed by the witnesses in the case make it
particularly revealing:

> Dr Robinson corroborated and said that although the grandfather had
> attended to the child in every way he could, yet it did not receive the
> attention which it needed from the mother.– Wilson Palmer, the hus-
> band, elected to give evidence, and said his wife had been giving way
> to inhabitants [*sic*] of intemperance for some time. She neglected the
> child, but the grandfather gave it good attention.– John Hinley, the grand-
> father, said the child had not been neglected. He had looked after it,
> and being an old army man he could do as well for it as its mother. He
> attended the child when it was taken ill and had carried out the doctor's
> instructions.– Defendant said she had not neglected the child, but left it
> in it's [*sic*] grandfather's care, because she went out to work as a baby linen
> manufacturer at Mrs Walkdens.[52]

This case provides an insight into a series of quite different ideas of care
and neglect. For the doctor and NSPCC inspector it was solely the mother's
duty to use her unique caring ability to protect the life of her child, in
line with the new ideas of 'professional motherhood' in which both child-
minding and medical provision were of the utmost importance. The Palmer
family, however, expressed views that appear to have been widely held in
Burnley, in which gendered roles were far from strictly defined, with men
being willing to take on caring responsibilities. It is interesting to note that
the grandfather in this case apparently took pride in his ability to 'do as well
for it as its mother'. There also seems to be a subtle difference in Wilson
and Ellen Palmer's definitions of the maternal role. While Ellen perceived
wage-earning to be a proper part of her responsibilities as a mother, Wilson's
evidence suggests that he considered that his wife was neglecting her maternal duty, but that in leaving the little girl in her grandfather's care the couple
were not abandoning their shared parental duty to their daughter. Nevertheless, Ellen Palmer was found guilty and sentenced relatively harshly to a fine
of 20 shillings and costs, or one month's imprisonment.[53]

Equivalent prosecutions were infrequent in Auckland and, significantly,
received far less detailed or sensational coverage than those cases reported

in the Burnley newspapers. In common with evidence from studies of child abuse in other localities, neighbours in both districts were the most frequent source of accusations of parental neglect.[54] However, it is important to emphasise that Burnley residents were overwhelmingly keen to protect mothers against suggestions that it was their work that harmed their offspring or that most parents were anything other than 'affectionate' towards their children. Furthermore, by purchasing patent medicines, parents sought to defend themselves against anxieties about the health and suffering of their children (which were emotively displayed in the barrage of advertisements), and against increasingly common accusations of neglectful parenting. This contrasted with Auckland where parental responsibilities were seldom a topic of debate and where gender-specific caring roles were rarely undermined. Therefore, a discourse of neglect that was potent and ubiquitous in the national prescriptive texts was transformed into contrasting and complex ideas of gendered social practices of caring at a local level.

Cultures of parental authority

Three conclusions can be drawn from this study of the negotiation of domestic power between mothers, fathers and children. First, cultures of parenthood in England between 1860 and 1905 were both locally diverse and in a state of flux. Despite the proliferation of advice literature offering instruction on how best to assert parental authority, these ideals were interpreted and adopted in contrasting ways in different localities. These two case studies have suggested that a model of skilled parenthood in which paternal, and especially maternal, duties were highly demanding was not widely adopted even by 1900 in the coal-mining district of Auckland, whereas expectations of parental authority in Burnley were far more challenging from the 1860s. It seems clear that neither childhood nor parenthood was a nationally uniform experience.

Second, it is not helpful to envisage domestic and public authority over children as necessarily in conflict. In some cases – particularly in the context of school attendance – the state was increasingly involved in bringing up children. However, this was neither universally the case, since ratepayers in Bishop Auckland explicitly attempted to avoid this involvement, nor did it go unchallenged. Parents extensively, and often voluntarily, intervened in the ways in which schools treated their offspring in order to further what they perceived to be their child's best interests outside the domestic sphere. The competitive, commercial and relatively weak nature of this pioneering state educational provision meant that parents had considerable power through their children to shape the implementation of nationally applicable legislation. Far from leading to a diminution in either paternal or maternal power, interaction with the welfare state could provide a further arena in which parents were expected to, and often chose to, actively assert their authority. Late nineteenth-century childhood could not simply be 'transformed' by non-familial institutions without the cooperation of, or conflict with, both mothers and fathers.

Third, marital and intergenerational authority was intimately linked. Late Victorian and Edwardian advice literature and advertisements increasingly overtly portrayed the rearing of children as an exclusively feminine responsibility in idealised households that were supported economically solely by the father's income. However, in practice a strict division of gendered responsibilities seems very rarely to have been adopted in either locality. As the chapter by Szreter and Fisher in this volume (Chapter 6) also demonstrates, this constant negotiation of roles could be a source of conflict. This was particularly the case where one parent or an external authority perceived a child to be endangered by a failure to perform proper parenting responsibilities. These increasingly formally demanding and complex identities as parents could contribute to domestic conflict and potentially to marital breakdown.

Above all, the ubiquity and potency of the language of neglect of parental authority is striking. The image of the suffering, innocent child had considerable, and increasing, influence in both localities between 1860 and 1905. However, the implications of this cultural ideal were locally diverse, so that good fatherhood and motherhood were interpreted and practised in subtly different ways in these two contrasting communities. Nevertheless, it is clear that the authority of fatherhood and motherhood was founded upon the constant threat of parental failure.

Notes

1. I should like to thank Simon Szreter, the anonymous reviewer, and the editors of this volume for their help and comments.
2. M. Langan and B. Schwarz (1985) *Crises in the British State 1880–1930* (London: Hutchinson); R. Cooter (1992) *In the Name of the Child: Health and Welfare, 1880–1940* (London: Routledge); M. L. Arnot (1994) 'Infant Death, Child Care and the State: The Baby-Farming Scandal and the First Infant Life Protection Legislation of 1872', *Continuity and Change*, 9, 271–311; H. Hendrick (1994) *Child Welfare: England 1872–1989* (London: Routledge); G. K. Behlmer (1998) *Friends of the Family: The English Home and its Guardians, 1850–1940* (Stanford: Stanford University Press); A. Fletcher and S. Hussey (1999) *Childhood in Question: Children, Parents and the State* (Manchester: Manchester University Press).
3. G. K. Behlmer (1982) *Child Abuse and Moral Reform in England 1870–1908* (Stanford: Stanford University Press); L. A. Jackson (2000) *Child Sexual Abuse in Victorian England* (London: Routledge); H. Ferguson (2004) *Protecting Children in Time: Child Abuse, Child Protection and the Consequences of Modernity* (Basingstoke: Palgrave Macmillan).
4. Influential studies that have focused upon aspects of this, predominantly working-class mothers: J. Lewis (1986) *Labour and Love: Women's Experience of Home and Family 1850–1940* (London: Basil Blackwell); E. Ross (1993) *Love and Toil: Motherhood in Outcast London, 1870–1918* (Oxford: Oxford University Press); A. Davin (1996) *Growing Up Poor: Home, School and Street in London 1870–1914*

(London: Rivers Oram Press); L. Murdoch (2006) *Imagined Orphans: Poor Families, Child Welfare and Contested Citizenship in London* (New Brunswick, NJ: Rutgers University Press). For important studies of fatherhood: C. Nelson (1995) *Invisible Men: Fatherhood in Victorian Periodicals, 1850–1910* (Athens, Georgia: University of Georgia Press); T. L. Broughton and H. Rogers (2007) *Gender and Fatherhood in the Nineteenth Century* (Basingstoke: Palgrave Macmillan).

5. G. Bock and P. Thane (1991) *Maternity and Gender Policies: Women and the Rise of the European Welfare States, 1880–1950s* (London: Routledge); S. Koven and S. Michel (1993) *Mothers of a New World: Maternalist Politics and the Origins of Welfare States* (New York: Routledge); C. Nelson and A. S. Holmes (1997) *Maternal Instincts: Visions of Motherhood and Sexuality in Britain, 1875–1925* (Basingstoke: Macmillan).

6. See also Nelson, *Invisible Men*; Broughton and Rogers, *Gender and Fatherhood*.

7. D. Rubinstein (1969) *School Attendance in London, 1870–1904: A Social History* (Hull: University of Hull), pp. 42–54, 117–19; Belfiore, 'Family Strategies in Essex Textile Towns 1860–1875: The Challenge of Compulsory Elementary Schooling' (unpublished PhD thesis, University of Oxford, 1986), pp. 173–204; S. Koven (1993) 'Borderlands: Women, Voluntary Action and Child Welfare in Britain, 1840 to 1914', in S. Koven and S. Michel (eds), *Mothers of a New World: Maternalist Politics and the Origins of Welfare States* (New York: Routledge), pp. 94–135; L. V. Marks (1996) *Metropolitan Maternity: Maternal and Infant Welfare Services in Early Twentieth Century London* (Amsterdam: Rodopi).

8. Evidence for this chapter is drawn from a 25 per cent sample of school log books for each locality. A detailed analysis of newspaper articles has been completed for 3 six-month snapshots from January to June 1860, 1880 and 1900 in the most long-running and widely read local newspaper in each study area.

9. R. Moore (1974) *Pit-men, Preachers and Politics: The Effects of Methodism in a Durham Mining Community* (Cambridge: Cambridge University Press), pp. 140–8; R. Church, A. Hall and J. Kanefsky (1986) *The History of the British Coal Industry, 1830–1913* (Oxford: Oxford University Press), Vol. 3, pp. 191–9, 261–97, 601–37; S. Szreter (1996) *Fertility, Class and Gender in Britain, 1860–1940* (Cambridge: Cambridge University Press), pp. 354–9, 526–7.

10. Only in 1900 was the Conservative candidate victorious. Parliamentary Papers (1861) *Census of England and Wales 1861*; Parliamentary Papers (1902) *Census of England and Wales 1901*; W. Bennett (1998 [1951]) *The History of Burnley from 1850* (Burnley: Burnley and District Historical Association); T. Griffiths (2001) *The Lancashire Working Classes c1880–1930* (Oxford: Oxford University Press).

11. Society for Promoting Christian Knowledge (1871) *Children: Addressed to Fathers and Mothers* (London: SPCK), p. 11.

12. J. Bailey (2003) *Unquiet Lives: Marriage and Marriage Breakdown in England, 1660–1800* (Cambridge: Cambridge University Press), pp. 132–4, 194; A. Shepard (2003) *Meanings of Manhood in Early Modern England* (Oxford: Oxford University Press), pp. 70–87.

13. Society for Promoting Christian Knowledge (1893) *Words to Mothers. Being a Series of Addresses to Educated Women* (London: SPCK).

14. J. R. Day (1904) *Childhood in Health and Sickness* (London: Kegan Paul, Trench, Trubner and Co.)

15. Mrs H. Drew (1888) *The Mothers' Union* (London: SPCK), pp. 5–14; E. Hopkins (1899) *The Power of Womanhood; or Mothers and Sons. A Book for Parents and Those in Loco Parentis* (London: Wells, Gardner, Darton and Co.), pp. 49–59.

16. T. L. Claughton (1864) *The Duty of Fathers Concerning the Education of Their Children. A Short Plain Sermon Addressed to the Working Classes* (Oxford: John Henry and James Parker); G. Stables (1894) *The Mother's Book of Health and Family Adviser* (London: Jarrold and Sons), p. 19; A. W. Thorold (1895) *On Children* (London: Isbister and Company Ltd.), pp. 63–4.

17. Lady I. Margesson (1894) *The Principles and Practical Working of the New Education. A Few Suggestions to Parents* (London: George Philip and Son).

18. SPCK, *Children*, pp. 3–4, 14–6; SPCK, *Words to Mothers*, p. 5.

19. Hopkins, *The Power of Womanhood*.

20. *The Bishop Auckland Herald and General Advertiser*, 1860; *The Auckland Times and Herald, and South Durham Advertiser*, 1880; *The Auckland Times and Herald*, 1900; *The Burnley Advertiser*, 1860; *The Burnley Gazette*, 1880; *The Burnley Gazette and East Lancashire Advertiser*, 1900.

21. Lancashire Record Office, SBBy1/1–SBBy1/8, Burnley School Board Minutes, 1871–1903.

22. Lancashire Record Office, SBBy2/21–SBBy2/23, Burnley School Board Rota Committee, 1880–1904.

23. Lancashire Record Office, SBBy2/19, Burnley School Board General Purposes Committee, Petition to Secretary of State for the Home Department, based on petition by Macclesfield School Board, 2 March 1896.

24. *The Auckland Times and Herald, and South Durham Advertiser*, 27 February 1880; Durham Record Office, E/SW, Auckland school log books, 1860–1905.

25. *The Auckland Times and Herald, and South Durham Advertiser*, 27 February 1880, report of meeting of Bishop Auckland and District Teachers' Association; Durham Record Office, E/SW, Auckland school log books, 1860–1905.

26. *The Auckland Times and Herald, and South Durham Advertiser*, 23 April 1880, report of meeting of School Attendance Committee of Board of Guardians; *The Auckland Times and Herald, and South Durham Advertiser*, 1880, 1900.

27. G. Sutherland (1973) *Policy-making in Elementary Education, 1870–1895* (Oxford: Oxford University Press), pp. 84–5, 111–12, 163–90; D. F. Mitch (1992) *The Rise of Popular Literacy in Victorian England: The Influence of Private Choice and Public Policy* (Philadelphia: University of Pennsylvania Press), pp. 149–55.

28. Durham Record Office, E/SW 19, St Anne's Church of England Girls' School, Bishop Auckland log book, 9 September 1881.

29. Durham Record Office, E/SW 89, St John's Church of England Mixed School, Old Shildon log book, 26 July 1872.

30. *The Auckland Times and Herald, and South Durham Advertiser*, 30 January 1880; *The Auckland Times and Herald*, 16 March 1900.

31. Lancashire Record Office, SBBy1/1–SBBy1/8, Burnley School Board Minutes, 1871–1903; Lancashire Record Office, SMBy, Burnley school log books, 1860–1905; *The Burnley Gazette*, 1860, 1880, 1900.

32. *The Burnley Gazette*, 22 May 1880.

33. Examples of regular advertisements in *The Burnley Gazette*: Marshall's cooling and soothing powders, 1880; Mrs Winslow's soothing syrup, 1880; Scott's Emulsion, 1900.

34. *The Burnley Gazette and East Lancashire Advertiser*, 6 January 1900.

35. *The Burnley Gazette and East Lancashire Advertiser*, 14 April 1900.

36. Evidence from longitudinal record linkage between Burnley censuses 1861–1901.

37. *The Burnley Advertiser*, 7 January 1860.

38. *The Burnley Gazette and East Lancashire Advertiser*, 24 January 1900.

39. *The Burnley Advertiser*, 7 April 1860.
40. *The Burnley Gazette and East Lancashire Advertiser*, 3 January 1900.
41. Burnley was used as an example of a site of these 'negligent' nursing practices in Parliamentary Papers (1871), VII, *Select Committee to inquire into means of preventing destruction of lives of infants put out to nurse for hire by their parents*, p. 372; Parliamentary Papers (1890) XI, *Select Committee of House of Lords on Children's Life Insurance Bill House of Lords*, p. 344; Parliamentary Papers (1896) X, *Select Committee of House of Lords on Infant Life Protection and Safety of Nurse Children Bills House of Lords*, p. 343, evidence from Mr Tatham MD.
42. Lancashire Record Office, SMBy, Burnley school log books, 1860–1905.
43. Durham Record Office, E/SW, Auckland school log books, 1860–1905.
44. *The Burnley Advertiser*, 7 April 1860; *The Burnley Gazette and East Lancashire Advertiser*, 23 May 1900.
45. *The Burnley Gazette*, 24 April 1880.
46. *The Auckland Times and Herald, and South Durham Advertiser*, 18 June 1880.
47. Durham Record Office, E/SW90, St John's Church of England Mixed School, Old Shildon log book, 27 March 1896.
48. Durham Record Office, E/SW127, Bishop Barrington Church of England Boys' School, Bishop Auckland log book, 11 March 1887.
49. Record linkage of a 10 per cent sample of these parents to the nearest census in Auckland and Burnley suggests that these complaining parents came from a wide spectrum of social backgrounds, but that they were predominantly drawn from skilled working-class families.
50. Durham Record Office, E/SW, Auckland school log books; Lancashire Record Office, SMBy, Burnley school log books, 1860–1905.
51. Durham Record Office, EP/Au SA14/34, Bishop Auckland Parish Magazine *Home Words*, article relating to St Luke's Church, Fylands, June 1900.
52. *The Burnley Gazette and East Lancashire Advertiser*, 26 May 1900.
53. Evidence from record linkage to Burnley censuses 1891 and 1901.
54. Behlmer, *Child Abuse and Moral Reform*; Jackson, *Child Sexual Abuse*; Ferguson, *Protecting Children in Time*.

11
Godfathering: The Politics of Victorian Family Relations

Valerie Sanders

> We christen an infant phaenomonon [*sic*] on Saturday, and expect
> a few friends in the evening in honor [*sic*] of the occasion.[1]

In Chapter 5 of Dickens' *Dombey and Son* (1848), Mr Dombey, who has longed all his married life for a son to inherit the family business, finally acquires one – at the cost of his exhausted wife – and is planning little Paul's christening ceremony. His sister Mrs Chick, promoting her friend Miss Tox as a potential second wife, hopes Dombey might make her a godmother, but worries that Miss Tox is too negligible for such an honour. '"Godfathers, of course," continued Mrs Chick, "are important in point of connexion and influence"' – implying that god*mothers* are less essential in buttressing a family's social position. Mr Dombey's tetchy reply is: '"I don't know why they should be, to my son."' He elaborates: '"The kind of foreign help which people usually seek for their children, I can afford to despise; being above it, I hope".' Miss Tox is therefore 'elevated ... to the godmothership of little Paul, in virtue of her insignificance.'[2]

The twisted logic of this episode, derived from Mr Dombey's determination to own and manage his son almost single-handedly, runs counter to the usual thinking of the period in relation to the appointment of godparents. Dickens himself clearly thought influential godparents were an advantage, naming his children after famous contemporary writers such as Alfred Tennyson, Walter Savage Landor, Sydney Smith, Francis Jeffrey, and Edward Bulwer Lytton. His daughter Kate's middle name was Macready, after the tragic actor, William Charles Macready, who was one of Dickens' closest lifelong friends. In return, Dickens was godfather to Macready's son Henry. Similar reciprocal arrangements existed in other circles of Victorian influential men such as the scientists, Charles Darwin, Joseph Hooker, and Thomas Henry Huxley. Although these are exceptional or atypical families, they exemplify a number of broader issues involving domestic power relations in the mid to late nineteenth century: the contest for religious authority between husband and wife, the husband's/father's responsibilities as religious head of the household, the semi-public ceremonial of introducing the child into the wider community, and the bolstering of the family with additional supporters whose role was generally seen in secular terms by the men, though a religious ceremony was meant to be the means of publicly demonstrating their Christian faith. In other words, what we have here is a collision between the secular and the spiritual, the maternal and the paternal, and the public and the private. The rich variety of ideological cross-currents created by these issues makes godparenting practices a fruitful source of information about Victorian domestic authority, though surprisingly little has so far been written about the negotiation of male/female roles in christening ceremonies.

According to John Gillis, family, for a significant part of the middle classes, became 'a major site of cultural work in the 1840s and 1850s.' Apart from household prayers led by the father, women were becoming increasingly involved in spiritual leadership in the home, especially with seasonal rituals such as Christmas when women were 'the chief ritualists of the Victorian family, carrying out the bulk of its newly acquired liturgical activity.' Gillis uses explicitly religious language to describe what Victorian women did, even when the occasion was not specifically sacred: for example, becoming the 'priestesses of the Victorian cult of domesticity, arranging its ceremonies and presiding over its icons, rarely the recipients of the sacraments they themselves prepared.'[3] So far as christenings were concerned, Gillis argues that the ceremony of baptism 'regained favour in the second half of the nineteenth century,' and 'was a family affair in which the central figure was the mother rather than the father.' The father, in effect, might be displaced as the orchestrator of an event which was designed to celebrate his position in the community and in relation to friends, family and work colleagues, fathers having up to the eighteenth century been more directly involved in welcoming a new child into the family.[4] While the mother in each of the families I discuss was undoubtedly the moral and emotional centre of the day, my examples demonstrate that the father found ways of managing the arrangements so as to register his dissent from the religious side of things, especially in his selection of godparents. It should be clear from the discussion that far more was at stake than the provision of spiritual guardians for newborn children. This, if anything, seems to have been the least important consideration in these families, despite – or perhaps because of – the atmosphere of religious doubt and controversy which pervaded the period under review. With the church at mid-century engaging in urgent debate about the issue of baptismal regeneration, through the so-called 'Gorham controversy,' apparent indifference towards the spiritual implications of the ceremony, compared with the strengthening of the father's professional ties, indicates that some prominent Victorians were mainly using this ritual for domestic and secular purposes of their own.[5]

So far as godparents were concerned, they gave the Victorian family an opportunity to supplement and strengthen the parental function in certain ways. Both the *Book of Common Prayer* and the Canon Law of the Anglican Church stipulate that wherever possible baptism should be a public ceremony, and 'for every Male-child to be baptized two Godfathers, and one Godmother [should be provided]; and for every Female, one Godfather and two Godmothers.'[6] The primary responsibility of the godparents was to 'answer for the child' as a Christian, and assist the parents in bringing him up as such; learned footnotes in the 1820 version of *The Book of Common Prayer* stress that this responsibility should not be accepted too casually, or 'merely in compliment' to the parents.[7] In fact, as Peter Jagger has shown, there was considerable concern at mid-century that many parents were failing to have their children baptised at all because they were unable to find three suitably qualified godparents. To be acceptable to the Anglican Church, a godparent had to have been baptised himself and to be willing to provide spiritual guidance to the child until at least the age of confirmation. Although neglect of baptism was more common in the urban working classes than elsewhere, Jagger suggests that 'in the mid-Victorian period the choosing of sponsors was generally done with little thought either about their functions or their suitability...Sponsorship, in many cases, was simply a friendly act done for that day, primarily to the parents of the infant.'[8] This impression is strongly borne out by interviews recently conducted with survivors of upper- and middle-class families from the late nineteenth century. One interviewee, Mrs Philpots, for example, when asked about godparents replied, 'Godparents? Never of any use – if I had them'; while Mr K. Vignoles commented, 'I don't think they meant very much to me personally, although I'm sure that they were of some support to my parents.'[9] In the examples to be discussed here, concern for the child's religious welfare is rarely mentioned in the correspondence between fathers and friends, nor is there much sense of the wider Christian family the public service of baptism was meant to create. Least often mentioned is the mother, though she was usually the driving force behind the ceremony, and the one most eager to make the arrangements. Daughters, again, were seen as less central to the father's concerns because of the lack of any perceived need to forge professional networks for them. The emphasis was primarily on the advantages that would accrue to the father, with some promise of collateral secular benefit to the sons.

Dean Stanley of Westminster, in an article on 'Baptism' for the *Nineteenth Century* (1879), refers to the ceremony in terms of the whole Christian community being an extended family: 'It teaches us the value of the purity of those domestic relations in which from childhood to old age all our best thoughts are fostered and encouraged.'[10] Tracing the history of baptism from the practice of immersing adults to sprinkling infants and providing sponsors for them, Stanley adds that this system of creating 'a new series of spiritual affinities' brings 'social and moral advantages' to those involved.[11] A similar idea of an extended family created by baptism is suggested by Dickens' friend and sub-editor W. H. Wills in a more secular essay on 'Baptismal Rituals' (1850) for *Household Words*. Deploring that the meaning has gone out of the godparent–godchild relationship, which seemed to him to be over with the presentation of gifts, Wills concludes, 'It is not to our praise that the ties between sponsors and god-children, were much closer, and held more sacredly in times which we are pleased to call barbarous. God-children were placed not only in a state of pupilage with their sponsors, but also in the position of relations.'[12]

Both these essays point to the way a religious family ceremony crosses the boundaries between private and public, family and not-family; like a wedding, it creates new relationships; it displays a family in a place that replicates the home; and it asks them to make a private profession of faith in a public place. The meaning of baptism was in fact constantly aired in the middle period of the nineteenth century, by churchmen of widely differing denominations, from the high-Church Tractarians, such as Keble and Pusey, to the Broad Churchmen like Stanley. Pusey explored the heated issue of baptismal regeneration, and what he called the 'privileges' of baptism, in an historical context in three *Tracts for the Times* (numbers 67–69 in 1835); while John Keble, who gave a series of 33 sermons on the Baptismal Service in 1849–50, reminded hearers of the Prayer Book's emphasis on the public nature of baptisms as ceremonies to be held on Sundays and other holy days in order to attract the maximum number of witnesses and spectators. For him, baptism was 'in some respects a coronation and a marriage,' and any parent deliberately neglecting to have his child baptised would be wilfully leaving himself and his family 'in the power of Satan and not in the family of God.'[13] Keble's contributions to debates about baptism are less technical than the correspondence between the Archbishop of Canterbury and Bishop Henry Phillpotts of Exeter over the doctrine of baptismal regeneration (1850), but like other commentators of the period, he was anxious to restore full spiritual meaning to the ceremony, as well as a sense that baptised children were entering into a privileged but extended Christian family. Unfortunately, in Keble's own case, the extended family was subject to ideological rift: Keble was Matthew Arnold's godfather, but his relationship with Dr Arnold was compromised when the latter attacked the Oxford Movement, of which Keble was a core member, in a series of articles in the 1830s.[14]

Relations between another father, Alfred, Lord Tennyson and an active apologist for baptism, Frederick Denison Maurice, who was godfather to Tennyson's elder son Hallam, were more cordial and lasting. Maurice, alienated by Pusey's suggestion that the newly baptised child enjoyed a moment of holy purity before again being liable to sin, believed 'that at baptism infants received the Holy Spirit and were made members of the Church.'[15]

He was especially interested in the relationship between family and church, and more widely the kingdom of God as a whole. These were connections he explored in *The Kingdom of Christ* (1838; revised 1842), where he states that to the modern philosopher, 'Baptism was unquestionably a bond of fellowship in certain periods; it did mean something to those who lived in them; but its significance is gone.' Maurice believed this significance was far from defunct: he defends the continuing importance of baptism by asserting that it testifies to men of all countries 'that they have a common friend and a common enemy.'[16] In Maurice's masculinist terms, the baptised form a kind of brotherhood expanding ever outwards from the domestic hearth: 'I was sent into the world,' he claimed, 'that I might persuade men to recognise Christ as the centre of their fellowship with each other, that so they might be united in their families, their countries, and as men, not in schools and factions.' Without this reminder of his connection with other people, he feared he might continually have been 'letting go friendships, and sinking into an unprofitable solitude.'[17] According to Jeremy Morris, *The Kingdom of Christ* argued that 'the family is a microcosm of the relations of mutual dependence which characterize the kingdom of God as a whole, and the primary form in which the perception of "spiritual things" is mediated in human beings.'[18]

This familial vocabulary is a regular feature of mid-century writing about baptism, though it tends to be deployed in a masculine context. Little is said about the mother's role in bringing her child to be baptised: according to Gillis, it had traditionally been the father who brought the child to the font while the mother was still recovering from childbirth.[19] The christening was thus the public, supposedly spiritual, male-dominated part of the baby's entrance into the world, the female part – the child's birth – being essentially intimate, physical, and domestic, with the focus on the body, not the spirit. Though many of the fathers discussed in this chapter did what they could to assist their wives through childbirth, they are essentially self-appointed mediators between the home and the gentlemen's club, announcing both birth and christening in a series of witty letters to their predominantly male friends. The father is often especially concerned with his own image as a begetter of children, with both Dickens and Darwin viewing with mixed pride and alarm the number of children for whom they were fast becoming responsible. In Mr Dombey's case, the shortage of children makes the christening of the only son all the more emotionally intense, and the significance of their trip to church a public statement of the father's importance. The narrator says pointedly, however:

> It might have been well for Mr Dombey, if he had thought of his own dignity a little less; and had thought of the great origin and purpose of the ceremony in which he took so formal and so stiff a part, a little more. His arrogance contrasted strangely with its history.[20]

The publication of *Dombey and Son* coincided with the beginnings of the Gorham controversy and the upsurge of public debates about the meaning of baptism. Both Dickens and Tennyson, who had sons born and baptised in this period, could have engaged in, or registered some interest in, the heated theological arguments going on around them, but both essentially saw the christening of their children as an occasion to invite their male friends to a good party; this despite Dickens' warning in the *Dombey* passage just cited. As Rosemarie Bodenheimer has recently argued, Dickens often seems more at ease with his male than his female correspondents, and more inclined to risk controversial opinions with them: 'Men are his confidants, his companions in play and in travel, his ways of measuring himself,' Bodenheimer suggests.[21] It is to men that he most frequently writes, inviting them to attend his children's christening parties, with the emphasis on the gathering of good friends which will occur after the ceremony, while practically nothing is said either about the ceremony itself or about the role of his wife and women friends, godmothers included, in any part of the proceedings.

Dickens was by all accounts a traditional Anglican who distrusted showy displays of religious feeling: he privately rewrote the gospels in a simplified form for his children, and recommended each of his sons, as they left home, to be guided by the morality of the New Testament. To a large extent he left them to reflect for themselves along generalised Christian lines. To his youngest, Edward, known as 'Plorn,' he wrote, 'You will remember that you have never at home been wearied about religious observances or mere formalities.'[22] Dickens largely avoids commenting in any detail on the spiritual implications of baptism.[23] There is no sign that he shared his wife's views – that the 'consequences of a child's dying without being baptized are very dreadful as they cannot be buried on consecrated ground';[24] nor that he thought baptism provided any kind of insurance policy against moral laxity, unlike Huxley's wife Henrietta, who, according to his biographer, Cyril Bibby, saw baptism as 'a kind of spiritual vaccination without which the youngsters might catch Sin in worse forms as they grew up.'[25]

Indeed, Dickens' invitations to his friends to attend each of his children's christenings were couched in decidedly secular as well as masculine language, as between male friends whose wives were no more than necessary adjuncts to the occasion. Dombey's wife was, of course, dead when the christening arrangements were made, but in Dickens' real domestic situation, his wife's role in the celebrations is minimised in his letters, and it is difficult to tell what the women were doing on the great day. Occasionally he mentions that Catherine has asked him to pass on an invitation, and on one occasion at least she invited people herself, but this was very much a matter of complying with his instructions. This was in 1852, when Dickens was away from home at a point when he wanted to invite Edward Bulwer Lytton to be his youngest son's godfather. 'We have a very great desire to give our youngest boy your distinguished name,' she wrote. 'Will you grant this favour to him and his parents, and will you be his godfather. I need not say how glad we shall be to have such a valued friend in this relation to the little boy.'[26] Though written at her husband's behest, the letter is clearly phrased in a less jocular style than his usual invitations. 'We christen an infant phaenomonon on Saturday, and expect a few friends in the evening in honour of the occasion,' he informed one friend when his eldest son Charley was baptised (1837) – the phrase 'infant phenomenon' anticipating its usage in *Nicholas Nickleby* (1838–39), where it refers to an over-exposed and overgrown child actress exhibited by her showman father. To another friend he explained that people were being invited in honour of the baby 'and his faith' to the very secular entertainment of 'music and a rubber.'[27] He already seems to be mocking the idea that a baby could have a 'faith'; of another son, Sydney, Dickens reported his habit of staring 'with a kind of leaden satisfaction, at his spoons, without afflicting himself much, about the established church.'[28] Like many of his other brief throwaway remarks about the Church, this shows that while Dickens was aware of Christian doctrinal matters, he found them hard to reconcile with the reality of a baby's self-absorbed infantile existence.

By the time of his second daughter's christening, Dickens was resorting to parody and burlesque: 'A babby is to be christened and a fatted calf killed on these premises on Tuesday the 25th. Instant. It (the calf; not the babby) is to be taken off the spit at 6.'[29] His casual reference to the return of the Prodigal Son (Luke 15: 11–32) in the context of his baby daughter's christening shows both his familiarity with the Gospels, and his natural, instinctive recourse to a distinctly masculine father/son parable, even when the occasion was his daughter's baptism. It was difficult for Dickens to move outside an implicitly male frame of reference even where his girls were concerned. Nor did he name them after women novelists to match his sons' compliments to the great male writers of the day. Possibly, this was because there were no contemporary women writers in the 1830s he would have considered worthy of the honour (it is hard to imagine a 'Harriet Martineau Dickens' for example, given his difficult relationship with the great populariser of political economy); more probably, even if there had been, he did not recognise the same need to create professional networks for them via baptismal parties and relationships, as they would presumably marry and be supported by their husbands. In this respect he was very different from Dr Arnold, who, having run out of female family names, christened his youngest daughter Frances Bunsen Trevenen Whately – after the Prussian ambassador Chevalier Bunsen, and Archbishop Richard Whately of Dublin. Mary (Mamie) Dickens (1838–96) was named after Dickens' recently dead 17-year-old sister-in-law Mary Hogarth; while the unfortunate Dora Dickens (1850–51) shared the name of his ill-fated character Dora Spenlow, David Copperfield's wife, who dies of a disease associated with pregnancy. Dickens had her christened hastily by James White, a playwriting clergyman friend, while he was attending a dinner-party at the Dickens house in February 1851; she survived only another two months, and less than a year after Dickens had casually talked about 'killing' his fictional Dora.

By this stage, Dickens had entered into reciprocal godfathering arrangements with his actor friend Macready. 'Anything which can serve to commemorate our friendship and to keep the recollection of it alive among our children is – believe me – and ever will be, most deeply prized by me,' he assures Macready in response to an invitation from him to be Henry Frederick Bulwer Macready's godfather.[30] Macready's own diary account of Henry's christening stresses the gender divisions and male professional networking of the arrangements; he had already, as he put it (in suitably theatrical terminology), 'engaged' the novelist and dramatist Edward Bulwer, who was evidently a popular choice of godfather: all the more so for Macready, who was working with him on the staging of his plays:

> Went to church with Dickens, Forster, Maclise – to meet Catherine and her party with darling little Henry, who was christened by Dr Morris. Dickens gave him a silver cup – as his godfather. He is one to be proud of.[31]

His description of the ceremonial implies that the husband and wife, or men and women, entered the church in two separate parties: the women with the baby, and the men forming a phalanx of friends and colleagues – in this case all writers and journalists who belonged to the father's world. While Macready was later happy to be Kate Dickens' godfather, and boasted in his diary of having given her a 'sponsorial offering of a watch and chain, which [he] was pleased to see very much admired,' he privately thought the tone of Dickens' christening parties was all wrong. 'Rather a noisy and uproarious day – not so much *comme il faut* as I could have wished,' he commented after the 'fatted calf' celebrations mentioned above.[32] Nevertheless, he joined Dickens and the sculptor Angus Fletcher on a visit to Cold Bath Fields Prison immediately after lunch on the christening day, and was shown around by the governor, Captain Chesterton. This, and a book-buying expedition, seems to have filled in the time for the men before the main dinner at Dickens' in the evening, while the women presumably stayed at home with the children.

Though Macready was unusual in this group in having more of a religious feeling about the ceremony of baptism, what seems to have mattered most to him at Henry's christening was the silver cup and the distinguished godfather. Moreover, it was not unusual for the men to form a separate party from the women on such occasions and devise some alternative secular entertainment. Henry Macready's christening was a two-day event, with Macready's male friends staying over with the family in Elstree. Macready notes in his journal that on the christening afternoon, he, Dickens, Maclise, and Forster (who was godfather to Macready's daughter Joan) 'went to the reservoir,' where he 'pulled on the water with Dickens.' Field sports were also available: 'Forster, Bulwer, and myself went into the field and shot with the bow for some time.' In quiet moments on both days, Macready 'talked much with Bulwer about a play.'[33] With no reference to what the women were doing while all this male bonding was taking place, one can only assume that Macready saw the christening primarily as an opportunity to spend more time with his own literary friends, and cement promising relationships in the theatrical world.

Dickens worked harder still to equip his sons with potentially useful god-fathers. As his family grew, he sometimes had to negotiate around the Christian issues in selecting men he found congenial and influential. One of his most extraordinary choices was for his second son Walter, born in 1841: Dr John Elliotson was not only a well-known physician, but also a celebrated mesmerist, whose religious position was anything but orthodox. Knowing this, Dickens reassured him in advance that he would not need to perform any religious duties towards the child. Elliotson replied in very explicit terms for a would-be godfather that he could not 'have spoiled him [Walter] for arithmetic by teaching him that three are one & one is three, or defaced his views of the majesty of God by assuring him that the master of the Universe once came down & got a little jewess in the family way.'[34] Walter fared only slightly better with his other godfather, the poet and critic Walter Savage Landor, whose published attacks on the church deplored the amount of money squandered on bishoprics, as measured against clergy-men's neglect of their flocks. Nor had he any time for quarrels about dogma. Landor did in fact accept Dickens' invitation with good grace, admitting that 'it creates in me a somewhat new sentiment, it makes me religious, to think of him,' but in choosing two such men as his son's godfathers, Dickens evidently felt their ability to provide spiritual guidance was relatively unim-portant, compared with what the connection could offer him. Even when the original godfathers had died, Dickens shamelessly exploited their for-mer reputation in his attempts to find his son's useful career openings. This was especially true of Francis Jeffrey Dickens, named after a founder of the *Edinburgh Review*. In trying to push the hapless Frank into the Regis-trar's Office in 1863, 13 years after Jeffrey's death, Dickens reminded Lord Brougham that his son was 'Jeffrey's godson, and Francis Jeffrey by name.'[35]

That he saw christening parties as inevitably divisive along gender lines is clear not only from his letters, but also from 'The Bloomsbury Christening' in his *Sketches by Boz* (1836) and 'The Formal Couple' from *Sketches of Young Couples* (1840), a series of satirical pieces published anonymously in the year of Queen Victoria's marriage to Prince Albert. In 'The Bloomsbury Christening,' the baby's father invites his misanthropic uncle Nicodemus Dumps to be a godfather; again, the wife and mother is a secondary figure, as the women guests fuss delightedly round the baby. Dumps offends his hear-ers by proposing a toast which largely warns of all the illnesses and mishaps that will probably befall the child, causing his mother to rush from the room 'with her handkerchief to her eyes, and accompanied by several ladies.'[36] For *Sketches of Young Couples* the starting-point was the comic notion of women making marriage proposals, as they were supposedly entitled to do in a Leap Year, and following the Queen's example. 'The Formal Couple,' one of Dickens' models of married life, do nothing but complain about the shortcomings of their friends' social arrangements, such as funerals and christening parties. 'We made one at a christening party not long since,' reports the narrator,

> where there were amongst the guests a formal couple, who suffered the acutest torture from certain jokes, incidental to such an occasion, cut ... by one of the godfathers; a red-faced elderly gentleman, who, being highly popular with the rest of the company, had it all his own way, and was in great spirits.

In observing the 'formal lady's' pained response to the godfather's ill-judged jokes about 'the time when he had dandled in his arms the young Christian's mother,' and to the possibility of 'the subject of that festival having brothers and sisters,' the narrator is clearly amused by her primness in the face of so much good-humoured, if slightly ribald gallantry. Indeed, she is in two minds whether she should have attended the party at all: 'encouraging, as it were, the public exhibition of a baby,' which to her is 'an act involving some degree of indelicacy and impropriety.' She too leaves the room in tears, under her husband's protection.[37]

Perhaps these sketches partly allude to the difficulties involved in celebrating anything with women around: certain kinds of joke are clearly inappropriate, and if they cause offence, women are apt to flounce out and spoil the harmony of the party. Dickens, in these sketches, was bound to make fun of women more than he does men, given his exaggerated alarm about the proposal 'conspiracy' and a certain jadedness about christenings, but his parting words in the 'Conclusion' make significant assumptions about the balance of domestic power in his public and private writing. 'We have purposely excluded from consideration the couple in which the lady reigns paramount and supreme,' he explains, 'holding such cases to be of a very unnatural kind, and like hideous births and other monstrous deformities, only to be discreetly and sparingly exhibited.' This type of comment presupposes an assenting male readership, and is difficult to position in relation to an implied woman reader. For Dickens, the notion of men being indisputably in charge of their own homes is both something to be taken for granted, and something to be worried about, in case it turns out not to be true. The wife's moral high ground when her children are born and their christening arrangements made becomes a cause of unease. It may be ungallant to tease women when they have just survived the trauma of giving birth, but Dickens overcompensates for any such conscientious scruples, both in his letters and in his published fictions, where the deployment of a coy and self-conscious wit predominates.

What exactly parents expected of godparents and their role in the upbringing of their children at this period is not entirely clear. Though the godparents' duties were meant to be primarily spiritual, they had the potential to be almost anything: a friend to the child at the very least, but also an additional guardian, especially if the parents should happen to die. The relationship between godparents and girls seems to have been particularly unclear, as indicated above in relation to Dickens' daughters, and very little is ever said in his letters about the role of godmothers. Few, one hopes, were as negligent as Jane Carlyle, who had forgotten that she had a goddaughter until she met her again some years later: 'Not one godmotherly thing had I ever done towards that child!' she confessed when she was reunited with Lydia Macready (1842–58), daughter of the actor, in 1849. When she invited Lydia to stay for a few days, she found the child a major domestic disturbance, as Jane '"ran horses" at her bidding,' shared a bed with her, and was kept awake all night by the child's kicking 'with her active little heels': 'I had not once closed my eyes and in this state to have to wash and dress her and play at horses again! It was a strange and severe penalty for being a Godmother.'[38] A religious sceptic, Jane Carlyle clearly has no sense of needing to make anything spiritual of the visit, though she presumably accepted the role knowing that she could offer the child only secular support (and that very rarely). Her acceptance implies more a compliment to the parents than an interest in the child. Even in a more pious family, like the Rossettis, there was uncertainty as to the role expected of the girls' godparents. Jan Marsh records that Christina was provided with exceptionally grand godmothers: Georgina Macgregor, whose governess Christina's mother had been, and Lady Dudley Stuart, formerly Princess Christina Bonaparte, Napoleon's niece, whose acquaintance her father, Gabriele Rossetti, had recently made. 'What benefits were intended to flow from such sponsors is unknown,' Marsh comments; 'neither seems to have featured in their goddaughter's later life, though one is thought to have given as christening gift a coral necklace she always treasured.'[39]

Victorian intellectuals and writers are particularly interesting cases in terms of godparenting choices, since, unlike the upper middle class, they had to form their own personal and extra-family connections by making themselves into desirable friends for the famous. In asking a celebrity, even another writer who had achieved public acclaim, to stand as godparent to one of their children, writers such as Dickens and Tennyson were inviting them into their families and establishing a lifelong personal link, with all the continuing sense of obligation, financial and social, this would entail.

It was pointedly as a concession to his more pious wife Emily that F. D. Maurice was asked to stand godfather to the Tennysons' elder son

Hallam, born in 1852 – ironically, a year before he was asked to resign from his Professorship at King's College London for declaring his disbelief in eternal punishment. Emily Tennyson had insisted on including a clergyman among the godparents in order to counteract the prevailing scepticism of her husband's other friends. 'I wish there were any chance of your being at his christening next Tuesday,' she wrote to one such friend, James Spedding, 'though in order to protect against all you naughty infidels we have been constrained to get Maurice to be one of the sponsors.'[40] Maurice himself told Charles Kingsley how honoured he was to have been asked (Tennyson was by now Poet Laureate), but he knew the poet himself might not have chosen him: 'I accept the office with real thankfulness and fear. It was to please his wife he asked me.'[41] Hallam's other male godparent was the historian Henry Hallam, father of the Arthur Hallam who had been Tennyson's closest friend at Cambridge until his sudden premature death – thus revitalising a formative relationship from Tennyson's own youth. Similarly, when their second son Lionel was christened two years later, another clergyman, Drummond Rawnsley, was brought in as godfather. 'Will you kindly consent notwithstanding your strong suspicions of our want of orthodoxy?' Emily Tennyson asked, repeating her earlier concerns about the generally unreligious tone of the Tennyson celebrations.[42]

The poet, however, clearly came to value Maurice as more than a showcase godfather, hired to put a respectable gloss on the occasion, though typically enough it was as a hearty male friend with a feel for good food, wine, and conversation that Tennyson most appreciated him. When Maurice was dismissed from his post, Tennyson wrote a poem, dated January 1854, 'To the Rev. F. D. Maurice,' addressing him as 'Godfather,' and heartily inviting him to visit the family on the Isle of Wight and spend time with his godson Hallam: 'Your presence will be sun in winter, / Making the little one leap for joy.' This, however, is all he says about the godfather/godchild relationship: Tennyson is primarily interested in Maurice as a friend of his own, with whom he can converse, over a good meal, about secular matters such as the Crimean War or Maurice's social reforms: 'You'll have no scandal while you dine / But honest talk and wholesome wine.' There is certainly no suggestion in the poem that Tennyson would go to him for spiritual advice on his own or his son's behalf, and the child's mother is by implication excluded from the male camaraderie celebrated in the poem.[43] Maurice, on the other hand, dedicated his 1853 book of *Theological Essays* to Tennyson, with a compliment to the poet's knowledge of the 'deepest thoughts and feelings of human beings' to which a true Theology should always respond. He concludes, 'As the hopes which I have expressed in this volume are more likely to be fulfilled to our children than to ourselves, I might perhaps ask you to accept it as a present to one of your name, in whom you have given me a very sacred interest.'[44] Possibly, this was a tacit acknowledgement that Tennyson himself was unlikely to read the essays (on such core Christian issues as sin, charity, 'the Evil Spirit,' and 'Regeneration') with the pious respect they merited, but Maurice was certainly more than fulfilling his duties as godfather.

The experiences of the Dickens and Tennyson circles in the 1840s were largely repeated, with increased confidence, by the scientists Charles Darwin, Thomas Henry Huxley, and Joseph Hooker 20 years later. Although their own religious belief was in steady decline, or – with the younger men – already gone by the time they became fathers, they still had their children christened, largely at their wives' behest. In this respect they were very different from the notable agnostic, Sir Leslie Stephen, Virginia Woolf's father, who gave his children 'secular godparents,' including the American ambassador, James Lowell, for Virginia ('He gave her a natal poem, a silver posset-dish and a bird in a cage,' Woolf's biographer Hermione Lee reports, 'For this, "Ginia" was much envied by the other children, whose godparents were less impressive').[45] Darwin, by contrast, constantly struggled to negotiate the gap between his wife Emma's steadfast religious belief and his own growing scepticism, which gained momentum from his daughter Annie's death in 1851. Darwin had long since abandoned the religious leadership of his own household, treating Sundays like a weekday, while his wife went to church and pursued her own religious needs. Their son Francis remembered many years later how odd it was to see his father enter a church to attend any kind of religious ceremony. Even his daughter's wedding cost him an effort; as for baptisms, 'I remember him many years ago at a christening; a memory which has remained with me, because to us children it seemed an extraordinary and abnormal occurrence.' Francis' draft version of these recollections reveals that the christening was actually that of Darwin's youngest son, Charles Waring, who died of scarlet fever at the age of two in 1858.[46] It seems surprising that he attended this last christening, when he had long since lost his faith, but this was presumably in compliance with Emma's wishes. Moreover, some, at least, of the Darwin children seem to have been baptised without godparents: 'not from any objection to their having such – but as we should in that case have been obliged to have stood proxies & we both disliked the statement of believing anything for another.' It is not entirely clear why he thought the godparents would be unable to attend, and the parents would have to speak for them, but he clearly disliked the notion of making any theological promises, whether for himself or another. Darwin himself explained these circumstances to his second cousin, William Darwin Fox, father of 11 children, who was so keen to secure Darwin as godfather that he wrote and invited him while he was away on his *Beagle* voyage. When the invitation was confirmed in 1841, Darwin replied at some length explaining his stance, which shows that he had no intention of taking part himself: 'with your deep feelings on religion, I thought possibly you might much dislike having a Godfather who could [not] stand in propriâ personâ as such.'[47]

Nevertheless, Darwin was clearly keen to cement relations with his cousin by recognising that godparenting gave them a connection. In Spain, he informed Fox, men standing godfather to each other's children call each other 'compadre.' This is such an attractive notion to Darwin that he repeats it in his next letter to Fox, extending the term experimentally to Fox's wife: 'Pray remember me very kindly to her, & as you seem to like the title of compadre, I hope she will not dislike being my commadre, which I have heard Spaniards, I know not whether in joke or earnest, call the wives of their compadres.'[48] What is noticeable here is that while 'compadre' is offered as a recognised term of comradeship between men, he is not at all certain whether 'commadre' is even a serious notion. In this respect Darwin's speculation follows the same lines as the language of the other fathers I have been discussing: bonding among friends at christenings seems to have followed strongly along gender lines, with men placing themselves at a remove from women in both spiritual and bodily terms.

Huxley and Hooker openly declared their scepticism in letters to each other while obeying their wives' insistence on arranging a christening. The most frank about it is Huxley, who in 1861 invited Hooker to be godfather to his son Leonard (Darwin consented to be another godfather): 'My wife will have the youngster christened, although I am always in a bad temper from the time it is talked about until the ceremony is over,' Huxley told his friend. 'The only way of turning the farce into a reality is by making it an extra bond with one's friends.' Like Darwin, he immediately thought of proxy godfathers, and offered to delegate Hooker's ceremonial promises to a clerk, rather than ask him to perform them himself: 'if you consent, the clerk shall tell all the lies for you, and you shall be asked to do nothing else than to help devour the christening feed, and be as good a friend to the boy as you have been to his Father.'[49] Put like this, the christening arrangements become a male conspiracy to turn a meaningless religious ritual into an opportunity for masculine cross-generational bonding beyond the boundaries of both family and Christianity. Fittingly enough, Leonard Huxley subsequently edited Hooker's *Life and Letters* (1918) as well as his own father's (1900), thereby becoming the guardian of both men's reputations in the very secular 'afterlife' of their scientific achievements. As with Dickens and Macready, the christening of sons, more than daughters, seems to have elicited this kind of division along gender lines: girls usually had only one male godparent, and it would of course have seemed indecorous for women, whether mothers or godmothers, to turn the occasion into an opportunity for anti-religious badinage, or even a jovial party. The published letters say little or nothing about the daughters' baptisms, though it is known that Annie Darwin's was held jointly with her cousin Sophy Wedgwood's at the parish church in the grounds of Maer, the Wedgwood family home in Staffordshire, in May 1841, with the ceremony performed by another Wedgwood cousin. Emma Darwin had clearly kept control of the christening arrangements by ensuring they happened at Maer and entirely within her own family. This was something she could perhaps do more easily for a daughter than for a son, where the father's importance loomed larger over the ceremony.

Hooker, himself the father of a large family, responded in kind, declining the offer of a deputy at the Huxley ceremony. Like Huxley, Landor, and Elliotson, he was prepared to endure the religious ritual for the sake of cementing his relationship with the child's father, and eventually the child himself. This becomes in fact a kind of secular alternative to the bond with God the Father and Christ the Son which the ceremony is supposed to construct. In accepting Huxley's invitation, Hooker tried to verbalise the exact nature of his feelings about the event:

> In the abstract I hate and despise the spiritual element of the ceremony, but in practice I do not care so much about it as conscientiously to plead any honest wish to shirk it....I assure you truthfully that the pleasure of being in any recognised relationship to your child will sweeten any pill of doctrine that may be offered, even if I could not manage to 'sham Abraham' at the responses, an unworthy and cowardly resort I affect on such occasions.[50]

The understanding among the men that none of them has any religious belief, and that they will attach a different symbolic meaning to the occasion from the one intended, restores some of the domestic authority they have lost through obedience to their wives. This loss of authority seems to have begun when their children were born, the husbands being largely powerless to help their wives through the ordeal. Once chloroform came into use, from the late 1840s onwards, the scientists regained some involvement by being able to administer the anaesthetic to their wives. In all the cases discussed in this chapter, however, the husbands seem to have been looking for a role in their household following the birth of a child. Huxley convinced himself that the birth of his first son Noel would somehow validate and ennoble his scientific ambitions. 'Waiting for my child,' he noted in his journal. 'I seem to fancy it the pledge that all these things [scientific ambitions] shall be.' His plans included avoiding petty personal controversies and giving 'a nobler tone to science.'[51] Being unable to share either their wife's physical involvement with the baby, or her religious convictions, Huxley and the other scientific fathers reclaim ground by going behind their wives' backs and sharing sceptical talk with other men – constructing a space where they can be entirely open about their dislike of the baptism ceremony.

The christening ritual, in that sense, becomes a means by which domestic authority changes hands. Though performed by a man within the all-male structure of the Victorian Church, the christening for these families at least was a female-driven ceremonial, as John Gillis suggests, in that the wives in most cases initiated it, and insisted that their children were properly baptised. Dickens confided to Angela Burdett Coutts, on the day of his youngest son's christening, that his wife also expected him to stay at home. 'We have been christening the baby today, and I *dare not* go out,' he told her conspiratorially. 'It would be considered heresy.'[52] Presumably Catherine by then had had enough of all-male excursions to the bookseller's and prisons on christening afternoons, let alone Macready's water and field sports. Bandying religious terms disrespectfully was as far as Dickens could go in disobeying his wife's more reverent feelings about the day. For the husbands and fathers, christenings worked only in terms of what F. D. Maurice called a 'bond of fellowship' among men and boys, intellectuals, and famous public figures, who determinedly secularised the occasion. Mothers and daughters, who wield all the spiritual power, lack a role in these networks, both by virtue of their situation as non-professionals whose future lies in the home rather than in the public sphere, and because they have no place in these newly created male fellowships. More than anything, perhaps, their commitment to the spiritual importance of the event, where even the baby seems edged out, excludes them. Despite all the promises to be a friend to one another's sons, the fathers were evidently more interested in promoting their relationships with one another. By the time it actually happened, the christening ceremony had been reclaimed by the husbands and fathers as an occasion for secular networking on their own and their sons' behalves, and covert undermining of both church and women's domestic authority. Ironically, they had recovered for themselves a central historical position at the heart of welcoming rituals for the newborn.

Notes

1. Madeline House and Graham Storey (eds) (1965) *The Letters of Charles Dickens. Vol. One: 1820–1839* (Oxford: Clarendon Press), p. 338.
2. Charles Dickens (1848, 1970) *Dombey and Son* (Harmondsworth: Penguin), pp. 101–3.
3. John R. Gillis (1989) 'Ritualization of Middle-Class Family Life in Nineteenth-Century Britain,' *International Journal of Politics, Culture and Society*, 3, pp. 214, 226.
4. John R. Gillis (1996) *A World of Their Own Making: Myth, Ritual, and the Quest for Family Values* (Cambridge: Harvard University Press), pp. 192, 170. Gillis also notes that in the seventeenth century the newly born child would be placed in its father's arms, and 'he would show it off to the gathered company,' ibid., p. 185.
5. A long-running controversy, beginning in 1847, when Bishop Henry Phillpots of Exeter refused to induct George Cornelius Gorham to the living of Brempton Speake because of Gorham's apparent belief in the doctrine of baptismal regeneration, that is, the notion that infants are regenerated by the sprinkling of holy water.
6. *The Book of Common Prayer* (London: J. Parker and F. C. and J. Rivington, 1820), p. 385.

7. Ibid., p. 405.
8. P. Jagger (1982) *Clouded Witness: Initiation in the Church of England in the Mid-Victorian Period 1850–1875* (Alison Parkes, Pennsylvania: Pickwick Publications), p. 80.
9. 'Middle and Upper Class Families in the Early 20th Century, 1870–1977,' SN 5404: http://www.data-archive.ac.uk; Mrs Philpots, p. 11; Mr Vignoles, p. 53.
10. A. P. Stanley (1879), 'Baptism,' *Nineteenth Century*, VI, 700.
11. Ibid., pp. 702–3.
12. [W. H. Wills], 'Baptismal Rituals,' *Household Words*, I (27 April 1850), 108.
13. John Keble (1849–50, published 1868) *Village Sermons on the Baptismal Service*, http://anglicanhistory.org/keble/bapt/sermon1.pdf, p. 2.
14. Arnold's most notorious article, 'The Oxford Malignants and Dr Hampden,' in the *Edinburgh Review* (April 1836), pp. 225–39, attacked the Oxford Movement for their campaign against the new politically liberal Regius Professor of Divinity at Oxford, R. D. Hampden.
15. Jagger, *Clouded Witness*, p. 31.
16. Frederick Denison Maurice (1838, revised 1842, 4th edn, 1891), *The Kingdom of Christ or Hints to a Quaker Respecting the Principles, Constitution, and Ordinances of the Catholic Church*, 2 vols (London: Macmillan), I, p. 333.
17. Frederick Denison Maurice (1884) *The Life of Frederick Denison Maurice*, 2 vols (London: Macmillan), I, p. 238.
18. Jeremy Morris (2005) *F. D. Maurice and the Crisis of Christian Authority* (Oxford: Oxford University Press), pp. 34, 76.
19. John R. Gillis, *A World of Their Own Making*, p. 163.
20. Charles Dickens, *Dombey and Son*, p. 115.
21. Rosemarie Bodenheimer (2006) 'Dickens, Fascinated,' *Victorian Studies* 48, p. 268.
22. Graham Storey (ed.) (2002) *The Letters of Charles Dickens. Vol. 12, 1868–1870* (Oxford: Clarendon Press), p. 188.
23. Though there are some signs that Dickens knew enough about Puseyism and baptism to make an 'in' joke about being born again on his birthday, to the clergyman who gave his ailing daughter Dora an emergency baptism. See Graham Storey, Kathleen Tillotson and Nina Burgis (eds) (1998) *The Letters of Charles Dickens. Vol. Six* (Oxford: Clarendon Press), p. 30.
24. Madeline House and Graham Storey (eds) (1969) *The Letters of Charles Dickens. Vol. Two, 1840–41* (Oxford: Clarendon Press), p. 209.
25. Cyril Bibby (1872) *Scientist Extraordinary: The Life and Scientific Work of Thomas Henry Huxley 1825–1895* (Oxford: Pergamon Press), p. 57.
26. *The Letters of Charles Dickens. Vol. Six*, p. 662.
27. *The Letters of Charles Dickens. Vol. One*, p. 339.
28. Graham Storey and K. J. Fielding (eds) (1981) *The Letters of Charles Dickens. Vol. Five, 1847–1849* (Oxford: Clarendon Press), p. 90.
29. *The Letters of Charles Dickens. Vol. Two*, p. 117.
30. *The Letters of Charles Dickens. Vol. One*, p. 571.
31. William Toynbee (1912) *Diaries of William Charles Macready*, 2 vols (London: Chapman and Hall), II, p. 21.
32. Ibid., p. 75.
33. Ibid., p. 21.
34. *The Letters of Charles Dickens. Vol. Two*, p. 210.
35. Graham Storey (ed.) (1998) *The Letters of Charles Dickens. Vol. Ten, 1862–1864* (Oxford: Clarendon Press), p. 195.

36. Charles Dickens (1836), 'The Bloomsbury Christening,' *Sketches by Boz* (London: The Caxton Publishing Co Ltd), p. 558.
37. Text available online through Project Gutenberg at http://www.gutenberg.org/dirs/etext97/yngcp10h.htm.
38. Kenneth J. Fielding and David R. Sorensen (eds.) (2004) *Jane Carlyle: Newly Selected Letters* (Aldershot: Ashgate), pp. 139–40.
39. Jan Marsh (1995) *Christina Rossetti: A Literary Biography* (London: Pimlico), p. 17.
40. James O. Hoge (ed.) (1974) *The Letters of Emily Lady Tennyson* (University Park and London: Pennsylvania State University Press), p. 61.
41. Cecil Y. Long and Edgar F. Shannon, Jr (eds) (1987) *The Letters of Alfred Lord Tennyson* (Oxford: Clarendon Press), II, p. 47.
42. James O. Hoge (ed.) (1974) *The Letters of Emily Lady Tennyson*, p. 67.
43. 'To the Rev. F. D. Maurice' in T. Herbert Warren (1971/1975) *Tennyson: Poems and Plays* (Oxford: Oxford University Press), p. 218.
44. Frederick Denison Maurice (1853, 1891) *Theological Essays*, 5th edn (London: Macmillan), Dedication.
45. Hermione Lee (1996) *Virginia Woolf* (London: Chatto and Windus), pp. 104–5.
46. Francis Darwin (1887) *The Life and Letters of Charles Darwin Including An Auto-biographical Chapter*, 2 vols (London: John Murray), I, p. 128. The draft of this chapter can be found in *The Complete Works of Charles Darwin Online*.
47. Frederick Burkhardt and Sydney Smith (eds) (1986) *The Correspondence of Charles Darwin. Vol. Two, 1837–1843* (Cambridge: Cambridge University Press), p. 303.
48. Ibid., p. 304.
49. Leonard Huxley (1900) *Life and Letters of Thomas Henry Huxley*, 2 vols (London: Macmillan and Co Ltd), I, p. 223.
50. Leonard Huxley (1918) *Life and Letters of Joseph Dalton Hooker*, 2 vols (London: John Murray, 1918), II, p. 59.
51. Leonard Huxley (1900) *Life and Letters of Thomas Henry Huxley*, I, p. 151.
52. *The Letters of Charles Dickens. Vol. Six*, p. 664.

12

"Beating Children is Wrong": Domestic Life, Psychological Thinking and the Permissive Turn

Deborah Thom

The question of who exercises domestic authority and how it is exercised remains interesting to academics, politicians, children and citizens.[1] Punishment of children is perhaps the most prominent amongst an array of parental practices, which expose changing concepts of legitimacy and power within the family. This chapter examines the norms, theories and practices of child punishment in order to explore debates about the autonomy of children, about the care and interest of parents and about the effectiveness of professional discourse coming out of emerging social sciences in the early twentieth century. These debates also expose a problem about chronology. How far does the 1960s mark a significant break between authoritarian parenting, especially by patriarchal fathers, and liberal permissive tolerance, increasingly applied by mothers? Historians have explained the apparent shift in parenting practices around the 1960s as underpinned by a new idea of the autonomous child body and psyche, constructed by childcare authorities. New ideas about children in turn gave rise to a new perspective – the idea of childhood as the site upon which society enacts its theories about the future, influenced by the development of new ideas of the self, deriving from the disciplinary possibilities of Freudian psychoanalysis. This notion has been particularly forcefully argued by Jacques Donzelot, writing about the twentieth-century development of family-centred practices of regulation in place of a legalistic framework of middle-class control of the working classes through state agencies.[2] This chapter will problematise the extent to which such a new concept of the child body circulated, and will thus question the broad periodisation of 'permissiveness' in parenting practices.

Child punishment provides a site of discussion and a place where discursive formations are often deployed to make forceful and clear arguments for changing cultural practices. The consensus about corporal punishment has become overwhelmingly opposed to bodily punishment in the home as well as in the school and the criminal justice system. For example,

Penelope Leach, author of the very successful manual, *Baby and Child*, first published in 1977, has been extremely prominent in campaigns to end domestic violence to children administered in the name of discipline. Her campaigning organisation calls itself 'Children are unbeatable'. She has been campaigning against the use of corporal punishment since it was the subject of her PhD thesis in 1964. More recent research has echoed her arguments. The Royal College of Paediatricians supported her arguments when it gave evidence to a recent government investigation into punishment for children and reported from an Ontario study of over 2000 adults in the 1990s which showed that

> Those who reported being slapped or spanked 'often' or 'sometimes' had significantly higher lifetime rates of anxiety disorders, alcohol abuse, or dependence and one or more externalising problems compared with those who reported 'never' being slapped or spanked.[3]

Another 2000 study cited by the Royal College found that of 403 British children of ages 1, 4, 7 and 11, an astonishing 97 per cent of 4- year olds had experienced some smacking; 75 per cent of infants aged less than 1 were smacked 'frequently to occasionally' and 38 per cent of those more than once a week.[4] Smacking had never really gone away although there was consensus that beating was damaging.

Leach based her argument on a variety of psychological and social authorities but mostly on the premise that no parent would use violent means to impose authority because it was wrong. Smacking was wrong in several ways: it was ineffective, it created inappropriate psychological developmental effects, and it affected parents badly as well as children. Yet but 40 years before in 1944, the magazine *Good Housekeeping* had published a short piece about smacking, in which the child benefited from the smack, and learnt quickly and safely to avoid danger. The parent benefited too since the punishment was held to be effective and fair: 'Children like discipline.'[5] How far do these contrasting views represent the development of a permissive turn in British culture in the 1960s? And how general or persistent was the change from smacking as just and beneficial to smacking as harmful and cruel?

The history of public discourse on parental punishment is rooted in material shifts to do with family size and economic opportunities for women, as much as it is an effect of the theories of psychology. However, the nature of popular understanding of psychology needs examination also. Histories of the 'psychological complex' or 'governing the soul' have tended to emphasise the psychometric, quantitative elements of psychology in Britain, emphasising measurement and regulation, whereas looking at the history of parenting advice shows that popular Freudianism, based on case-studies and ideas of individual fulfilment, has been more important than people have often assumed in thinking about children and therefore in thinking about parenting. One of the key factors in the transformation of acceptable parental practice was the replacement of shame about the child's misbehaviour by shame about the parents' skills. The use of shame and humiliation was integral to the practice of corporal punishment but then became associated with its use at all rather than its desired effects. Parenting became the place where ideas about competence and science were increasingly applied. What had created this transformation of the fundamental morality of parental authority and how far did it reflect changing attitudes to adult sexuality and child bodies? The law had not flogged girls since 1820, nor provided the birch for boys since 1948.[6] But, despite campaigns against beating in both home and school going back to the 1890s parental punishment remained legally untouched until 2004, based upon the notion of 'reasonable chastisement'.[7] Cultural change preceded law in that parents were increasingly discouraged from beating. Right wing commentators have written about 'the 60s', as a period when there was a 'permissive turn' in which traditional methods of punishment and discipline were rejected, leading to social breakdown and social atomisation. So too have the followers of Canguilhem, writing about the complex of law and social regulation they call governmentality, especially Jacques Donzelot on France and Nikolas Rose on the United Kingdom.[8] Yet historical research demonstrates that there has not been a unitary culture of child discipline in the United Kingdom in the twentieth century, nor in the nineteenth century as Siân Pooley's chapter in this book (Chapter 10) shows, nor was there a complete transformation in the 1960s. Schools retained the legal power to use corporal punishment until 1983 when the Department for Education and Skills removed it as part of the armoury of school punishment, a ruling enforced in 1986 (except in private schools which continued, with parental permission, until 1996). However, parents and most local authorities had begun to abandon school punishment before the permissive 1960s. The change to an idea of discipline as a part of emotionally as well as physically healthy practices began with the growth of a literature of parental advice in the 1920s. Permissiveness of the child's will and acceptable naughtiness became acceptable in this period among progressives, based upon a Freudian notion of development as much as upon ideas of 'mental and moral hygiene'.

The interwar years

Mrs Sidney Frankenburg's *Common Sense in the Nursery*, a very popular, much reprinted book, first suggested in 1922 that 'in the case of boys who have been allowed to get out of hand and become defiant [corporal punishment] may occasionally be permissible. For girls I am sure it is always an unqualified evil', because, she went on to explain, ' a deeply rooted instinct of physical privacy is violated'.[9] Mrs Frankenburg was a professional journalist whose appeal to common sense was very characteristic of manuals in the interwar period. Her credentials were her own middle-class motherhood and a desire to cut through professional expertise and reach a common core of populist rhetoric and understanding that symbolised the new interwar motherhood of middle-class households in which families were practising birth control, educating girls and containing working women. The nursery in her title is the one vacated by the nursery nurse who became increasingly only available to the very rich, or for the users of local authority day nurseries. Increasingly, middle-class women were expected to practise motherhood throughout the day and not leave it to the servants.

The appeal to a general practical common sense in popular texts contrasted to a science of parenting but in practice showed the same principles at work. All were dominated by an idea of normal development which could be observed, monitored and measured. What was new in the 1920s was the psychological expertise that accompanied the medical advice about bodily fitness that came out of childcare manuals from medicine and nursing. The new psychology was elaborating the idea of the healthy psyche not just the good citizen. The healthy psyche was one in which desires should not be frustrated or repressed but encouraged to find expression. It was based upon the central principle of the unconscious, and more controversially, on the dynamics of childhood sexuality. Increasingly, these ideas were presented in a form that made them accessible to a wider public. Susan Isaacs was probably the most successful populariser of Freudian ideas in the interwar years. She wrote regular columns under the penname Ursula Wise in *The Nursery World* and reproduced these in her *Behaviour of Young Children* in 1933 as well as in the popular 1948 book *Troubles of Children and Parents*.[10] Her attitude to discipline and punishment in these pieces of advice, which were written mostly, as she admitted, for the middle-class readership of *The Nursery World*, was reflecting most directly the range of possible anxieties of concerned active parents who showed a strong interest in discipline. But it also reflected an understanding of normal health which came out of a Freudian notion of the unconscious bases of behaviour and the dangers of repression of drives and instincts. Discipline was one of the commonest questions raised by parents' letters. Chapter 2 of the book reflected this level of interest and was titled 'Obedience, Discipline and Punishment'. Isaacs starts, engagingly as always, with a presentation of the child's point of view which explained a child's sense of time, the need for clarity and how easily bad habits can set in and be reinforced: 'It is so easy to let a child slip into tyranny and ourselves into helpless worry'.[11] One mother who wrote was worried about her wilful child and said, 'Is a slap on the hand that persists in touching the forbidden object a very mistaken method? Sometimes I can see no other way.'[12] Isaacs responded tartly, 'We have no need to have things within reach of a child that are really dangerous to her'; and when another asked if she should smack her young child, as her own mother asked her to do, Isaacs simply ignored the question and turned the reader again and again to the child. The next time a parent used the same argument of slapping as the only feasible way to react, Isaacs described the claim that smacking a child hurts the parent more than it hurts the child as 'complete humbug'. She strongly challenged the idea that the child's buttocks were 'the correct place' for smacking, arguing

> It is also true of course that it is possible to develop in a child a definite, though hardly desirable, pleasure in being smacked on the buttocks and in the case of children who know that 'only Mummy can smack them' this is liable to happen.[13]

[Isaacs concluded:]

> What those who advocate the smacking of little children do not realize is that by having recourse to this method they simply coarsen the child's responses and make him insensitive to other more normal and delicate methods of control, the worst is assumed from the start, instead of the best, and all the ordinary motives for doing things to please other people or because other people demand them ... are all cut out from the start and they cannot grow in that atmosphere.[14]

This language concentrates on the child's memory and its capacity to learn morality as essentials in any idea of learning which must lie behind discipline. The child is to learn to be self-governing for its own happiness. In the same year, Isaacs published her more technical book, *Childhood and After*, in which she spelled out more theorised versions of some of these arguments. For example, she reported on a four-year-old child who was always very good and charming and funny. This was not at all grounds for self-congratulation for his parents. He had been a good child 'because his need for punishment for his unconscious libidinal wishes was so great'.[15]

Others deployed a direct Freudianism to influence styles of parenting. In particular Mary Chadwick, an early analyst (who worked with the poet Hilda Doolittle, known as HD), who described herself as a nurse on the title page of her book, produced popular, lucid and eloquent arguments for recognition of the perversity of beating and the damage it did to parents who did it, as well as to the child. 'A taste for Flagellation was a dangerous consequence of the process, but more important was the destruction of the child's trust in its parent'.[16] She suggested that corporal punishment represented a failure of care as well as of authority. Chadwick also pointed out the illogicality of telling a child that violence was wrong and using violent means to enforce this rule. She was more explicit, writing in the 1920s, than many of her successors but her arguments remained pertinent throughout the interwar period. She instructed parents about the powerful unconscious motives behind beating and reported that perversity would follow, mostly in the spanking parent but also in the child.[17]

Psychology in general shared the ideas of psychoanalysis, and indeed, there is little distinction between the two styles of argument in the interwar period. However, the distinction between psychology and psychoanalysis proper lay in the primacy of the home as the formative institution for children. Cyril Burt, one of the most influential contemporary psychologists, who taught teachers alongside Isaacs at the London Training College, as well as writing numerous newspaper columns for publications ranging from the *Times* to the *Daily Worker*, wrote *The Young Delinquent* (1925) partly to explain delinquency as 'an extreme of ordinary childish naughtiness'. He rejected corporal punishment except as a punishment for offences involving unimaginative physical cruelty – for 'brutality to other children, animal cruelty or endangering the lives of railway passengers' as 'it did more harm than good'.[18] For Burt the advice to parents was not distinguished from the advice to teachers or psychologists, since he saw home and school as well as the courts as all part of one culture of child care. Child care remained a public space only insofar as it developed the child's potential as a citizen. The home was not separate in this endeavour and was seen as a legitimate object of public concern. For Burt the parents who needed to learn better parenting were insignificant compared to the public need for child negligence to be compensated for by official agencies, especially the psychological clinic. Here psychology has a separate domain of its own helping to create psychological health by counteracting bad influences including the home, as one site amongst many. In some respects psychology thus stepped back from the parent as the primary source of society's patterns. Burt addressed parents rarely. Home was a place where official writs did not run, still private and undisturbed. But home was also a place where the reading parent needed to know what should be done. Donzelot's account of the home as the place of regulation does not seem very relevant yet in the British context. Psychology informed public practice more directly for the majority of children than psychoanalysis or psychiatry.

Others also saw the school as the place where children could become good citizens and improve social and individual health. The most extreme opponent of punishment as itself a cause of social damage was A. S. Neill, author and creator of a progressive school, Summerhill.

> The parent's attitude to the child is a subjective one; it is not selfless, it is selfish. The child is a chattel something owned; it must be a credit to its owner.[19]

and, he added,

> The disciplining of the child is fundamentally the parental disciplining of the self. The self disapproving mother or father will spank.[20]

The problem is hatred of the body...Every disciplinarian is a humbug when he isn't a sadist.[21]

Here he was repeating the even more vehement argument of his earlier book, *The Problem Child*, written in the 1920s:

It [beating] certainly frightens the child but the wrong part of the child; it terrifies the conscious and leaves untouched the unconscious.[22]

One of the most disturbing things for readers, especially anxious parents, about the popular Freudianism of the new psychology of the 1920s was the way in which innocence was no longer possible, where home became the place of greatest risk as well as greatest power. Although the link is not explicit, one of the reasons for this would appear to be the emphasis on the mother as an active agent in her child's life, an emphasis that became all the stronger as residential domestic child care became less and less common. If, as Chadwick and Neill suggested, the child was malformed by punishment, even corrupted by it, the complacency of advice which assumed the child was only a problem because of the embarrassment it caused by inexpert behaviour could no longer be allowed. This is often attributed to status anxiety – to being a matter of class and class aspirations – and certainly there are suggestions in some manuals that the child of the parent reading them is far removed from the slum child who went untended and unmonitored. But the uncertainty about appropriate parenting was evident in the pages of the press, as well as the books which were much more likely to be used by the middle class. Women's magazines also routinely discussed parental dilemmas as did the vestigial personnel and institutions of pre-World War social management, the schools for mothers, health visitors and the nursery nurses who looked after the children of working mothers in nurseries.

The interwar period also saw the elaboration of an entirely contradictory notion of the child based upon a simple calculus of reward and punishment – behaviourism. Here, famously, Watson asserted that parents should

Treat them as though they were young adults. Dress them and bathe them with care and circumspection. Let your behaviour always be objective and kindly firm. Never hug and kiss them, never let them sit on your lap.[23]

This American text had little impact in Britain at the time of its first publication but extended into the British life in the 1960s, as psychology and education courses created a wide diffusion of such theories.

War

The outbreak of war in 1939 helped to accentuate concerns about discipline and about the domestic environment as a place of security rather than fear. It also emphasised the division of domestic responsibility as, although women were registered after 1943, men were conscripted as soon as war was declared. Parental status had limited effect on male eligibility for military service. War also raised fears about aggression, about delinquency, about authority and about the change of the home into a more public space. The language of control became very evident in the 1940s and here beating was stigmatised as showing a lack of parental attention, being a seductive quick fix with dangerous long-term consequences. C. W. Valentine, professor of psychology at Birmingham, made punishment and discipline a central feature of his discussion of *The Difficult Child* (1940). He deployed recent research published in the *British Journal of Educational Psychology* in 1939 as his authority for children's own preferences for corporal punishment over detention or lines, but noted that girls rejected it at all ages, whereas boys preferred it until the age of 15. He rejected Freudian arguments about the sexual origins of emotional and behavioural development but commended Isaacs for her practical suggestions for the education of young children, 'quite independent of her excessive concentration on the sex factor'. He went on to report feeling 'a certain squeamishness' over using it on girls. 'Girls have a greater reverence for their bodies than have boys'.[24]

Others have written of the radio programmes Winnicott, Isaacs and Burt produced in the war years as part of the most paternalist welfarist regime of the twentieth century at the BBC. Denise Riley in *War in the Nursery* shows how these means conveyed complex theoretical structures in easy, accessible, populist ways.[25] Their advice spread more widely still through the training programmes of childcare professionals and in the infant welfare, child guidance and paediatric clinics of the new National Health Service after 1948. There was something of a crisis of delinquency during the war years, especially in areas where bomb damage turned city streets into adventure playgrounds. Official response to this varied widely. Magistrates resurrected birching, administered by policemen for some 500 young boys in war-time, and schools were using it in desperate attempts to control large classes and distressed, difficult children.[26] No guidance was given to evacuee billets about whether or not to punish evacuees as they would punish their own children; oral histories indicate that mostly they did so or were more cruel to their visitors than to their own. The general assumption was that the domestic practices of British homes were in general acceptable and needed neither monitoring nor advice. Corporal punishment using instruments such as canes and rulers was effectively discredited by the end of the Second World War as far as childcare professionals and most educators who elaborated theoretical justifications for their practices were concerned. But it was not discredited in the homes of Britain nor in many schools. The question of slapping, or smacking, especially for infants, was still debated, but most advice manuals suggested more desirable alternatives. However, both went on being practised in many homes for far longer. Not all experts agreed in any event; Lt Col Ford Thomson as late as 1950, basing his arguments on a lifetime of administration in Madras (now Chennai), used the other popular psychology of the day, behaviourism, to argue on the contrary, that rewards were not as successful as punishments in changing behaviour.

Post-war

What changed in the late 1960s and early 1970s was the acceptability in public discourse of corporal punishment as parental discipline. This was partly a result of prescript as well as changing traditions of parental control. What also changed was the balance of authority between parents when mothers, who had always been those with most daily concern for children's behaviour, became the main focus of social work, of psychology, of child study and paediatric medicine. This in its turn came from two sources: the Freudianism popularly circulating in Britain, with its notions of repression, and sociology, which privileged the home over the school, and the street or the court as the location of 'society'. R. S. Illingworth, the Sheffield paediatrician and author of several texts on child care, included a chapter on discipline in *The Normal Child* of 1964, which culminated in a measured indictment of corporal punishment for children rather than infants. He addresses parents, usually implicitly as mothers, but here the punitive parent is assumed to be male. The beating father 'finds release from the repressions of his childhood. He fails to realise that the whipping he received has made him the sort of father he is and has led to rebellion in his children.'[27] But interestingly, Illingworth suggests that infants *can* be punished this way, as it is an immediate response to someone without long-term memory but that the parent should ask if it were justifiable; concluding 'It is usually not'. The measure of the practice should be, he argued, whether punishment made the child better or worse. Just as the interwar bodily measures of children's growth and feeding had been assessed by parents as 'scientists in their own lives', so punishment was to be assessed by monitoring its effects on the child's behaviour not its emotions nor those of the parent. Illingworth put the child first rather than the parent. This humane and thoughtful but somewhat uneven approach contrasts strikingly with a text of ten years before by American author A. H. Chapman MD, in which the technique of beating was forcefully outlined as was the insistence that it must be on the bare buttocks which were he argued 'admirably designed for character building purposes'.[28] Chapman did argue that no child should be beaten after puberty. But he still clearly believed that there was a simple model of good character, which could be made, just as Baden Powell had argued in 1908 in *Scouting for Boys*. This argument demonstrates that Imperial discipline and American militarism both provided continuing contest for liberal European notions of the importance of the liberated psyche for social discipline and health in the 1950s.

There was little expert consensus in the United States compared to that which existed in the United Kingdom concerning punishment of children who could speak and reason; most agreed that smacking was undesirable for both child and parent. Mrs Frankenburg, who had argued for a light smack to prevent immediate danger in the 1920s, was still publishing some 50 years later, and now argued in 1970 that at any age it was to be unreservedly condemned. She pointed out that Solomon, so often cited as the biblical authority for beating, was not a good example and Rehoboam, his son, was not a good advertisement for the habit; in fact he was 'a typical result, being determined to pass it on in aggravated form "My father chastised you with whips I will chastise you with scorpions" '.[29] She cited the Bible rather than more secular authorities, a rare occurrence in child advice texts, which were predominantly and explicitly secular. But Dr Ginott, who agreed about the reprehensible effects of corporal punishment, made the very Foucauldian point that it was ineffective because it relieved guilt too easily. 'The child having suffered the punishment has not repented and feels free to repeat the offence.'[30] There is a language of sin, shame and remorse here but it is no longer addressed to the parent. The enlightened reader of this text is assumed to be someone who needs neither authority nor evidence to agree that beating is a failure in parental authority, rather than a rational or rationalised mode of discipline.

The key text for this intellectual as well as practical shift was J. W. B. Douglas' *The Home and the School* of 1968 to explain how far children could be good citizens, contributors to the economy and the society. Douglas located the origins of success and failure in school firmly back to the emotional and social life of the household. This was to some extent echoed by psychiatry when Michael Rutter, who produced several influential books on the origins of child mental and social development, challenged some of the assumptions of development theory made by the developmentalists, in particular John Bowlby, whose *Child Care and the Growth of Love* had located disordered development in the childhood of an insecurely attached infant separated for too long from his primary caregiver, the mother. Bowlby had first argued this in his account of 44 juvenile thieves in work done before the Second World War. Rutter's critique of attachment theory in its 1950s form reached as wide an audience as the original theories.[31] Rutter argued that the caretaking parent was not the only person concerned with a child's socialisation and that the normative assumptions of Bowlby's critique of nurseries needed to be placed in the context of a wider social world. Children's social experience was increasingly being seen away from the nursery, and located out in the public world. Bowlby had sought to explain thieving by a critique of the lack of domestic care for children and extended his critique to the institutions of non-domestic care in his *Child Care and the Growth of Love*.

The publishing house, Penguin, played an important part in circulating these ideas, with numerous texts written for a popular but educated market, made up of the larger number of couples with children that the post-war baby boom had brought into the population.[32] Texts on education, sociology and psychology were sold in large numbers to both professionals and parents. The university expansion helped to fuel this growing consensus against corporal punishment by creating large numbers of young parents who had experienced the first systematic parenthood education in schools as well as the life of the new universities. University education no longer led to a choice between parenthood and employment for young women and they benefited from free education, university grants, and the development of both large numbers of new degrees and new universities. Many went into teaching and acquired a rudimentary notion of child psychology from teacher training courses, which had contained this version of popular Freudianism since Agatha Bowley had described it in her 1942 popular bestseller *The Natural Development of the Child*.[33] From its foundation, Penguin Education extended this general diffuse knowledge, which focused theoretically on the idea of repression and inhibition rather than the Oedipus complex or the unconscious. Of all the Penguin authors, perhaps the most successful populariser of Freud was Donald Winnicott through his 1964 Penguin publication *The Child, the Family, and the Outside World* (a compressed version of two volumes previously published by Tavistock in 1957) which was quite explicitly aimed at a lay audience and written very artfully in everyday language without technical jargon. Winnicott had no index entry for discipline or for punishment but his book is full of powerful advice on these subjects. He argued that child delinquency indicated that some hope remained for the child behaving in this way, because the child was still acting autonomously. What such children showed by their delinquency was that 'antisocial behaviour is an S.O.S. for control by loving confident people'.[34] Winnicott described the roots of aggression, using a typical paradox, characteristic of much of his writing, in suggesting that aggression was a central part of development and that controlling it from inside was a useful part of growing up into stable happy adulthood. A lack of aggression was as much a problem as too much. Winnicott's whole emphasis was on getting parents to trust to their own understanding and to recognise that most parents knew very well what they were doing. Famously he wrote about the mother as 'good enough' and urged mothers to recognise that their own instincts were right. But the instincts he recommended were for loving attention, not for punitive control. His emphasis had shifted from policing parenthood to celebrating it.

Community sociology developed by Michael Young in his account of working-class life in Bethnal Green and published by Penguin was to some extent to do the same in the 1960s.[35] The interwar sociology that stressed the inadequacies of working-class parenting was increasingly being seen as outmoded, and being replaced by Bowlby's strong assertion of the central role for the loving support and continuous attention of a mother for healthy emotional development. This book was criticised by others later for overemphasising the ideal amounts of time spent by mothers with their children and thus confining women to domestic life, but part of its effects were to emphasise the importance of parents and ultimately of mothers in particular. Its descriptions of working-class life carried a powerful sense of recommendation about the strengths and continuities of working-class female culture.

Much of the guidance for parents made this same shift in the 1960s. The British Medical Association produced guidance for parents in pamphlets available in infant welfare clinics which were aimed at parents of babies but provided advice for parents of older children too. Penguin Publishing was very important in this change in the tenor of guidance, but was certainly not the first to attempt to redraw the boundaries of acceptable public morality applied in the privacy of people's homes. However, it is not at all clear that professional advice mattered more than existing domestic and familial culture. Women's magazines were one of the bridges between books and daily life, so too were authors of popular fictions such as Catherine Cookson who wrote extensively about authoritarian parents and the problems they created for their children.

Theories

There were, then, divergences between precepts and practices. What did popular commentators recommend for parental discipline, and is it possible to identify how far these cultures were changing? Historians of discursive practice do not as such use the term very much, seeing any control as part of a wider project of socialisation and happiness. Nikolas Rose calls this *Governing the Soul*. Jacques Donzelot saw parental control as the crucial site for intervention within the family relocating power between family members where women benefited from the contribution of social work, of psychoanalysis and of Marxism.[36] His analysis has been much criticised for assuming an exact fit between precept and practice, and for assuming a generality of European experience from the particularities of the French welfare state. It also presents a problem of chronology in that the changes to the modern family he describes cover a broad period. Certainly, the impact of social work professionals was not so great in quantity or quality and psychological thinking arrived more slowly and less generally in Britain than in France. But Donzelot was right to turn a critical eye to the claims for emancipation and improvement for children created by juvenile courts, social workers and welfare provision that were key institutions of 'permissiveness'. Nonetheless, this idea of a new governmentality of the home opened up to intervention by a nanny state looks implausible set against the resistance of entrenched cultural practice to social and psychological theory in many homes. Donzelot and Rose also tend to ignore political factors as well as a wider socio-economic context – both ignore the substantial developments arising out of the language of human rights. Feminists and trade unionists had also used the language of rights since the 1968 revival of a notion of improvement of society through the improvement of the position of women. The language of women's rights quickly began to develop into children's rights. Liberal parenting was the place where new practices could have been perceived. The literature of guidance on child management was less copious in the interwar period and often aimed as much at nursery nurses and nannies as it is at parents but it does include the narrative of appropriate punishment often attributed to Dr Spock in the 1960s. The most extreme liberal view is earlier – that of A. S. Neill whose provocative little books from the 1930s were designed to expose the hypocrisy of much parental treatment of children and were harsh on the subject of punishment rather than love as the mechanism. Many writers talk about the damage that punishment can do both to discipline itself and to normal development. Truby King has been mentioned often in looking at the 1930s, as if his contentious critical narrative of over feeding and spoiling was the only model of child care available. King's precepts were however contested, especially by psychologists, who looked to mind rather than body alone.[37] All write as if reader and caregiver alike are female.

One of the changes charted here was the end of domestic service, explored within this volume by Judy Giles (Chapter 9). Child care in the home was limited to the very rich after the 1950s except for the growing number of au pairs who were rarely described as exercising any domestic discipline and seen as adjuncts to parents rather than alternatives. Nannies remained professionalised at training schools and uniformed but less and less available to the middle class. Middle-class mothers worked for wages as university education, teacher training and medical schools gradually feminised over the 1960s but in the period from 1930 to the late 1950s, middle-class mothers of young children were more likely than at any other time in British history to be full time housekeepers and child carers. Young fathers on the other hand started being seen as parents slightly later after national service which took men away from the domestic from 1938 until it ended in 1960, with the last man serving leaving in 1963.

Parenthood advice

Does the literature of childcare advice demonstrate this shift? Certainly, childcare regulation became increasingly sophisticated theoretically and well informed psychologically in the post-war period. Home was seen in the post-war world as a place of safety – one where the market place had less effect than an emotional economy. Some saw discipline as training for harsh reality, others as protection from it. Working parents often argued that the labour market was the place where discipline would be developed but rarely saw their role as the production of disciplined future workers. Certainly, Bourdieu's idea of cultural capital seems useful in assessing post-war British family patterns. There was clearly substantial variation in the material, emotional and cultural resources available to children in British homes. Labour market imperatives are inadequate explanations for those variations. Elizabeth Roberts argued that it was a notion of general morality rather than economic urgency that lay behind family norms of behaviour.[38]

Paul Thompson's study *The Edwardians* echoed the argument that moral rather than political economy lay behind family ideas.[39] He argued that family life then was not a microcosm of the future but a place of here and now where citizens were being created rather than workers. Parental authority did become more affectionate than it had been for the Victorians and it was mostly a result of mothers becoming more liberal in treatment of their children. The institution that made child care very different for rich and poor was the division between those who employed and those who were domestic servants. For the middle class visible public decorum was as important as ethical behaviour and status related to that decorum. Both notions were highly gendered. Girls were less disciplined than boys, and were much less likely to be beaten. These two studies in oral history looked at the period before the First World War and they show a sense of change in the period and of wide cultural differences within it. The permissive turn was beginning before the war but was not universal.

Did feminism provide the intellectual resources to rethink the punishment of children? In the period before the First World War it had been assumed that to advance the interests of women would be to advance the interests of children.[40] Feminism developed an account of the primacy of motherhood and of historical accounts in the 1960s. This was more of an intellectual project of historical recovery and description seeking to analyse patriarchy. Jane Lewis' 1980 book *The Politics of Motherhood* was an account of maternity services rather than a form of political activism as far as child care was concerned.[41] When there was political activism around child care it focused on the provision of childcare facilities and challenging the absence of local authority day nurseries. The general thrust of humanitarian reform was over the question of how to be a mother and how to develop a more humanised social and political order. But children were seen more as labour than love. Denise Riley cited the description of children as the 'burdens of love'.[42] Feminism was thus not offering much of a narrative about social reform to provide a more human social democracy but more arguing for an improvement in the conditions of household labour.

The evidence from popular and political discourses suggests that 'body to mind' is a shift that never really took place in relation to punishment. The idea of the unconscious was used to explain ideas of guilt, sexual fantasy and repression but mostly these were carefully normalised so that parents were being enlisted in a common pursuit of a happier world rather than one that was more just. However, this humanisation did not come with Dr Spock nor did it come from professionals in the main – the most popular of these writers in the 1970s was still probably Mrs Frankenburg, who had argued for her qualifications as an ordinary mother with common sense for 50 years. The psychoanalysts did not by and large speak the name of their discourse nor did they mention Freud, Anna or Sigmund, although the common currency of Freudianism is evident to the reader. It was Melanie Klein who most influenced Isaacs and Winnicott who continued to be the most widely read theorists in thinking about child development in this period. Sexuality was thus downplayed in favour of thinking about mothers and feeding rather than fathers and incestuous desire.

Practice

What did children experience? Questions of management or theory showed a child's own social theory of parental trust or control. Most adults do not, in remembering childhood discipline, retain a very elaborate account of punishment unless it is in relation to their own sense of justice or injustice. 'Were you smacked as a child? No I was beaten, there's a hell of a difference.'[43] The historical account demonstrates that the experience of serious punishment often makes its sufferers hostile to using it themselves. To examine the history of its effects is difficult because those that speak in later life are able to comment only if they do not feel stigmatised by having endured it. If they have been beaten, they are those least likely to have been traumatised. Since one of the intended effects of punishment was shame, the recollection is likely itself to be shameful. Testimonies and newspapers indicate a powerful sense of justice and injustice before the First World War which lead many children to challenge teachers who beat children, but fewer challenged those who punished them at home. Children have, and had, a strong sense of culture and community but also a sense of isolation and foreshortening because their own experience is so limited. Hence gathering accounts of parental punishment is often a very political process requiring the historian to assess the arguments of witnesses as well as the history of their experiences.

Another factor that affected the transmission of new standards of ethical behaviour in the 1960s became the development of more informal teaching practices starting with advanced models in progressive education from Montessori and Froebel and extending through the work of the teacher training institutions in the 1930s onwards. Here again Isaacs was a key figure as she contributed along with Cyril Burt to the programme of what became the London Institute of Education. School practices of punishment correspondingly changed in the 1960s. But the practice of parents did not reflect such consistent cultural trends. We still do not know how far culture consciously instituted through Parentcraft coincided with cultural patterns transmitted through family tradition, popular cultural sources such as novels and magazines, and parental practice. Social science became interested in parenting in the 1960s using a variety of research methods with a strong emphasis on self-report. The Newsons' investigation in the 1960s was the most systematic attempt to investigate this subject in the study *Four Years Old in an Urban Community*, published and widely circulated by Penguin in 1968. The Newsons asked parents what they did with their four-year-old children and by careful construction of their questionnaire managed the only systematic account of practice rather than attitudes of the period. They approached the question with caution since they pointed out,

> Parents' emotional involvement in the control of the child, coupled with feelings of anger, humiliation and violence which can arise on both sides during conflict, are apt to invest any direct discussion of discipline with a certain amount of guilt, even where the mother believes she is doing the best she can.[44]

They demonstrate that practice varied very widely within social groups but that a majority of their respondents did use mild corporal punishment with young children. But most importantly they pointed out that this varied practice reflected this punishment as part of a sequence of events. Counting the number of incidents was therefore not as helpful as understanding the 'pattern of understanding' in a culture of parenting. Their findings show that no one class beat more than any other although the two extremes of a class distribution beat less than the middle. They also looked at religion, finding that some groups were slightly more punitive, especially Roman Catholics, but not everywhere. This may reflect schooling, migrant communities with their tendency to self help or the prominence of guilt characteristic of religions where shame is embedded in the notion of the individual's relationship to the moral order. They were later to record that the long-term effects of corporal punishment were likely to lead directly to delinquency,

> The measures which stand out as being most predictive of criminal record before the age of 20 are having been smacked or beaten once a week or more at 11, and having had a mother with a high degree of commitment to formal corporal punishment at that age.[45]

Thus 40 years of investigation demonstrated change in other institutional locations and very limited use of implements to punish children but continued and significant smacking remained central in a minority of homes and extensive, occasionally, in a majority.

The anthropologist, Geoffrey Gorer, took a similar model of investigation from social science when he analysed punishment practices as part of his *Exploring English Character: A Study of the Morals and Behaviour of the English People*. He had asked the readers of his 6 newspaper columns in *The People* to fill out questionnaires, which many did, and then he analysed 5000 of them, apparently selected at random. One of his six articles was about children's treatment and thus respondents reported on their attitudes to and practices of corporal punishment. These results were summed up to describe national character. His organisation of his findings makes comparative work difficult because he uses an idiosyncratic version of the registrar general's class distribution, which he believed to be central to variations of the national life. He believed that aggression and its repression was the core emotional element to English national culture. He found a more distinct class difference than the Newsons did later, with the middle class opposed to cruelty and brutality to the highest degree. He also argued that 'at heart some English parents find pleasure without conscious guilt in inflicting severe pain on children as a punishment'.[46] As a legitimate account of social science this populist writing does and did deserve some criticism as it is loosely constructed and analysed.[47] However, Gorer's choice of punishment as a peculiarly interesting English characteristic demonstrates its place in popular culture. Others asked the question about the practice at the same time. Ian Gibson's *The English Vice*, a history of beating in English culture which looked primarily to flagellation as a cultural pursuit, was published in 1978 and this too wanted to see English culture bound up a particular punitiveness towards children but in this case mainly through an account of the public schools rather than domestic cultures.[48]

Histories

Historians have addressed the particular nature of English or British culture and its attitudes to children as well. A leading advocate of the history of children as an inspiration for policy change, Harry Hendrick, argued in a book published in 2003 that 'The welfare of a substantial proportion of children is fairly grim.'[49] His view that improvement has not continued unabated since the Victorian period is quite controversial but he looks in particular to the lack of protection for children from cruelty as one of the ways in which British society does not demonstrate universal progress. Others have attempted to investigate the question of authority and control in the home as well as on the street and in the school.

Those who have looked at social history in a quantitative way have been particularly interested in looking at the long roots of corporal punishment and its particularities. Paul Thompson, interested in trying to understand social facts in Britain and believing, in general, in progressive social change, had asked his Edwardians about their disciplinary practices and found that there was a range from the Shetlands where beating was very rare to the daily violence of some Londoners. He argued that since the period before the First World War there has been a decline of parental authority. My analysis of the narratives indicates that there had been more of a shift from fathers to mothers and a decline of direct authority – in particular, a greater notice of the child's point of view, if not the child centredness often attributed to Dr Spock in the 1950s.[50] The Lancashire working-class women interviewed by Elizabeth Roberts similarly showed support for punishment or rejection of it in roughly equal measure, and described both children who resented the practice or valued it when interviewed in adulthood.[51] Roberts reported in her second study *Women and Families: An Oral History 1940–1970* that nearly all parents said they were less strict than their own parents although they varied in how much they agreed that this was a good development. Roberts quotes one witness:

> You were smacked as a child? No, I was beaten, there's a hell of a difference. I never did to my children the way I was beaten.[52]

In the life histories collected for the national sound archive of 2000 life histories, 156 reported an experience of corporal punishment but more in school than at home and very few at home after the 1960s. These are, however, subject to all the criticisms of testimony in that to have experienced corporal punishment has become less respectable in itself and the naming of the practice as child abuse makes a personal history increasingly uncomfortable.[53] Members of the House of Lords may find it easy to say 'It made me the man I am today' but most people recognise the essential ambiguity of that comment.[54] For example, Lord Swinfen in the debate on the Children's Bill in 2004 compared the caning he had at school to a friend who could not be beaten, for medical reasons, who had had to translate 1000 lines into Latin:

> In my view the punishment was very much heavier and harder than the three strokes of the cane that I had. In fact the strokes warmed me up on a cold winter's evening. I am certain that I benefited from it far more than my colleague whose punishment lasted several days.[55]

Louise Jackson reported parental rejection of others punishing their children in the Victorian period while Roberts saw it as common among Edwardians.[56] In the end the testimony about change in parental practices is varied and inconclusive and one must agree with Thompson that it shows many cultures of child-rearing, not just one. Stephen Humphries' books assessing parenthood provide oral histories of the experiences of life in twentieth-century working-class households which support this idea of diversity of practice and attitudes.[57] One of the extraordinary things about this mixed history is the way in which the idea of the 'bad old days' of parental cruelty and excess is only recently in the past, yet generational change has not been uniformly progressive nor uniformly theoretically sophisticated.

The question of what age a smack becomes an assault remains contentious. The majority of parents would accept in principle that beating is unacceptable but a large number in Britain continue to believe there is a substantial difference between a slap and a flogging. Yet when this was discussed in Parliament in 2004, despite the representations of all charity and research organisations concerned with children except one, which was formed to protect the right of parents to punish as they choose, called Families First, Parliament ended up only outlawing corporal punishment where 'visible damage' is caused to the child's body, ignoring the bruise to the spirit that may come from the experience of physical assault.

The emergence of Supernanny and other television programmes of the new century demonstrates one of the ways in which modernity is not necessarily teleological. Here the mass media prescribe extensively how children should be reared and demonstrate from within the privacy of homes the actual practices of the parents who are doing it wrong. The parent is chastised and made responsible and the child is considered absolutely predictable and standard. Guilt without any hint of a Freudian tinge re-emerges to make the watcher reflect on the practice of child care and accept a simple behaviourism which goes back to the behavioural techniques of 1930s writers. There is no smacking and in the internet forum developing out from the programme it becomes clear that parents' anger and aggression is increasingly pathologised here. However, the management techniques are far more corporeal than psychological. The child is held then placed firmly on the naughty step or in the naughty chair. Mary Chadwick's simple and pertinent assertion that attention rewards bad behaviour by giving a response, *even if it is a punitive one*, might never have existed. The return to a utilitarian calculus of pleasure and pain ignores the fundamental Freudian insight that pain is not always something that we flee. The website talks of firm discipline and techniques of management less bodily punishment but not corporal:

> You know that smacking your children and verbally abusing them.... will lead to a repetition of mimicked behavior from your children. What is much needed here is respect on all sides. You need to recognize that only YOU can make that choice and decide to break the dysfunctional cycle – so you can bring up your children in a new generation that think and behave in a healthier manner.[58]

This language from 2007 demonstrates that discourse has not changed that much. Parental responsibility has not been replaced by a more liberal and collective view of the nation's children in which their welfare is the concern of all, despite the prevalence of such views in the 1930–1980 period. Child care remains individualised, privatised and a source of guilt rather than pride. Consensus of a liberal kind has not become dominant, and nor does popular understanding of unconscious motives reflect the Freudian model which seems to have receded, replaced by a crude behaviourism also characteristic of the 1930s. The difference is that it is both parents who are depicted as lacking in authority or knowledge, and that the expert portrays parental inadequacy publicly in the televisual market place rather than privately between the pages of a book read and thought about at home.

The question of how far the state should protect children or the rights of parents to punish them as they thought fit has been raised over the years by concerned bodies usually coming out of the psychological and teaching professions. STOPP (The Society of Teachers Opposed to Physical Punishments) was founded in 1968 to get punishment out of schools and EPOCH (End Punishment of Children) took over from it when school punishment was banned and the ban enforced in 1986. Tackling punishment at home was always a more difficult campaign than the one against school beatings but it was successful in enabling a reform to be put before Parliament in 2004. The result, however, was a decision in which the rights-based discourse of law ended up privileging parents' rights to be free from state intervention and policing, trumping the rights of the child to be free from punishment. The opposition to this point of view came from the defence of the freedom of the home from government intervention. Richard Reeves MP commented,

> Smacking is another example of how we would only restrict someone's personal freedom if it could be shown that somebody else was being harmed by that individual freedom.

MPs were urged to vote according to conscience. As one dryly said, 'I genuinely hope the government will have the common sense to allow a free vote and not whip it', adding, 'It's not a question of whether [the banning of smacking] will happen but just a question of when'.[59]

When the BBC reported this Parliamentary discussion and its conclusions for their child audience they emphasised the positive outcome. 'The government didn't want a complete ban on smacking as they thought parents should be able to decide how to punish their children themselves. But smacks which cause bruises, redden the skin or harm you mentally will be made illegal, to protect children.'[60]

Thus the public discourse in the twenty-first century still needed to present competing needs of parents and children and the physicality of smacking in discussing the household practices of British parents. Practice and precept remained to some extent disjointed and corporeal punishment remained still central to the processes of parental discipline. The idea of governmentality which has become so general does not seem to be at play here. The home remains a place of private unregulated behaviour in which the child, often depicted as monarch of the small domestic world, remains an ideal not realised in actual social practices. The idea of a recent past as a bad period when punishment was cruel and corporal to be succeeded by a modern society where children are 'reasonably' chastised keeps recurring, despite a willingness to turn to the behaviourist solutions of that 'past'. Precept has changed irreversibly but practice remains mixed, with damaging effects for the social and cultural life of Britain.

Notes

1. By which I do not mean to imply that these are exclusive categories.
2. J. Donzelot (1980) *The Policing of Families*, trans. M. Hurley (London: Hutchinson).
3. D. Elliman and M. A. Lynch (2000) 'The Physical Punishment of Children', *Archive Diseases of Childhood*, 83, pp. 196–8.
4. G. Nobes, M. Smith (1997) 'Physical Punishment of Children in Two Parent Families', *Clinical Child Psychology and Psychiatry*, 2, pp. 271–81.
5. *Good Housekeeping*, 1944.
6. V. Bailey (1987) *Delinquency and Citizenship: Reclaiming the Young Offender 1914–1948* (Oxford: Clarendon Press).
7. D. Thom (2003) 'The Healthy Citizen of Empire or Juvenile Delinquent? Beating and Mental Health in the UK', in M. Gijswijt-Hofstra and H. Marland (eds), *Cultures of Child Health in Britain and the Netherlands in the Twentieth Century* (Amsterdam, New York: Rodopi), pp. 189–212.
8. N. Rose (1999) *Governing the Soul* (London: Free Association Press); (1985) *The Psychological Complex: Psychology, Politics and Society in England, 1869–1939* (London: Routledge & Kegan Paul); Donzelot, *The Policing of Families*.
9. Charis Barnett (Mrs S. Frankenburg) (1922) *Common Sense in the Nursery* (London: Christopher's), p. 246.
10. S. Isaacs (1948) *Troubles of Children and Parents* (London: Methuen); idem (1933) *Behaviour of Young Children* (London: Tavistock).
11. Isaacs, *Troubles*, p. 27.
12. Ibid., pp. 28–30.
13. Ibid., p. 37.
14. Ibid., p. 39.
15. S. Isaacs (1948) *Childhood and After. Some Essays and Clinical Studies* (London: Routledge, Kegan Paul), p. 5.
16. M. Chadwick (1937) *Difficulties in Child Development* (London: Allen and Unwin).
17. Ibid.
18. C. Burt (1925) *The Young Delinquent* (London: University of London Press), Vol. 1 *The Sub-normal Schoolchild*, pp. 14, 121.
19. A. S. Neill (1932) *The Problem Parent* (London: H. Jenkins Ltd), p. 39.
20. Ibid., p. 40.
21. Ibid., p. 51.
22. A. S. Neill (1929) *The Problem Child* (London: Jenkins), p. 154.
23. J. B. Watson (1928) *Psychological Care of Infant and Child* (New York: Norton), pp. 81–2, cit Graham Richards (1996) *Putting Psychology in its Place* (London: Routledge), p. 134.
24. C. W. Valentine (1940)'The problem of corporal punishment', *The Difficult Child and the Problem of Discipline* (London: Methuen) Chap. VIII, p. 82.
25. D. Riley (1984) *War in the Nursery* (London: Virago).
26. See Thom, 'The Healthy Citizen of Empire...', pp. 189–212.

27. R. S. Illingworth (1964) *The Normal Child: His Problems, Physical and Emotional* (London: W. Heinemann Medical Books), p. 221.
28. A. H.Chapman (1962) *Management of Emotional Disorders, A Manual for Physicians* (London: Pitman medical publishers), p. 157.
29. Mrs S. Frankenburg (Charis Ursula Barnett) (1970) *Common Sense about Children: A Parents' Guide to Delinquency* (London: Arco).
30. H. C. Ginott (1969) *Between Parent and Child: New Solutions to Old Problems* (London: Staples Publishing), p. 142.
31. M. Rutter (1972) *Maternal Deprivation Reassessed* (Harmondsworth: Penguin Education).
32. The first title specifically in the series 'Penguin Education' was published in 1966 but they had earlier published Winnicott, Isaacs and the Newsoms as Pelicans. *Children in Distress* by Sir Alec Clegg and Barbara Megson was published in 1968; Barbara Furneaux (1969) *The Special Child*; Pelican published C. W. Valentine (1962, 1963, 1964, 1967, 1968, 1970) *The Normal Child and Some of His Abnormalities: A General Introduction to the Psychology of Childhood*; J. A. Hadfield (1964) *Childhood and Adolescence*; John Bowlby (1965) *Child Care and the Growth of Love*.
33. A. Bowley (1942) *The Natural Development of the Child (a Guide for Parents, Teachers, and Others)*, with a foreword by D. R. MacCalman (Edinburgh: E. & S. Livingstone).
34. D.Winnicott (1964) *The Child, the Family, and the Outside World*, Penguin, p. 229.
35. M. Young and P. Wilmott (1962) *Family and Kinship in East London* (Harmondsworth: Penguin).
36. Rose, *Governing the Soul*; Donzelot, *The Policing of Families*.
37. C. Hardyment (1984) *Dream Babies: Child Care from Locke to Spock* (Oxford: Oxford University Press); see also C. Urwin and E. Sharland (1992) 'From Bodies to Mind in Childcare Literature: Advice to Parents in Inter-war Britain', in Roger Cooter (ed.), *In the Name of the Child: Health and Welfare, 1880–1940* (London: Routledge), pp. 174–99. But see some criticism of an entirely maternal focus in T. Fisher (2005) 'Fatherhood and the British Fathercraft Movement, 1919–39', *Gender & History* 17(2), 441–62.
38. E. Roberts (1995) *Women and Families: An Oral History, 1940–1970* (Oxford: Blackwell), p. 158.
39. Thompson interviewed in six locations using a sample standardised on the British population as a whole to assess social change. He and his researchers carried out some 444 interviews to appraise the processes of social and cultural change.
40. C. Dyhouse (1989) *Feminism and the Family in England, 1880–1939* (Oxford: Basil Blackwell).
41. J. Lewis (1980) *The Politics of Motherhood: Child and Maternal Welfare in England, 1900–1939* (London: Croom Helm).
42. D. Riley (1983) ' "The Serious Burdens of Love"? Some Questions on Childcare, in *Feminism*, and *Socialism*', in N. Segal (ed.), *What is to be Done about the Family?* (London: Penguin), pp. 129–56; repr. A. Phillips (1987) *Feminism and Equality* (London: Macmillan), pp. 176–97.
43. Roberts (1995) *Women and Families*, p. 161.
44. J. and E. Newson (1969) *Four Years Old in an Urban Community* (London: George Allen and Unwin, paperback (1970) (Harmondsworth: Pelican), p. 413.
45. Newsons (1990) *The Extent of Physical Punishment in the UK* (London: Approach).
46. G. Gorer (1955) *Exploring English Character: A Study of the Morals and Behaviour of the English People* (London: The Cresset Press), p. 195.

47. See the review by P. Stirling in (1956) *American Anthropologist*, Vol. 54. pp. 1157–60.
48. I. Gibson (1978) *The English Vice Beating, Sex and Shame in Victorian Britain and After* (London: Duckworth).
49. H. Hendrick (2003) *Child Welfare: Historical Dimensions, Contemporary Debate* (Bristol: The Policy Press), p. 247.
50. Dr Benjamin Spock, *Baby and Child Care* appears to have been first published in Britain in 1955 by the Bodley Head but paperback copies by Pocket books were circulating from its 1951 version in the 1950s. It was originally published in the USA as *Commonsense Guide to Parent and Child Care*.
51. E. Roberts (1984) *A Woman's Place: An Oral History of Working Class Women, 1890–1940* (Oxford: Blackwell).
52. E. Roberts (1995) *Women and Families: An Oral History 1940–1970* (Oxford: Blackwell), pp. 158–64, quote is from p. 161.
53. J. E. Durrant, PhD (2006) 'Researching the Prevalence of Corporal Punishment of Children: A Working Paper', Department of Family Social Sciences University of Manitoba, offers a lucid comparative exposition of these difficulties.
54. Despite this being a cliché of this debate it has reappeared verbatim in speeches in the House of Lords since 1936 including the one in the 2004 debate.
55. *Hansard*, 20 May 2004, col. 902.
56. L. Jackson (2000) *Child Sexual Abuse in Victorian England* (London: Routledge).
57. S. Humphries (1981) *Hooligans or Rebels? : An Oral History of Working-Class Childhood and Youth, 1889–1939* (Oxford: Blackwell); S. Humphries and P. Gordon, *A Labour of Love: The Experience of Parenthood in Britain, 1900–1950* (London: Sidgwick & Jackson); M. Akhtar and S. Humphries (1981) *The Fifties and Sixties: A Lifestyle Revolution* (London: Boxtree).
58. *Supernanny* website, accessed July 2007. www.supernanny.co.uk.
59. David Hinchcliffe, Today programme BBC archive, 6 July 2004.
60. *Newsround*, 6 July 2006.

Index

abolitionism, *see* anti-slavery
Adam Bede (1859), 198
Adams, Annmarie, 114
Altick, Richard, 186
The Amazing Philanthropists (1916), 75
anthropology, 276
anti-slavery, 200
   see also slavery
aristocracy, 5, 114, 115, 120, 199, 206, 209
Armstrong, Nancy, 63
Arnold, Matthew (1822–88), 246, 249
August, A., 87
autobiography, 86–7, 88, 91–2, 96, 97, 113–14, 119, 123, 195, 206, 218
Ayer, Pat, 14

Baby and Child (1977), 262
Bacon, Francis (1561–1626), 191
Baden-Powell, R.S.S. (1889–1977), 269
Bailey, Peter, 18
Barthes, Roland, 192
BBC, 207, 280
   see also television
Beeton, Isabella Mary (1836–65), 187, 190, 191, 192, 194
behaviourism, 267, 269, 279, 281
Behaviour of Young Children (1933), 264
Bell, Vanessa (1879–1961), 212, 213
Bentham, Jeremy (1748–1832), 62, 65, 66, 74
Bevin, Ernest (1881–1951), 208
Bibby, Cyril, 248
birth control, 132, 160, 264
   see also family
Bland, Hubert, (1855–1914), 199
Bodenheimer, Rosemarie, 248
Book of Common Prayer, 245
Book of Household Management (1861), 187, 190, 194
   see also Beeton, Isabella Mary
Bourdieu, Pierre (1930–2002), 274

British Journal of Educational Psychology, 268
British Medical Association, 272
Burnley Gazette, 229, 230
Burt, Cyril (1883–1971), 266, 268, 275

Canguilhem, Georges (1904–95), 263
Carlyle, Jane (1801–66), 187, 253
Carlyle, Thomas (1795–1881), 187
Carpenter, Mary (1807–77), 67, 70, 74
Carter, Philip, 6
Catholic Church
   and anti-Catholicism, 74
   in England, 155–75
   and Holy Family, 156, 158–60, 168, 171
   in Ireland, 61, 62, 64, 65, 67–9, 76–7, 164
   and St Joseph, 155, 156, 170–2, 174, 180n96
   and Virgin Mary, 156, 161–3, 165–7, 169–70, 174
   see also Church of England; femininity; Leo XIII; Pius IX; Pius XII; religion; state
Catholic Herald, 160, 163
Central Committee on Women's Training and Employment, 208
de Certeau, Michel, 193, 195, 196, 200, 201
Chadwick, Edwin (1800–90), 65, 66, 74
Chadwick, Roger, 31
Chartism, 11, 90
The Child, the Family, and the Outside World (1964), 271
Childhood and After (1948), 265
children
   and boarding out, 68, 70, 71, 73, 76
   and Catholic Church, 61, 67–9, 76–7
   and childcare, 10, 227, 233–4, 261, 264–73, 273–4
   and child protection, 95
   corporal punishment, 224, 261–81
   delinquency, 266, 268, 271

and district schools, 62, 66–7, 71, 73–4
and domestic authority, 61–3, 76–7, 77, 111–13, 121–3, 124–7, 225, 235–7
and domestic space, 113, 114–24, 126–7
experience, sources of, 113
illegitimate, 28–48, 63
and industrial schools, 66, 94
and infanticide, 30–2, 64
and infant mortality, 64, 70, 71
medical care, 70, 72–3, 75, 230, 235
orphans, 61–77
and 'ragged schools', 67
Romantic idea of, 67
and state, 61, 77
and workhouse schools, 63, 70, 101
see also domesticity; education; individualism; Ireland; material culture; men; parenthood; Scotland; welfare; women; workhouse
Children's Bill (2004), 278
Christie, Agatha (1890–1976), 206, 215, 216
Church of England, 156
and advice literature, 9
and evangelicalism, 10
and marriage, 10
see also Catholic Church; evangelicalism; marriage; religion; state
citizenship, 14, 62, 85, 86, 89–90, 93, 100, 101, 103, 150, 205, 261, 264, 266, 270, 274
see also individualism; state; taxation class
class
and domestic space, 122–3
formation, 6, 11, 12, 113, 187
and Industrial Revolution, 6
lower-middle, 12, 28, 32, 70, 115, 121, 123, 127, 205, 210
middle, 111–27, 264, 274
and post-Second World War period, 18
upper, 112, 122, 193, 200, 205, 209
upper middle, 111–12, 120–1, 253
working, 14, 16, 27–8, 186, 210, 212–13, 245, 271–2

see also domesticity; family; fiction; marriage; nursery; men; women
Cobbe, Frances Power (1822–1904), 67, 70
Cobb, J., 87
Collins, Marcus, 13, 133, 134
Collins, Wilkie (1824–89), 193
colonization, 62
Common Sense in the Nursery (1922), 263
communism, 171, 212
see also Fabianism; Labour Party
The Companionate Marriage (1927), 133, 157
Conekin, Becky, 15
Conley, Carolyn, 28
contraception, *see* birth control
Cookson, Catherine (1906–98), 272
Cruse, Amy, 199, 200
culture
mass, 210
material, 111–12, 113, 117, 120–1, 125–6

Daily Telegraph, 189
Daily Worker, 266
Daniel Deronda (1876), 43
Darwin, Charles (1809–82), 243, 247, 255–6
Davidoff, Leonore, 1, 5–6, 11, 18, 112, 113, 125, 133, 150, 151
Davies, Margaret Llewelyn (1861–1944), 195
Day, Susanne (1875/6–1964), 75
The Diary of a Nobody (1892), 12
Dickens, Charles (1812–70), 61, 72, 99, 189, 213, 243, 246, 247–53, 255, 256, 258
see also Household Words
Dickens, Monica (1915–92), 206, 213–15
The Difficult Child (1940), 268
Dombey and Son (1848), 243, 247–8
domesticity
and advice literature, 9, 13
and Catholic teaching, 163–4
and children, 113
and domestic space, 111–27, 205, 207, 209
and evangelicalism, 5, 6, 9, 10–11, 12, 157
and family, 7, 155–6, 160

domesticity – *continued*
  and mass press, 185–6
  and religious belief, 10
  twentieth-century, 14
  Victorian cult of, 244
  and violence, 11, 27–48, 88, 94
  see also class; domestic service;
      femininity; masculinity; men;
      paternalism; women
domestic service, 70, 88, 113, 121, 123,
    163
  and domestic authority, 14–15, 185,
      187, 189–90, 193–5, 198, 205–6,
      208–9
  and historical record, 204, 206
  and men, 14, 192–3, 194, 207
  and reading, 185–7, 187–8, 190,
      193–4, 195–201
  and 'servant problem', 2, 15, 187, 207
  and women, 194–5, 204–18, 264
  see also domesticity
Domestic Workers Union, 208
Donzelot, Jacques, 261, 263, 266, 272–3
Dublin Statistical Society, 69, 70
  see also Social Science Association
Dyhouse, Carol, 207

Edinburgh Review, 251
education, 228–9, 234–7, 238
  early nineteenth-century, 66
  and local government, 228
  progressive, 275
  see also children
The Edwardians, 274
egalitarianism, 10, 14, 148, 149, 208,
    213
eighteenth century, 6–7, 209, 244
Eliot, George (1819–80), 196, 198
Elliotson, John (1791–1868), 251, 257
Ellis, Sarah Stickney (1899–1872), 9,
    10, 13
End Punishment of Children, 280
  see also children: corporal punishment
The English Middle Classes (1949),
    209–10
The English Vice, 277
Englishwoman's Domestic Magazine
    (1852), 190
  see also Beeton, Isabella Mary

evangelicalism, 5, 6, 9–12, 21n42,
    67, 157
  and domestic authority, 12–13
  see also Church of England; religion
Evans, Wainwright, 133, 157
Evening Post, 68

Fabianism, 102
  see also communism; Labour Party
family
  and domestic authority, 157, 173, 175
  and generational change, 17–18,
      155–6, 239, 278
  and godfathers, 245, 250–1, 255
  and godmothers, 243, 245, 253
  and god-parenting, 243, 245, 253
  and law, 89
  middle-class, 18, 114–15, 122–3, 160,
      244
  poor, 39, 85, 91, 100
  and professional discourses on, 18
  and reading, 189
  and social science movement, 69
  and state, 77, 157
  and workhouse, 95–6
  working-class, 86–7, 173, 261, 278
  see also baptism; Catholic Church;
      class; marriage; men; Social
      Science Association; welfare;
      women
Family Fortunes (1987), 5, 13
Family Friend, 189
Family Herald, 186–7, 189, 200
femininity, 6, 15, 16
  and the Catholic Church, 156, 162–7,
      170, 174
  conduct literature, 9, 13
  and 'modern girl', 162
  and motherhood, 63, 64, 66, 68, 69,
      264, 269, 271–2, 273, 274, 276
  and state, 75, 164
  see also Catholicism; marriage;
      masculinity; men; patriarchy; *The
      Politics of Motherhood*; separate
      spheres; welfare; women
feminism, 63, 75, 101, 192, 273, 274
fiction, 43, 190, 206, 209, 210, 216,
    217, 272
  'condition of England', 87
  working-class, 92

Finch, Janet, 157
Fink, Janet, 113
Fish, Stanley, 192
Flint, Kate, 114
Fordyce, Rev. James (1720–96), 191
Four Years Old in an Urban Community
    (1968), 276
Fox, Barbara, 92
Fox, W. J. (1786–1864), 10
Foyster, Elizabeth, 11
France, 193, 263, 272
franchise
    female, 90
    male, 86, 89, 90
Freeman, 68
Fremlin, Celia, 206, 212–13, 215
Freudianism, 165, 261–9, 271, 275,
    279–80
friendly societies, 90–1, 100, 102, 103
    see also welfare

Galsworthy, John (1867–1933), 43–4
Gathorne-Hardy, Jonathan, 122
Gibson, Ian, 277
Gillis, John, 244, 257
Gladstone, Helen (1849–1925), 113
Gladstone, William (1809–98), 113
Good Housekeeping, 262
Goodlad, Lauren, 62
Gordon, Eleanor, 112, 113
Gordon, Linda, 92
Gorer, Geoffrey (1905–85), 276–7
'Gorham controversy', 244, 248, 258n5
Gosford Park, 205
Greenwood, Walter (1903–74), 212
Grierson, John (1898–1972), 212–23
Grossmith, George (1847–1912) and
    (Walter) Weedon (1854–1919), 12

Hale, Matthew (1609–76), 44
Hallam, Arthur (1811–33), 254
Hallam, Henry (1777–1859), 254
Hall, Catherine, 1, 5–6, 11, 112, 125
Hearth and Home, 189
Henderson, Nigel, 204
Hendrick, Harry, 277
hereditarianism, 73
The Hidden Injuries of Class, 87
Hilton, Boyd, 10
Holden, Katharine, 113

Holton, Sandra Stanley, 10
The Home and the School (1968), 270
Hooker, Joseph (1817–1911), 243, 255,
    256, 257
House Architecture (1880), 115
Household Words, 189, 246
Howitt, Mary (1799–1888), 200
Howitt, William (1792–1879), 200
Humphries, Stephen, 278
Huxley, Leonard (1860–1933), 256
Huxley, Thomas Henry (1825–95), 243,
    248, 255, 256, 257

Illingworth, R. S. (1909–90), 269
individualism, 62
    and children, 67, 73–4, 77
    and women, 63
    see also citizenship; state
Industrial Revolution, 6
infanticide, *see* children
inter-war Britain, 204–5, 207, 263–7, 271
Ireland
    famine, 66
    and Irish poor Law, 64
    and orphans, 61–77
    see also Catholic Church; children
Isaacs, Susan (1885–1948), 264, 268, 275

Jagger, Peter, 245
Jeffrey, Francis (1773–1850), 243, 251

Keble, Thomas (1793–1875), 246
The Kingdom of Christ (1832), 247
Kingsley, Charles (1819–75), 254
King, Truby (1858–1938), 273
Klein, Lawrence, 7
Klein, Melanie (1882–1960), 275

Labour Party, 90, 208
    see also Fabianism; trade unionism
Ladies Sanitary Association, 193, 198
Lady, 207
Landor, Walter Savage (1775–1864), 243,
    251, 257
Lang, Andrew (1844–1912), 196
Leach, Penelope, 262
Lee, A. J., 198
Lee, Hermione, 255

Leo XIII, Pope (1878–1903), 155
  see also Catholic Church; Pius IX;
    Pius XII
Lewis, Jane, 274
Lewis, Roy, 209
library, public, 189
  see also reading
Light, Alison, 1, 204, 205, 218
Lindsey, Ben, 133, 157
literacy, 186
literary theory, 192
  see also de Certeau, Michel; reading
Lloyds Paper, 199
Longman's Magazine, 196
Lytton, Edward Bulwer (1803–73), 243,
    248, 251

McBride, Teresa, 113, 115, 122, 123
McCormack, M., 89
Macready, Lydia (1842–58), 253
Macready, William Charles (1793–1873),
    243, 250–1, 256, 258
magazine, 187, 189, 196
  women's, 187, 190, 197, 199, 267, 272
  see also fiction; newspaper; reading
Malthus, Thomas (1766–1834), 63, 66
The Man of Property (1906), 43
  see also Galsworthy, John (1867–1933)
marriage
  and caring, 140, 142–3, 148, 149, 151
  and Catholic Church, 155–64, 167–8,
    173, 174–5
  and Church of England, 10
  companionate marriage, 13–14, 132–4,
    138, 148, 150, 156, 157–61
  and divorce, 44–54, 159, 160
  and individual autonomy, 138–9
  and law, 3, 30, 89
  and love, 132–4, 139, 141, 143, 145,
    149–51
  marital violence, 43–54
  and sexuality, 132, 133, 138, 147, 149,
    150–1, 159
  twentieth-century, 15, 133, 148–51
  and women's employment, 88
  see also birth control; men; women
Martineau, Harriet (1802–76), 249
Marxism, 272

masculinity, 6, 11, 12, 14, 16, 156
  and domestic authority, 13, 28, 38,
    84–5, 87–90, 103, 112, 126,
    168–73
  and fatherhood, 27–33, 38–48, 69,
    119, 168–70, 243–4, 247–53, 256,
    257–8, 269, 273, 277–8
  and state, 75
  and violence, 28–48
  see also femininity; marriage; men;
    paternalism; separate spheres;
    women
Maude, Angus, 209
Maurice, Frederick Denison (1805–72),
    246–7, 253–5, 258
du Maurier, Daphne (1907–89), 206,
    215, 218
Mayhew, Henry (1812–87), 199
Meldrum, Tim, 113
men
  and domestic authority, 10, 13, 85,
    88–93, 94, 95, 97–100, 112, 120,
    257
  and domestic sphere, 7
  and employment, 14, 88, 91, 145–8
  and fatherhood, 112, 156, 160, 167–9,
    172–3, 224, 227
  as husbands, 12–13, 118, 132, 140–8,
    157–9, 210
  lower-middle-class, 32
  and marriage, 10
  middle-class, 13, 38, 54, 189
  poor, 27, 38, 54, 62, 89
  and religion, 10
  upper-class, 198
  and welfare, 90–3
  and workhouse, 85
  working-class, 12, 30, 38, 54, 85–7, 89,
    173
  see also children; class; domestic
    service; family; femininity;
    franchise; individualism;
    masculinity; marriage;
    parenthood; patriarchy; welfare;
    women
Mill, John Stuart (1806–73), 10,
    43, 62
missionary work, 62
Modleski, Tania, 200
The Moonstone (1862), 193

Morning Post, 198
Morris, Jeremy, 247
Mort, Frank, 18

Nair, Gwyneth, 112, 113
National Health Service, 268
national identity, 217
National Marriage Guidance Council (NMGC), 155, 157, 160
National Society for the Prevention of Cruelty to Children (NSPCC), 95, 237
The Natural Development of the Child (1942), 271
Neil, A. S. (1883–1973), 266, 273
Nesbit, Edith (1858–1924), 199
newspaper, 50–1, 98, 185–6, 189, 196, 227, 230, 275
   see also reading
Nicholas Nickleby (1838–9), 249
Nightingale, Florence (1820–1910), 199
Nineteenth Century, 245
Nonconformism, 10–11, 114, 119, 224
Nooks and Corners (1889), 115
The Normal Child (1964), 269
Northcliffe, Lord (1865–1922), 191
novel, *see* fiction
nursery, 111, 114–18, 126, 128n19, 263–4, 267, 268, 270, 273
   see also children; material culture; women: nurses
Nursery World, 264

Oedipus complex, 271
One Pair of Hands (1939), 206, 214–15
On Liberty (1859), 62
   see also Mill, John Stuart (1806–73)
oral history, 86, 132–3, 149–51, 151–2, 156, 223, 278
orphans, *see* children
Orwell, George (1903–50), 212
Owen, Robert (1771–1858), 10
Oxford Movement, 246

Pamela (1740), 189–90, 199
Panton, Jane Ellen (1847–1923), 115
parenthood, 224, 225–7, 230–8, 261–8, 269, 271–6

Parliament, 4, 70, 73, 207, 234, 279, 280
   1832 Reform Act, 11
   and women's rights, 11
Pateman, Carole, 44
paternalism, 31, 93
   see also masculinity
patriarchy, 69, 119, 132, 148, 149
   see also masculinity; men
pauperism, 87–8, 99, 101, 102, 103
People, 276
Picture Post, 168–9
Pius IX, Pope (1846–78), 170
Pius XII, Pope (1939–58), 171, 173
political economy, 63, 67, 69–70, 77
The Politics of Motherhood, 274
Poor Law, 23n64, 30, 61, 85–6, 91, 96, 97–100, 103, 227
   1834 New Poor Law, 28, 63–4, 67, 74, 95, 100
   1909 Poor Law enquiry, 101, 102
   Irish Poor Law, 64, 69, 70
   reform, 101, 102
   Scottish Poor Law, 66
popular press, 185, 186, 188, 189
   see also newspaper; reading
post-modernism, 193
The Problem Child (1926), 266
psychiatry, 270
psychoanalysis, 266, 272, 275
psychology, 262, 264, 266–7, 271, 273
public and private spheres, 7, 156, 174, 244, 246, 266, 268
Punch, 187
Pusey, Edward (1800–82), 246

reading
   advice on, 185, 187, 190, 194, 198
   dangers of, 190–2
   men, 189
   women, 188–9, 195–201, 215–16
   see also library; literary theory; magazine; newspaper; popular press
Rebecca (1938), 206, 215, 217
religion, 10
   and baptism, 244, 245–8, 251–2, 257–8
   and female authority, 244, 252, 257–8
   and male authority, 10, 89, 243–4, 252

religion – *continued*
　　see also Catholic Church; Church of
　　　England; evangelicalism;
　　　Nonconformism
*Report of the Committee Appointed to
　Enquire into the Present Conditions as
　to the Supply of Female Domestic
　Servants* (1923), 208
*Report of the War Cabinet Committee on
　Women in Industry* (1919), 208
Reynolds News, 199
Richardson, Samuel (1689–1761),
　　189, 199
Riley, Denise, 268, 274
Roberts, David, 112
Roberts, Elizabeth, 274, 278
Robinson Crusoe (1719), 193, 198
Rose, Jonathon, 195
Rose, Nikolas, 263, 272–3
Royal College of Paediatricians, 261
Royal Commission on Population (1949),
　　173

Sandford, Elizabeth (1797/8–1853), 9
Scheff, T. J., 87
Scotland
　　and boarding out, 66, 69
　　see also Poor Law
Scouting for Boys (1908), 269
Segal, Lynn, 167
Senior, Jane (1828–77), 73–4
Senior, Nassau (1790–1864), 74
Sennett, Richard, 87
'separate spheres', 5–6, 10–12, 13, 118,
　　148n7
　　see also femininity; masculinity
servants, *see* domestic service
The Seven Chars of Chelsea (1940), 206,
　　213, 215
sexology, 133, 160
Sketches by Boz (1836), 251
Sketches of Young Couples (1840), 251–2
slavery, 62
　　see also anti-slavery
Smith, Sydney (1771–45), 243
social democracy, 205, 206, 212, 217
socialism, 86, 100, 101
Social Science Association, 70
Society for Promoting Christian
　　Knowledge, 225

Society of Teachers Opposed to Physical
　　Punishments, 280
　　see also children: corporal punishment
sociology, 133, 173, 269, 271
Southgate, Henry (1818–88), 191
Spock, Benjamin (1903–98), 273, 275,
　　278
Stanley, Arthur (1815–81), 246
Stanton, Elizabeth Cady, 43
state, 86
　　and Catholic Church, 68
　　and children, 63, 67, 69, 73, 77
　　and Church of England, 7
　　and citizenship, 62
　　and family, 77
　　and local government, 8, 86, 224, 228
　　and orphans, 61
　　and Protestantism, 65, 67–8, 69
　　see also Catholic Church;
　　　individualism; Poor Law; taxation;
　　　welfare; workhouse
Steedman, Carolyn, 1, 88
Stephen, Leslie (1832–1904), 255
Stevenson, J. J. (1837–1908), 115
Stowe, Harriet Beecher (1811–96), 200
Strange, Julie-Marie, 27
The Subjection of Women (1869), 10, 43
　　see also Mill, John Stuart (1806–73)
suffrage, *see* franchise
Summerfield, Penny, 157
Summerhill, 266
　　see also education: progressive
Swan, Annie (1859–1943), 197
Sweethearts, 199
Tadmor, Naomi, 7

taxation, 207
　　Taxes on Knowledge, 186, 188–9
　　see also citizenship; reading; state
Tebbutt, Melanie, 16
television, 279–80
　　see also BBC
Tenant of Wildfell Hall (1848), 43
Tennyson, Alfred (1809–92), 243, 246,
　　248, 253–4, 255
Thane, Pat, 18
Theological Essays (1853), 254
Thompson, Paul, 274, 277
Thompson, William, 43
the Times, 31, 45, 266

Tit-Bits, 191
Todd, Selina, 17, 207
Tosh, John, 7, 112, 118
To Those Getting Married (1946), 164
Tractarianism, 246
Tracts for the Times (1835), 246
trade unionism, 63, 100, 101, 273
    see also Fabianism; Labour Party
Troubles of Children and Parents (1948),
    264
Tufnell, Edward (1806–86), 73–4
twentieth century, 113, 155–6, 158, 200,
    261

Uncle Tom's Cabin (1852), 200
Upstairs Downstairs, 205

Valentine, C. W. (1879–1964), 268
Vickers, George, 30
Vickery, Amanda, 6
Vincent, David, 186

Wahrman, Dror, 8, 11
Wales, 12, 104n6, 159, 207
war
    Crimean, 254
    First World, 86–7, 158, 195, 207–8,
        209, 210, 212, 274, 275, 277
    of Independence, American, 8
    Second World, 155–7, 157–8, 160, 161,
        164, 165–7, 168, 206, 208, 267–8,
        270
War in the Nursery, 268
Webb, Beatrice (1858–1943), 1
welfare
    child, 63–78, 92, 93–5, 101, 161,
        261, 280
    and domestic authority, 92
    family, 85, 91–3
    and masculinity, 90
    state, 86, 167, 217, 272
    women's, 92–3, 103
    see also children; femininity; friendly
        society; men; women
What Every Lady Would Like to Know
    (1876), 191
What's Wrong with Domestic Service?
    (1930), 208
Wiener, Martin, 39
Wilson, Linda, 10

Winnicott, Donald (1896–1971), 271
Woman at Home, 197
Womankind (1876), 190
women
    and child-bearing, 152
    and domestic authority, 3, 5, 6, 9–15,
        89, 90, 95, 97–100, 112, 120, 126,
        258
    and employment, 12, 14, 15, 17,
        207–8, 211, 233
    and individualism, 63
    and marriage, 10
    middle-class, 14, 63, 112, 163, 187,
        212, 217, 264
    and motherhood, 112, 140–3, 156,
        161–7, 170, 226–7, 233, 244, 264,
        273
    'new women', 161
    nurses, 14, 31, 47, 71–2, 74, 111, 122,
        263–4, 267, 270, 273
    and philanthropy, 8, 61, 62, 63, 70,
        74, 75, 77, 92–3, 102–3
    and the poor law, 61, 63, 66, 67, 69,
        70, 71, 72–6, 77, 100
    and public life, 7, 14, 61
    and religion, 10
    as wives, 132, 140–8, 157–9, 167–8,
        210–11
    and women's rights, 14, 90, 273
    working, 16, 63, 162–3, 264, 273
    working-class, 163, 171, 173, 188, 191,
        195–6, 207–8, 213, 272
    see also children; class; domestic
        service; family; femininity;
        franchise; individualism;
        masculinity; men; parenthood;
        welfare
Women and Families, 278
Women's Cooperative Guild, 101, 195,
    201
Wood, J. Carter, 38
Woolf, Virginia (1882–1941), 205, 212,
    213, 255
workhouse, 47, 85, 95–6, 97–100, 101–2
    and orphans, 61–7, 68–72, 74–7
    see also state

Yonge, Charlotte (1823–1901), 190, 198
The Young Delinquent (1925), 266
Young, Michael (1915–2002), 271